I0361023

GOD AT PLAY

Comparative Theology / *Thinking Across Traditions*

SERIES EDITORS

*Loye Ashton and John Thatamanil*

This series invites books that engage in constructive comparative theological reflection that draws from the resources of more than one religious tradition. It offers a venue for constructive thinkers, from a variety of religious traditions (or thinkers belonging to more than one), who seek to advance theology understood as "deep learning" across religious traditions.

# GOD AT PLAY

## *Līlā* in Hindu and Christian Traditions

DANIEL SOARS, EDITOR

*Fordham University Press* NEW YORK 2025

Fordham University Press also publishes its books in a variety of electronic formats. Some content that appears in print may not be available in electronic books.

Visit us online at www.fordhampress.com.

For EU safety / GPSR concerns: Mare Nostrum Group B.V., Mauritskade 21D, 1091 GC Amsterdam, The Netherlands, gpsr@mare-nostrum.co.uk

Library of Congress Cataloging-in-Publication Data available online at https://catalog.loc.gov.

Printed in the United States of America

27 26 25 5 4 3 2 1

First edition

# CONTENTS

Introduction. *God at Play: Līlā* in Hindu and Christian Traditions 1
DANIEL SOARS

**Part I: *Līlā* as Divine Will and Divine Creativity**

1 Play in East and West 21
DOUGLAS HEDLEY

2 Creating without a "Why": Divine Play as Metaphor for Creation in John Scottus Eriugena, Thomas Aquinas, and Meister Eckhart 43
BERNARD McGINN

3 God's Will and the Creative Act: Origen on Divine Volition and the Intelligibility of the Cosmos 63
DANIEL J. TOLAN

**Part II: Grace, Compassion, and Suffering: Some Pastoral Connotations of *Līlā***

4 Creation, Vision, Bliss: *Līlā* as Grace according to Rāmānuja, with Reference Also to Thomas Aquinas and Gregory Palamas 89
FRANCIS X. CLOONEY, SJ

5 *Līlā* and Divine Mercy in the *Hundred Verses to Compassion* of Vedānta Deśika 109
SUCHARITA ADLURI

6 What Does It Mean for the Goddess to Play? *Līlā* (or Its Absence) in the Śākta Traditions 135
RACHEL FELL McDERMOTT

## Part III: Some Aesthetic and Dramatic Dimensions of *Līlā*

7 "You have made me endless, such is thy pleasure": The *Līlā* of Love in the Metaphysical Poetry of Rabindranath Tagore 153
ANKUR BARUA

8 The Metaphysics of Emotion: Divine Play in Caitanya Vaiṣṇava Philosophy 178
JESSICA FRAZIER

9 The Making of the Sacred City: *Līlā* as God's Violence in a Tamil Śaiva *Talapurāṇam* 197
SRILATA RAMAN

## Part IV: Human Playfulness as Imitation of Divine *Līlā*

10 Looking to the Leader: The Divine Dance in Neoplatonism 221
STEPHEN R. L. CLARK

11 *Serio Ludere!* Divine Lessons from Tricksters and Holy Fools 244
PETER TYLER

12 The Serious Subject of Play: Play in Dance and Music 264
DOMINIC WHITE, OP

Afterword: Divine *Līlā* and Human Play 289
MICHELLE VOSS

Contributors 299

Index 303

# GOD AT PLAY

# God at Play

## *LĪLĀ* IN HINDU AND CHRISTIAN TRADITIONS

## INTRODUCTION

*Daniel Soars*

This volume presents a theological exploration of the multifaceted motif of *līlā* in Hindu and Christian contexts. Given its ubiquity in Hindu theologies and life-forms, *līlā* offers a rich comparative framework for exploring certain ways of understanding divine and human action as expressed in Hindu and Christian sacred texts, philosophical theology, and devotional practices. By focusing on *līlā* and resisting any uniform translation of this term, we also seek to avoid a tendency to which some styles of comparative theology can be prone: namely, of using predominantly Western/Christian categories to understand the Hindu other. The primary motivation behind the volume is to explore how *līlā* functions in a variety of distinctive philosophical, theological, and devotional ways across Hindu traditions, and to listen for echoes in Christian understandings of the gratuitousness of the created order in relation to God. In these ways, the volume is a genuine experiment in deep learning across traditions. As far as I am aware, it is also the first such comparative treatment of the "ludic features" of Hindu-Christian landscapes.[1]

The inchoate beginnings of this experiment stretch back some years.[2] I was becoming increasingly aware of the importance of *līlā* in Hindu universes as a way of talking about the relation between the Supreme Reality and the world but was struggling to find a neat counterpart for *līlā* in Christian theology, so varied were the contexts in which it appeared across Sanskritic and Indian vernacular landscapes. Douglas Hedley pointed me toward Bettina Bäumer's doctoral thesis, "Schöpfung als Spiel. Der Begriff *līlā* im Hinduismus, seine philosophische und theologische Bedeutung" (1969),[3] and I was familiar with common English renderings of *līlā* as "divine play." Although I suspected even then that *līlā* could not simply be translated as "play" in any straightforward manner,

I was curious about how its various connotations might or might not be present in Christian traditions. These connotations range across a broad semantic field spanning at least some of the following: freedom, lack of constraint, effortlessness, spontaneity, joy, wonder, and mystery. *Līlā* seems to encapsulate or gesture toward all of these in more capacious and subtle ways than does "play," but one has to start somewhere. As such, in early 2019 I convened a workshop in Cambridge to discuss the broad themes of "play and creation" in Hinduism and Christianity.

Despite the somewhat loosely defined remit of the conference, the discussions that day did end up having a certain thematic consistency, and participants all agreed that the rich comparative potential of the themes that arose were worthy of further exploration. In my callow exuberance, I decided to take on the task, with the gentle warning of a more experienced colleague ringing in my ears: "I don't envy you making a coherent volume out of it!" The more I thought about a future volume and the more I read back through the papers delivered, the more I started to worry that he was right. Part of the problem, as this same colleague pointed out to me, is that "creation" is a substantive topic in its own right, not the same as "creation and/as play," and "play" as a topic can be discussed distinctly from the theme of "creation." So also "play" is not the only way to think about unmotivated creation that is "free."

Trying to work out how to hold all this together—and wondering at times whether it really *did* all hold together—is part of the reason why this volume is appearing several years after that 2019 workshop.[4] I was also conscious that the conference was dominated by Christian thinkers (or, at least, thinkers with Christian backgrounds) commenting on play and creation—as is often the way with comparative endeavors—and I knew that the volume would be richer and more helpful as a piece of scholarship with more input from Hindu scholars and their expertise on *līlā* in Hindu traditions. This all meant allowing time for the original participants to rework and finesse their thoughts into book-worthy chapters and also for new contributors to improve on what we already had. I am particularly grateful to Srilata Raman and to Sucharita Adluri for agreeing to write chapters for the volume despite not being part of the initial conversations. Michelle Voss also generously agreed to write an Afterword, which does much to enrich the volume and to suggest fruitful paths for further research.

If I am honest, I still think the volume has a somewhat incomplete feel to it, in terms of what is discussed and what is not, and the thematic consistency between chapters is more obvious in some cases than in others. However, I have come to think that this may reflect something quite important about the subject matter. A volume about "creation" in Hinduism and Christianity would have been one thing,[5] and a volume about "play" would have been another, but this is not quite either of those. I now think that the main reason it has sometimes felt as if this volume lacked clearly defined boundaries is because it was at root *inspired by a concept without clearly defined boundaries* or, at least, a concept without a straightforward meaning which fits across all contexts: namely, the concept of *līlā*.

In a major recent reexamination of the concept of *līlā* in Hindu philosophy and theology, as revered an authority as Julius Lipner argues that there simply is no "universal fit." *Līlā*, he shows in the article, "is a context-sensitive term whose translation must reflect its polysemic nature. I do not think it can be 'defined' *sensu stricto*."[6] Given its broad semantic range and context-specific connotations, even an analysis of *līlā* like Lipner's, which focuses solely on its Hindu usages, is inevitably "many-streamed,"[7] with some nuances emphasized more in some contexts than in others, and some meanings overlapping while others appear quite discrete. Lipner recognizes, therefore, that even the sort of considered discussion he offers "is far from exhaustive of the philosophical and theological nuances and functions of *līlā* (not to mention *krīḍā* and *khelā*) in Hindu thought."[8] In an earlier collection of essays, *The Gods at Play: Līlā in South Asia*, William S. Sax and his contributors came to a similar conclusion.[9] Rather than trying to fix on an "essence" of *līlā*, Sax argues that it is better in this case to settle for a Wittgensteinian "family resemblance" approach, where we recognize that there are partially overlapping similarities in different usages of *līlā*, even if there is no one definition that fits them all.[10] Across texts and performances, contributors to Sax's volume found that the most important *līlā*-shaped themes that recurred in different contexts were freedom, spontaneity, and playfulness. Even here, though, Sax sounds a cautionary note similar to that of Lipner: "It is important to remember that precisely what freedom, spontaneity, and playfulness might entail in different contexts and at different times in Indian history is not necessarily self-evident and certainly not always the same."[11]

Inviting comparative reflection on such a theme is only likely to complicate this picture even further, for there will be resonances heard by some Christian thinkers not heard by others and vice versa. The echoes picked up by the particular contributors to this volume cannot, therefore, claim any degree of completeness. Like all comparative theology, the particular choices of which texts and themes to engage with have a degree of arbitrariness. In this case, these choices reflect the idiosyncratic responses of particular Hindu and Christian thinkers to certain shades of meaning they have picked up in their understandings of *līlā* in Hindu texts and life-forms.

I have come to think that the incompleteness of the volume is more of a virtue than a vice, though. It reflects the multifaceted and inherently polyvalent nature of its subject matter. A longer comparative Hindu-Christian volume about *līlā* could be more exhaustive of the range of possible meanings of this term, but it would still be difficult to know where to draw the boundaries; a more internally consistent volume would also be possible but would, I think, risk straitjacketing the semantic range of *līlā* for the sake of greater overall coherence. I am inclined, therefore, to say, along with Lipner, and without too much of an apology, that "we have made a start, and others can add to or modify the semantic range distinguished here."[12]

## The Semantic Range of Līlā

The *locus classicus* for theological discussions of *līlā* in Hindu traditions is the passage in Bādarāyaṇa's *Vedāntasūtras* at 2.1.32–34.[13] The verses form part of a lengthy section on the origin of the world and at this point, an opponent objects that Brahman (the Supreme Reality) cannot have produced the world because Brahman would have no motive (*na prayojanavattvāt*) to create (or indeed, to do anything else). The belief, drawn from Upaniṣadic testimony, is that Brahman lacks nothing and is self-fulfilled, and would therefore have no *reason* to create. The Vedāntic reply given in the following verse (2.1.33) is that creating for Brahman is *līlākaivalyam*, comparable to instances we see in the world (*lokavat*). But what does it mean to say that the production of the world from Brahman is *līlā*?

In his commentary on this verse, Śaṃkara (ca. eighth century CE) explains as follows:

> As in the world it is seen that though a king or some councillor of the king who has got all his desires fulfilled, may still, without any aim in view, indulge in activities [in their pleasure-halls/*krīḍā-vihāreṣu*] in the forms of sports and pastimes [*kevalaṃ līlārūpāḥ pravṛttayaḥ*], as a sort of diversion, or as inhalation, exhalation, etc. proceed spontaneously

> [*svabhāvād*] without depending on any external motive, so also God can have activities of the nature of mere pastime out of His spontaneity without any extraneous motive. For any motive imputed to God can have neither the support of reason nor of the Vedas.[14]

*Līlā* here, then, connotes divine freedom in creating; God is self-fulfilled and lacks nothing, and yet chooses to create despite there being no compulsion or ulterior motive, just as someone might choose to do some activity for the pleasure of doing it, even though one is already perfectly satisfied. Creating for Brahman is as natural and spontaneous as breathing in and out. As Lipner puts it:

> The Lord's creative act is conscious, premeditated, as when a king engages in a game in his pleasure-hall. But it is spontaneous in the sense that it is not forced in any way or subservient to some ulterior purpose; it springs freely from the power of His nature (*svabhāvād*) just as breathing in and out springs from our natural constitution (*svabhāvād*).[15]

Given their seminal status in discussions of *līlā*, it is no surprise that several chapters in this volume focus on the themes of divine will and divine freedom and creativity raised by the aphorisms in *Brahmasūtra* 2.1.32–3. Most individual chapters are not comparative in their own right but focus on specific *līlā*-related themes in Hinduism or in Christianity—thus making the volume comparative when taken as a whole. Douglas Hedley's chapter, however, is a comparative tour de force, touching on many of the different connotations of *līlā* in Hindu contexts which I have addressed in this introduction and highlighting echoes in certain themes and figures in the Neoplatonic and Christian traditions. His chapter thus serves as a fitting opening to the volume and might usefully be read first in order to gain a broad sense of the landscape which is mapped out in fine-grained detail in the other chapters.

Though he does not analyze the *Brahmasūtra* passage as such, Bernard McGinn addresses its echoes in Christian theology in his chapter on three medieval theologians (John Scotus Eriugena, Thomas Aquinas, and Meister Eckhart) who each argue in different ways that God creates "without a why." Creation *is* willed by God, McGinn insists, but for God "willing is not purposeful like the particular actions of created intellectual beings. This "willing" is transcendental, an absolute spontaneity of life flowing out of the divine ground."[16] There is no "why" in the sense of an ulterior motive or external compulsion; God creates just like a horse spontaneously gambols in a meadow.[17] What is more, Eckhart invites us to share in this divine *līlā*: "It is 'living without a why' (*âne warumbe, sunder warumbe*), a share in the inconceivable freeness in which God created the universe, something more like play than purpose."[18]

In his chapter, Daniel Tolan offers a close analysis of the nature of divine volition as understood by the early Christian thinker Origen of Alexandria (ca. 185–253 CE). Tolan notes that Origen does not use the imagery of "play" in a positive light and does not discuss "play" at all in relation to creation because he is concerned to demonstrate the rationality and intelligibility of God's will in creating. This is a good example of why Lipner is right to caution us against *starting* "our inquiry into the meaning of *līlā* by exploring the semantics of the English word "play" and its putative substitutes."[19] For Origen, "play" has negative connotations, perhaps similar to the madman in *Brahmasūtra* 2.1.32 whose actions are purposeless due to the derangement of his brain. Śaṃkara would have no hesitation in agreeing with Origen that this is not how we should picture God's activity in creating.[20] God is certainly free in Origen's understanding, but there is no hint of randomness or whimsy. As Tolan puts it, "If, by 'divine play' [*līlā*], one has in mind a non-compelled creative act, then this squares with what Origen has in mind. However, when it comes to creation itself, all things within creation have a 'why,' an 'account,' a 'reason,' or, more succinctly, a 'logos' for creation, and this is God."[21]

Rāmānuja (ca. eleventh century CE) follows Śaṃkara in his commentary on *Brahmasūtra* 2.1.32–3, emphasizing the free and voluntary nature of divine creation in his *Śrī Bhāṣya*. Lipner comments on Rāmānuja as follows: "By invoking the contingency of the creative act—its superfluity in terms of the divine nature—*līlā* is inherently *a relational term* signifying the dependent nature of all 'added' being, which derives *per se* from the Absolute Being and exists as entirely reliant on Its free will."[22] This is another example of why "play" is only a partially adequate rendering of *līlā*, and explains why two chapters in this volume focus on Rāmānuja and highlight quite different connotations of his understanding of our key term.

Francis Clooney brings this Śrīvaiṣṇava understanding of *līlā* into conversation with Christian theology and focuses on how Rāmānuja invites us to see the world as a sacramental embodiment of God's presence. Clooney underscores the ongoing, continual aspect of creation ex nihilo—not as the production of the world at some one originary point, but as the sustaining activity of a loving God. Thus understood, *līlā* "characterizes creation as a graced site, a sheer gift . . . and the mutual delight of God and God's people."

Sucharita Adluri discusses *līlā*'s function in the welfare of beings, especially their liberation from the cycle of birth and rebirth (*saṃsāra*). In their commentaries on *Brahmasūtra* 2.1.34, both Śaṃkara and Rāmānuja explain that the Lord is guided by the law of *karma* in producing the sort of world we see around us, showing that *līlā* is a weightier notion than "play" might suggest.[23] Adluri explains how Rāmānuja highlights a merciful and gracious aspect of *līlā*, and then turns to the writings of one his disciples, Vedānta Deśika (thirteenth–fourteenth centuries CE) to explore this connection further. Undergirded by Viśiṣṭādvaita Vedānta, the Śrīvaiṣṇava imagination of *līlā* expands its primary denotation as spontaneous divine activity to envision it as an emancipatory act and as intimately connected with divine compassion, mercy, and grace (*dayā/krpā/karuṇā/anukaṃpā*).

Rachel Fell McDermott continues in a similar vein to Adluri and Clooney by exploring some pastoral connotations of *līlā* and its resonances with themes related to grace, compassion, and suffering. She does this by focusing on the presence (and absence) of *līlā* in the Goddess-centered Hindu Śākta tradition. She argues that *līlā* as "playfulness" is not viewed as positively in the Goddess tradition as it is in the Kṛṣṇa-centered Vaiṣṇava tradition. *Līlā* is rather associated with the transcendent inscrutability of divine action. McDermott questions whether *līlā* thus understood can provide a pastorally sensitive response to human suffering, especially when the illusory—and sometimes even deliberately *delusory*—nature of the divine becomes enmeshed with human beings caught in *saṃsāra* and the outworkings of *karma* and release.[24]

*Līlā*, then, is often used in the context of creation or world-production—for example, in *Brahmasūtra* 2.1.33–34 and commentaries on these passages in Advaita and Śrīvaiṣṇava Hindu traditions. This use of *līlā* is picked up and discussed in various ways in the volume, especially in the chapters by Hedley, McGinn, and Tolan. As well as a certain notion of playfulness, the connotations of *līlā* in these contexts span a wide range: from spontaneity, effortlessness, and lack of constraint to compassion, mercy, and grace. Adluri, Clooney, and McDermott focus particularly on these latter connotations and on how *līlā* is connected to theodicy; in the context of *saṃsāra* and the outworkings of *karma*, *līlā* means something more like the inscrutability of the divine, and suffering becomes part of the mysterious *līlā* of God.

A different development of these nuances of *līlā* can be found in post-Vedic purāṇic literature, where the term is used in the context of divine descents or *avatāras*.[25] Here, *līlā* "signifies the arrival or activity of the divine *avatāra* and, by this token, reveals the Deity's involvement with the phenomenal world, which in some traditions has given rise to the concept of the *līlā-avatāra*."[26] The *Harivaṃśa Purāṇa* (ca. 300 CE), for example, contains stories about Kṛṣṇa which are retold a century later in the *Viṣṇu Purāṇa* where his antics are called *līlā*s and the whole of his earthly time is described as *manuṣyalīlā* (5.7.38). Around the ninth century these antics were fully elaborated in the tenth book of the *Bhāgavata Purāṇa*.[27] It is not too much of a stretch to see how *līlā* here can describe the playfulness of the deity who descends to interact with humans, just as it was used in the earlier Vedāntic literature to convey the spontaneity and ease of accomplishment with which God produces the world.

> After all, this is what God is supposed to do by His mighty powers and inscrutable ways—challenge the limits of human expectation, sometimes in a guise that would in normal circumstances be unequal to the task (here, that of a youth) and often in response to the devotee's supplication, to vindicate the faith of those who have eyes to see.[28]

Ankur Barua focuses on the paradigmatic narrative of Kṛṣṇa and the cowherd women (*gopī*) found in the *Bhāgavata Purāṇa* (10.29–33). The agonized quest of the cowherd women to be united with their divine lover, during which they discern vivid signs of Kṛṣṇa's absence everywhere, is followed by their reunion with Kṛṣṇa and their rejoicing when Kṛṣṇa joins them in a circle dance (*rāsa līlā*). Barua explores some expressions of these motifs in the devotional songs of Rabindranath Tagore (1861–1941), in whose poetry *līlā* becomes entangled with the languages of longing, desolation, separation, joyfulness, love, and fulfilment.

Jessica Frazier thinks about the metaphysics of creative powers from the perspective of sixteenth- to eighteenth-century Vedāntic philosophers in the Caitanya Vaiṣṇava tradition and highlights some of the more dramatic and aesthetic dimensions of *līlā*. Rūpa Gosvāmī, Jīva Gosvāmī, and Baladeva Vidyābhūṣaṇa defend the idea that the ground of the world is replete with generative power that naturally tends toward open-ended development in what they thought of as divine *līlā* or "play." They utilize the notions of ontological fullness (*pūrṇa*) and infinite power (*śakti*) alongside the *satkāryavāda* theory of immanent causation, and the *rāsa* theory of emergent aesthetic significance. What results is a metaphysics that seeks to celebrate the complex, creative, animating powers that lie at the root of the world we know.[29]

In her chapter, Srilata Raman focuses on the Śaivite tradition—how it is part of Śiva's *līlā* to create sacred landscapes and cities on earth as is shown specifically in the South Indian and Tamil literatures (*talapurāṇa/sthalapurāṇa*).

As well as being a theological concept, *līlā* also refers to a certain kind of theatrical performance found throughout India which dramatizes the lives and actions of divine *avatāras* and epic figures (e.g., *Pāṇḍav-līlā*, *Rām-līlā*, and *Rāsa-līlā*). In these role-plays, setting, characters, and story are all important because "the actors, as well as the viewers, are usually thought of as participants in an actual *re-presentation* of the 'past' action"[30] or sacred episode which is being play-acted. There are several excellent studies of specific plays in this genre in Sax's collected volume, which we have not sought to repeat here,[31] but a number of our contributors have taken this more performative aspect of *līlā* as inspiration for their discussions. Stephen Clark and Dominic White both explore in different ways music and dance as a response to the divine. For Clark, these are spiritual and metaphysical concepts drawn from Plotinus, who, at his death, "joined the dance of immortal love." By putting aside our merely sensory attachments and looking toward the divine leader of the chorus (not a conductor, but the musician or lead dancer in the center), we can return to the companionship in the divine from which we fell. White examines medieval French Cathedral dances, with their choreography mirroring the Angelic Dance, and the "play of the impossible" in the visionary and playful religious music of Olivier Messiaen, especially his adoption of Hindu rhythms. He argues that music and dance enable a return to knowledge through the senses as a basis for theology.

Peter Tyler picks up on this idea of human playfulness as an imitation of divine *līlā* in his examination of the figure of the "trickster" or "holy fool." He takes the work of Carl Jung and Paul Radin as his starting point and asks what role there is for such figures in contemporary Christian worship and practice. Further comparative work might usefully reflect on some of God's surprising (playful?) interactions with the world in the Jewish and Christian scriptures: One thinks of many of the unlikely characters God uses to convey his message—the hundred-year-old Abraham who laughs when God promises him a son (Genesis 17:17); Moses who is "slow of speech and tongue" and yet tasked with speaking to Pharaoh (Exodus 4:10); the shepherd boy David defeating the soldier

Goliath (1 Samuel 17); or the locust and honey-eating character of John the Baptist who is chosen to prepare the way for Christ (Mark 1:1–8).[32]

The thematic trios into which I have organized the volume should not be seen as hard and fast. They emerged more or less organically as people revised their essays in dialogue with other chapters, but the divisions have the same fuzzy edges and multiple overlapping areas one would expect given what we have said about the polysemic nature of the subject matter. Each "trio" does form a thematic conversation, but they could doubtless be organized differently.

## Why Does *Līlā* Matter?

More than half a century has passed since the publication of Johan Huizinga's seminal work *Homo Ludens* (1949) on the importance of play in human culture and society.[33] Much like *līlā*, Huizinga shows that "play" is not straightforwardly reducible or translatable into other terms, but some of its key characteristics overlap with many of the chapters in this volume. It is voluntary and free, but nevertheless ordered and rule-bound; it sometimes involves elements of pretend and make-believe (often in a special place and for a limited period); and it promotes the formation of social groupings.[34] Indeed, "the great archetypal activities of human society [such as language, myth, and ritual] are all permeated with play from the start," meaning that human culture can only be understood *sub specie ludi*.[35] This is all the more true of religious traditions, where ideas of ritual, sacrifice, liturgy, sacrament, and mystery can all be seen to fall under the concept of "play"/*līlā*.[36]

Two of the most sustained treatments of the relevance of play-related tropes in Christianity appeared in German in the second half of the twentieth century: Hugo Rahner's *Man at Play* and Jürgen Moltmann's *Theology of Play*.[37] If there is a parallel to *Brahmasūtra* 2.1.32–34 in the Jewish and Christian scriptures, it is surely the figure of divine Wisdom (*hochmah*/*sophia*) "dancing" or "playing" before the face of God in Proverbs 8:27–31.[38] Rahner shows how these verses have often been interpreted in the same vein as Vedāntic commentators' interpretations of the *Brahmasūtra* aphorisms—i.e., that creation is "meaningful but not necessary."[39] In a similar way to the *līlā-avatāra* in Hinduism, Rahner also refers to God's incarnation in the human person of Jesus as a "game" because there is "nothing here of compulsion or calculation."[40] Such divine playfulness is a reminder, Rahner argues, of the importance of *eutrapelia* in Christian living. Indeed, Rahner was inspired to write his book by Aquinas's comparison of play with contemplation—both give pleasure and both are ends in themselves—and by Aristotle's notion of the person who strikes a balance between buffoonery and boorishness (the *eutrapelos*), as well as by references to play in some of the Church Fathers.[41] In an article on the role of laughter in the Christian life, Terry Lindvall reminds us that Evagrius identified *hilaritas* as a key Christian virtue—at the right time and place, laughter is part of what it means to live in the Spirit.[42] Perhaps one of the more obvious gaps in this volume is a chapter specifically on humor.

Playful man knows two things and holds them in creative tension: that his life has meaning and yet that he is not the product of necessity. In imitation of our Creator, we ought thus to go about life with appropriate seriousness but also with the spontaneity and lightness of touch of a skilled actor or musician.[43]

> The nature of the inward gaiety of the man who truly plays, and for whom earnest and jest are sisters, is at bottom a religious problem, and this peculiar quality can only be attained by one who is both of heaven and of earth.[44]

Moltmann, likewise, suggests that the contingent nature of the created world can either lead to nihilism and despair or to playfulness. I quote the following passage at some length because the echoes of Vedāntic understandings of *līlā* are striking:

> The world as free creation cannot be a necessary unfolding of God nor an emanation of his being from his divine fullness. God is free. But he does not act capriciously. When he creates something that is not God but also not nothing, then this must have its ground not in itself but in God's *good will* or *pleasure*. Hence the creation is God's play, a play of his groundless and inscrutable wisdom. It is the realm in which God displays his glory. . . . God created the world neither out of his own essence nor by caprice. It did not have to be, but creation suits his deepest nature or else he would not enjoy it. This may be expressed symbolically in the categories of play.[45]

Like Rahner, Moltmann takes the *Deus ludens* as a pattern for human living. The category of play is a crucial counterbalance to the tendency in capitalist societies to measure a person's worth by what they produce or achieve:

> Play as world symbol goes beyond the categories of doing, having, and achieving and leads us into the categories of being, of authentic human existence and demonstrative rejoicing in it. It emphasizes the creative against the productive and the aesthetic against the ethical. Earthbound labor finds relief in rejoicing, dancing, singing, and playing. This also does labor a lot of good.[46]

Indeed, forgetting this balance has serious consequences. Moltmann is surely not overstating the case when he says: "When a man sees the meaning of life only in being useful and used, he necessarily gets caught in a crisis of living, when illness or sorrow makes everything including himself seem useless."[47]

In one of the most recent treatments of *līlā*-related themes in Christian contexts, Brian Edgar makes the case for his work not on grounds of originality but due to a focus on "the needs of the present day":

> In the contemporary world it is a rare thing to find *any* sustained theological reflection upon play or the spiritual importance of a playful attitude (or, perhaps to a lesser extent, its associated concepts such as humor, dance, creativity, relaxation, spontaneity and joy).[48]

This "playful attitude" is what the Greeks saw as the essential virtue of *eutrapelia*—getting the right balance between work and leisure, between seriousness and fun. Edgar is not the first or only commentator to have noticed that industrialized societies often get this balance wrong and are reaping the psychological consequences.[49] He argues that Christians in particular need to develop a "play ethic" to complement the positive elements of the more culturally dominant "work ethic."[50]

Robert K. Johnston takes a similar position in his 1997 book, *The Christian at Play*, where he claims that "the person at play is expressing his or her God-given nature."[51] Johnston shows how Josef Pieper's case has become ever more relevant half a century later. Leisure is no longer a luxury only for a social elite because the twentieth century has seen an increase in available time and disposable income for leisure in developed economies, and yet people struggle to enjoy their leisure time in meaningful ways, often just reducing it to consumption or idleness.[52] Economic abundance ironically seems to leave less space for true leisure. Even for a younger generation that seems to prize self-development over work, the only thing that has changed, Johnston argues, is the object—external achievement has been replaced by a culture of narcissism and internal achievement. The result is that leisure is placed under the "tyranny of a work mentality."[53] Just as Pieper called for a reappraisal of the value of leisure, Johnston urges us to reconsider play as a possible remedy for this cultural *dis*-ease.[54] More than two decades on since Johnston's book, the cultural landscape has changed unrecognizably (and probably irrevocably) due to the ubiquity of the internet, social media, and smartphones—especially among children and adolescents. As I write this introduction, Jonathan Haidt's book *The Anxious Generation*[55] is topping the *New York Times* bestseller list: A central tenet of his argument is that the developed world has created an epidemic of mental illness,[56] partly due to losing what he calls "play-based" childhood. Just as the UN Convention on the Rights of the Child identifies the right to "relax and play" (Article 31) as central to a child's basic development and flourishing, so Haidt insists that play is crucial to health and well-being.

In short, there are at least three reasons why this comparative volume on *līlā* is important. First, and perhaps most obviously, its ubiquity in Hinduism makes a nuanced understanding of the polyvalence of *līlā* a crucial part of understanding these religious traditions. Second, by resisting a uniform translation of the term merely as "play," we are able to uncover its importance in Christian belief and practice as well: From the contingent nature of creation to the mystery of the incarnation, from the exuberance of grace to the joy of dance and music, *līlā*-shaped themes permeate Christian landscapes as well. Finally, by reflecting on God's *līlā*, we can allow ourselves to imitate this divine ease by approaching life with a certain "lightness" and allowing for a degree of what Gadamer called *Spielraum*.[57] Just as there needs to be some "play" in a structural joint so that it is neither too tight nor too loose, so we need some "play" in our lives lest they become suffocated by a perceived need to plan, produce, and control. Reflecting on *līlā* reminds us that theology is hollow if it remains at a purely conceptual level; it is also meant to help us to live well. Perhaps this rather serious academic tome can remind us to listen in our day-to-day life for the celestial laughter heard by Dante as he follows Beatrice into Paradise.

## References

Bäumer, Bettina. "Schöpfung als Spiel: Der Begriff *līlā* im Hinduismus, seine philosophische und theologische Bedeutung." Unpublished doctoral thesis, University of Munich, 1969.

Boyd Brown, Christopher. "*Deus Ludens*: God at Play in Luther's Theology." *Concordia Theological Quarterly* 81, no. 1–2 (2017): 153–170.

Brown, Stuart, with Christopher Vaughan. *Play: How It Shapes the Brain, Opens the Imagination, and Invigorates the Soul.* New York: Avery, 2009.

Caillois, Roger. *Man and the Sacred.* Glencoe, IL: Free Press, 1959.

Caillois, Roger. *Man, Play, and Games.* New York: Free Press, 1961.

Coomaraswamy, Ananda K. "Līlā." *Journal of the American Oriental Society* 61 (1941): 98–101.

Cox, Harvey. *The Feast of Fools: A Theological Essay on Festivity and Fantasy.* Cambridge, MA: Harvard University Press, 1969.

Edgar, Brian. *The God Who Plays: A Playful Approach to Theology and Spirituality.* Eugene, OR: Cascade, 2017.

Frazier, Jessica. *Reality, Religion, and Passion: Indian and Western Approaches in Hans-Georg Gadamer and Rūpa Gosvāmī.* Lanham, MD: Lexington Books, 2009.

Gambhirananda, Swami, trans. *Brahma Sūtra Bhāṣya of Śaṅkarācārya.* 13th ed. Kolkata: Advaita Ashrama, 2016.

Guardini, Romano. *The Spirit of the Liturgy.* London: Sheed & Ward, 1935.

Haidt, Jonathan. *The Anxious Generation: How the Great Rewiring of Childhood Is Causing an Epidemic of Mental Illness.* New York: Penguin.

Huizinga, Johan. *Homo Ludens: A Study of the Play-Element in Culture.* Kettering, OH: Angelico Press, 2016.

Johnston, Robert K. *The Christian at Play.* Eugene, OR: Wipf and Stock, 1997.

Kane, Pat. *The Play Ethic: A Manifesto for a Different Way of Living.* London: Macmillan, 2004.

Keen, Sam. *Apology for Wonder.* New York: Harper and Rowe, 1969.

Keen, Sam. *To a Dancing God.* London: Fontana, 1971.

Kinsley, David R. *The Divine Player: A Study of Kṛṣṇa Līlā.* Delhi: Motilal Banarsidass, 1979.

Lindvall, Terry. 'The Role of Laughter in the Christian Life." In *Knowing and Doing: CS Lewis Institute* (Spring 2015), accessed here: The Role of Laughter in the Christian Life—C. S. Lewis Institute (cslewisinstitute.org).

Lipner, Julius J. "A God at Play? Reexamining the Concept of *Līlā* in Hindu Philosophy and Theology." *International Journal of Hindu Studies* 26 (2022): 283–326

Miller, David L. *Gods and Games: Toward a Theology of Play.* 1970. Stillpoint, 2013/1970.

Moltmann, Jürgen. *Theology of Play.* Translated by Reinhard Ulrich. New York: Harper and Row, 1972.

Neale, R. E. *In Praise of Play: Toward a Psychology of Religion.* New York: Harper and Row, 1969.

Pieper, Joseph. *Leisure: The Basis of Culture.* Translated by A. Dru. London: Faber and Faber, 1952.

Rahner, Hugo, SJ. *Man at Play.* 1964. Providence, RI: Cluny Media, 2019.

Raj, Selva, and Corinne Dempsey. *Sacred Play: Ritual Levity and Humor in South Asian Religions.* Albany: SUNY Press, 2010.

Sax, William S., ed. *The Gods at Play: Līlā in South Asia.* New York: Oxford University Press, 1995.

Schweig, Graham M. *Dance of Divine Love: The Rāsa Līlā of Krishna from the Bhāgavata Purāṇa, India's Classic Sacred Love Story, Introduced, Translated, and Illuminated.* Princeton, NJ: Princeton University Press, 2005.

Schweig, Graham M. "*Līlā*." Oxford Bibliographies Online.

Valpey, Kenneth R. "Viewpoint: Reflections on Ludic Dimensions in Hindu-Christian Scholarship." *Journal of Hindu-Christian Studies* 25 (2012): Article 10.

## Notes

1. Kenneth R. Valpey suggested more than ten years ago that there should be "more such work (or play) in the area of the ludic, as an important means of stretching our understanding of where these two traditions—Hindu and Christian—meet, where they part company, and how persons (including scholars of Hindu-Christian studies) go about relating the two traditions." Valpey, "Reflections on Ludic Dimensions," *Journal of Hindu-Christian Studies* 25 (2012): 51. Valpey was reflecting on the volume edited by Selva Raj and Corinne Dempsey titled *Sacred Play: Ritual Levity and Humor in South Asian Religions* (SUNY, 2010).
2. The seeds of the volume began in conversations I was having with Douglas Hedley and Ankur Barua about divine and human creativity in Hinduism and Christianity.
3. Bettina Bäumer, "Schöpfung als Spiel: Der Begriff līlā im Hinduismus, seine philosophische und theologische Bedeutung" (University of Munich, unpublished doctoral thesis, 1969)—"Creation as Play: Philosophical and Theological Meanings of the Concept of *Līlā* in Hinduism" (my translation).
4. The arrival of a global pandemic in the intervening period certainly contributed to the delay as well, though it did provide valuable time for rumination.
5. Of course, the doctrine of creation *has* proven to be a fruitful resource for comparative Hindu-Christian theological reflection in the work of figures like Brahmabandhab Upadhyay, Bede Griffiths, and Raimundo Panikkar.
6. Julius J. Lipner, "A God at Play? Reexamining the Concept of *Līlā* in Hindu Philosophy and Theology," in *International Journal of Hindu Studies* 26 (2022): 323.
7. Lipner, "A God at Play?" 302.
8. Lipner, "A God at Play?" 321.
9. William S. Sax, ed., *The Gods at Play: Līlā in South Asia* (New York: Oxford University Press, 1995).
10. See Sax, *Gods at Play*, 4–5. The volume came out of a 1989 conference at Harvard whose aim was to unite theological and anthropological approaches to see if there was any common ground in understandings of *līlā* across these textual and performative boundaries.
11. Sax, *Gods at Play*, 5. He points out that some *līlā* performances can also involve grief and sorrow, or can have connotations of terror, deception, subversiveness, or the erotic, which are certainly not common to all usages of *līlā*.
12. Sax, *Gods at Play*, 5. For further resources on *līlā* in Hindu traditions, see Graham M. Schweig's Oxford Bibliographies entry.
13. This text, also known as the *Brahmasūtras*, is a distillation of the key teachings of Vedānta, and is generally dated to the early centuries of the Common Era. For more

detail on early uses of *līlā*, see Ananda K. Coomaraswamy, "Līlā," *Journal of the American Oriental Society* 61 (1941): 98–101, and Lipner, "A God at Play?" 288n15.

14. Swami Gambhirananda, trans., *Brahma Sūtra Bhāṣya of Śaṅkarācārya*, 13th ed. (Kolkata: Advaita Ashrama, 2016), II.i.33 (p. 361). Abbreviated hereafter to BSBh.
15. Lipner, "A God at Play?" 291.
16. Bernard McGinn, "Creating without a 'Why'," in this volume.
17. Meister Eckhart's image for God's *līlā* (see McGinn, "Creating without a 'Why'").
18. McGinn, "Creating without a 'Why'"
19. Lipner, "A God at Play?" 285.
20. BSBh. II.i.32 (p. 361).
21. Daniel Tolan, "God's Will and the Creative Act: Origen on Divine Volition and the Intelligibility of the Cosmos."
22. Lipner, "A God at Play?" 297.
23. Cf. Lipner, "A God at Play?" 292, 302.
24. Lipner responds to some of McDermott's concerns in his article already cited (cf. 299–300).
25. For more on this, see Clifford Hospital, "*Līlā* in Early Vaiṣṇava Thought" in Sax (1995), 21.
26. Lipner, "A God at Play?" 306.
27. For more detail on this development in the purāṇic literature, see Norvin Hein, "*Līlā*," in *The Gods at Play*, ed. Sax, 15–18.
28. Lipner, "A God at Play?" 307.
29. See also Jessica Frazier's comparative consideration of Rūpa Gosvāmī's concept of *līlā* and Hans-Georg Gadamer's notion of *Spiel* in her work *Reality, Religion, and Passion: Indian and Western Approaches in Hans-Georg Gadamer and Rūpa Gosvāmī* (Lanham, MD: Lexington Books, 2009).
30. Lipner, "A God at Play?" 314. See also John S. Hawley, "Every Play a Play within a Play," in *The Gods at Play*, ed. Sax, 115–30; David R. Kinsley, *The Divine Player: A Study of Kṛṣṇa Līlā* (Delhi: Motilal Banarsidass, 1979); Graham M. Schweig, *Dance of Divine Love: The Rāsa Līlā of Krishna from the Bhāgavata Purāṇa, India's Classic Sacred Love Story, Introduced, Translated, and Illuminated* (Princeton, NJ: Princeton University Press, 2005).
31. See the chapters by D. Wulff, N. Kumar, V. Narayanan, and A. Hiltebeitel, as well as those by J. S. Hawley and W. Sax mentioned above.
32. Christopher Boyd Brown shows how the images of God as a father playing with his children and Christ playing with his disciples are important to Luther's theology; see "*Deus Ludens*: God at Play in Luther's Theology," *Concordia Theological Quarterly* 81, no. 1–2 (2017): 153–170 (esp. 163–167).
33. Johan Huizinga, *Homo Ludens: A Study of the Play-Element in Culture* (Kettering, OH: Angelico Press, 2016).
34. Huizinga, *Homo Ludens*, 7.
35. Huizinga, *Homo Ludens*, 4.
36. Huizinga, *Homo Ludens*, 18. See also Romano Guardini, *The Spirit of the Liturgy* (London, 1937), especially "The Playfulness of the Liturgy," 85–106.
37. Hugo Rahner, SJ, *Man at Play*, trans. B. Battershaw and E. Quinn (Providence, RI: Cluny Media, 2019/1964)—originally *Der spielende Mensch*; Jurgen Moltmann, *Theol-*

*ogy of Play*, trans. Reinhard Ulrich (New York: Harper and Row, 1972)—originally *Die ersten Freigelassenen der Schöpfung*. See also Harvey Cox, *The Feast of Fools: A Theological Essay on Festivity and Fantasy* (Cambridge, MA Harvard University Press, 1969); David L. Miller, *Gods and Games: Toward a Theology of Play* (California: Stillpoint, 2013/1970); R. E. Neale, *In Praise of Play: Toward a Psychology of Religion* (New York: Harper and Row, 1969); Sam Keen, *Apology for Wonder* (New York: Harper and Row, 1969), and *To a Dancing God* (London: Fontana, 1971).

38. Rahner discusses various possible translations of the Hebrew and Greek (Septuagint) in some detail in ibid., 24–29.
39. A phrase used throughout by Huizinga, Rahner, and Moltmann.
40. Rahner, *Man at Play*, 61–62.
41. Rahner, *Man at Play*, 29–31, 117–133. For original sources, see Aquinas, *Expositio super Boethium, "De Hebdomadibus"* (Paris: Mandonnet, 1927), 165f. and *Summa Theologiae* II–II, q.168, aa.2–4. See also Maximus, *Ambigua*, 261a.
42. Terry Lindvall, "The Role of Laughter in the Christian Life," in *Knowing and Doing: CS Lewis Institute* (Spring 2015), accessed here: The Role of Laughter in the Christian Life—C. S. Lewis Institute (cslewisinstitute.org). See also Valpey, "Reflections on Ludic Dimensions," 52.
43. Rahner, *Man at Play*, 36–38. Moltmann (*Theology of Play*, 34) makes the interesting point that emphasizing incarnation as God's solution for sin makes it sound necessary (and leads to all sorts of questions like why then, why there, etc.)—and we forget the joy of God *wanting* to become man (i.e., neither necessary nor capricious).
44. Rahner, *Man at Play*, 45.
45. Moltmann, *Theology of Play*, 17 (original emphasis).
46. Moltmann, *Theology of Play*, 23–24. Josef Pieper made a similar case in his seminal work *Leisure: The Basis of Culture*, trans. A. Dru (London: Faber and Faber, 1952). Perhaps "leisure" would be another useful rendering of *līlā* in certain contexts.
47. Moltmann, *Theology of Play*, 19.
48. Brian Edgar, *The God Who Plays: A Playful Approach to Theology and Spirituality* (Eugene, OR: Cascade, 2017), 2.
49. See also, Roger Caillois, *Man and the Sacred* (Glencoe, IL Free Press, 1959), and *Man, Play, and Games* (New York: Free Press, 1961); Pat Kane, *The Play Ethic: A Manifesto for a Different Way of Living* (London: Macmillan, 2004); Stuart Brown with Christopher Vaughan, *Play: How It Shapes the Brain, Opens the Imagination, and Invigorates the Soul* (New York: Avery, 2009).
50. Edgar, *The God Who Plays* 73.
51. Robert K. Johnston, *The Christian at Play* (Eugene, OF: Wipf and Stock, 1997), vii.
52. Johnston, *The Christian at Play*, 7–15.
53. Johnston, *The Christian at Play*, 20–21.
54. Johnston, *The Christian at Play*, 28.
55. Jonathan Haidt, *The Anxious Generation: How the Great Rewiring of Childhood Is Causing an Epidemic of Mental Illness* (New York: Penguin, 2024).
56. Haidt focuses in particular on evidence of increased social anxiety, sleep deprivation, attention fragmentation, addiction, and depression in adolescents in North America, Canada, and Europe.
57. Miller, *Gods and Games*, xii.

PART I

# *Līlā* as Divine Will and Divine Creativity

# 1 Play in East and West

*Douglas Hedley*

> *Līlā* appears to mark a delightful difference between European and South Asian traditions, embodying a ludic dimension in Indian religious life that is muted or even absent in the dominant religions of the West. Though there may be examples of "playfulness" in Judaism, Christianity, or Islam, still it seems fair to say that Hinduism has developed the doctrine of play more than any of the other so-called world religions, and that this idea has supported, particularly in the more recent religious history of the subcontinent, a pervasive attitude of joy and delight in God's *līlā*.[1]

Although William Sax is clearly correct that the concept of *līlā*, or play, is a dominant principle in South Asian thought, its parallels in Western thought are instructive. In this essay I shall concentrate on the metaphysical, the aesthetic, and the mystical-soteriological dimensions of the notion of play. That is to say that I will explore the idea of the playful spontaneity of the first principle, the significance of the aesthetic dimension of play, and finally the notion of the experience of blissful participation in creative play or activity of the divine in the world. We shall see that models of play, spontaneity, and theater are closely linked in the Greek as well as the Sanskrit traditions.

I concentrate on the figure of Plotinus. His work is the unique instance of ancient philosophy for which we possess the entire works and a detailed account of their production in the *Vita Plotini* of Porphyry. It was the particular fusion of Platonism, Aristotelianism, and Stoicism in Plotinus that deeply influenced Christian and Muslim thought to such a degree that H. G. Gadamer could even speak of the "platonisch-plotinische

Wirkungseinheit"—the "Platonic-Plotinian unitary legacy."[2] I argue that play was a powerful component of this legacy.

The comparison with Plotinus serves a useful purpose in this comparative context. Several significant scholars claim that creation is a uniquely Christian concept, often relying on a rather simplistic opposition of "creation" and "emanation."[3] If one takes this narrow view of creation, then the comparison with Indian thought becomes highly problematic. But ironically, St Augustine—no minor figure in the history of Christian thought—took a different view: For Augustine the difference between Christian theology and pagan Neoplatonism resides in the doctrine of incarnation, not in the doctrine of creation (*Confessions*, 7, 9, 13–14). The Plotinian doctrine of the world as a production of the One provides a theoretical model for the procession of the physical cosmos from the divine Mind or Intellect, in contrast to the absence of such a theory in either Plato or Aristotle—at least explicitly. Plato uses the myth of the demiurge in the *Timaeus*, but he has no theory of creation as such. Aristotle has no need of a doctrine of creation since God is the final but not the efficient cause of the cosmos. Of course, Plotinus thinks that he is merely expounding the philosophy of Plato. In fact, he replaces the demiurge of the *Timaeus* with his model of the Intellect and the world soul. The question around the monistic or theistic interpretation of Plotinus cannot be addressed here. It suffices to note that the enormous influence of Plotinus on the Christian and Muslim worlds would have been impossible without the theistic interpretation of his legacy by Augustine, or by the Arabic interpreters of the metaphysics of Plotinus in the so-called *Theology of Aristotle*.

One might envisage the popular images of the idea of *līlā* as exemplifying a licentious paganism. The frolics of Krishna in Brindaban with the *gopīs* as the divine love play looks like a heathenish fantasy. Of course, such episodes tend to be spiritualized as the joyful drama of the eternal play of God with humanity. This is significant, since dialogue between South Asian and Western thought can be obscured by such misapprehensions. Preconceptions, such as that creation is a uniquely Christian concept or thought of in terms of human manufacture, or that Indian thought is polytheistic or world-renouncing, can preempt serious discussion of genuine parallels.

I begin with a citation of the Cambridge Platonists within the Bengal renaissance, which neatly illustrates the parallel between the Platonizing mode of thought in Western theology and some strands of Vedānta.

## The Bengal Renaissance and the Cambridge Platonists

The *Tattvabodhini Patrika*—"The Truth-Enlightening Journal"—was one of the most influential organs of the Bengal Renaissance. It was the expression of the ideas of a group around Debendranath Tagore called the *Tattvaranjini Sabha* or "The Society of Those Who Delight in Truth." The context was one of intense proselytizing in colonial Calcutta and the Society, or *Sabha*, was pursuing the soi disant Father of modern India, Rammohan Roy. This was a vision of a renewed Vedantic theism, and the monotheistic Hindu Brahmo Samaj was disrupted by the death of Rammohan Roy in Bristol in 1833. Faced with the prospect of answering the challenge of evangelists such as Alexander Duff, whose combination of educational institutional activity and Christian zeal rather paradoxically ignited a vigorous response from the Hindu reformers, *Tattvabodhini Patrika* published Debendranath's own interpretations of the *Upanishads* alongside extracts from Rammohun's translations of the *Upanishads*. Among the critiques of the attacks of Christian missionaries on Hinduism as a pantheistic, monistic, and idolatrous religion, we find in 1864 the following passage:

> Our reverend friends maintain that it was Christ who first revealed correct notions of religion to mankind, and that they did not possess them before his appearance. Now this is a statement contradicted by all history.
>
> I would recommend, Gentleman to your attentive perusal the "Intellectual System of the Universe" by old Dr Cudworth, whose liberal Christianity the revered gentlemen in question would do well to imitate. This book contains innumerable proofs of the existence of correct notions of the godhead prevailing among the ancient Greeks and Romans.[4]

Why do we find a reference to the Cambridge Platonists, "old Dr Cudworth" and his "liberal Christianity," one the great schools of Western philosophy, and the most significant Platonic school in Europe between the Renaissance and the Romantic era?[5] These figures of the Bengal elite do not want to fall into the arms of the Enlightenment agnosticism of Hume and Gibbon. Cudworth represents that Alexandrian strand of Christianity that happily drew upon pagan Hellenic thought, and what might be called a more fluid or mystical monotheism as opposed to the exclusive monarchical theism of high Protestant or Catholic orthodoxy. To use the language of John Kenney, "exclusive theism" concentrates on the numerical singularity of deity, while the more "inclusive theism" of Hellenic monotheism laid stress on the ultimacy and unity of the supreme principle.[6] Much of Cudworth's *True Intellectual System of the Universe*, in particular the enormous fourth book, is devoted to showing that monotheism was the foundational religion of the Egyptians and the rest of the ancient world, and this primordial monotheism lapsed into polytheism and pantheism.[7] It is no accident that one of Cudworth's liberal Christian successors, B. F. Westcott, should have been a driving force behind the foundation of St Stephen's College in Delhi. Westcott was a great admirer of Plotinus and Origen and the Cambridge Platonists as their successors in the modern world.

Cudworth was regarded as an antiquarian, but his concern was philosophical and theological. His was a period of a Neoplatonic revival in Cambridge, fueled by the reception of the Eckhart school via the *Theologia Germanica*, Boehme, and Origen, and the critique of theological voluntarism. The Platonists themselves, who all hailed from a puritan background, were reacting against the Augustinianism of the Westminster Confession, in particular the doctrine of double predestination. Origen was preferred to Augustine, the spontaneity of divine goodness over the absolute sovereignty of divine will. The paragraph from the lecture "Defence of Brahmoism and the Brahmo Samaj" is from Raj Narayan Bose, the maternal grandfather of Aurobindo Ghose. As we will note later, Aurobindo plays a significant role in the argument of this essay. One can appreciate that for certain Western missionaries in India, the appeal to divine "play" looked like raw heathenism. How can such a serious matter as salvation be considered as play?

A more recent successor to Cudworth might be Dom Bede Griffiths. Initially a student of C. S. Lewis at Oxford, and with a profound knowledge of English literature and philosophy, he developed a frame of thought that drew upon Indian thinkers such as Aurobindo as well as the Western tradition. Griffiths observes that

> all activity is a lila, a play of God. This is the view of Ramakrishna. The great mother is playing, and all that goes on in this world is her play. By itself that is hardly satisfactory for it means that all the suffering of the world is ultimately meaningless. The concept of lila, however, can also be interpreted in the way towards which the Gita is working and which the modern Hindu certainly supports, namely that this lila of God has a meaning and purpose. In this view God is not merely at play but is pur-

> posefully active in the world. . . . This is consistent with the Christian understanding of the activity of God. The Crucifixion reveals that suffering is redemptive.[8]

Bede Griffiths's debt to the English Romantics is especially evident:

> Wordsworth had taught me to find in nature the presence of a power which pervades both the universe and the mind of man. Shelley had awakened me to the Platonic idea of an eternal world, of which the world we see is a dim reflection. Keats set before me the values of "the holiness of the heart's affections and the truth of the imagination." These were for me not merely abstract ideas but living principles, which were working in me over many years and which I tried to comprehend in a reasoned philosophy of life.[9]

Aurobindo also admired the English Romantics. He recognizes Coleridge as a fine poet and "a great metaphysician." He says, moreover, about Plotinus: "Yes, Plotinus was not a mere philosopher—his philosophy was founded on Yogic experience and realisation."[10]

One could see the concept of *līlā* as attempting to bridge two extremes that recur in Western theology: extreme voluntarism and necessitarianism. Is the world the product of arbitrary and brute will or the mechanical and inexorable emanation of the absolute? Neither alternative is theologically attractive: In the first, the divine becomes willful and anthropomorphic; in the second, a sub-personal or impersonal agency. The notion of "play" could be viewed as a middle position between these two options. God is not "constrained" or needful in his activity but neither is the divine work wanton or groundless. The concept of *līlā* forms a link between the "aesthetic" concepts of play employed in relation to dance and architecture and the abstract metaphysics of the *Brahma Sutras*. How do the many hold together? Because of the sustaining and adhesive power of the One. How should this sustaining activity of action be viewed? Cosmic play. How do images of dance and play in Hindu life and practice fit into the complex and conflicting theories of God and the world in the nondual and dualist traditions of Indic metaphysics?

## Plotinus on Contemplation

> Meanwhile, while our Plato discusses often in a hidden manner the duty belonging to mankind it sometimes seems as though he is joking and

> playing. But Platonic games and jokes are much more serious than the serious things of the Stoics. For he does not disdain to wander occasionally through certain humble matters, if only gradually to guide his listeners, who grasp humble things more easily, to more elevated matters. With the most serious purpose he often mixes the useful with the sweet, by which the most grace of charming speech he may lure minds that are naturally prone to pleasure to sustenance with the bait of pleasure itself. And he often composes fable in a poetic manner, for in fact the style itself of Plato seems not so much philosophical as poetic. For he sometimes raves and wanders, as a *vates*, all the while paying no attention to a human order but to one prophetic and divine.[11]

In this passage the most important interpreter of Plato in the European Renaissance, Marsilio Ficino, expounds explicitly on the playfulness of Plato and the theme of *serio ludere*, or serious play—a key theme in Renaissance philosophy.

Johan Huizinga's (1872–1945) seminal work *Homo Ludens, or Man Playing*, is perhaps the most important work on play in the last century. Huizinga notes the particular significance of Plato, especially *Laws* 803c. There, play is presented as a metaphor for human existence, where God is said to be the object of seriousness and humanity a toy of the divine. The point would be that the appropriate relation to the divine is essential for human happiness. Plato also discusses the literal play of children in the *Laws* 797a–798d, and this fits his central concern for *paideia*. In *Republic* VII in relation to the critique of philosophy, Plato presents philosophy as play and notes that children should be nourished by play (*pazontas trephe*—537a 1).[12]

Plotinus is the most significant Late Antique interpreter of Plato; it is perhaps unsurprising that Plotinus should draw in this salient aspect of Plato's thought and that Plotinus explicitly developed the notion of play in a paradoxical relation to the serious exercise of philosophy. A relevant text is that of Ennead 3.8. A century ago, Émile Bréhier wrote: "Nous avons en ce traité la production la plus caractécteristique et peut-être la plus achevée, au point de vue de la forme et de la pensée, de toutes les oeuvres de Plotin."[13] In this text, Plotinus commences by combining the Platonic theme of play with the strongly Aristotelian emphasis on contemplation:

> Suppose we said, playing at first before we set out to be serious, that all things aspire to contemplation, and direct their gaze to this end—not

only rational but irrational living things, and the power of growth in plants, and the earth which brings them forth—and that all attain to it as far as possible for them in their natural state, but different things contemplate and attain their end in different ways, some truly, and some only having an imitation and image of this true end—could anyone endure the oddity of this line of thought? Well, as this discussion has arisen among ourselves, there will be no risk in playing with our own ideas. Then are we now contemplating as we play? Yes, we and all who play are doing this, or at any rate this is what they aspire to as they play. And it is likely that, whether a child or a man is playing or being serious, one plays and the other is serious for the sake of contemplation, and every action is a serious effort towards contemplation; compulsory action drags contemplation more towards the outer world, and what we call voluntary, less, but, all the same, voluntary action, too, springs from the desire of contemplation.[14]

This is not the caricature of Neoplatonism as a sterile dogmatic scholasticism critiqued by Walter Bröcker, the "Platonismus ohne Sokrates" (*Platonism without Socrates*). On the contrary, the playful Socratic element is striking: "Well, as this discussion has arisen among ourselves, there will be no risk in playing with our own ideas"—this is presumably a reference to the seminar context of the circle of Plotinus and questions that emerged from the group.

The participle Παίζοντες (*Paizontes*) is the first word of the text. The use of the δή is used nowhere else in Plotinus at the beginning of a treatise. The sense is: playing now, at first before striving to be serious. The passage commences by asserting the close link between play and gravity.

ἆρ' ἄν τις ἀνάσχοιτο τὸ παράδοξον τοῦ λόγου;
—"Could anyone endure the paradox of this reasoning?"[15]

Plotinus seems to be suggesting that play is a good model or paradigm for thinking about nature's production.

Ἆρ' οὖν καὶ ἡμεῖς παίζοντες ἐν τῷ παρόντι θεωροῦμεν;
—"Are we playing as we contemplate?"

His answer is yes. Plotinus is arguing for the superiority of contemplation over practice. This is a nuanced and deeply Plotinian theme. Prima facie, it elicits the familiar objections: This is the downgrading of praxis by the elitism of Hellenic culture or the characteristic arrogance of a leisured class. Yet centrally this is a metaphysical claim, more specifically a critique of materialism. We should be open, Plotinus, insists, to various forms of causation and making, and the productions of nature raise specific questions, especially in relation to the physicalism of the Epicureans, who denied value and teleology to a nature envisaged as wholly mechanical. Yet he is also dissatisfied with the attempts of the Aristotelians and the Stoics to answer the Epicurean challenge.

Play is presented as superior to seriousness as a means of engaging with the counterintuitive and paradoxical claim that nature is slumbering contemplation. Presumably, this is because Plotinus is inviting the reader, or the participant in the seminar, to engage in an imaginative thought experiment. Second, the stress on play is calculated to draw the mind away from an unreflective view of the mundane world, away from seeing reality itself as only a collection of material objects and transient events. Against the reductionism of the Epicureans, Plotinus wishes to invoke a top-down principle. He considers the Stoic and Aristotelian deployment of the divine as an explanatory principle as the proper route to criticize the materialists, but rejects the Stoic and Aristotelian proposals. The Stoics concede too much in making their divinity material, and the Aristotelian deity is effectively divorced from the sublunary world. The divine as rapt self-contemplation as in the classic book Lambda of Aristotle's *Metaphysics* is radicalized by Plotinus when he envisages nature itself as engaging in contemplation dimly, that is, as a mirror or image of the contemplation of the divine Intellect or Nous. In *Ennead* III 8, each level of being is productive—*poiesis* through contemplation is a form of efficient causation. There is no philosophical precursor to the thesis of Plotinus that nature contemplates. Plotinus is proposing that nature is not a set of blind mechanical irrational powers but is the work of soul. The soul of the world as nature is contemplating Intellect, just as Intellect contemplates the One.

Plotinus's own playful manner is evident when he imagines nature speaking and enjoining silence:

> And if anyone were to ask nature why it makes, if it cared to hear and answer the questioner it would say: "You ought not to ask, but to understand in silence, you, too, just as I am silent and not in the habit of talking.[16]

Kevin Corrigan notes the Platonic dimension in this passage: Just as Plato employs various devices, like myths or changes of scene in the Dialogues, "so Plotinus provides a dramatic enactment for us to see through it to the sort of living contemplation in nature for which he has been arguing."[17]

Nature, talking in the thought experiment of Plotinus, proceeds to compare its productions with the work of geometers. Armstrong notes the "intuitive spontaneity of the process":

> Understand what, then? That what comes into being is what I see in my silence, and object of contemplation which comes to be naturally, and that I, originating from this sort of contemplation have a contemplative nature. And my act of contemplation makes what it contemplates, as the geometers draw their figures while they contemplate. But I do not draw, but as I contemplate, the lines which bound bodies come to be as if they fell from my contemplation. What happens to me is what happens to my mother and the beings that generated me, for they, too, derive from contemplation, and it is no action of theirs which brings about my birth; they are greater rational principles, and as they contemplate themselves I come to be.[18]

This is a puzzling passage. Nature itself is explaining that it is the inferior product of the Divine ideas in the intellect: the resplendent beauty of nature is not the result of the fortuitous concourse of atoms but the result of the productive power of the intelligible world. Plotinus is making a profoundly serious point about the limitations of any attempt to explain nature in materialistic or mechanistic terms, while illustrating his intent in a playful manner. One might compare this argument with a thought exercise as in V.8.9.9 where Plotinus proposes the "shining imagination of a sphere" of the visible universe, whereby the mind strips the physical cosmos of its body and mass: Plotinus invokes the intelligible world through a process of imaginative apprehension.

Plotinus is contrasting the inward silent vision with the outward spectacle. The playful development of the dialectic is subordinated to the serious pursuit of the Good. In the awareness of nature as contemplative, the soul is quietened by its increasing unity with the logos: "We must already be serious" (III.8.6.16). The realization that nature is not a composite of value-neutral stuff, but the image of the divine mind, should provoke reverence and awe. We should, perhaps, note that this key concept of contemplation in Hellenic philosophy has a background in pilgrimage. A *theoros* was a state ambassador sent to the oracle or games. *Theorein* was originally looking at the gods, and Plato and Aristotle note this explicitly:[19]

> As we go to the Olympian festival for the sake of the spectacle (θεᾶς), even if nothing more should come of it—for the theoria (θεωρία) itself is more precious than money; and just as we go to theorize (θεωροῦμεν) at the festival of Dionysus not so that we will gain anything from the actors (indeed we pay to see them) . . . so too the theoria (θεωρία) of the universe must be honoured above all things that are considered to be useful.[20]

Whether Plotinus is conscious of this ancient backdrop to the concept of contemplation, he certainly employs the model of theater play as a philosophical theme, with the image of life as a stage.

## The Spectacle of Drama, the Image of the Stage and the Problem of Evil

Life in the physical cosmos is symbolized by Plotinus as a drama. Like a director, the *logos* bestows order upon the cosmos, whereby each soul plays a part.[21] The idea of life as a stage is to be found in Seneca, Epictetus, and Marcus Aurelius. The metaphor of the stage can convey the relative insignificance of the physical in relation to the intelligible cosmos, and indeed the ancient theme of the vanity of so many human ideas and obsessions. It can also apply to the variety and complexity of the world. Plotinus hovers between the view of evil as a means to an end and the privation model by which it is merely an aspect of the phenomenal world but not the intelligible world.

> It is like on the stage, when the actor who has been murdered changes his costume and comes on again in another character. But [in real life, not on the stage,] the man is really dead. If, then, death is a changing of body, like changing of clothes on the stage, or, for some of us, a putting off of body, like in the theatre the final exit, in that performance, of an actor who will on a later occasion come in again to play, what would there be that is terrible in a change of this kind, of living beings into each other?[22]

The imagery of the stage is rather different in the Platonists than in the Stoics because of the clash of metaphysics. The pantheism and the determinism of the Stoics furnishes their imagery with a more fatalistic tone. For Plotinus, the motif of the theater is connected to the intelligible world. This is an evident distinction between him and the Stoics. The participation in the drama has a different resonance because of the Platonic metaphysics whereby the lower receives its significance through its participation in the higher. The individual soul has a middle position in the cosmos, straddling the physical world and yet partaking in a higher principle.[23]

Although the theater image is initially suggestive of an attitude of Stoic resignation, Plotinus wishes to bring to the fore the life-affirming aspect of his metaphysics of the *theatrum mundi*. It is better than if there had been no world at all:

> For that way there would be a barren absence of life and no possibility of a life which exists in something else; but as it is a manifold life exists in the All and makes all things, and in its living embroiders a rich variety and does not rest from ceaselessly making beautiful and shapely living toys (μὴ ποιοῦσα ἀεὶ καλὰ καὶ εὐειδῆ ζῶντα παίγνια).[24]

Just as painting contains colors that are not intrinsically beautiful but add to the overall beauty of the work, a narrative contains villains as well as heroes to form an overarching beauty:

> For though it is at war with itself in its parts it is one thing and on good terms with itself in the same way that the plot of a play might be; the plot of the play is one though it contains in itself many battles. Of course, the play brings the conflicting elements into a kind of harmonious concordance, by composing the complete story of the persons in conflict; but in the universe the battle of conflicting elements springs from a single rational principle; so that it would be better for one to compare it to the melody which results from conflicting sounds, and one will then enquire why there are the conflicting sounds in the rational proportions [of musical scales]. If, then, in music the laws of rational proportion make high and low note and come together in a unity.[25]

Plotinus is proposing that just as in music the overall unity is composed of conflicting sounds, so too life is a pattern of apparently incongruous and clashing elements. Finite beings, however, possess agency and "providence ought not to be blamed for the doings of souls" (III.2.7.29–10). Mankind "has the middle place between gods and beasts" (III.2.8.9). Indeed, "Providence ought not to exist in such a way as to make us nothing. If everything was providence and nothing but providence, the providence would not exist; for what would it have to provide for? There would be nothing but the divine" (III.2.9.2–3). Here Plotinus is steering the middle path between the Aristotelian denial of sublunary providence and the deterministic immanentism of the Stoics.

> Men, too, are principles; at any rate they are moved to noble actions by their own nature, and this is an independent principle.[26]

Although life can be seen as a theatrical play, this is not meant to imply that there is no freedom. The qualities of agents become clear through their actions. The actor is given a role, but this can be done well or badly.

> And as the sound of the voice and the gestures of the actor are beautiful or ugly as he makes them, and either adorn the poet's creation further, as one might think, or by adding the badness of the actor's own voice, do not make the play other than what it was, but the actor makes a grotesque exhibition of himself, and the author of the play sends him off in deserved disgrace, behaving in this like a good judge of acting, but promotes the good actor to higher rank, and if he has any, to finer plays, but puts the bad actor into any worse play that he has; in this way the soul, coming on the stage in this universal poetic creation and making itself a part of the play, supplies of itself the good or the bad in its acting; it is put in its proper place on its entrance.[27]

Plotinus presents the world as an artistic work: His theodicy is linked to aesthetic images. Somewhat akin to his suggestion to imagine nature as contemplating, Plotinus is putting forward the image of the productive source of the world as being like a poet and the structure of the cosmos being like a musical harmony.

> So the activity of life is an artistic activity, like the way in which one who is dancing is moved; for the dancer himself is like the life which is artistic in this way and his art moves him, and moves in such a way that the actual life is somehow of this [artistic] kind.[28]

The paradigm of the dance is given a theological dimension in Treatise VI.9. (9).

> And in this dance the soul sees the spring of life, the spring of intellect, the principle of being, the cause of good, the root of the soul; these are not poured out from him with the result that they diminish him; for there is no bulk; otherwise the things generated from him would be perishable. But, as it is, they are eternal, because their principle remains the

same, not divided up into them but abiding as a whole. So they also abide; just as the light abides if the sun abides. For we are not cut off from him or separate, even if the nature of body has intruded and drawn us to itself, but we breathe and are preserved because that Good has not given its gifts and then gone away but is always bestowing them as long as it is what it is.[29] (VI.9.9.1ff.)

The One, moreover, "is gentle, kindly, and gracious, and present to anyone when one wishes" (5.5.12.33–34). Here the image of the dance is linked to the sense of the One, the principle of being, as the giver and sustainer of life. Stephen Clark in his book *Plotinus: Myth, Metaphor, and Philosophical Practice* draws an analogy with Vaiṣnavite theater in the notion of possession or participation.[30] Perhaps the image of theater, like that of the dance, was meant to convey the sense of participation in the divine life. The images of the theater and dance tend to reinforce the anti-Gnostic polemic in Plotinus: In opposition to the cosmic pessimism of the Gnostics, Plotinus is presenting a vision of life grounded in the Good who is continually bestowing life, like the generous demiurge of Plato's *Timaeus.*

## Returning to Līlā

The late Sanskrit notion of *līlā* (sport, dalliance, play, pastime, or drama) is a complex and polyvalent term. It is employed in related but distinct fields from theology to aesthetics and finds myriad forms of expression in South Asia.[31] In speculative terms, *līlā* becomes a model for the existence of the world. How can an Absolute or First Principle that is perfect and self-sufficient come to generate an inferior or imperfect world? Invocations of love or will seem crudely anthropomorphic. *Līlā* becomes a rationale for, or vindication of, the created realm. Coomaraswamy argued that even if the term is late, the idea finds expression in Vedic materials, and the felicitous freedom of the supreme Being and the idea of unity with that being as joy plays a role in the *Upanishads.*[32] The idea of *līlā* is generally associated with Hindu monotheism. The idea was more fully explored in the *Purāṇas*, notably the tales of Krishna in the *Bhāgavata Purāṇa*. Whereas classical Indian monism tends to deploy the concept of *māyā* or illusion for the world, *līlā* is the counterpart notion, both terms expressing different aspects of the relation between Brahman and the world. For Advaita Vedānta, *līlā* is a *façon de parler* linked to the inescapable fact of *māyā*. For the monotheistic systems, *līlā* has a theophanic quality. Creation as such manifests the divine. Two of the most important Indian writers of the twentieth century, Tagore and Aurobindo deploy the idea of *līlā*. Aurobindo presents the idea as endorsing and affirming rather than rejecting the world.

> All exists here, no doubt, for the delight of existence, all is a game or Lila; but a game too carries within itself an object to be accomplished and without the fulfilment of that object would have no completeness of significance. A drama without denouement may be an artistic possibility, existing only for the pleasure of watching the characters and the pleasure in the dubious balance of solution; the drama of the earth evolution might conceivably be of that character, but an intended or inherently predetermined denouement is also and more convincingly possible.[33]

The sport of *līlā* is meant to aid humanity in its ascent to superior degrees of consciousness. Tagore found the ancient doctrine of *līlā* to express the rapture of participating in the joy of divine creativity. *Līlā* is the infinite delight of the divine.

It is in the late *Vedānta Sūtra* of Bādarāyaṇa (2.1.33) that the idea of creation is defended against the (atheistic) argument that this presupposes some inadequacy on the part of the creator. The challenge is that a perfect deity cannot be producing what he does not in some sense already possess. Here the argument is from the analogy of acts of spontaneity that do not serve a particular end but are performed out of ebullience, the sheer delight of the activity. Rāmānuja much later employs the image of a king enjoying sport, and Baladeva relates the idea of *līlā* to a man waking up and dancing in high spirits.[34]

The worship of Śiva as the Lord of Dancers, the Naṭarāja, is an obviously playful-aesthetic symbol of divine immanence. "He creates, sustains and dissolves the world by his rhythmic dance, and the whole cosmic order is nothing but this dance of Siva."[35] Bengali Shaktism and Kashmir Śaivism have developed hermeneutics of *līlā*.[36]

It is, however, in the Vaiṣnavite tradition that *līlā* occupies a central role, especially in popular piety, with the veneration of Krishna as the cowherd.[37] These legends of Krishna are associated with the Braj area around Mathura.[38] In Sanskrit aesthetic theory, drama encompasses the arts, and Krishna is the deity most often depicted in Indian dance, art, and music. Such expressions fit well with the view that life is the upshot of divine play, or *līlā*. The experience of God is created through the aesthetic experience, or *rasa*, of the drama that imaginatively relives the divine play. The terrestrial city Mathura is regarded as an image of the heavenly world. The carnivalesque ambience of the *Holi* festival is a representation of the joy of the transcendent realm.

From a theological perspective, *līlā* is primarily the divine play in the sense that the Godhead is not forced in any way to create or act in the world: The plenitude of divine bliss is the very incentive for creation.[39] This aspect of *līlā* is of particular significance for the dualist-theistic traditions within Hinduism to refer to both the deity and the adherent, and where salvation means access to the realm of *līlā* rather than identification with the Absolute. *Līlā* is connected to *māyā*. To ask about the "why" of creation is not just pointless but meaningless for Śaṃkara. Yet *līlā* has only a limited value for Śaṃkara: He is primarily an epistemologist and interested in *jñāna-marga*. The concept of *līlā* is, for Śaṃkara, bound to a provisional sense of reality. Moreover, the playful and the artistic have no role in his thought. Dasgupta writes:

> All creation is illusory maya. But accepting it as maya, it may be conceived that God (Isvara) created the world as mere sport; from the true point of view there is no Isvara who creates the world, but in the sense in which the world exists, and we all exist as separate individuals, we can affirm the existence of Isvara, as engaged in creating and maintaining the world. In reality all creation is illusory and so the creator also is illusory.[40]

Rāmānuja, the preeminent Vedānta commentator of the eleventh century, develops *līlā* in the later Vedānta with a distinctive theistic slant; this is no longer a way of talking about *avidya*, but is the positive form of self-realization of the deity. Rāmānuja wants to attack Śaṃkara's doctrine of avidya

There is, moreover, a sense of being dazzled. Rāmānuja identified *prakriti* with *māyā*. The word "māyā" can mean the wonder or miracle that captivates mortals, whereby *māyā* is not unreal but wonderful.[41] For Rāmānuja, *Isvara* is a person who plays with his body—i.e., the world is material for divine play (Sri Bh. II, 1, 15).[42] In this sense *māyā* is not illusion but the play of the Lord, as the development of his bliss (*ananda*) and his wonder (*ascarya*). For a worshipper of Vishnu like Rāmānuja, *māyā* must be more real than it is for Śaṃkara: for Rāmānuja *Māyā* is a synonym for *jñāna* (the wisdom of the Vedic gods).

Sri Aurobindo follows Rāmānuja rather than Śaṃkara. Aurobindo considers that divine Brahman can emerge as empirical reality through *līlā*, or divine play. He denies the idea that the empirical world is an illusion (*māyā*):

> The world, as God has made it, is not a rigid exercise in logic but, like a strain of music, an infinite harmony of many diversities, and his own existence, being free and absolute, cannot be logically defined. . . . Maya is one realisation, an important one which Shankara overstressed because it was most vivid to his own experience. For yourself leave the word for subordinate use and fix rather on the idea of Lila, a deeper and more penetrating word than Maya. Lila includes the idea of Maya and exceeds it.[43]

*Līlā* including and exceeding *māyā* shows the marked important of the former concept for Aurobindo.

## Theodicy and Play?

The notion of *līlā*, however, might be seen to conflict with the model of the righteous deity of the *Bhagavad Gītā*. In the words of Gloucester in Shakespeare's *King Lear*:

> As flies to wanton boys are we to the gods.
> They kill us for their sport.

Rather than a world structured by divine justice, mankind could be viewed as inhabiting a domain that is the playground of fathomless cruelty as an amusement for the divine and savage sport. Caitanya (1486–1533) viewed God as only acting without advantage for creatures, whereas most Vaishnava thinkers attempted to present the play of God as compatible with supportive grace. Aurobindo is no exception. In *The Life Divine* he writes that

> there is always possible the retort that a God, himself all-blissful, who delights in the suffering of creatures or imposes such suffering on them for the faults of his own imperfect creation, would be no Divinity and against him the moral being and intelligence of humanity must revolt or deny his existence. But if the human soul is a portion of the Divinity, if it is a Divine Spirit in man that puts on this imperfection and in the form of humanity consents to bear this suffering, or if the soul in humanity is meant to be drawn to the Divine Spirit and is his associate in the play of imperfection here, in the delight of perfect being elsewhere, then Lila may still remain a paradox, but it ceases to be a cruel or revolting paradox; it can at most be regarded as a strange mystery and the rea-

> son inexplicable. To explain it there must be two missing elements, a conscious assent by the soul to this manifestation and a reason in the All-Wisdom that makes play significant and intelligible.[44]

"The strangeness of play" diminishes, Aurobindo avers, once we accept both a "progressive assent of souls" and a "progressive divine manifestation."[45]

For Sri Aurobindo. the *līlā* of Brahman is the objective aspect of the subjective evolution of consciousness toward *Saccidānanda*. Aurobindo does seem conscious that the mystery of evil cannot be resolved: he writes:

> The Vaishnava idea of the play of God, striking as it does into the secret of hidden delight at the core of things, is a luminous ray shot into the very heart of mystery; but isolated, it cannot solve all its enigma. (16 119)

Consider how close this is to the Cambridge Platonist Henry More:

> The Theatre of the world is an exercise of Mans wit, not a lazy *Polyantheia* or book of Common places. And therefore all things are in some measure obscure and intricate, that the sedulity of that divine Spark the Soul of Man, may have matter of conquest and triumph when he had done bravely by the superadvenient assistance of his God.[46]

Just as in Aurobindo, More wishes to emphasize the interplay between the soul and the divine spirit, and the rousing of the divine spark within the human soul.

## Aesthetic Performance and Divine Possession

The model of the theater is another point in common among Plotinus, later Platonists like Henry More, and the Vaiṣnavite tradition. For Plotinus, the image of the *theatrum mundi* is pivotal. Moreover, Plotinus uses images of dance and theater, somewhat akin to the Vaiṣnavite theater, in relation to the notion of possession or participation in the divine. This is a model for a life grounded in the transcendent source of being. We should not be surprised that a recent thinker such as Aurobindo should express his admiration for Plotinus. Theater is one of the great achievements of Hindu culture, and drama is commonly regarded as the pinnacle of Sanskrit literature. It is striking, and yet unsurprising, that in both the Hellenic and Indic metaphysical contexts the motif of theater should assume such significance; yet theater also furnishes a model of inspiration or possession by the deity. For the Platonist philosophy is the practice of becoming "like

God." The model of theater, whether as an actor or an audience, offers a way of thinking about identification with the divine. As an actor identifies with a role, or the audience identifies with a character, so too the human agent can imagine participation in the divine realm. In devotional icons, Krishna plays his overpowering lute and is frequently bidding the gopīs, who symbolize human souls.[47] The thought would be that yielding to play and theater, and to cultivate the sense of life itself as play will foster a deeper appreciation of reality, whether in the Holi festival of Mathura or the dramatic representations of Krishna. Aurobindo writes:

> The Vaishnavites accept the world as a Lila, but the true Lila is elsewhere in the eternal Brindavan. All the religions which believe in a personal Godhead accept the universe as a reality, a Lila or a creation made by the Will of God, but temporal and not eternal. The aim is the eternal status above.[48]

A similar sentiment is given expression by Tagore:

> Thou hast made me endless, such is thy pleasure,
> this frail vessel thou emptiest again and again,
> and fillest it ever with fresh life.[49]

Tagore is referring to the blissful drama of eternal play of God with humanity, rather than the detachment of the Krishna of the *Bhagavad Gītā*.

## Conclusion

The distinctive centrality of the notion of *līlā* in Hindu thought is undeniable. Less obvious are the parallels with Plotinus and, by extension, with "the Platonic-Plotinian legacy," as Gadamer called it. It is striking that the parallels are with Vaiṣnavite theology rather than with the austere monism of Śaṃkara. Parallels between Plotinus and Indic thought have been frequently remarked upon, especially since the writings of Émile Bréhier, and his *La Philosophie de Plotin*.

The philosophy of the Vaiṣnavite tradition was one of differentiated unity. The distinction between the individual devotee and the supreme being is on this model not just *māyā* or illusion as in Śaṃkara's monism. For the Vaiṣnavite, the liberated soul is not extinguished, even though remaining a manifestation of the divine sovereignty:

> Without entering into any discussion regarding the meaning of this term or the distinctive metaphysical features of the different systems of Vaish-

> navism, I can here say only that all these systems in a manner agree as to the duality of God and man. They consider man as a manifestation of the power of God. Though ultimately sustained and always controlled by God, man is for all his empirical purposes different from Him. This psychological, logical and ontological difference between God and man is the basis of devotion and worship.[50]

Although one might imagine the deeper parallels between Neoplatonism and Vedānta to be with the monist Śaṃkara than the theistic Rāmānuja, on the issue on "play" it is not so. For Śaṃkara, *līlā* is subordinated to the idea of *māyā*. Part of the reason for the surprising overlaps rests on the insistence in Plotinus upon the goodness of the world, and whose polemic against the Gnostics is coupled with a world-affirming dimension to his metaphysical vision of a transcendent principle whose "giving" is spontaneous and non-instrumental. This idea is common to both traditions. Huizinga writes, "Play consecrated to the Deity, the highest goal of man's endeavour—such was Plato's conception of religion".[51] We concur with his view that:

> The Platonic identification of play and holiness does not defile the latter by calling it play, rather it exalts the concept of play to the highest regimes of the spirit. . . . In play, we may move below the level of the serious, as the child does; but we may also move above it—placements in the realm of the beautiful and the sacred.[52]

For the Christian Platonists, whether in Alexandria, the Rhineland, or in Cambridge, creation is the play of wisdom (Proverbs 8.30–31) and this play can be legitimately viewed as a biblical trope. Yet it is also instructive to see the parallels with the Hindu world. Or perhaps vice versa. After all, Huizinga was first an Indologist. It is not implausible that the greatest of the twentieth-century writers of play came to his theme through a study of *līlā* as a young Sanskrit scholar.

## Bibliography

Adamson, P. *The Arabic Plotinus: A Philosophical Study of the "Theology of Aristotle."* London: Duckworth, 2002.

Augustine. *Confessions*. Translated by R. S. Pine-Coffin. Harmondsworth: Penguin, 1961.

Aurobindo. *Centenary Library Writings*. Pondicherry: All India Press, 1972.

Ardley, G. "The Role of Play in the Philosophy of Plato." *Philosophy* 42 (1967): 226–244.

Barua, Ankur. *The Vedantic Relationality of Rabindranath Tagore: Harmonizing the One and Its Many*. Lanham, MD: Lexington Books, 2019.

Bäumer, Bettina. *Schöpfung als Spiel, Der Begriff Līlā in Hinduismus, seine philosophische und theologische Bedeutung.* Munich: UNI-Druck, 1969.

Bonin, Therese. *Creation as Emanation: The Origin of Diversity in Albert the Great's On the Causes and the Procession of the Causes.* Notre Dame, IN: University of Notre Dame Press, 2017.

Bréhier, Émile. *Ennéades III.* Paris: Les Belles Lettres, 1925.

Bryant, E. F., ed. and trans. *Krishna: The Beautiful Legend of God.* London: Penguin, 2003.

Charrue, J.-M. *Néoplatonisme. De l'existence et de la destinée humaine.* Paris: L'Harmattan, 2014.

Corrigan, Kevin. *Reading Plotinus: A Practical Introduction to Neoplatonism.* West Lafayette, IN: Purdue University Press, 2002.

Coomaraswamy, Ananda. "Līlā." *Journal of the American Oriental Society* 61, no. 2 (June 1941): 98–101.

Dasgupta, Surendranath. *The History of Indian Philosophy.* 5 vols. Cambridge: Cambridge University Press, 1969.

Deck, John. *Nature, Contemplation and the One: A Study in the Philosophy of Plotinus.* Burdett, NY: Larson Publications, 1992.

Festugière, A. J. *Contemplation et vie contemplative selon Platon.* Paris: Librarie Philosophique J. Vrin, 1978.

Griffiths, Bede. *The Marriage of East and West.* Norwich: Canterbury Press, 2003.

Griffiths, Bede. *River of Compassion: A Christian Commentary on the Bhagavad Gita.* New York: Amity House, 1987..

Hedley, Douglas. "Gods and Giants: Cudworth's Platonic Metaphysics and His Ancient Theology." *British Journal for the History of Philosophy* 25, no. 5 (2017): 932–953.

Hein, Norvin. "Līlā." In *Encyclopedia of Religion.* 2nd ed. Vol. 8. Edited by Lindsay Jones, 550–554. New York: Macmillan, 2005.

Kenney, John Peter. *Mystical Monotheism: A Study in Ancient Platonic Theology.* Eugene, OR: Wipf and Stock, 2010.

Lipner, Julius. *Hindus: Their Religious Beliefs and Practices.* 2nd ed. Abingdon: Routledge, 2009.

Narbonne, Jean-Marc. "Traité 30 (III 8), Sur La Contemplation". In *Plotin, Oeuvres Completes. Tome II, Volume III: Traités 30 a 33.* Edited by Lorenzo Ferroni, Zeke Mazur, Jean-Marc Narbonne, John D. Turner, and Kevin Corrigan. Paris: Les Belles Lettres, 2021.

Nightingale, Andrea Wilson. *Spectacles of Truth in Classical Greek Philosophy: Theoria in Its Cultural Context.* Cambridge, UK: Cambridge University Press, 2009.

*Plotinus.* Translated by A. H. Armstrong. 7 vols. Cambridge, MA: Harvard University Press, 1966–1988.

Pollock, Sheldon. *A Rasa Reader: Classical Indian Aesthetics.* New York: Columbia University Press, 2016.

Ramanuja. *Brahma-Sutras.* Kolkata: Sri-Bhasya, 2008.

Robichaud, Denis J.-J. *Plato's Persona: Marsilio Ficino, Renaissance Humanism, and Platonic Traditions.* Philadelphia: University of Pennsylvania Press, 2018.

Sandford, A. Witney. "Don't Take It Badly, It's Holi. Ritual Levity, Society and Agriculture." In *Sacred Play,* edited by Selva J. Raj and Corrine G. Dempsey, 37–56. Albany: State University of New York Press, 2010.

Sax, William S., ed. *The Gods at Play: Līlā in South Asia.* Oxford: Oxford University Press, 1995.

## Notes

1. William S. Sax, ed., *The Gods at Play: Lila in South Asia* (Oxford: Oxford University Press, 1995), 3–4.
2. H. G. Gadamer, Gesammelte Werke (Tübingen: Mohr Siebeck, 1990), 7, 409.
3. For a sophisticated account of these matters see Therese Bonin, *Creation as Emanation: The Origin of Diversity in Albert the Great's On the Causes and the Procession of the Causes* (Notre Dame, IN: University of Notre Dame Press, 2017).
4. The 1864 issue of the *Tattva-bodhini Patrika*, p. 78. (the PDF has ninety-nine pages), https://fid4sa-repository.ub.uni-heidelberg.de/1286/.
5. I am grateful to my colleague Ankur Barua for putting me onto this.
6. See John Peter Kenney, *Mystical Monotheism: A Study in Ancient Platonic Theology* (Eugene, OR: Wipf and Stock, 2010), 91.
7. See my article, "Gods and Giants: Cudworth's Platonic Metaphysics and His Ancient Theology," *British Journal for the History of Philosophy* 25, no. 5 (2017): 932–953.
8. Bede Griffiths, *River of Compassion: A Christian Commentary on the Bhagavad Gita* (New York: Amity House, 1987), 87.
9. Bede Griffiths, *The Marriage of East and West* (Norwich, Eng.: Canterbury Press, 2003), 43.
10. Aurobindo, *Centenary Library Writings* (Pondicherry: All India Press, 1972), 9:546.
11. Denis J.-J. Robichaud, *Plato's Persona: Marsilio Ficino, Renaissance Humanism, and Platonic Traditions* (Philadelphia: University of Pennsylvania Press, 2018), 54–55.
12. G. Ardley, "The Role of *Play* in the Philosophy of *Plato*," *Philosophy* 42 (1967): 226–244.
13. Émile Bréhier, *Ennéades III* (Paris: Les Belles Lettres, 1925), 149.
14. Plotinus, *Enneads*, trans. A. H. Armstrong, 3.8 (30) 1, 1ff.
15. See Jean-Marc Narbonne, "Traité 30 (III 8), Sur La Contemplation," in *Plotin, Oeuvres Completes. Tome II, Volume III: Traités 30 a 33*, ed. Lorenzo Ferroni et al. (Paris: Les Belles Lettres, 2021), 268.
16. Plotinus, III.8 (30) in A. H. Armstrong, *Plotinus* (Cambridge, MA: Harvard University Press, 1980), vol. 3, p. 369.
17. Kevin Corrigan, *Reading Plotinus: A Practical Introduction to Neoplatonism* (West Lafayette, IN: Purdue University Press, 2002), 123.
18. Plotinus, *Enneads*, III 8 (30) in A. H. Armstrong, *Plotinus*, (Cambridge, MA: Harvard University Press, 1980), vol. 3, p. 369.
19. John Deck, *Nature, Contemplation, and the One: A Study in the Philosophy of Plotinus* (Burdett, NY: Larson Publications, 1992).
20. Andrea Wilson Nightingale, *Spectacles of Truth in Classical Greek Philosophy: Theoria in its Cultural Context* (Cambridge, UK: Cambridge University Press, 2009), 18. See also A. J. Festugière, *Contemplation et vie contemplative selon Platon* (Paris: Librarie Philosophique J. Vrin, 1978).
21. J.-M. Charrue, *Néoplatonisme. De l'existence et de la destinée humaine* (Paris: L'Harmattan, 2014), 208–220.
22. Plotinus, *Enneads*, III.2.15.30–34. A. H. Armstrong, *Plotinus*, vol II, p.91.
23. Lela Alexidze, "Are We, as Actors on the Stage, Still Free? Plotinus' Ennead on Providence III 2 (47)," in *The Caucasus between East and West* (Tbilisi, 2021), 378–391.
24. Plotinus, *Enneads*, III.2.15.30–34. A. H. Armstrong, *Plotinus*, vol. II, p. 91.

25. Plotinus, *Ennead*, III.2.15.30–34. A. H. Armstrong, *Plotinus*, vol. II, p. 97
26. Plotinus, *Ennead*, II.2.10.19f, Armstrong, III, p. 79.
27. Plotinus, *Ennead*, III.2.17.42–53, Armstrong, III, pp. 103–104.
28. Plotinus, *Ennead*, III.2.16.23ff., Armstrong, III, p. 97.
29. Plotinus, *Ennead*, VI.9. (9), 9, 1ff., Armstrong, p. 335.
30. Stephen R. L. Clark, *Plotinus: Myth, Metaphor, and Philosophical Practice* (Chicago: University of Chicago Press, 2016).
31. Sheldon Pollock, *A Rasa Reader: Classical Indian Aesthetics* (New York: Columbia University Press, 2016).
32. Coomaraswamy, "Līlā," *Journal of the American Oriental Society*. 61, no. 2 (June 1941): 98–101. See also Bettina Bäumer, 'Schöpfung als Spiel, Der Begriff Līlā in Hinduismus, seine philosophische und theologische Bedeutung' (Munich: UNI-Druck, 1969).
33. Aurobindo., *Centenary Library Writings* (Pondicherry: All India Press, 1972),19.835.
34. Norvin Hein, "Līlā," in *Encyclopedia of Religion*, 2nd ed., vol. 8., ed. Lindsay Jones (New York: Macmillan, 2005), 551.
35. Griffiths, *The Marriage of East and West*, 21.
36. Sax, *Gods at Play*, 6ff.
37. E. F. Bryant, ed. and trans, *Krishna: The Beautiful Legend of God* (London: Penguin, 2003).
38. A. Witney Sandford, "Don't Take It Badly, It's Holi. Ritual Levity, Society, and Agriculture," in *Sacred Play*, ed. Selva J. Raj and Corrine G. Dempsey (Albany: State University of New York Press, 2010), 37–56.
39. Julius Lipner, *Hindus: Their Religious Beliefs and Practices*, 2nd ed. (Abingdon: Routledge, 2009).
40. Surendranath Dasgupta, *The History of Indian Philosophy*, 5 vols. (Cambridge: Cambridge University Press, 1969), I, 438.
41. Ramanuja, *Brahma-Sutras* (Kolkata: Sri-Bhasya, 2008), III, 2, 3. pp. 331–332.
42. Max Müller, *Sacred Books of the East*, 442.
43. Aurobindo, *Centenary Library* (Pondicherry: All India Press, 1970), vol. 16, 428–429.
44. Aurobindo, *Centenary Library*, 18, 408.
45. Aurobindo, *Centenary Library*, 18, 409.
46. Henry More, in *The Cambridge Platonists*, 262.
47. Lipner, *Hindus*, 279ff.
48. Aurobindo, *Centenary Library*, 22, 83.
49. Tagore, *Gitanjali* (Stilwell, KS: Digireads, 2005), 1:17. See Ankur Barua, *The Vedantic Relationality of Rabindranath Tagore: Harmonizing the One and Its Many* (Lanham, MD: Lexington Books, 2019), 57ff.
50. Surendranath Dasgupta, *Hindu Mysticism* (New York: Frederick Ungar, 1959), 129.
51. Huizinga, *Homo Ludens*, 19.
52. Huizinga, *Homo Ludens*, 19.

# 2 Creating without a "Why"

## DIVINE PLAY AS METAPHOR FOR CREATION IN JOHN SCOTTUS ERIUGENA, THOMAS AQUINAS, AND MEISTER ECKHART

*Bernard McGinn*

In 2008 I taught a two-week seminar at Fu-Jen University in Taiwan on Augustine's *Confessions.* I had about a dozen students. Although Fu-Jen is a Catholic University, the majority of the students were Buddhist or Confucian, so the course was an exercise in ecumenism. We covered the whole thirteen books of Augustine's masterpiece, including the last three, Book XI on the meaning of creation and temporality, and XII and XIII on the interpretation of the creation account in Genesis. As we surveyed these final books, I sensed a change in the attitude of the students. Finally, I had some discussions with the non-Christian students, who told me that they could not understand why Augustine got so concerned about creation. They said they could relate to his life story, his struggles against sin and temptation, and his conversion, but they could not make sense out of why he was so bothered about creation. One student said to me, "We Buddhists don't worry about creation!"

I wish I could share this equanimity. I do worry about creation. The issue of "Why is there something instead of nothing?" seems important to me and to the Christian tradition. In the history of Christian theology, a considerable amount of energy has been devoted to thinking about creation. This may be a minority view today. Many of our contemporaries may wonder *when* the "Big Bang" occurred, but they might be puzzled by the question, "Why a Big Bang?" Their answer might be, "There just *was* a Big Bang. It happened and that's it." Period. End of questioning. I am not going to speak to this attitude directly, but I would like to address it obliquely by posing some questions about creation to three medieval theologians: John Scottus Eriugena (800–877), Thomas Aquinas (1225–1274), and Meister Eckhart (1260–1328). The main questions are: (1) What is the meaning of the term "creation"? (2) Is creation free? and (3) What is the point of creation, that is, what is it for? Along the way, I hope to revisit the notion of creation as play that I mentioned in an article written almost three decades ago.[1]

## The "Four D's"

Over many decades teaching the history of Christian thought about creation, I identified what I call the "Four D's" as a pedagogical tool for approaching the meaning of creation. Various theologies of creation have had to deal, willy-nilly, with the God-world relation in terms of the dyad of *distinction* and *dependence*, and a second dyad of *decision* and *duration*. I would now like to add a fifth "D," that of *dialectic*. Let me explain. Unlike the ancient philosophers, Christian theologians and their Jewish and Muslim counterparts held that the universe was not a given, something always there, nor was its First Principle (God, the Good, the First Cause, etc.) a part of the world system, albeit the biggest and best part. The world was *distinct* from God. God was conceived of as absolutely independent of the world system. Further, the world as contingent (something that need not have been), must therefore be *dependent* on God as the ground, or cause, of its existence. The world need not have existed at all, and therefore it requires an explanation that is not part of its own system, but that lies outside it.[2] The monotheistic faiths find that explanation in the one God on whom the world *depends* for its existence and maintenance. Many arguments for this absolute dependence have been advanced by thinkers in all three faiths, some based on their revealed scriptures, but many also appealing to human reason and philosophy. From this creationist perspective, the reality of the world adds nothing to the reality of God. God and the world are not more than God taken alone, an issue that makes for some interesting intellectual problems for monotheistic creationism, as we will see below.

The second dyad concerns *decision* and *duration*. In ancient philosophy, once again, if the First Principle is described as making some sort of decision about how to fashion the world (see, e.g., the Demiurge in Plato's *Timaeus*), this act is not absolutely foundational but is merely something within the established world system. In the monotheistic faiths, however, *that* the world itself exists is seen as an originating and transcendental action determining that there should be "something" instead of "nothing." To be sure, ascribing something like determining or *decid-*

*ing* to the First Principle is not easy to comprehend and involves dangers of anthropomorphic projection onto the Supreme Power. Still, the absolute freedom that the monotheistic faiths ascribe to "the Holy One, Blessed be He," seems to necessitate something analogous to human choosing in the Creator. God's "decision" to create is not like human choosing between alternatives, but is an expression of the absolute freedom by which God establishes a relation to the world, dare we say even a personal relationship.

What, then, is the relation of the divine "decision" to create to the question of the *duration* of the dependent universe? Again, the Greek philosophers such as Aristotle (and probably Plato), had no difficulty in conceiving of the world as eternal, and eternally dependent on the First Principle. The philosophers and theologians of the revealed religions were split on the issue. For Jews and Christians, the creation account in Genesis seemed to indicate that the universe began to exist in and with time, and therefore its *duration* was temporal. Nonetheless, it was possible to accept Aristotle's arguments for the eternity of the universe as either probative for the philosophically astute as contrasted with simple believers (e.g., Maimonides), or to grant an eternal universe as not impossible, but factually wrong due to the teaching of revelation (e.g., Thomas Aquinas). Other thinkers mounted rational arguments that Aristotle was just plain wrong (e.g., Bonaventure).

These four "D's" are helpful for sorting through the various positions that Christian theologians advanced regarding their belief in *creatio ex nihilo*, that is, that God created everything from nothing in the first moment of time. But it may be helpful to add a fifth "D," that of *dialectic*. Dialectic is an attempt to deal with the paradox involved in using the seemingly antithetical terms of both immanence and transcendence about the God-world relation. The monotheistic faiths advance the aporia that God is somehow totally distinct from the world, that is, transcendentally beyond it, and yet at the same time completely immanent within it. The world's existence is totally dependent on God; it has no reality *in itself*; its being is God's being, though God as manifested, participated, shared out in all things. How God is both beyond and within all things is a problem that many thinkers found demanded some kind of dialectical solution. I call such solutions dialectical in the sense that the logic involved consists of three steps: first, an assertion that God is absolutely transcendent to the world; second, a contradictory assertion that God is totally immanent in the world; and third, some kind of *Aufhebung*, or transcendentalizing move, that solves the aporia by moving it to a higher level, such as the assertion that God is the more transcendental to the world the more immanent he is, and vice versa.

## Three Thinkers on Creation

### JOHN SCOTTUS ERIUGENA

John Scottus Eriugena's daring form of Christian Neoplatonism at first glance might seem to challenge a number of aspects of traditional Christian teaching on *creatio ex nihilo*, especially with regard to issues such as the status of "nothing" (*nihil*), the divine freedom in creating, and the distinction between Creator and creature.[3] As is well known, the system expressed in Eriugena's *summa*, the *Periphyseon*, rests on the universal definition of the *genus generalissimum*, that is, *natura*, as comprising all that exists and all that does not exist. The *genus naturae* contains four *species* defined in terms of their relation to creation: (1) what creates and is not created; (2) what creates and is created; (3) what is created and does not create; and (4) what neither creates nor is created. All four *species* can be seen as aspects of God and divine causality. What creates and is not created is God as efficient cause of all things. What creates and is created is the unity-in-multiplicity of the Divine Ideas in the *Verbum*, or Divine Wisdom. These are the formal causes of things. This second *species* is God's eternal and unitary awareness of the manifold ways in which his total simplicity can be manifested. What is created and does not create is the multiplicity of the universe as divine manifestation (*theophania*), analogous to the material cause. What neither creates nor is created is the unknown God as the final end of the whole process of emanation and return (*exitus/reditus*).

The inner logic of this universal perspective led the Irish thinker to advance a number of bold claims and seemingly contradictory assertions. The first is the affirmation that God is "the essence of all things" (*essentia omnium*), a teaching he took over from Pseudo-Dionysius (ca. fifth–sixth century CE).[4] As he put it: "So when we hear that God makes all things we ought to understand nothing else than that God is in all things, that is, that he is the essence of all things."[5] Yet more boldly, "Therefore, we ought to understand God and creatures not as two things distant from each other, but as one and the same."[6] Such statements have led to accusations of pantheism against Eriugena, but that is scarcely fair, as thinkers such as Etienne Gilson recognized long ago.[7] God is the essence of all things, but you cannot reverse the statement to say that all things are God's essence. No, God is transcendentally beyond the world as the first and especially the fourth *species* of *natura*. Thus, the statements "God is all things" and "God is not all things" call out for a higher resolution in some dialectical way. For Eriugena, the higher resolution is found in the language of *superessentialitas*, the eminent language that enables us to posit that God is simultaneously and reciprocally within and beyond all things. It is positive in form, but negative in content. *Superessentialis* "says that God is not one of the things that are, but that he is more than the things that are, but what that 'is' is, it in no way defines."[8] Both Eriugena, and after him Meister Eckhart, have a distinctive Neoplatonic solution to the problem of the God-world relation—a dialectical one that insists that this relation is different from all others in that God is the more transcendent the more immanent he is, and vice versa.

Eriugena heightens the paradox in his analysis of the two aporiae that govern his treatment of the nature of creation: the claim that God both creates and is created,[9] and the corollary that all things are therefore both eternal and made.[10] God creates as the efficient and formal cause of the universe, and God is created because the reality of the world is neither more nor less than God made manifest. This is well expressed in a series of nineteen antitheses about the God-world relation in Book 3 of *Periphyseon*. These begin: "Everything that is understood and sensed is nothing else but (1) the apparition of what is non-apparent (*non apparentis apparitio*), (2) the manifestation of the hidden, (3) the affirmation of the negated, (4) the comprehension of the incomprehensible, (5) the utterance of the unutterable," and so forth.[11] What we are dealing with here are not objective genitives, but subjective genitives in which the first negated member of each phrase (*non-apparentis*) points to the hidden divinity while the positive second member (*apparitio*) in the nominative indicates God as processing into his theophanies and then returning to Godself. James McEvoy paraphases the first antithesis as "coming out of the non-appearing there is the appearing, which moves ineluctably to its goal that is also its source."[12]

What this implies, as the third antithesis states ("the affirmation of the negated"), is another of the surprising aspects of Eriugena's understanding of creation. *Creatio ex nihilo* for the Irishman means creation from the *nihil*, or nothingness, that is God.[13] Eriugena, like thinkers as far back as Aristotle, recognized a negating sense of *nihil* as lack or privation; far more important, however, was his discernment of the eminent meaning of *Nihil*, the God beyond all categories and affirmations who, as the source of all, must be nothing of what they are. Of this God it is more correct to avoid all language of existence insofar as it pertains to the beings we apprehend. As Eriugena says in one place, "God neither was, nor shall be, nor has become, nor becomes, nor shall become, nor indeed *is*." This eminent *nihil* is another way of speaking about the divine superessentiality. A passage in *Periphyseon* 3 says: "[God] makes all things from nothing, that is, he produces essences from his superessentiality, lives from his supervitality, understands from his superintellectuality, from the negation of all things which are and which are not [comes] the affirmation of all things which are and which are not."[14]

The way in which the Irishman deals with the aporia of how creation is eternal-yet-made begins from his distinction of two understandings of "creature." "Creature," he says, "can be understood in two ways, the one relating to its eternity in the divine knowledge, in which all things truly and substantially abide, the other to its temporal establishment which was, as it were, subsequent in itself."[15] The most real existence of things is in their eternal aspect in the Mind of God, but this does not rule out the fact that creatures also come to subsist in multiplicity and temporality in the third *species* of nature. So, both predications are true: "'There was not a time when they were not,' because they always subsist in the Word of God," that is, causally, "and 'there was a time when they were not,' because in time they begin through generation to be that which they were not, that is, to become manifest in forms and species."[16]

The question about the freedom of creation is closely tied to the issue of the purpose of creation. Eriugena does not discuss the issue of God's freedom in creating very much, although he does say, "Everyone of the things that are made he made willingly."[17] I would suggest that the freedom of the Creator is not a major issue for him because he conceives of creation as a transcendental form of divine self-expression. God freely expresses himself in order to come to know himself in a new way. Prior to creation God cannot be said to "know" himself, although he is transcendentally aware of his Nothingness and of his capability of being multiplied by way of the Divine Ideas or Primordial Causes. For Eriugena, God does not know himself, because knowing is always knowing some *thing* and God is not a thing until he manifests himself in the third *species*. Through creation (*exitus*) God comes to know himself as the creative principle of the other,[18] and when he draws all things back to himself in the universal *reditus*, the end will be different from the beginning, both for God in Godself and for God as manifested. God in Godself will now "contain" the actual, not just possible, differentiating unity of all the divine manifestations. The end will be different from the beginning also for the creatures, which, now perfectly unified in the Word, will be conscious of their destiny as a constant, ever-deepening journey into the silence of the divine mystery, the fourth *species* of *natura*.[19] For Eriugena the paradigm for creative emanation and final return is not so much play (*ludus*) as the dialectical relation of speech and silence.

## THOMAS AQUINAS

Aquinas's treatment of creation, primarily as seen in *Summa theologiae* Ia, qq. 44–46, is an admirable illustration of how *sacra doctrina* can make use of reason while also demonstrating reason's limits.[20] Thomas was certainly deeply influenced by Aristotle, but the hoary picture of an Aristotelian-Thomistic philosophy has fortunately vanished like the snows of yesteryear. Aristotle, of course, was an unlikely resource for a Christian teaching on creation, because the philosopher's universe is eternal and his First Cause is not an efficient cause but a final one. Hence, as Joseph de Finance pointed out ninety years ago, Thomas's doctrine of creation combines a modified Aristotelian teaching on act and potency with a modified Platonic doctrine of participation.[21] This is evident in the fact that Thomas has no hesitation in using both the term *creatio* and *emanatio* to describe the God-world relation.

Thomas's view of this relation is both admirably clear and often more complex than its surface perspicacity suggests. In the relatively brief analysis found in Questions 44–46, Thomas takes up the questions about creation that exercised the great Scholastic thinkers of his time. What is creation? What does *creatio ex nihilo* mean? Is creation a form of change? Must God create? Must God create in a certain way? Did God create in time? Can we prove on the basis of reason that God created in time? What kind of causality did God exercise in creating? Such questions and Thomas's answers can be analyzed from the perspective of my five "D's" of Christian creation theology.

Question 44 addresses "The Procession of Creatures from God and the First Cause of all Things," that is, the realm of dependence and distinction. To the issue of whether it is necessary that every existing being (*ens*) be created by God, Thomas answers in terms of his fundamental teaching about the difference between God as *ipsum esse per se subsistens* and all other beings (*entia*). "If something is found in anything by way of participation, it is necessary that it be caused in that thing by the one to whom it belongs essentially. . . . Therefore, it remains that all things other than God are not their existence itself (*suum esse*), but participate in existence" (q. 44, a. 1 c). So, the dependence of all things on God is clear in that everything that has existence but that is not existence itself must *depend* on what is existence itself. So too, is the difference between God and creature. In God alone essence (what God is) is identical with existence (that God is)—to be God is to be, while to be a creature is to be a something. In everything created the essence, or whatness (*quidditas*) of the thing, is a particular form which does not entail necessary existence.[22] The remainder of Question 44 demonstrates that God is not only the efficient cause, but also the formal and final cause of all things. Question 45 takes up the mode of the emanation of all things from the First Principle and gives a quasi-definition of creation by speaking of "the emanation of the entirety of being from the Universal Cause, which is God, and this emanation we designate as creation" (q. 45, a. 1c). Here Aquinas, in distinction from Eriugena, also makes it clear that *creatio ex nihilo* means creating from absolute lack, that is, from nothing at all (*Idem est nihil quod nullum ens*).

Both in the eight articles of Question 45 and the three articles of Question 46 Thomas answers objections to his exposition of what *sacra doctrina* teaches about *creatio* on the basis of three essential distinctions. The first is the difference between creation and change (*motus*). Change presupposes something to be changed, a passive potency in a thing; but there is no passive potency in *nihil*.[23] Thus, creation can be best understood under the category of relation—it is the beginning of a relation of absolute dependence on God.[24] The second distinction concerns the difference between an *agens naturale*, that is, a natural agent that must act in a certain way (e.g., fire must burn), and an *agens intellectuale*, one that decides to act. As Thomas says in Question 46, a. 1c, "The will of God is the cause of things. . . . Absolutely speaking, it is not necessary for God to will anything except himself. It is therefore not necessary that God willed the world to have always existed, but the world exists in the way that God willed it to be" (see also ad 6, ad 9, and ad 10). The third distinction is that between a particular cause and God as the Universal Cause. Trying to make an analogy between the particular causes bound to space and time and God as Universal Cause inevitably leads to error, Thomas says (e.g., q. 45, a. 1c; q. 46, a. 1, ad 6).

With regard to dependence and distinction, and even decision, Thomas is arguing on the basis of reason. When it comes to the question of the duration of the universe taken up in Question 46, he has to prove that reason cannot prove either that the world must be eternal or that it is necessarily temporal. Its duration is an article of faith known only on the basis of revelation. In showing that reason cannot demonstrate that the world must be eternal (q. 46, a. 1) Thomas gives an unusually full rebuttal to ten objections based on Aristotle (especially *Physica* 8, and *De caelo* 1), essentially by appealing to God as an *agens intellectuale*. In article 2 of Question 46 Thomas responds to Bonaventure and other Augustinian theologians by showing the world's beginning in time cannot be demonstrated by reason, because neither from the perspective of the world itself (which scientific reason considers only by abstracting from the here and now), nor from that of God as an agent who can act how and when he chooses, are there *necessary* reasons that the world must have had a beginning.

If we shift to the issue of *dialectic*, we can see that the God-world relation in Thomas Aquinas is conceived of as involving both transcendence and immanence, but that the Dominican's solution to this aporia is different from Eriugena's and later Meister Eckhart's. Thomas's solution is not so much by way of a strict dialectic that posits a higher synthesis of the opposed terms, but by an *analogy* of participation, that is, the claim that all things are *different* from God because they participate in *esse* while he is *esse* itself. Nonetheless, all things are totally *dependent* on God because without participation in *esse* they would not exist. For Thomas, an analogical notion of *esse* allows for both transcendence and immanence.

It is not for us to know the reason why God chose to act in a certain way and decided to create a temporal universe. There is, however, one aspect of Thomas's theology of creation that may provide food for further thought on the divine "intention." Thomas's theology is essentially a sapiential one, as I have tried to show elsewhere.[25] Our *sapientia* is a participation in the divine Wisdom which is God (*STh* IIaIIae, q. 23, a. 2, ad 1). All three persons of the Trinity are *sapientia essentialis*, although Wisdom is appropriated to the Son, so that the Second Person incarnate in Jesus Christ becomes the mediator between the eternal sapiential flow of the processions in the Trinity and the origin of the world from Divine Wisdom, as well as the restoration of fallen humanity.[26] If God created the universe through his Wisdom, and, if by coming to share in the *donum sapientiae* given by the Holy Spirit, we make our journey back to God, then what we know about wisdom here below has its root in the divine *sapientia essentialis* and may give us some hints about it. One aspect of wisdom, both divine and human, that Thomas stresses is its spontaneity, sheer delight, yes, even its ludic quality. In his brief *Commentary on the "De Hebdomadibus" of Boethius*, Thomas says that striving after wisdom is its own reward that allows us to take full possession of our minds. Invoking Wisdom 8:16, he notes that the mind should call its powers within "and there play" (*et illic lude*). He continues: "The contemplation of wisdom is suitably compared to play on two counts. . . . First, because play is delightful, and the contemplation of wisdom possesses maximum delight. . . . Second, because things done in play are not ordered to anything else, but sought for their own sake, and this same trait belongs to the delights of wisdom."[27] We might say, then, that the Divine Wisdom that created the universe was an expression of the divine inner delight spilling over in ludic joy. This is one way of expressing the purpose for which God made the world—to play with it.

## MEISTER ECKHART

Like Eriugena, Eckhart was deeply influenced by Neoplatonic dialectical thinking, but the German Dominican also knew Thomas Aquinas well. His teaching on creation, set out primarily in his Latin scriptural commentaries, but also sometimes appearing in his Latin and vernacular sermons, was controversial.[28] Articles relating to the eternity of creation and the nothingness of creatures were condemned in the papal bull *"In agro dominico"* issued after his death.[29]

Eckhart defines creation much like other Scholastics—creation is "the giving of existence" (*collatio esse*), or "the production of things from nothing," or "Creation is to give existence out of nothing."[30] *Esse* is the "ground of creatability" (*ratio creabilitatis est esse*: *Ex. Sap.* n. 24), and the final cause of creation: "He created all things so that they might be" (Wis. 1:14). The emphasis on *esse* sounds much like Thomas Aquinas, but the distinctive nature of Eckhart's teaching on creation begins to emerge when we observe how he links the *esse* of creation with two other essential terms in his vocabulary: *principium* and *unum*.[31] A passage from his *Commentary on John* says: "Existence (*esse*) is a principle (*principium*) under the idea or the property of the One (*proprietate unius*) and from it proceeds the universe and the entirety of all created being."[32] This means that God as Creator is to be understood in terms of God as the formal cause, ideal reason, or *principium* of all things. "You must recognize," says Eckhart, "that the *principium* in which God created heaven and earth (Gen. 1:1) is the ideal reason," that is, the Logos.[33] Thus Genesis 1:1 and John 1:1 are in agreement that it is the formal causality of the Word in which creation takes place. If Thomas Aquinas stressed God as the efficient cause of the universe, Eckhart emphasizes God as formal cause. Indeed, in some places he goes further by favoring the Neoplatonic term *causa essentialis*, which denotes "a principle in which there is Logos and Idea . . . an essential agent that precontains its effect in a higher way and exercises causality over the whole species of its effect."[34] The essential cause is a universal agent and must be intellectual in nature—"Every true essential agent is spirit and life."[35]

For Thomas Aquinas God is *ipsum esse subsistens* and therefore the transcendental cause of the limited participations of *esse* that are creatures. Eckhart also speaks of God as *ipsum esse subsistens*, but he prefers terms like *esse absolutum* and *esse indistinctum*, and he understands these not so much in terms of a model of participation, but through a form of dialectical thinking best revealed through an analysis of the transcendental predicate *unum*. "Thus," he says in one place, "the term 'one' adds nothing beyond existence (*esse*), not even conceptually, but only according to negation. . . . For this reason, it is most immediately related to existence in that it signifies the purity and core and height of existence, something which even the term 'existence' does not do."[36] *Unum* demonstrates the dialectical nature of the God-world relation, as we see in a passage from the Dominican's *Commentary on Wisdom* in which he exegetes Wisdom 7:27a ("Since it is one, it can do all things"). God as one with all things is *indistinct* (not-other), that is, immanent in the world. But since such oneness belongs to God alone, it is what makes him *distinct* from all things and thus absolutely transcendent. This reveals a new dialectical logic: "Everything which is distinguished by indistinction is the more distinct the more indistinct it is, because it is distinguished by its own indistinction. Conversely, it is the more indistinct the more distinct it is, because it is distinguished by its own distinction from what is indistinct."[37]

Grasping that creation takes place in the *principium* under its causal formality/essentiality as the One (*unum*) allows us to see where creation fits into the three forms of "principial activity" that Eckhart mentions in several places, but especially in Latin Sermon XLIX.[38] Eckhart distinguishes the formal emanation, or "inner boiling" (*bullitio*), by which the three Persons of the Trinity proceed within the divine realm as one and the same God from the efficient emanation, or "boiling over" (*ebullitio*), by means of which the divine *principium* produces what is different from itself. There are two kinds of *ebullitio*: the universal form, which we call *creatio*, and the particular, which is any kind of *factio*, or making. Thus, there is an essential Trinitarian isomorphism among all forms of activity as rooted in the divine *principium*.[39] Eckhart cited Psalm 61:12 (Vg.) as proof: "God has spoken once and for all, and I have heard two things." That means in one and the same speech-act God spoke the emanation of the Second Person in the Trinity and the creation of the world.[40]

The implications of this doctrine are many, but I will only spell out four here. The first is the eternity of creation, which was the source of so much controversy. The first three articles condemned as heretical in the papal bull deal with Eckhart's teaching on eternal creation, summarized in Article 3: "In one and the same time when God was, when he begot his coeternal Son as God equal to himself in all things, he also created the world."[41] Eckhart affirmed that God can only create in his eternal "now" (*nû, nunc*), that is, the timeless divine present—no past or future is possible for him. To deny this, Eckhart said, is heretical. The eternal "nowness" of creation also implies that creation takes place *in God* and that it must *always* be taking place (*creatio continua*). Nothing can be outside of, or distinct from, God. "Everything that happens in nothing, is surely nothing. . . . By creating, God calls all things out of nothing, and from nothing into existence."[42] Since he does this "in the Principle," he does it in himself. There is no before and after for God, therefore, the act of creating is present and continuous. In Sermon (Predigt) 30 Eckhart says: "That all creatures should pour forth and still remain within is very wonderful. . . . The more He is in things, the more He is out of things: the more in the more out, the more out the more within. I have often said God is creating the whole world now in this instant."[43] And yet Eckhart also says that "exterior creation is subject to time which makes things old."[44] How does he square this with the eternity of creation?

The answer to this paradox brings us to the second implication, which is the Dominican's distinction of two levels of creation and the existence of creatures: the virtual and the formal. In the *Commentary on Wisdom* he says: "All things are in God as in the First Cause in an intellectual way and in the mind of the Maker. Therefore, they do not have any of their formal existence (*esse formale*) until they are produced and extracted on the outside in order to exist."[45] This is not unlike what we have seen in

Eriugena's teaching on how everything is both eternal and made. On the level of their virtual existence (*esse virtuale*) in God all things must be one and eternal, but on the level of their formal existence in the world they are distinct and temporal. The relation of the two levels obviously privileges the *esse virtuale*, as we can see from Eckhart's appeal to the example of the mirror. A face is always a face, whether or not a mirror is present. So too, the virtual existence of things is always present in God. When a face is reflected in a mirror, there is certainly a reflection, a different and formal existence; but the reality of the reflection is totally dependent on the "realer" face, that is, the *esse virtuale*.[46]

A corollary of this, and the third of the implications of Eckhart's view of creation, is the nothingness of creatures *taken in themselves*. This had also been asserted by Thomas Aquinas,[47] but Eckhart's formulations are so radical and frequent that one of them wound up condemned in the bull, although not as heretical, but only as "dangerous and evil-sounding." The twenty-sixth article is an extract from Eckhart's German Sermon 4: "All creatures are one pure nothing. I do not say that they are a little something or anything, but that they are pure nothing."[48] The same teaching is found in the Latin works, as when Eckhart says, "Every created being taken or conceived apart as distinct in itself from God is not a being, but a nothing."[49] There is another implied dialectic regarding the God-world relation hinted at here that I will just mention but not analyze. If God is *esse absolutum* and creatures in themselves are *purum nihil*, the dialectic will reverse itself when we look at it from the other direction. That is, if we conceive of creatures as some kind of being (*esse hoc et hoc* Eckhart often calls it), then God must be characterized as *nihil* in opposition to the limited being of creatures. Poised between two forms of *nihil*, the *nihil* of eminence that is God and the *nihil* of defect that is the creature, Eckhart's mystical way is an invitation to detach ourselves from the nothingness of the created self so that we can come to realize our oneness with the divine Nothingness that is also all things.

A fourth implication concerns the question of why God creates. Eriugena's answer to this was intellectualist, framed in the language of self-expression and silence. Eckhart does not exclude all intellectual dimensions, but he stresses willing and not willing in the question of motivation. His teaching about "breaking-through" into the divine ground (*durchbrechen in den Grund*), as found for example in German Sermon 52, shows how the self-divestment of wanting nothing, knowing nothing, and having nothing allows the soul to attain the "God" beyond God and become so one with God that the transcendental "I" can say: "There

I myself was, there I *willed* myself and *committed* myself to create this person" (my italics).[50] At this deep level, however, willing is not purposeful like the particular actions of created intellectual beings. This "willing" is transcendental, an absolute spontaneity of life flowing out of the divine ground. It is "living without a why" (*âne warumbe, sunder warumbe*),[51] a share in the inconceivable freeness in which God created the universe, something more like play than purpose.

Eckhart was not the first to talk about "living without a why." The Flemish Cistercian mystic, Beatrice of Nazareth, used it in her *Seven Manners of Loving* (ca. 1215). The expression was probably developed from Bernard of Clairvaux's language about the spontaneous disinterestedness of pure love—"I love that I may love; I love in order to love" (*Sermons on the Song of Songs* 83.4; *On Loving God*, Prol. 1.1). Eckhart himself says that "love has no why" (e.g., Pr. 28 in DW 2:59.7). "Living and acting without a why," which Eckhart uses about twenty times, pertains first of all to God, and then to the person ("the noble, just, or godlike person") who has become one with God in the ground. Predigt 59 says: "A Master says, 'Everything has a why, but God has no why, and the person who prays to God for anything other than himself makes God have a why.'"[52] As a Latin sermon puts it: "God, and therefore the divine person, does not act for why or wherefore" (*non agit propter cur aut quare*).[53] This is because the just person (*justus in quantum justus*) acts out of the ground: "Out of the innermost ground you shall do all you do without a why" (Pr. 5b in DW 1:90.11–12).

One interesting way Eckhart presents his teaching about God and the soul as acting without a why is by imaginary dialogues. In Predigt 26 he has a discussion during which someone asks "the good person" why he does what he does. Because "everything that is in time has a why," the good person can respond in terms of purpose about temporal things, such as "Why do you eat?" "In order to gain strength." But this is not so with regard to divine things. "Why do you love God?" "I don't know—because of God." "Why do you love the truth?" "Because of the truth." The dialogue concludes: "Why do you live?" "Truly, I don't know—I'm happy to live."[54] Eckhart also uses some striking images for acting without a why. In Predigt 12 the Dominican has a passage about how all things are alike in God and are God. "Here in this sameness (*Glîchheit*)," he says, "God finds it so pleasant that he lets his nature and his being flow in this sameness in himself." Eckhart compares this inner flowing with a horse that is allowed to run loose in a meadow, because it is his nature "to jump about in the meadow." So too, God "finds it a joy to pour his nature and his being completely into the sameness, for he is this sameness himself."[55] Without using the phrase "without a why," this is a good illustration of divine spontaneity. Another noted image is found in the expression, "The rose is without a why." This does not appear in Eckhart's work, but is used by the seventeenth-century German poet and mystic Angelus Silesius, who was influenced by Eckhart: "The rose is without a why; it blossoms because it blossoms. / It does not care for itself, nor asks if someone sees it."[56]

In conclusion, we can say that the notion of play does enter into the Christian theology of creation, but certainly not among all theologians. Thomas Aquinas (perhaps surprisingly to some) has a place for it in his understanding of creative wisdom, as does Meister Eckhart with his stress on the total spontaneity of the divine action (and of the "divine person" in God). John Scottus Eriugena, on the other hand, does not.

## Appendix: Some Further Christian Reflections on *Līlā*

In reading the other essays in this collection, I have discovered something of the surprising richness and diversity of the Hindu conception of *līlā*. I do not believe that we have anything *quite* like it in Christian thought on creation. Still, I think a distinction may be helpful. It seems we may be able to take *līlā* in two ways: a narrow sense as "play/playfulness," or in a broad way as "freedom, spontaneity, plenitude, vital activity, etc." In the narrow sense, there are a few parallels with Christian understandings of creation that I have tried to point out above. These seem limited. In the broader sense, however, there are obviously many analogies and parallels in Christianity to *līlā* taken as freedom, spontaneity, and the like. Thus, I found a number of passages in Daniel Soars's introduction and in Jessica Frazier's wide-ranging essay that sounded like statements to be found in Christian theologians and philosophers. It is quite possible that some broadly analogous view of God's spontaneity in creating as conceived by Christian thinkers could be helpfully compared with what some Indian thinkers have said about *līlā*. It strikes me that this would be a worthwhile, if difficult, enterprise to take on.

I do want to give a further word of explanation about my own essay and its provocative title, "Creating without a 'Why.'" Eriugena never said this, nor did Thomas Aquinas. Nor, I hasten to add, did Meister Eckhart, at least explicitly. Eckhart did, however, constantly affirm that God acts *sine cur aut quare* ("Without why or wherefore"), so I take this title as not untrue to his thought. "Without a why" means that God acts *without compulsion, without an external purpose, without discourse*

("Should I do this?"), *without drama* (*pace* Hinduism), and even *without a final cause* in the strict Aristotelian sense. Although my three authors have significant differences, they all thought of God's creative activity as totally spontaneous and completely self-determining. Modern investigation of Aquinas's view of God as absolute *esse* has shown that his fundamental assertion, *Deus est esse*, is logically tautological. Because God's essence is his existence, *God is what he is.* That's as much as we can really say. My presentation of three medieval thinkers on creation suggests a parallel tautology: *God does what he does because he does it*, whether we want to think of this as play or as in some way purposive. The critic might ask: "Well, what does that tell us?" My authors might well respond: "It tells us the limits of what we can ever really know about creation."

## Primary Sources


### JOHN SCOTTUS ERIUGENA

*Iohannis Scotti Eriugenae "Periphyseon."* Edited by Éduard Jeauneau. 5 vols. Turnhout: Brepols, 1996–2003.

### MEISTER ECKHART

Meister Eckhart. *Die deutschen und lateinischen Werke.* Various editors. *Die deutschen Werke.* 5 vols. *Die lateinischen Werke.* 5 vols. Stuttgart-Berlin: Kohlhammer, 1936–.

### THOMAS AQUINAS

*S. Thomae Aquinatis Scriptum super libros Sententiarum Magistri Petri Lombardi.* Edited by R. P. Mandonnet. 4 vols. Paris: Lethielleux, 1929–1947.

*Sancti Thomae Aquinatis Summa Theologiae.* 4 vols. Madrid: Biblioteca de Autores Cristianos, 1952–1956.

*St. Thomas Aquinas. The Exposition "On the Hebdomads" of Boethius.* Introduction and translation by Janice L. Schultz and Edward A. Synan. Washington DC: Catholic University Press, 2001.


## Secondary Sources


Beierwaltes, Werner. "*Negati Affirmatio* or the World as Metaphor: A Foundation for Medieval Aesthetics from the Writings of John Scottus Eriugena." *Dionysius* 1 (1977): 127–59.

Connolly, John M. *Living without Why. Meister Eckhart's Critique of the Medieval Concept of Will.* Oxford: Oxford University Press, 2014.

de Finance, Joseph. *Être et agir dans la Philosophie de Saint Thomas.* 2nd ed. Rome: Gregorian University Press, 1960.

Duclow, Donald. "Divine Nothingness and Self-Creation in John Scottus Eriugena." *Journal of Religion* 57 (1977): 109–23.

Gilson, Etienne. *History of Christian Philosophy in the Middle Ages.* New York: Random House, 1955.

Goris, Wouter. *Einheit als Prinzip und Ziel: Versuch über die Einheitmetaphysik des "Opus Tripartitum" Meister Eckharts.* Leiden: Brill, 1997.

McEvoy, James. "Biblical and Platonic Measure in John Scottus Eriugena." In *Eriugena East and West,* edited by Bernard McGinn and Willemien Otten. Notre Dame: University of Notre Dame, 1994.

McGinn, Bernard. "*Contemplatio sapientialis:* Thomas Aquinas's Contribution to Mystical Theology." *Ephemerides Theologicae Lovanienses* 95 (2019): 317–334.

McGinn, Bernard. "Do Christian Platonists Really Believe in Creation?" In *God and Creation: An Ecumenical Symposium,* ed. David Burrell and Bernard McGinn. Notre Dame: University of Notre Dame Press, 1990.

McGinn, Bernard. *The Growth of Mysticism: Gregory the Great through the Twelfth Century.* New York: Crossroad, 1994.

McGinn, Bernard. *Meister Eckhart: Teacher and Preacher.* New York: Paulist Press, 1986.

McGinn, Bernard. "Meister Eckhart on God as Unity." In *Neoplatonism and Christian Thought,* ed. Dominic O'Meara. Albany: SUNY Press, 1982.

McGinn, Bernard. *The Mystical Thought of Meister Eckhart.* New York: Crossroad, 2001.

McGinn, Bernard. *Thomas Aquinas's "Summa Theologiae": A Biography.* Princeton, NJ: Princeton University Press, 2014.

Silesius, Angelus. *Cherubinischer Wandersmann.* Zurich: Manesse Verlag, 1986.

Sokolowski, Robert. *The God of Reason and Faith: Foundations of Christian Theology.* Notre Dame: University of Notre Dame Press, 1982.

Teasdale, Wayne. "'Nihil' as the Name of God in John Scottus Eriugena." *Cistercian Studies* 19 (1984): 232–247.

Wojtulewicz, Christopher M. *Meister Eckhart on the Principle.* Leuven: Peeters, 2017.

## Notes

1. Bernard McGinn, "Do Christian Platonists Really Believe in Creation?" in *God and Creation: An Ecumenical Symposium,* ed. David Burrell and Bernard McGinn (Notre Dame: University of Notre Dame Press, 1990), 197–225.
2. Helpful here is Robert Sokolowski, *The God of Reason and Faith: Foundations of Christian Theology* (Notre Dame: University of Notre Dame Press, 1982).
3. Besides the article cited in note 1, I shall draw also on material in Bernard McGinn, *The Growth of Mysticism: Gregory the Great through the Twelfth Century* (New York: Crossroad, 1994), "Chapter 3. The Entry of Dialectical Mysticism: John Scottus Eriugena" (80–118).

4. Eriugena cites this often; e.g., *Periphyseon* 1 (443B, 454A, 518A); *Periphyseon* 2 (559B); and *Periphyseon* 4 (759A). The edition of the *Periphyseon* used here is that of Éduard Jeauneau, *Iohannis Scotti Eriugenae "Periphyseon"*, 5 vols. (Turnhout: Brepols, 1996–2003). I will cite by book of the *Periphyseon* with the Migne column number used by Jeauneau in parentheses.
5. I will generally use the translation by I. P. Sheldon-Williams and John O'Meara, *Eriugena: Periphyseon (The Division of Nature)* (Montréal/Washington: Bellarmin/Dumbarton Oaks, 1987).
6. *Periphyseon* 3 (678C).
7. Etienne Gilson, *History of Christian Philosophy in the Middle Ages* (New York: Random House, 1955), 116–17.
8. *Periphyseon* 1 (462D).
9. Eriugena discusses this aporia in many places in *Periphyseon*; see especially *Periphyseon* 1 (453C–55B).
10. See the long discussion in *Periphyseon* 3 (638C–87A).
11. *Periphyseon* 3 (632D–33B): "Non apparentis apparitio, occulti manifestatio, negati affirmatio, incomprehensibilis comprehensio, ineffabilis fatus."
12. James McEvoy, "Biblical and Platonic Measure in John Scottus Eriugena," in *Eriugena East and West*, ed. Bernard McGinn and Willemien Otten (Notre Dame: University of Notre Dame Press, 1994), 153–77; see also Werner Beierwaltes, "*Negati Affirmatio* or the World as Metaphor: A Foundation for Medieval Aesthetics from the Writings of John Scottus Eriugena," *Dionysius* 1 (1977): 127–159.
13. See the long "Quaestio de Nihilo," in *Periphyseon* 3 (634A–690B), especially 663CD, 681C, 683B, 686D. There is considerable literature on God as *nihil* in Eriugena; see especially Donald Duclow, "Divine Nothingness and Self-Creation in John Scottus Eriugena," *Journal of Religion* 57 (1977): 109–23; and Wayne Teasdale, "'Nihil' as the Name of God in John Scottus Eriugena," *Cistercian Studies* 19 (1984): 232–247.
14. *Periphyseon* 3 (683B).
15. *Periphyseon* 3 (677A); see also 639C.
16. *Periphyseon* 3 (655C).
17. *Periphyseon* 3 (673B).
18. On God as the creative principle of the other, see Beierwaltes, "*Negati Affirmatio*," 140.
19. Eriugena stresses the need for silence before the ineffable mystery of God in this life: "patiens esto, divinaeque virtute incomprehensibili locum da, eamque silentio honorifica, quoniam, dum ad eum pervenitur, omnis ratio deficit et intellectus" (*Periphyseon* 5, 951C). Since, God remains a mystery even after the *reditus* is complete, there must be an eternal role for silence as well.
20. Aquinas also treats creation in his *Scriptum super Libros Sententiarum II*, dd. 1–20, which, like Eriugena's *Periphyseon*, includes a long commentary on the Hexaemeron. There is a translation by Steven E. Baldner and William E. Carroll, *Aquinas on Creation* (Toronto: Pontifical Institute of Mediaeval Studies, 1997).
21. Joseph de Finance, *Être et agir dans la Philosophie de Saint Thomas*, 2nd ed. (Rome: Gregorian University Press, 1960). The book was written between 1927 and 1938, but not published until 1942. The modification of Aristotelian act-potency is achieved on the basis of conceiving God as *ipsum esse subsistens* and therefore Universal Agent, while the modification of Platonic/Neoplatonic views of participation is based

on Thomas's shift to a participation of *esse* rather than the Platonic participation of form.

22. This outlook is at the root of the *tertia via* of Thomas's noted five ways for "proving" God's existence in *STh* Ia, q. 1, a. 3—the existence of the contingent demands the necessary.
23. This principle appears in, e.g., q. 45, a. 1, ad 2; q. 46, a. 1, ad 6; q. 46, a. 2, ad 1.
24. *STh* q. 45, a. 3c: "Unde relinquitur quod creatio in creatura non sit nisi relatio quaedam ad Creatorem, ut ad principium sui esse."
25. Bernard McGinn, *Thomas Aquinas's "Summa Theologiae": A Biography* (Princeton, NJ: Princeton University Press, 2014); and "*Contemplatio sapientialis:* Thomas Aquinas's Contribution to Mystical Theology," *Ephemerides Theologicae Lovanienses* 95 (2019): 317–334.
26. This is based on Paul, who in 1 Corinthians 1:24 and 30 spoke of "Christ as God's Wisdom and Power . . . who became for us wisdom from God." The role of the Incarnate Word in the cycle of Wisdom is set forth in Thomas's Prologue to his *Scriptum super Sententias*, probably dating from 1252, as found in *S. Thomae Aquinatis Scriptum super libros Sententiarum Magistri Petri Lombardi*, ed. R. P. Mandonnet, 4 vols. (Paris: Lethielleux, 1929), 1:1–5.
27. For the Latin text and translation, see *St. Thomas Aquinas. The Exposition of the "On the Hebdomads" of Boethius*, introduction and translation by Janice L. Schultz and Edward A. Synan (Washington, DC: Catholic University Press, 2001), chap. 1. For more on Thomas on the nature of play, see *STh* IIaIIae. q. 168, aa. 2–4.
28. Eckhart's works appear in *Meister Eckhart: Die deutschen und lateinischen Werke* (Stuttgart-Berlin: Kohlhammer, 1936–). There are two main sections, LW (*Lateinischen Werke*), which will be cited by volume and page (e.g., LW 1:157), and DW (*Deutschen Werke*), cited the same way. In addition, the Latin works have numbered sections (n. and nn.). Four main discussions of creation are: (1) *Prologus generalis in Opus Tripartitum (Prol. Gen.)* nn. 12–22 in LW 1:156–65; (2) *Expositio Libri Genesis (Ex. Gen.)* nn. 1–28 in LW 1:185–206; (3) *Liber Parabolorum Genesis (Par. Gen.)* nn. 8–40 in LW 1:479–507; and (4) *Expositio Libri Sapientiae (Ex. Sap.)* nn. 19–40 in LW 2:339–362.
29. Along with the material on Eckhart in the article "Do Christian Platonists Really Believe in Creation" (see fn. 1), I will also use my treatment of creation in Bernard McGinn, *The Mystical Thought of Meister Eckhart* (New York: Crossroad, 2001), especially 100–106.
30. *Prol. gen.* n. 12: "Creare quippe est dare esse ex nihilo" (LW 1:157).
31. *Principium* as one of the keystones of Eckhart's thinking has been recently studied by Christopher M. Wojtulewicz, *Meister Eckhart on the Principle* (Leuven: Peeters, 2017). There is a good treatment of *unum* in Eckhart by Wouter Goris, *Einheit als Prinzip und Ziel: Versuch über die Einheitmetaphysik des "Opus Tripartitum" Meister Eckharts* (Leiden: Brill, 1997).
32. *Expositio S. Evangelii secundum Iohannem (Ex. Io.)* n. 514 (LW 3:445): "Restat videre quomodo esse sub ratione sive proprietate unius principium est et ab ipso procedit universitas et integritas totius entis creati."
33. *Ex. Gen.* n. 3 (LW 1:186–187).
34. *Ex. Io.* n. 31 (LW 3:25). On the *causa essentialis*, which goes back to Proclus and Dionysius, see Burkhard Mojsisch, "'Causa essentialis' bei Dietrich von Freiburg und Meister

Eckhart," in *Von Meister Eckhart zu Meister Dietrich*, ed. Kurt Flasch (Hamburg: Meiner, 1984), 106–114.

35. *Par. Gen.* n. 45 (LW 1:512).
36. *Ex. Sap.* n. 148 (LW 2:486).
37. *Ex. Sap.* n. 154 (LW 2:490). There is a translation of the whole comment on Wis. 7:27a (*Ex. Sap.* nn. 144–157) in Bernard McGinn, *Meister Eckhart. Teacher and Preacher* (New York: Paulist Press, 1986), 166–71. This passage is at 169. See Bernard McGinn, "Meister Eckhart on God as Unity," in *Neoplatonism and Christian Thought* , ed. Dominic O'Meara (Albany: SUNY Press, 1982), 128–39.
38. *Sermo (S.)* XLIX.3 (LW 4: 26); see also *Par. Gen.* nn. 9–20 (LW 1:479–491).
39. This is a daring claim, but Thomas Aquinas also said that the processions of the Persons in the Trinity were the *rationes productionis creaturarum inquantum includunt essentialia attributa* (*STh* Ia, q. 45, a. 6).
40. Eckhart often cites the Psalm verse in this connection; see, e. g., *Ex. Gen.* nn. 7, 16; *Ex. Io.* n. 73; and *Predigt (Pr.)* 53.
41. *"In agro dominico,"* art.3, as translated in Edmund Colledge and Bernard McGinn, *Meister Eckhart. The Essential Sermons, Commentaries, Treatises and Defense* (New York: Paulist Press, 1981), 78. The article is taken from *Ex. Gen.* n. 7.
42. *S.* XXIII n. 223 (LW 4: 208). See also *Ex. Sap.* n. 122; and *Prol. gen.* n. 17.
43. *Pr.* 30 (DW 2: 94). *Creatio continua* occurs both in the German sermons and especially in the Latin works. The notion of *creatio continua*, also found in a number of other medieval and Early Modern theologians, has interesting affinities with the modern scientific category of evolution that cannot be pursued here.
44. *Ex. Io.* n. 323 (LW 3: 271); see also *Par. Gen.* n. 62 (LW 1: 529); *S.* XV (LW 4: 147–48); and many other texts.
45. *Ex. Sap.* n. 21 (LW 2: 342). The two levels of existence are found throughout Eckhart's writings, especially in his Latin works. See McGinn, *The Mystical Thought*, 237, n. 195.
46. *Pr.* 57 (DW 2: 600–02).
47. Thomas Aquinas, STh IaIIae, q. 109, a. 2, ad 2: "Unaquaeque autem res creata, sicut esse non habet nisi ab alio, et in se considerata est nihil."
48. *Pr.* 4 (DW 1: 69–70).
49. *Expositio Exodi* n. 40 (LW 2: 45), and elsewhere.
50. *Pr.* 52 can be found in DW 2: 486–506. I cite from the translation in Colledge-McGinn, *Meister Eckhart. The Essential Sermons*, 202.
51. See John M. Connolly, *Living without Why. Meister Eckhart's Critique of the Medieval Concept of Will* (Oxford: Oxford University Press, 2014).
52. Pr. 59 (DW 2:625.7–626.2). The "Master" here is probably Avicenna, who speaks of God's action as not having a why (*Metaphysics* 8.4). See also Pr. 41 (DW 2:289.1–6).
53. *Sermo* IV, n. 21 (LW 4:22.12). Other passages in the Latin works include *In Ex.* n. 247 (LW 2:201); *In Eccli.* n. 59 (LW 2:287–288); *In Sap.* n. 187 (LW 2:253); *In Io.* nn. 50 and 743 (LW 3:41 and 641); and *Sermo* VI n. 59 (LW 4:58).
54. Pr. 26 (DW 2:27.1–0); see also Pr. 27 (DW 2:45.11–46.6).
55. Pr. 12 (DW 1:199.8–200.3).
56. Angelus Silesius, *Cherubinischer Wandersmann* (Zurich: Manesse Verlag, 1986), book 1, no. 289 (p. 96).

# 3 God's Will and the Creative Act

## ORIGEN ON DIVINE VOLITION AND THE INTELLIGIBILITY OF THE COSMOS

*Daniel J. Tolan*

This chapter lays out Origen's account of creation through divine volition. With an eye to the notion of divine "*līlā*," we begin with a brief overview of how Origen understands words related to "play"; notably, he does not present words related to play in a positive light, and he does not discuss play in relation to creation. Before we consider Origen's account of divine volition, a brief example of "emanation" is given from Proclus; after this, through reference to Plotinus, it is argued that a strict separation between creation by "willing," as opposed to by "emanation," is more elusive than certain polemicists would like it to be. The investigation continues with a careful analysis of Origen's note that the Son is the will of the Father, and points to the fact that it is not just through the Son that God creates, but it is through His will. Given that advocates of creation through divine "willing" often hold this position because they wish creation to be intentional, the further connection to the intelligibility of this intentionality will be made. On the basis of God's will being intelligible in the world, a belief Origen holds in tandem with a commitment to human freedom, the further point is made that for God's will to be "done on earth," and for this will to reach the depths of creation one must invite God into the deepest recesses of one's being, into the hidden man of the heart,[1] by harmonizing one's own will with the will of God, which is made manifest in creation. The chapter concludes by pointing out the similarities between Origen's understanding of creation and "*līlā*" on the grounds of divine freedom; however, for Origen, creation itself most certainly bears a "why."

### Play and παίγνιον (*paignion*)

Whenever Origen uses terms related to "play," they do not normally have a positive connotation. More broadly, in Greek, words such as παίζειν (*paizein*), a verb that means to "play," "sport," or "jest," and the related noun, παίγνιον (*paignion*), which means "plaything," "toy," or "game," are closely tied to the words παῖς (*pais*, child) and, thus, παιδεία (*paideia*, education).[2] However, in the Origenian corpus, words surrounding the notion of play bring with them a negative implication. One finds in the *Contra Celsum* that Celsus plays with (παίζειν, *paizein*) or, perhaps more accurately, mocks Jesus,[3] the Cross,[4] and even the blood spilled upon the Cross.[5] Likewise, when Origen strikes out at various Greek thinkers, he notes that the Prophets reduce them to child's play (παίγνιον, *paignion*).[6] The only neutral use of the term appears to be Origen's note that Leviathan, the dragon of the one-hundred-and-third Psalm, was crafted by God as a plaything (παίγνιον, *paignion*),[7] a comment made about the creation psalm's depiction of the forming of the sea: "There go the ships, there is Leviathan, whom thou hast formed to play [ἐμπαίζειν, *empaizein*] therein."[8] Yet one must bear in mind that this negative connotation of "play," comes from a mind ensconced in the biblical idiom; accordingly, Origen might well have the thirty-seventh Psalm in mind, wherein one reads, "For my loins are filled with mockings [ἐμπαιγμάτων, *empaigmatōn*], and there is no soundness in my flesh."[9] Given this understanding of "play" and Origen's commitment to God's goodness, it is not surprising that Origen does not describe the creative act as "play."

## Literature on Divine Volition in Origen

Much has been written about Origen's understanding of the Trinity and his understanding of human freedom; however, when it comes to divine freedom, this topic is best treated by Harald Holz's article 'Über den Begriff des Willens und der Freiheit bei Origenes." This article begins with discussions of Trinitarian thought, noting Origen's adherence to "orthodox subordinationism."[10] Moreover, Holz notes that, for almost all apologists, being is thought to originate from the will (*Willens* = θέλημα, *thelēma*) of the Absolute,[11] a point that is also true of the genesis of the *Logos*.[12] Holz specifies that in this discussion "will" refers not merely to the process of the unfurling of the absolute but to an expression of this principle, which leads to a personalist understanding of God.[13] Holz concludes his article with seven principles, all of which center on God's essence being self-communication; moreover, by self-communication, Holz has in mind the "will of the absolute" (*Wille des Absoluten*).[14] In relation to the notion of "*līlā*," it is important to note that this understanding of the will pivots on the non-arbitrary nature of creation: There is always a "why" in the creative act; however, the will of the absolute is also entirely self-determining.[15]

More recently, Christian Hengstermann, in his monograph *Origenes und der Ursprung der Freiheitsmetaphysik*, has brought out the connection between divine and human freedom in Origen's thought. For Origen, freedom is the principle of being.[16] Moreover, in contrast to Aristotle's "unmoved mover,"[17] Hengstermann points out the way in which Origen portrays God as *moving* in the revelation of his being.[18] A key point to Hengstermann's case is that Origen calls God, the Father, *libertas ingenita*.[19] Moreover, leaning on *fragmentum* 118 from *Fragmenta in evangelium Joannis*, Hengstermann notes that the Son is the *voluntus ex mente* of the Father.[20] Thus, it is the Son who makes known the will of the Father by having a will that is unified with the Father's will.[21]

Finally, it is worth noting that much, if not all, of modern scholarship on Origen is indebted to Henri Crouzel. While not a central focus to Crouzel's work, there are nevertheless clear points at which Crouzel reflected on the status of God's will. For instance, Crouzel notes that, for Origen, God's will is an "objective reality," and that this will plays a decisive role in the generation of the Son, creation, providence, the functions of angels, and the roles of the prophets and apostles.[22] Moreover, Crouzel notes that it is God the Father who guides the Trinity's "unity of will."[23] Thus, we are able to see that God's will plays a defining role in the Trinity's identity and God's creative act.

## Divine Exemplarism and Divine Volition

Origen lays out a well-defined notion of divine exemplarism throughout his corpus,[24] a doctrine which, for some Platonists, leads to an emanationist framework. Nevertheless, Origen is committed to a clear notion of divine volition. In testimony to this, one might consider Origen's claim that the Son is the will (θέλημα, *thelēma*) of the Father.[25] Thus, verses such as "all things were made through Him,"[26] which normally refer to Jesus, can also be understood in reference to God's will. In addition to being identified with God's will, the Son is also crucial to Origen's divine exemplarism, which is made clear in his *Commentary on John*, wherein he notes,

> For I think, just as a house and a ship are built or framed according to architects' plans, the *arche* of the house and of the ship having their

> respective plans [τύπους, *typous*] and reasons [λόγους, *logous*] in the craftsman; thusly, all things come about according to the reasons [λόγους, *logous*] made clear in advance by God in wisdom [σοφίᾳ, *sophia*], "for He made all things in wisdom." And it must be said, if I might say it thusly, that God made ensouled wisdom, He entrusted to her the moulding [πλάσιν, *plasin*] and the forms [εἴδη, *eidē*] for existence [οὖσι, *ousi*] and matter [ὕλη, *hylē*] from the plans [τύπων, *typo¯n*] which exist in her, but I stop short of saying if this is also their essences [οὐσίας, *ousias*]. Thus, therefore, it is not difficult to say that, roughly, the *arche* of beings [ὄντων, *onto¯n*] is the Son of God, as it says, "I am the *archē* and the *telos*, the A and the Ω, the first and the last." But it is necessary to know that He Himself is not called the *archē* according to all that He is called.[27]

This appeal to divine exemplarism, which places the divine paradigm in the Son, makes clear that the Son, synonymous with God's will, is the principle of all being.[28] This is important because thinking and willing coincide.

Yet it is not self-evident that divine exemplarism results in divine volition.[29] Consider proposition twenty-six of Proclus's (412–485 CE) *Elements of Theology*, "Every productive cause produces that which comes after it and the subsequent while remaining in itself,"[30] which develops into the notion of creation "by being itself" (αὐτῷ τῷ εἶναι, *auto¯ to¯ einai*). This notion is employed in various ways across Proclus's system. In contrast to Origen, Proclus understands the forms to produce "by being itself"; he notes, "For also if all the forms produce that which comes after them by being itself, and they always have their being just so, that which is produced from them will also have their being just so and will be eternal."[31] Thus, this is a clear example of a divine exemplarism wherein the forms, by their mere existence, create that which comes after them. In another proposition Proclus makes the same point when he notes that soul proceeds from *nous* because *nous*, unmoved, produces all "by being itself."[32] Production "by being itself" also extends to souls, which, Proclus notes, "by being itself" enliven (ζωοποιεῖται, *zōopoieitai*) that which comes from them; Proclus, in this instance, applies this concept to the soul's vehicle (ὄχημα, *ochēma*).[33] From this, one can see that there are differing understandings of divine exemplarism, and not all place emphasis on divine volition.

Creation "by being itself," in contrast with divine volition, proved an important point for Christian polemic against Platonism. Indeed, the distinction between "emanation" and "creation" was important enough to make it into a Byzantine critique of Proclus. Nicholas of Methone, in his *Ἀνάπτυξις*, accused Proclus of rejecting the divine will (θέλημα, *thelēma*), in favor of creation by mere existence.[34] Nicholas found this problematic because it seemed to render God as "unwilling" to create. This consequent unwillingness of God to create, Nicholas avers, is the reason why Proclus talks about *production* (παραγωγή, *paragōgē*) rather than *creation* (ποίησις, *poiēsis*). Thus, from Nicholas's perspective, creation "by being itself" is incompatible with divine intentionality.

## Plotinus: By Will or by Essence?

Despite what appears to be a clear distinction between creation "by being itself" and divine volition, this narrative is confounded by Plotinus's understanding of divine volition, as laid out in *Ennead* 6.8. Consider the statement:

> For if we were to grant activities to him, and ascribe his activities to what we might call his will [οἷον βουλήσει, *hoion boulēsei*]—for he does not act without willing—and his activities are what we might call his substance, *his will* [βούλησις, *boulēsis*] *and substance* [οὐσία, *ousia*] *will be the same thing.*[35]

Here, by refusing to acknowledge any difference between the "substance" and the will of the One, Plotinus does not fit squarely into a category of "emanation" or "volition," for it is not clear whether one ought to consider this an "emanation" from the One's essence, or an act of the will. One must bear in mind that the One is a perfect being, or, perhaps more accurately, a *beyond* perfect being, so it is not surprising that the One is difficult to classify; after all, this *Ennead* sees Plotinus develop a strong apophaticism,[36] and it is here that he stresses the use of οἷον (*hoion*) "as if" when employing divine predicates.[37]

Plotinus restates his commitment to the identity of the One's will with its essence when he notes that the One has a "freely willed [ἑκούσιος, *hekousios*] substance which comes to it in accordance with its will [θελήσει] and is *one and the same thing* as its will and is established in existence through its will."[38] Moreover, given that the One's will is identical with its essence, this also means that "its will [βούλησις, *boulēsis*] is its thought [νόησις, *noēsis*]."[39] Yet one ought not to be surprised that the One's will is identical with its existence and its thought because the One "brought himself into existence; so that he is not what he happened to be but what he himself willed."[40] Plotinus's insistence that the One wills all it is is born from a commitment to the One being maximally free. In his exegesis of *Republic* 509b9, Plotinus notes that the One is beyond being (ἐπέκεινα τῆς οὐσίας, *epekeina tēs ousias*) because the One is free from the "slavery" to substance (οὐσία, *ousia*).[41] Plotinus has, thus, placed the One beyond even the determination of activity (ἐνέργεια, *energeia*) by essence (οὐσία, *ousia*),[42] the One's act and will coming from pure freedom. Thus, without an essence, or substance (οὐσία, *ousia*), to determine the One's activity, Plotinus is able to say that the One is "primarily his will."[43] The One is also unique in that it is maximally self-determined: It is the cause of its own existence, and everything posterior to the One exists on account of the One.

In his article "Plotinus's Metaphysics: Emanation or Creation?" Lloyd Gerson argues that Plotinus is not an emanationist. This article, which brings Plotinus into conversation with Aquinas's understanding of creation, has a couple of cruxes. The first is an analysis of the use of "necessity" in relation to creation. On the surface, one finds that, for Plotinus, that which exists does so by necessity, while, for Aquinas, God does not create by necessity. However, "necessity" does not mean the same thing in these two cases. For Plotinus, that which the One creates is "necessary" insofar as the process of creation does not employ discursive reasoning (λογισμός, *logismos*);[44] it remains the case that the One acts by its will. Thus, on the one hand, for Plotinus, necessity is contrasted with discursive thought, which would imply imperfection, since one must be ignorant of the thing toward which one reasons, otherwise there would be no reasoning process. Aquinas, on the other hand, contrasts acting by necessity with acting by will. This leads Gerson to assert that "this should lead us to conclude that the "necessity" as attributed to creation by Plotinus and "necessity" as denied of God's acting by Aquinas do not mean the same thing.[45] Plotinus does not intend to say that the One creates due to some sort of external necessity. Gerson also distinguishes between creation *per accidens* and creation *per se*. He defines these sorts of creation as follows: "In a *per accidens* causal series, as opposed to a *per se* causal series, A is the cause of B, B is the cause of C, and so on. In a *per se* causal series, A would be the cause of C, and B would be an instrument of A's causal activity."[46] Gerson concludes that, if instrumental creationism counts as "creation," namely a *per se* causal series, Plotinus is a creationist rather than an emanationist.[47] Finally, it is worth noting that Gerson begins his article with the note that it is a category error to take any of Plotinus's metaphorical language about "flowing" as an indication that he is an emanationist.[48]

In light of Plotinus's equating the One's essence with its will, it should now be apparent that the distinction between "emanation" and "creation" is not quite as clear as it would be made to appear by those who wish to make "creation" by God's will a crucial difference between Christianity and Platonism.[49] Moreover, as Gerson points out, it is not enough to say that divine necessity is the clear distinction between "creation" and "emanation."[50] The question of necessity is also important when considering the notion of creation in the Platonic and Christian traditions in relation to "*līlā*." In what we have just seen, it is clear that, for Plotinus, creation is an intentional, but unnecessitated action; for, on the one hand, the One clearly wills what it does, but, on the other hand, there is nothing external to the One that can impose necessity upon the One. Yet since this remains a point where some wish to delineate Christianity from other late-antique "schools" of thought, let us turn our attention to Origen's understanding of God's volition.

## Origen on Divine Volition

Origen is the first thinker in the Christian tradition to pen a treatise in defense of human self-determination;[51] moreover, it would appear that Origen's commitment to human self-determination is simply a reflection of his commitment to divine freedom.[52] Although others before him, such as Irenaeus,[53] noted that God creates freely, Origen continuously develops this notion throughout his corpus. The notion of divine willing centers, for Origen, around the Father's relationship to the Son, whom Origen explicitly calls the will of the Father.[54] Origen uses the traditional, biblical language of the Son being the "image of the invisible,"[55] but he also moves beyond this when he notes the Son to be an emanation (ἀπόρροια, *aporroia*), which Rufinus translates as *manatio*, of the Father.[56] Also of note, Origen applies the phrase, found in Isaiah,[57] the "soul of God," to the Son.[58]

Origen's declaration that the Son is the will of the Father is found in his *Commentary on Ephesians*. Origen, reflecting on the first verse of the first chapter, which reads, "Paul, an Apostle of Jesus Christ through the will of God," notes, "And you will also understand, concerning 'the will of God,' whether it is possible to apply this to Christ; granted that it is just as He is 'the power of God and wisdom of God' (1 Cor. 1:24), on this supposition it is in this way he is also His will, he himself having his hypostasis from God."[59] God's will, moreover, plays a crucial role in each and every one of God's actions, Origen notes:

> As much as God enacts, does, and completes, He enacts all these things according to the proper "deliberation [ἰδίαν βουλὴν, *idian boulēn*] of His own will [θελήματος, *thelēmatos*]." For there is nothing which is able to make him act beside the "deliberation of his will," for he controls and rules all [πάντων γὰρ κρατεῖ καὶ ἄρχει τῶν ὅλων, *pantōn gar kratei kai archei*].[60]

Origen, moreover, turns to the language of will when discussing how one ought to understand what it means for the Son to be in the Father's image. Origen states, "Therefore, to a greater extent, just as the will proceeds from the mind neither cutting any part from the mind nor separating or dividing any part from it, it is in such a manner that the Father is thought to have begotten (the Son), who is clearly his image."[61] From what we have just cited, we see that Origen's understanding of divine volition has two key elements: First, God is almighty, ruling over all by his will;[62] second, that the Son, as the will of God, does not divide or reduce God's will in any way, proceeding directly from the divine mind, namely *nous*.

Earlier, we observed the claim of Plotinus, Origen's younger peer, that things have come about necessarily. For Plotinus, this does not express any form of constraint or compulsion on the divine, but, rather, it is a way to rule out any discursive thought or "development" in the divine. Origen shares this commitment. Consider *De Principiis* 1.2.10:

> Let us now look into the saying that wisdom is "an effluence," that is, an emanation, "of the clear glory of the Almighty," and if we first consider what "the glory of the Almighty" is, we shall then understand what its "effluence" is. Now as one cannot be a father apart from having a son, nor a lord apart from holding a possession or a slave, so we cannot even call God almighty if there are none over whom he can exercise his power. Accordingly, to prove that God is almighty we must assume the existence of the universe. For if anyone would have it that certain ages, or periods of time, or whatever he cares to call them, elapsed during which the present creation did not exist, he would undoubtedly prove that in those ages or periods God was not almighty, but that he afterwards became almighty

from the time when he began to have creatures over whom he could exercise power. Thus God will apparently have experienced a kind of progress, for there can be no doubt that it is better for him to be almighty than not to be so.[63]

Here, Origen is explicit that any sort of "progress" or development in Godself challenges God's status as the "Almighty." This is a standard problem in philosophy of religion: If God has room to improve, God is not almighty; if God has improved and is now supremely powerful, then there was a time when God was not almighty. This, of course, spawns the doctrine of divine immutability. In relation to creation, Origen gets around this problem by asserting that God, qua Father, has always begotten a Son, and that God, qua creator, has always created the universe. Hengstermann comments on this passage from *De Principiis*, noting that any change in God cuts against Origen's commitment to "aktualistischen Gottesbegriff."[64] In later, scholastic thought this is what came to be known as *actus purus*, which expresses God's perfection by removing potentiality from the divine. Clearly, this is at odds with the open-ended sort of development that Jessica Frazier outlines in the Caitanya Vaiṣṇava tradition in this volume. We have already observed, above, that Origen calls God, the Father, *libertas ingenita*; however, in what we have just cited, we read that "to prove that God is almighty we must assume the existence of the universe." These two claims dovetail together when we recall the way in which Plotinus understood "necessary creation": This term does not denote any compulsion on the divine, but, rather, it signals that God is *actus purus*. The cited passage clearly engages with notions vital to the dyad of "decision and duration," which Bernard McGinn discusses in his chapter in this volume with reference to the decision to create. Here, the "decision" and "duration" are from all eternity, a point vital to God's status as the "almighty."

The divine perfection of God the Father is reflected in the Son through a unity of will. Origen emphasizes this unity in the *Contra Celsum*, when he writes,

And if one should be vexed by these words, we should in no way desert our belief for those who deny there to be two *hypostases*, Father and Son: let him attend to the verse, "I and the Father are one." Therefore, we worship one God, Father and Son, as we have explained, and the account remains unbending for us against the others, and we do not worship superstitiously one who appeared recently as if he did not exist before. For

> we believe him who says "before Abraham was I am," and says, "I am the truth." . . . We worship, therefore, the Father of the truth and the Son, who is the truth, being two distinct things with respect to *hypostasis*, but one with respect to oneness of mind [ὁμονοίᾳ, *homonia*] and oneness of voice [συμφωνίᾳ, *symphōnia*] and identicality of will [βουλήματος, *boulēmatos*].[65]

Elsewhere, Origen notes that the Son shapes himself into the Father's will:

> It is the fitting food for the Son of God when he becomes a doer of the paternal will [θελήματος, *thelēmatos*], doing exactly what was in the will of the Father in himself, so that the will of God is in the will of the Son; and the will of the Son has become indistinguishable from the will of the Father, until there are no longer two wills but one will. That there is precisely one will was the cause of the Son saying, "I and the Father are One" (Jn. 10:30), and because of this will the one who has seen him has seen the Son, and has also seen the one who sent him.[66]

The Son is, thus, in a privileged position when it comes to doing the will of the Father, because He is the only one to know the full will of the Father, and it is this comprehension and doing of God's will that makes the Son the "Image of the Father."[67] This leads Origen to note that "for also the will in him is an image of the first will, and the divinity in him is an image of the true divinity."[68] Thus, "the will of the Father is whole when it is brought about by the Son, it comes about when the will in the Son does these things exactly as the will of God wishes."[69]

Nevertheless, this apparent harmony between the wills of the Father and the Son gets confounded through other statements. Consider Origen's note, "This was never the will [θέλημα, *thelēma*] of the Father, which was wiser than the intention [βούλημα, *boulēma*] of the Son, ordering things [οἰκονομοῦντος, *oikonomountos*] in a way and order beyond that which the Saviour was seeing."[70] This claim, moreover, seems to parallel Origen's note that the Father's contemplation of Himself gives Him more glory than the Son's contemplation of the Father.[71] Yet one might be able to counterbalance such claims with others, such as Origen's statement that the Father and the Son have one work,[72] or assertions that combine these claims, such as "both of these are the one proper food of Jesus, both to do the will of the one who sent him and to consummate His work."[73]

## Volition, Intentionality, and Intelligibility

But yet why should we care about God's will in relation to creation? If we recall the concern raised by Nicholas of Methone, it would appear that intentionality is the crux of this discussion. God's "creation" of the world through an act of the will, as Nicholas understands it, ensures that God's creation is freely willed (ἑκούσιος, *hekousios*). One suspects that his polemic against creation "by being itself" (αὐτῷ τῷ εἶναι, *autō tō einai*) also intimates a desire for there to be purposiveness behind the design of the cosmos. Yet in what we have observed with Origen, both exemplarism and the divine will coincide in the Son. The Son is, thus, identified both as the will and Logos of the Father. This is particularly important for biblical statements such as "all things were made through Him,"[74] for, as Logos, the Son endows creation with its intelligibility, and, as will, the Son expresses God's intentionality.

For Origen, God's will is reflected in creation. Moreover, Origen insists on the fact that God doesn't will anything contrary to nature; he notes,

> Thus, if anyone says evil is contrary to nature [αρὰ φύσιν, *para physin*], we also say that God does not wish [βούλεται] things that are contrary to nature, nor that which comes from vice, nor the things which come about irrationally [ἀλόγως, *alogōs*]. But if the things which come about according to the Logos of God are also the things that come about according to his wish [βούλησιν, *boulēsin*], it is necessary these things come about naturally, not contrary to nature. For the things done by God are not contrary to nature, even though they may be paradoxes or *seeming* paradoxes to some.[75]

This strikes a particular blow to those who wish, in a fideistic manner, to stress that God is beyond this world in such a fashion that God is, in every way, a paradox. Origen is clear: These are only *seeming* paradoxes; one can rest assured that God wills nothing contrary to nature (παρὰ φύσιν, *para physin*).

Elsewhere, Origen, in an attempt to make clear that God does not will the sin one finds in the world, makes clear that God wills *the administration* of the world.

> For how is it said that "all things are administered [διοικεῖσθαι, *dioikeisthai*] according to God's will [κατὰ γνώμην, *kata gnōmēn*]," this must be examined, and whether the administration also reaches the sins that

> are committed or not. For thus, if the administration reaches also to the sins committed not only by humans but also by daemons and if any other of those who are out of body is disposed by nature to sin; let the one who says this see it is out of place with the claim "all things are administered according to God's will [κατὰ γνώμην, *kata gnōmēn*]." For it follows this account also that the sins and all that is from evil [κακίας] is "administered according to the will [γνώμην, *gnōmēn*] of God," yet this very claim is not the same as the claim "these things come to pass without the hindrance of God." But if one were to hear "administered" properly, then one would say that the things administered from evil are "administered"—that is to say all things are administered according to God's will [γνώμην, *gnōmēn*]—, and all of the sins do not transgress the administration of God.[76]

Here, Origen has provided a theodicy. By asserting that God wills the administration of the world, Origen is attempting to remove God from the implication that he might will sins, or anything else that is untoward in the *cosmos*. Moreover, in another passage, in an even more positive manner, Origen notes that God not only administers all, but that he has arranged the whole world for humanity's spiritual progress, "the one who is well pleased with what happens is free from all bondage of that which comes to pass and does not raise his hands in contestation against God, who has ordained that which he wills [βούλεται, *bouletai*] as our training ground [γυμνάσιον, *gymnasion*]."[77]

As we have already seen, God's will is the catalyst for creation. Thus, it is God who wills the natural order of the *cosmos*. It thus follows that God can do nothing contrary to nature. Yet this is not enough to say that everything is natural or to say that everything is willed by God. In order to prevent the conclusion that God wills evil, or that God wills anything contrary to nature, we have seen Origen add the *provisio* that God wills the *administration* of the world. Thus, when one glimpses nature correctly, it is possible to discern the maker's meaning in creation, for, as we have already seen, God's essence is self-communication. Given that this is the case, the *cosmos* can be understood as a training ground, wherein one comes to better know and shape oneself in accordance with God's will.

## Creation as Revelation

Origen points to two ways of knowing God: through revelation in Scripture and through creation. Both the created order and the Bible are sources of knowledge about God, because they are both produced by the one and the same God.[78] At one point in *De Principiis*, Origen uses an analogy to explain how one can glimpse God through the *cosmos*. In this analogy, Origen notes that our eyes cannot look upon the light of the sun itself, but we can see its brightness and rays; thus, we can contemplate these rays and infer from them just how great the sun is. In like fashion, we cannot behold God in our minds, but we can come to understand Him from the beauty of his creation.[79] This lines up with McGinn's dyad of "distinction and dependence"; although the cosmos is, indeed, distinct from God, it is, nevertheless, dependent on Him. Likewise, with respect to the divine-cosmos relationship raised by Frazier in this volume, we might note that the cosmos, for Origen, is a symbol pointing beyond itself to the divine.[80] Accordingly, through bringing oneself into harmony with the world, one can be understood as bringing oneself into harmony with God.[81] Therefore, one's progression in the spiritual life can be seen as a journey to know and come into conformity with God's will. To this end, Origen notes, "and the one holy being, inspired by the paternal will, will dwell to a greater degree, or more fully, or more distinctively in it by comparison to another; and again, there will be something else living even more pre-eminently in it than that one."[82] Thus, one, in one's own distinct manner, can come to know and live in accordance with the divine will.

As a Christian, Origen also understands Jesus as a specific revelation. Just as Moses is the Hebrew lawgiver, Jesus is the one who introduces the saving doctrines of Christianity.[83] All divine revelations, for Origen, are instances of the divine will;[84] this is most emphatically the case with the incarnation.[85] The Son also has the unique task of making known the Father's will, leading Origen to ask, "But who announces the will [βουλὴν, *boulēn*] of the Father to those of the creatures who are worthy and who has come to exist alongside them other than the Saviour"?[86] This, no doubt, reinforces the centrality of self-communication to who God is.

The creative act through the Logos ensures that God's will is rational, and it also ensures that all of creation is undergirded by rationality. This means that those who truly worship the Logos will be fully rational; this leads Origen, in one place, to note that the saint is the only, properly speaking, rational person.[87] In line with this, if one worships the Logos, one will do nothing irrational:

> But also the miracles [παράδοξα, *paradoxa*] he did were not trickery, as Celsus thinks, but they were done by divinity, as foretold by the prophets,

> who have their testimony from God, in order that the "one who honours the Son," who is the Logos, does nothing irrational [ἄλογον, *alogon*] and benefits from honouring Him, and honouring Him, who is the truth, one might become better from honouring Truth, but also thusly from honouring wisdom and righteousness and all the divine attributes, which the divine words affirm to be the Son of God.[88]

One of the results of God willing rationally is that those who truly worship God will, likewise, only act rationally. Thus, already in the divine, we see that thought and will are inseparable. Moreover, the imitation of God's will is central to how Origen interprets the Lord's Prayer; he notes:

> Still being "upon earth" while praying, we consider that which comes to pass "in heaven" to be "the will" [θέλημα, *thelēma*] of God in the hands of those who are inhabitants of heaven, let us pray also that we who are "upon earth" might, similarly to them, carry out all things according to the "will" of God. This will happen when not one of us does anything contrary to His "will."[89]

It remains, however, that one must be *converted* to the Logos, and this conversion is one of persuasion, not compulsion. Persuasion, undoubtedly, points to the logocentric nature of conversion for Origen. He notes, concerning church officials:

> And in this way they worship God truly and teach as many as possible, they become a mix of the Logos of God and the divine law and thusly are unified with the God of all through the Son of God, the Logos, and Wisdom, and Truth, and Righteousness, who unites to himself all who have been persuaded to live in accordance with God [κατὰ θεὸν, *kata theon*] in all things.[90]

The wish for God's will to be done on earth is something actualized by those who, united with the Logos, harmonize their own wills with God's will.

God's will is essential to the creation and continuance of the cosmos for Origen, and the ability to discern this will is pivotal in the soul's return to God. Indeed, even God's will rejoices in our salvation; consider Origen's note in his *Commentary on Ephesians* that God's "will was also well pleased at His 'glory being praised' on account of His grace for those being saved."[91] God both shares the truth with each of us, to the extent that we are worthy,[92] and He comes and makes his dwelling in those whom He wishes.[93] So, in a certain way, the consummation of creation can be found in the striving of each individual to purify his or her self in order that God might penetrate the deepest recesses of his or her being, such that God might be "all in all."[94]

## Conclusion

Origen's commitment to divine freedom is the clearest way in which his understanding of creation converges with the Indic notion of "*līlā*." In *A Dictionary of Hinduism*, we read that "*līlā*" is "the spontaneous, unpremeditated act of creation or destruction," and, elsewhere in the same entry, that "*līlā* primarily means free motion or movement, whether regular or irregular, like the 'play' of water in a fountain."[95] We have already seen that, for Origen, God is *libertas ingenita*, a claim that is most congruous with the definition of "*līlā*" we have just cited. For Origen, there is no compulsion in the divine. Moreover, any sort of "necessity" in creation must be understood in line with Gerson's discussion of necessity in Plotinus: This terminology can only be used to denote the non-discursive nature of God's creative act, for God is *actus purus*. In the same entry for "*līlā*," we also read that "*līlā* is carried out through the abundance of the Supreme Being's bliss, and hence the world is said to originate from bliss." A parallel can be drawn with Origen's thought on the grounds that God creates as a form of "self-expression" or self-communication.[96] There is no reason for God's creation outside of the fact that God wishes to share his goodness with others. Moreover, we have seen that there is divine joy when God's creatures turn back to God.

There remains, however, one clear point at which Origen's understanding of creation does not square with the definition of "*līlā*," and this depends on how far one wishes to push the language of play. By now it should be clear that Origen's account of creation is logocentric. In Greek, λόγος (*logos*) has a variety of meanings, such as "word," "account," "proportion," "explanation," "theory," "reason," "speech." If, by "divine play," one has in mind a non-compelled creative act, then this squares with what Origen has in mind. However, when it comes to creation itself, all things within creation have a "why," an "account," a "reason," or, more succinctly, a "logos" for creation, and this is God. Thus, creation itself and nature most certainly bear a "why" or a purpose, and this is because they have come into existence "through" the Logos.

# Bibliography

## Ancient Authors


Angelou, Athanasios D., ed. *Nicholas of Methone, Refutation of Proclus' Elements of Theology.* Corpus Philosophorum Medii Aevi—Philosophi Byzantini 1. Athens: Academy of Athens, 1984.

Blanc, Cécile, ed. *Origène, Commentaire sur saint Jean.* Sources Chrétiennes 120, 157, 222, 290, 385. Paris: Le Cerf, 1966–1992.

Borret, Marcel, ed. *Origène, Contre Celse,* 4 vols. Sources Chrétiennes 132, 136, 147, 150. Paris: Éditions du Cerf, 1967–1969.

Borret, Marcel, ed. *Origène, Homélies Sur Le Lévitique, vol. 1.* Sources Chrétiennes 286. Paris: Cerf, 1981.

Bywater, Ingram, ed. *Ethica Nicomachea.* Oxford Classical Texts. Oxford: Clarendon Press, 1962.

Dodds, Eric R. *Proclus: The Elements of Theology.* 2nd ed. 1963. Oxford: Clarendon Press, 1977.

Görgemanns, H., and H. Karpp. *Origenes vier Bücher von den Prinzipien.* Darmstadt: Wissenschaftliche Buchgesellschaft, 1976.

Gregg, J. A. F., ed. "Documents: The Commentary of Origen upon the Epistle to the Ephesians." *Journal of Theological Studies* 3 (1902): 234–244, 398–420, 554–576.

Harl, Marguerite, and Nicholas de Lange, eds. *Origène. Philocalie, 1–20 et Lettre à Africanus.* Sources Chrétiennes 302, Paris: Cerf, 1983.

Harvey, W. Wigan, ed. *Irenaeus, Libros Quinque Adversus Haereses.* Cantabrigiae: Typis Academicis, 1857.

Klostermann, Erich, ed. *Commentarium in evangelium Matthaei.* In *Origenes Werke,* vol. 10.1–10.2. *Die griechischen christlichen Schriftsteller* 40.1–40.2. Leipzig: Teubner, 1935–1937.

Koetschau, Paul, ed. *Exhortatio ad Martyrium.* In *Origenes Werke,* vol. 1. *Die griechischen christlichen Schriftsteller* 2, 3–47. Leipzig: Hinrichs, 1899.

Koetschau, Paul, ed. *De Oratione,* in *Origenes Werke,* vol. 2. *Die griechischen christlichen Schriftsteller* 3, 297–403. Leipzig: Hinrichs, 1899.

Leonine edition. *Thomas Aquinas, Summa Contra Gentiles.* Vol. 13 in *Sancti Thomae de Aquino Opera omnia.* Rome, 1918.

Migne, Jean P., ed. *Origen, Homilies on Genesis.* Patrologia Graeca 12: 145–280. Paris, 1857–1886.

Ross, W. David, ed. *Aristotelis, Physica.* Oxford Classical Texts. Oxford: Clarendon Press, 1950.

Ross, W. David. *Aristotelis, Metaphysica.* Oxford: Clarendon, 1958.


### TRANSLATIONS


Plotinus. *Enneads, Volumes I–VI.* Translated by A. Hillary Armstrong. Loeb Classical Library 440–445, 468. Cambridge, MA: Harvard University Press, 1969–1988.

Origen. *On First Principles*. Translated by G. W. Butterworth. London: SPCK, 1936.

Origen. *Contra Celsum*. Translated by Henry Chadwick. Cambridge: Cambridge University Press, 1980.

Origen. *Commentary on the Gospel according to John: Books 13–32*. Translated by Ronald E. Heine. Washington, DC: Catholic University of America Press, 1993.

## MODERN AUTHORS

Beierwaltes, Werner. *Das wahre Selbst: Studien zu Plotins Begriff des Geistes und des Einen*. Frankfurt am Main: Vittorio Klostermann, 2001.

Crouzel, Henri. *Origène*. Paris: Lethielleux, 1985.

Crouzel, Henri. *Origène et Plotin: Comparaisons Doctrinales*. Paris: Téqui, 1991.

Dillon, John, and Daniel J. Tolan. "The Ideas as Thoughts of God." In *Christian Platonism: A History*, edited by Alexander J. B. Hampton and John Peter Kenney, 34–52. Cambridge: Cambridge University Press, 2020.

Doolan, Gregory T. *Aquinas on the Divine Ideas as Exemplar Causes*. Washington, DC: Catholic University of America Press, 2008.

Gerson, Lloyd P. "Plotinus's Metaphysics: Emanation or Creation?" *Review of Metaphysics* 46, no. 3 (1993): 559–574.

Hengstermann, Christian. *Origenes und der Ursprung der Freiheitsmetaphysik*. Adamantiana; Band 8. Münster: Aschendorff Verlag, 2016.

Holz, Harald. "Über den Begriff des Willens und der Freiheit bei Origenes." *Neue Zeitschrift für Systematische Theologie und Religionsphilosophie* 12, no. 1 (1970): 63–84.

Lollar, Joshua. *To See into the Life of Things: The Contemplation of Nature in Maximus the Confessor and His Predecessors*. Turnhout: Brepols, 2013.

McFarland, Ian A. *From Nothing: A Theology of Creation*. Louisville, KY: Westminster John Knox Press, 2014.

Sterling, Gregory. "Prepositional Metaphysics in Jewish Wisdom Speculation and Early Christian Liturgical Texts." In *The Studia Philonica Annual: Studies in Hellenistic Judaism. Jewish Wisdom Speculation and Early Christian Liturgical Texts*, IX:219–38. Brown Judaic Studies 312. Atlanta: Scholars Press, 1997.

Stutley, Margaret, and James Stutley. *A Dictionary of Hinduism: Its Mythology, Folklore and Development 1500 B.C.–A.D. 1500*. Routledge Library Editions. London: Routledge, 1977.

Tolan, Daniel. "The Impact of the Ὁμοούσιον on the Divine Ideas.". In *Platonism and Christian Thought in Late Antiquity*, edited by P. G. Pavlos, L. F. Janby, E. K. Emilsson, and T. T. Tollefsen, 129–50. Studies in Philosophy and Theology in Late Antiquity. London: Routledge, 2019.

Tolan, Daniel. "Ὁ Θεὸς Ἔρως Ἐστί: Origen and the Attribution of Ἔρως to God." *International Journal of the Platonic Tradition* (2022), https://doi.org/10.1163/18725473-bja10024.

Δημητράκος, Δημήτριος. 1936. *Μέγα Λεξικόν Ὅλης Τῆς Ἑλληνικῆς Γλώσσης*. Vol. 10. ΑΘΗΝΑΙ: ΕΚΔΟΣΕΙΣ ΔΟΜΗ Α.Ε.

# Notes

1. 1 Peter 3:4.
2. Δημητράκος 1936, 10: s.v. παιδεύω; s.v. παίζω.
3. Origen, *Cels.* 2.33.3; 2.34.2.
4. Origen, *Cels.* 6.36.30.
5. Origen, *Cels.* 1.6.12.
6. Origen, *Cels.* 7.7.9; cf. 8.39.3.
7. Origen, *Cels.* 6.25.1–10.
8. Psalm 103:26 (LXX): ἐκεῖ πλοῖα διαπορεύονται, δράκων οὗτος, ὃν ἔπλασας ἐμπαίζειν αὐτῇ. While this is a neutral reference to play, it is, nevertheless, a description of a sea monster. All translations are the author's own, save for citations of Plotinus.
9. Psalm 37:8 (LXX): ὅτι αἱ ψόαι μου ἐπλήσθησαν *ἐμπαιγμάτων*, καὶ οὐκ ἔστιν ἴασις ἐν τῇ σαρκί μου·
10. Harald Holz, "Über den Begriff des Willens und der Freiheit bei Origenes," *Neue Zeitschrift für Systematische Theologie und Religionsphilosophie* 12, no. 1 (1970): 65: "orthodoxen Subordinatianisimus."
11. Holz, "Über den Begriff des Willens und der Freiheit bei Origenes," 66–67: "Man kann sagen, daß in dieser Auffassung—die im Einzelnen mehr oder weniger, aber doch im Wesentlichen von fast allen Apologeten geteilt wird—innerhalb einer Theorie des Absoluten ontologische Daten als Resultate eines ursprünglichen Willens im Absoluten interpretiert werden."
12. Holz, "Über den Begriff des Willens und der Freiheit bei Origenes," 69.
13. Holz, "Über den Begriff des Willens und der Freiheit bei Origenes," 70: "Der Begriff des Willens ist hier ein Indiz nicht nur für die Art und Weise des absoluten Prozesses selbst, sondern noch mehr für das entsprechende Prinzip . . . Der 'heilsgeschichtliche Trinitarismus,' von dem man gesprochen hat mit Bezug auf das Denken des Origenes, ist so nichts anderes als ein 'personalistisch' konzipiertes System: sowohl der Beziehungen, die in Gott selbst herrschen, als auch der Beziehungen, die zwischen Gott und der Welt bestehen."
14. Holz, "Über den Begriff des Willens und der Freiheit bei Origenes," 84: "Was hier soeben als Mitteilung bezeichnet wurde, ist aber im Grunde nichts anderes als der Wille des Absoluten: sowohl als Prinzip wie auch als dessen Aktuierung."
15. Holz, "Über den Begriff des Willens und der Freiheit bei Origenes," 70: "So ist mit dieser Art von Willen, dem die Notwendigkeit immanent ist, nur die absolute und vollkommene Selbstbestimmung Gottes jenseits aller Willkür—die dem Begriff der absoluten Güte widerstreiten würde—gemeint."
16. Christian Hengstermann, *Origenes und der Ursprung der Freiheitsmetaphysik*, Adamantiana; Band 8 (Münster: Aschendorff Verlag, 2016), 89–93.
17. Aristotle, *Metaphysica* XII.
18. Hengstermann, *Origenes und der Ursprung der Freiheitsmetaphysik*, 143–168.
19. *HomLev* 16.6, 502.15. In *Origène, Homélies Sur Le Lévitique, vol. 1*, ed. Marcel Borret. Sources Chrétiennes 286 (Paris: Cerf, 1981).
20. Frag. 118: *natus est autem ex ipsa patris mente, sicut uoluntas ex mente.*

21. For more see Hengstermann, *Origenes und der Ursprung der Freiheitsmetaphysik*, 207–229.
22. Henri Crouzel, *Origène* (Paris: Lethielleux, 1985),101: "Il est maintes fois question de la volonté de Dieu dans le Peri Archon et dans le Contre Celse et cette volonté est considérée souvent comme une réalité objective, sans que soit examiné comment comprendre cette faculté de vouloir. Elle est attribuée pareillement au Fils et à l'Esprit. Elle s'exerce dans la génération du Fils, dans la création accomplie par bonté, dans le gouvernement du monde afin de pourvoir au bien des hommes, dans les fonctions et les noms attribués aux anges, dans la prophétie et dans l'apostolat des disciples: pareillement dans de nombreuses citations de textes néotestamentaires qui parlent de la volonté de Dieu ou du Christ."
23. Crouzel, *Origène*, 241: "Certes, Dieu agit dans le monde, comme nous allons le voir, par l'intermédiaire de son Fils et de son Esprit. Mais Origène est cependant fort loin de la conception du "Dieu oisif" auxquels aboutissent certains courants de la philosophie grecque, exagérant l'impassibilité de Dieu. Car à travers le Fils, son ministre, et l'Esprit, c'est lui qui agit. De lui proviennent en quelque sorte les décisions concernant l'action de la Trinité, il est le centre de cette unité de volonté qui dirige l'activité des trois personnes. Son rôle est primordial, aussi bien dans les opérations intratrinitaires, génération du Fils et procession de l'Esprit, que dans la création, la Providence, la divinisation des créatures raisonnables, l'eschatologie."
24. Exemplarism is both an ontological and an epistemological doctrine. It posits archetypes of being, such as the Platonic "forms" or "ideas," as thoughts in the mind of God, and it understands created being as a copy of this archetype. Ontologically, this doctrine justifies existence by explaining that all being is rooted in the mind of God. Epistemologically, this doctrine grounds cognition by basing the intelligibility of objects external to one's mind, and the ability to connect particulars to universals, in the fact that these objects depend upon the contemplation of the divine mind for their being. For more on the origins of this notion, see Dillon, John, and Daniel J. Tolan. "The Ideas as Thoughts of God." In *Christian Platonism: A History*, edited by Alexander J. B. Hampton and John Peter Kenney (Cambridge: Cambridge University Press, 2020), 34–52.
25. Origen, *Comm. Eph.* P. 235, §1.12–18.
26. John 1:3a: πάντα δι' αὐτοῦ ἐγένετο; Cf. 1 Cor. 8:6.
27. Origen, *Comm. in Io.* I.19.114–116. Translation taken from Daniel Tolan, "The Impact of the Ὁμοούσιον on the Divine Ideas," in *Platonism and Christian Thought in Late Antiquity*, edited by P. G. Pavlos, L. F. Janby, E. K. Emilsson, and T. T. Tollefsen, Studies in Philosophy and Theology in Late Antiquity. (London: Routledge, 2019), 129–50.
28. Origen also makes the Son the *arche* of being in his *Homilies in Genesis*, wherein he takes what seems like a temporal claim, "in principium," or ἐν ἀρχῇ, as a reference to "the Saviour" (Origen, *Hom. in Gen.* 1.1; *PG* 12:145c: "Non ergo hic temporale aliquod principium dicit: sed in principio, id est in Salvatore factum esse dicit coelum et terram, et omnia quae facta sunt").
29. While being mindful of the difficulties one comes across in separating God from God's will, as noted in the section on Plotinus below, it is worth considering the way in which exemplarism develops differently in Greek East and Latin West. More

specifically, the consideration as to whether or not Divine Exemplarism is based in the divine essence. For example, in his discussion of the λόγοι Maximus appeals to Dionysius in order to make the point that his λόγοι, understood as Divine Ideas, are God's wills (*Amb. Io.* 7 1085A: Τούτους δὲ οὕς ἔφην τοὺς λόγους ὁ μὲν Ἀρεοπαγίτης ἅγιος Διονύσιος "προορισμοὺς" καὶ "θεία θελήματα" καλεῖσθαι ὑπὸ τῆς Γραφῆς ἡμᾶς ἐκδιδάσκει), while Aquinas places the ideas in the divine essence (*Summa contra Gentiles* 1, c. 53 (Leonine ed., vol. 13.151): "Sic ergo per unam speciem intelligibilem, quae est divina essentia, et per unam intentionem intellectam, quae est verbum divinum, multa possunt a Deo intelligi."). While this might be a question of emphasis when one is talking about a perfect, or beyond-perfect, being, consider chapter three of Doolan's monograph on Aquinas's divine exemplarism (Gregory T. Doolan, *Aquinas on the Divine Ideas as Exemplar Causes* [Washington, DC: Catholic University of America Press, 2008]. 83–122), which is devoted to reconciling the multitude of the ideas with divine simplicity; it is not clear that one would need to argue this case if the ideas are in God's will, or, more precisely, if the ideas are understood as proper to God's ἐνέργεια (*energeia*, activity) of contemplation, rather than positing them in God's οὐσία (*ousia*, essence).

30. Πᾶν τὸ παρακτικὸν αἴτιον ἄλλων μένον αὐτὸ ἐφ' ἑαυτοῦ παράγει τὰ μετ' αὐτὸ καὶ τὰ ἐφεξῆς. (Proclus, *Elements*, Pr. 26 30.10–11).
31. Proclus, *Elements*, Pr. 178 156.30–32: καὶ γὰρ εἰ αὐτῷ τῷ εἶναι πάντα τὰ εἴδη παράγει τὰ μετ' αὐτά, τὸ δὲ εἶναι αὐτῶν ἀεὶ ὡσαύτως ἔχει, καὶ τὰ ἀπ' αὐτῶν ὡσαύτως ἕξει καὶ ἀΐδια ἔσται.
32. Proclus, *Elements*, Pr. 194 168.31–32: εἰ γὰρ ἀπὸ νοῦ πρόεισι καὶ νοῦς ὑποστάτης ψυχῆς, καὶ αὐτῷ τῷ εἶναι ἀκίνητος ὢν πάντα ὁ νοῦς παράγει . . .
33. Proclus, *Elements*, Pr. 209 182.28–31: διότι γὰρ αὐτῷ τῷ εἶναι τὰς ψυχὰς ζωοποιεῖται παρ' αὐτῶν καὶ ἔστι συμφυῆ ἐκείναις, παντοίως συμμεταβάλλει ταῖς ἐκείνων ἐνεργείαις καὶ συνέπεται πάντη . . .
34. N76 78.30–79.1: οὗτος δὲ τὸ θεῖον θέλημα παραιτούμενος καὶ τὴν παραγωγὴν τοῦ γινομένου τῷ εἶναι μόνῳ τοῦ ποιοῦντος ἀφοριζόμενος ἀκούσιον ἔοικε τῷ ποιοῦντι τὴν ποίησιν εἰσάγων• διὸ οὐδὲ ποίησιν ἀλλὰ παραγωγὴν αὐτὴν ὀνομάζει.
35. Plotinus, *Enneads* 6.8.13.5–8, trans. Armstrong (italics added).
36. E.g., Plotinus, *Enneads* 6.8.9.
37. Plotinus, *Enneads* 6.8.13.50. For discussion of the οἷον *provisio*, see Werner Beierwaltes, *Das wahre Selbst: Studien zu Plotins Begriff des Geistes und des Einen* (Frankfurt am Main: Vittorio Klostermann, 2001), 112.
38. Plotinus, *Enneads* 6.8.13.18–20 (emphasis added).
39. Plotinus, *Enneads* 6.8.6.36.
40. Plotinus, *Enneads* 6.8.13.56–59.
41. Plotinus, *Enneads* 6.8.19.10–20.
42. E.g., Aristotle, *Physics* II.3; *Nic. Eth.* I.7. Perhaps Origen's repeated claim that God is not "material substance" (*De Prin.* I.1.2; I.1.5; I.6.4; II.2.; II.4.3) is, at least in part, outlining this position with an eye to divine freedom. The suggestion is not being made that Origen is conflating "material substance" with "substance," but rather that substance is a way of delineating God from creation; take, for example, Origen's note "Quod autem a deo uniuersa creata sint, nec sit ula substantia qua non ab eo hoc ipsum ut esset acceperit . . ." (*De Prin.* 1.3.3, 50.14–15). Thus, out of concern for divine

freedom, Origen might be making the same move as Plotinus, divorcing God from Substance. Consider also Origen's note that intelligible natures have never existed separately from material substance: "necessitas consequentiae ac rations coartat intelligible principaliter quidem creatas esse rationabiles naturas, materialem uero substantiam opinione quidem et intellectu solo separari ab eis et pro ipsis cel post pisas effectam uideri, sed numquam sine ipsa eas del uixisse del uiuere: solis namque trinitatis incorporea uita existere recte putabitur" (*De Prin.* 2.2.2, 112.17–22).

43. Plotinus, *Ennead* 6.8.21.16; Also consider 6.8.13.21: but in that it possesses the Good it wills itself; 6.8.13.29–31: and that his willing to be himself by his own agency is concurrent with his being what he wills, and his will and he himself are one"; 6.8.13.38: "For the nature of the Good is in reality the will of himself"; 6.8.21.12–13: "Now his will is in his substance; so there is nothing different from his substance."
44. *Enn.* 3.2.3.1–5.
45. Lloyd P. Gerson, "Plotinus's Metaphysics: Emanation or Creation?" *Review of Metaphysics* 46, no. 3 (1993): 561.
46. Gerson, "Plotinus's Metaphysics," 562.
47. Gerson, "Plotinus's Metaphysics," 574.
48. "The first remark I wish to make about these passages is the obvious one that to think of emanating or flowing in contrast to creating is to make a sort of category mistake. For metaphors are not properly contrasted with technical terminology" (Gerson, "Plotinus's Metaphysics," 559).
49. It has become a commonplace to juxtapose Christianity with Platonism by saying that the former believes in creatio ex nihilo, whereas the latter believes in emanation. One recent example can be found in McFarland:
"In others, the [creation] stories have a more naturalistic cast, in which the world is birthed from a cosmic egg (e.g., certain Hindu and Taoist traditions, the Finnish *Kalevala*), or is understood as an emanation from the divine (Plotinus's *Enneads*, Jewish kabbalistic thought). Notwithstanding these significant differences, however, all these cosmogonies share the presupposition of a fundamental ontological continuity between Creator and creature: the world and its inhabitants derive from divinity in such a way that the visible cosmos includes traces of divinity, however obscure or deformed these may be.... Nevertheless, with extraordinary rapidity the early church rejected the claim that such language had anything other than purely metaphorical significance, insisting instead on the radical ontological discontinuity between Creator and creature encapsulated in the doctrine of creation from nothing" (Ian A. McFarlane, *From Nothing: A Theology of Creation* (Louisville, KY: Westminster John Knox Press, 2014), xii–xiii).
50. Gerson's conclusion about Plotinus's relationship to creation and emanation disrupts the clean division McFarland makes between Christianity and Platonism: "Returning to the question with which I began this paper, Is Plotinus's metaphysics creationist or emanationist? If it is allowed that instrumental creationism is a legitimate species of creationism, then I think the answer is the former. If, on the other hand, one insists that there is no common genus for a metaphysics that holds that the existence of everything depends on the first principle and a metaphysics that holds that the being of everything depends on the first principle, then Plotinus's metaphysics is not accurately called creationist. But it is not emanationist either. I do not have a convenient label to offer for this alternative" (Gerson, "Plotinus's Metaphysics," 574).

51. Origen, *De Prin.* III.1, περὶ αὐτεξουσίου.
52. Note that this is also part of Plotinus' reasoning throughout 6.8, where he notes that since humans are self-determining (αὐτεξούσιον), the One must be maximally self-determining.
53. One might also wish to consider Irenaeus's claim that God "libere fecit omnia" (He made all things freely) (Irenaeus, *Adversus Haereses* 2.1.1).
54. Origen, *Comm. Eph.* P. 235, §1.12–18.
55. Origen, *De Prin.* 1.2.5; cf. Col. 1:15.
56. Origen, *De Prin.* 1.2.5.101.
57. Isaiah 1.14.
58. Origen, *De Prin.* 2.8.5.
59. Origen, *Comm. Eph.* P. 235, §1.12–18: ἐπιστήσεις δὲ καὶ περὶ τοῦ θελήματος τοῦ Θεοῦ εἰ δύναται τάσσεσθαι ἐπὶ Χριστοῦ• ἵν' ὥσπερ ἐστὶ Θεοῦ δύναμις καὶ Θεοῦ coφία, οὕτως ᾖ καὶ θέλημα αὐτοῦ, Θεοῦ ὑπόστασιν ἔχον αὐτόν• ἐὰν δέ τινι ἀπεμφαῖνον φαίνηται οὐσιῶσθαι λέγειν τὸ τοῦ Θεοῦ θέλημα, ἐπιστησάτω εἰ μὴ ἡ δοκοῦσα ἀπέμφασις παραπλήσιός ἐστι καὶ ἐπὶ δυνάμεως Θεοῦ καὶ coφίας Θεοῦ καὶ λόγου Θεοῦ, καὶ ἀληθείας καὶ ἀναcτάcεως καὶ ὁδοῦ• παραπλήσιος γάρ μοι δοκεῖ τυγχάνειν περὶ πάντων τούτων, ὡς οὐσιωμένων ἐν τῷ μονογενεῖ Λόγῳ (The publication of this text retained the lunate sigma found in the manuscript. Here, the ἵνα and οὕτως are taken as setting up a supposition, in contrast to Heine, who appears to leave both terms untranslated: "And you will take note also if the phrase 'will of God' can be applied to Christ so that as he is 'the power of God and the wisdom of God' [1 Cor 1: 24], so he may also be his 'will,' himself having the substance of God.") The last part of this translation has been rendered "himself having his hypostasis from God" in distinction to Heine's "himself having the substance of God," on account of Origen's claim that the Son is *not* the same essence as the Father (*Com Jn* 20.157). Origen notes, elsewhere, that the will of the Father is enough to substantiate (perhaps *hypostasise*, in Greek) whatsoever he wills and that it is in this very way that the Son is begotten; in this passage, Origen continues to use the language of "deliberation of his will," perhaps invoking the language from Ephesians for his readers to bear the Epistle in mind for context: Si enim omnia quae facit pater, haec et filius facit similiter, in eo quod omnia ita facit filius sicut pater, imago patris deformatur in filio, qui unique natus ex eo est helt queaedam uoluntas eius ex mente procedens. Et ideo ego arbitro quad sufficere debeat uoluntas patris ad subsistendum hoc, quod uult pater. Volens enim non alia uit utitur, nisi qua concilie uoluntatis profertur. Ita ergo et filii ab eo subsistentia generatur (Origen, *De Prin.* 1.2.6, 34.23–35.7).
60. Origen, *Comm. Eph.* P. 241–242, §7.1–5.
61. Origen, *De Prin.* 1.2.6 48.134–136: Magis ergo sicut uoluntas procedit e mente et neque partem aliquam mentis secat neque ab e separatur aut diuiditur: tali quadam specie putandus est pater ilium genuisse, imaginem scilicet suam, ut sicut ipse est inuisibilis per naturam, ita imaginem quique inuisibilem genuerit.
62. Note the phrase πάντων γὰρ κρατεῖ (*pantōn gar kratei*). The "Almighty" in Greek is Παντοκράτωρ (*pantokratōr*).
63. Origen, *De Prin.* 1.2.10 (trans. Butterworth).
64. Hengstermann, *Origenes und der Ursprung der Freiheitsmetaphysik*, 185: "Anstatt also, was dem aktualistischen Gottesbegriff widerspräche, anzunehmen, Gott sei in

der Schöpfung nach einem nicht näher bestimmten Zeitraum untätiger Muße 'vom Schlechteren zum Besseren gelangt,' ist die 'Einsicht' notwendig, dass der Vater in seiner Allmacht stets Lenker von 'ihm angemessenen Geschöpfen' gewesen ist, 'denen er,' wie es seinem Wesen entspricht, 'Gutes tun konnte.'"

65. Origen, *Contra Celsum* 8.12.12–26. On oneness of will, etc cf. Origen, *Comm. in Matt.* XVII.14; *Comm. in Io.* 10.37.21, *Comm. in Io.* 2.10; *De Oratione.* 15.1. Chadwick suggests that this phrase is echoed in the Second Creed of Antioch (AD 341) (*Contra Celsum*, 461 N1).
66. Origen, *Comm. in Io.* 13.36.228.1–9.
67. Origen, *Comm. in Io.* 13.36.231.1–3: Μόνος δὲ ὁ υἱὸς πᾶν τὸ θέλημα ποιεῖ χωρήσας τοῦ πατρός• διόπερ καὶ εἰκὼν αὐτοῦ.
68. Origen, *Comm. in Io.* 13.36.234.2–3.
69. Origen, *Comm. in Io.* 13.230.3–5.
70. Origen, *Ex. Ad Martyr.* 29.37–40.
71. Origen, *Comm. in Io.* 32.350: ζητῶ δὲ εἰ ἔνεστιν δοξασθῆναι τὸν θεὸν παρὰ τὸ δοξάζεσθαι ἐν υἱῷ, ὡς ἀποδεδώκαμεν, μειζόνως αὐτὸν ἐν ἑαυτῷ δοξαζόμενον, ὅτε ἐν τῇ ἑαυτοῦ γινόμενος περιωπῇ, ἐπὶ τῇ ἑαυτοῦ γνώσει καὶ τῇ ἑαυτοῦ θεωρίᾳ, οὔσῃ μείζονι <τῆς> ἐν υἱῷ θεωρίας, ὡς ἐπὶ θεοῦ χρὴ νοεῖν τὰ τοιαῦτα, δεῖν λέγειν ὅτι εὐφραίνεται ἄφατόν τινα εὐαρέστησιν καὶ εὐφροσύνην καὶ χαράν, ἐφ' ἑαυτῷ.
72. Origen, *De Prin.* 1.2.12.
73. Origen, *Comm in Io.* 13.37.246.1–3.
74. John 1:3a: πάντα δι' αὐτοῦ ἐγένετο; Cf. 1 Cor. 8:6: ἀλλ' ἡμῖν εἷς Θεὸς ὁ Πατήρ, ἐξ οὗ τὰ πάντα καὶ ἡμεῖς εἰς αὐτόν, καὶ εἷς Κύριος Ἰησοῦς Χριστός, δι' οὗ τὰ πάντα καὶ ἡμεῖς δι' αὐτοῦ. Notably, such verses are instances of "prepositional metaphysics" (Gregory Sterling, "Prepositional Metaphysics in Jewish Wisdom Speculation and Early Christian Liturgical Texts,"i *The Studia Philonica Annual: Studies in Hellenistic Judaism. Jewish Wisdom Speculation and Early Christian Liturgical Texts*, 9:219–38. Brown Judaic Studies 312. [Atlanta: Scholars Press, 1997], e.g., 236).
75. Origen, *Cels.* 5.23.19–25: ὅτι εἰ μὲν παρὰ φύσιν τὴν κακίαν τις λέγει, καὶ ἡμεῖς λέγομεν ὅτι οὐ βούλεται τὰ παρὰ φύσιν ὁ θεός, οὔτε τὰ ἀπὸ κακίας οὔτε τὰ ἀλόγως γινόμενα• εἰ δὲ τὰ κατὰ λόγον θεοῦ καὶ βούλησιν αὐτοῦ γινόμενα, ἀναγκαῖον εὐθέως εἶναι μὴ παρὰ φύσιν• οὐ <γὰρ> παρὰ φύσιν τὰ πραττόμενα ὑπὸ τοῦ θεοῦ, κἂν παράδοξα ᾖ ἢ δοκοῦντά τισι παράδοξα. While I have added the italics in my translation, it seems to capture well the intention behind the Greek.
76. Origen, *Cels.* 7.68.18–30–451.
77. Origen, *De Oratione* 10.1.8–10.
78. Origen, *Philokalia* 2.5, pp246–8; Cf. *Comm. Rom.* 2.7.1.
79. Origen, *De Prin.* 1.1.6.
80. Consider Jessica Frazier's query, "whether the world should be seen as a real transformation (*pariṇāma*) of the divine, expressing its innately 'full' (*pūrṇa*) generative power (*śakti*), or a lower level (*vyāvahārika*) reality downgraded to a merely apparent (*māyā*), seeming (*ābhāsa*) or limited (*upādhi*) kind of truth" ("The Metaphysics of Emotion: Divine Play in Caitanya Vaiṣṇava Philosophy," in this volume).
81. For more on this theme, see Joshua Lollar, *To See into the Life of Things: The Contemplation of Nature in Maximus the Confessor and His Predecessors* (Turnhout: Brepols, 2013).
82. Origen, *Comm. in Io.* 13.49.232.1–4.

83. Origen, *De Prin.* 4.1.1.
84. Origen, *Hom. Lk.* 3.1.
85. Origen, *Hom. Lk.* 28.1.
86. Origen, *Comm. in Io.* 1.38.283.1–3.
87. Origen, *Comm. in Io.* 2.114.
88. Origen, *Cels.* 8.9.23–30.
89. Origen, *De Oratione* 26.1.6–10.
90. Origen, *Cels.* 8.75.22–27.
91. Origen, *Comm. Eph.* (§3 P238.38–39, *Eph.* 1:5b).
92. Origen, *Comm. in Io.* 1.186.
93. Origen, *Cels* 4.5.15–19: Ἐπιδημεῖ δὲ δύναμις καὶ θειότης θεοῦ δι' οὗ βούλεται καὶ ἐν ᾧ εὑρίσκει χώραν, οὐκ ἀμείβοντος τόπον οὐδ' ἐκλείποντος χώραν αὑτοῦ κενὴν καὶ ἄλλην πληροῦντος.
94. 1 Cor. 15:28. Also consider Origen's *Comm. in Io.* 10.221 for more on God's indwelling in the individual.
95. Margaret Stutley, and James Stutley. *A Dictionary of Hinduism: Its Mythology, Folklore and Development, 1500 B.C.–A.D. 1500*, Routledge Library Editions (London: Routledge, 1977), s.v., *līlā*.
96. For more on God's erotic outpouring of self in Origen's thought, see Daniel Tolan, "Ὁ Θεὸς Ἔρως Ἐστί: Origen and the Attribution of Ἔρως to God," *International Journal of the Platonic Tradition* (2022), https://doi.org/10.1163/18725473-bja10024.

PART II

# Grace, Compassion, and Suffering: Some Pastoral Connotations of *Līlā*

# 4 Creation, Vision, Bliss

## *LĪLĀ* AS GRACE ACCORDING TO RĀMĀNUJA, WITH REFERENCE ALSO TO THOMAS AQUINAS AND GREGORY PALAMAS

*Francis X. Clooney, SJ*

In this essay I wish to show that *līlā* refers importantly, even if not always, to the free action of God in the world, unmotivated other than by mercy and love toward the world and its living beings. *Līlā* is grace, in a context in which we better understand creation, freedom, beatitude, and the vision of God as interrelated concepts. To shed light on my thesis, I first recollect the understanding of *līlā* found in the Rāmānuja school of Vedānta. I consider Rāmānuja's teaching regarding the nature of God's creative action in a world that has been created as God's self-manifestation in material and spiritual complexity, so that in the world humans might encounter God. I will show that here *līlā* is tantamount to the free and gracious action of God (Nārāyaṇa) and, by extension, the world as *līlāvibhūti, the realm in which that grace is enacted and humans, by grace, enabled to see God.* In this section, I presume as very useful context and background the recent essay by Julius Lipner, on the semantics of *līlā*.[1] My reflections in the first part of this essay are also complemented and very ably extended by Sucharita Adluri's essay in this volume,[2] where she provides more detail regarding Rāmānuja's views on *līlā*, and then shows how his views on *līlā* are further developed by Vedānta Deśika, several centuries after Rāmānuja.

Thereafter, I develop a comparative angle, focusing on creation in Thomas Aquinas and Gregory Palamas of the Latin and Greek Christian traditions, not with reference to an act of *ex nihilo* production, but as regarding creation as the graced, dependent reality of the world. I rely on Hans Boersma's *Seeing God* to show us how to think about Palamas and Aquinas together, and both of them alongside Rāmānuja, as we move toward a more adequate understanding of the material world as the act and site of gracious divine self-manifestation and thus, even in Christian tradition, as *līlā*—grace.

## Creation, Vision, and Delight in the Theology of Rāmānuja

In a recent essay, Julius Lipner has masterfully surveyed uses of the word *līlā* in wide range of Hindu religious literature, and pushed back against a monolithic conceptualization of that *līlā* as "play." He rightly shows that in many cases, *līlā* does not entail "play" and the "playful," but rather an uncontestable freedom that is nonetheless purposeful, aimed at a divine intention to help living beings in this world, particularly through making it possible for humans to encounter God in the materiality of human existence. *Līlā* in this sense is a matter of grace. With Lipner's overview in mind, the central part of this essay aims to show how *līlā* as grace is enacted in the writings of one Hindu theologian, Rāmānuja.

Rāmānuja was a philosopher and a theologian; a proponent of the harmony of Tamil and Sanskrit traditions; a premier leader of the south Indian Hindu Śrīvaiṣṇava community and a reformer of its ritual practices; a devotee of the deity Nārāyaṇa who brilliantly theorized what "love of God" means. Nine works are attributed to him.[3] Rāmānuja's understanding of the vision of God within creation makes plausible the claim that humans really can see God in this world. Indeed, the point of creation is that in this temporal and spatial realm humans can begin to see God, in a vision that culminates in the supreme bliss of eternity with God. All of this is without compulsion on either the divine or the` human side, and so we must add that Rāmānuja cultivates a very rich sense of divine freedom, of the grace that makes the human and divine accessible to each other.

The *Viśiṣṭādvaita Kośa* is a theological dictionary in Sanskrit which quotes amply from theological sources in Rāmānuja's Vedānta tradition. It elaborates the meaning of *līlā* by quoting the verse that opens Rāmānuja's *Śrībhāṣya*, his great commentary on the *Brahma Sūtras*, to show that *līlā* is effortless action whose motive is simply one's own purpose, what a free person wishes to do:

> He whose *līlā* is the birth, steadiness, and destruction, etc. of the whole world,
> Whose sole dedication is the protection of the host of various worshipping beings,

> Who is the apex of the śruti, radiant, Brahman, on whose breast
> rests Śrī—
> May my dedication, in the form of devotion, be on that highest one.

The *Kośa* adds that by the word "*līlā*" is meant God's status as "fully perfect, driven by no other, acting only in accord with his own volition, etc."[4]

The act of creation is *līlā*'s primal enactment, but that act is inscribed with a complex set of purposes including purification, facilitating the capacity and realization of the vision of God, and superlative happiness. All of these points are succinctly related to Rāmānuja's view of the purpose of creation. As the Kośa adds, citing the *Darśanodaya*, "Evolved creation, which is the site (of that līlā), is secondarily indicated by the word 'līlā.'"

The *Vedārthasaṃgraha*, Rāmānuja's first composition, helps us understand what he has in mind. This treatise is heavily exegetical argumentative. The *Vedārthasaṃgraha* presumes that right interpretation of scripture is a key to understanding creation properly, and to seeing God: from right interpretation to right practice and full vision. The treatise is built around arguments defending the nature of the world, its source in God alone, and its importance to the devotional life.

The well-known creation account found in *Chāndogya Upaniṣad* 6 is crucial background for the whole of the *Vedārthasaṃgraha*. Here Uddālaka teaches his son Śvetaketu in this way:

> In the beginning, son, this world was simply what is existent, one only, without a second. . . . And it thought to itself: "May I become many. May I propagate myself." It emitted heat. The heat thought to itself: "May I become many. May I propagate myself." It emitted water. Whenever it is hot, therefore, a man surely perspires; and thus it is from heat that water is produced. The water thought to itself: "May I become many. May I propagate myself." It emitted food. Whenever it rains, therefore, food becomes abundant; and thus it is from water that foodstuffs are produced. (*Chāndogya Upaniṣad* 6.2.1–4)[5]

Several points are key for our purposes. First, the creation of the world is based simply on a decision of the original Existent to become many; there is no other reason for this free, gracious act; it is *līlā* as gracious creativity in a strong sense. Second, the original, simple Existent becomes many with respect to both material and spiritual realities, as fire, water, and earth evolve from that original, single source, with a certain consciousness driving their complexification.

Rāmānuja interprets the *Chāndogya* text as elucidating the glories of the Lord, but also the creation that arises from him and as it were extends beyond him, without becoming entirely separated from him:

> Thus challenged by his son Śvetaketu, Uddālaka explains: "This alone is concealed in the heart, having the single proper form of knowledge, bliss, and purity, having great unlimited glory, possessing hosts of innumerable auspicious qualities, flawless and superabundant, mingled in accord with his will, which is always accomplished. This is the highest Brahman, whose proper form is without change, whose body is all conscious and non-conscious beings, subtle and not susceptible to divisions by name and form. By his own will, simply for the sake of *līlā*, the entire configuration of the world in the form of the moving and unmoving, endless and varied, is established as a portion of him. By knowing this part as known, he is also stating all else that is to be known."[6]

A few paragraphs later Rāmānuja emphasizes the intimate relationship of God and the world, alluding to a subsequent statement from a few verses later in *Chāndogya* 6, *tat tvam asi* ("you are that [reality]"), in the course of his explanation:

> Thus, by passages such as, "All these creatures are rooted in Being, my son, have their abode in Being, and are founded in Being" (*Chāndogya* VI.8.4–6), he expounds in detail how the entire expanse of emitted creation, comprised of conscious and non-conscious beings, has Being as its material and efficient cause, its foundation. It is controlled by Being, and exists for the sake of Being. He explains texts such as, "All this is made of that," and "all this is Being" (*Chāndogya* VI.8.4–6), with attention to the relationship of effect and cause, showing that the entire world is comprised of Brahman, and Brahman is the self of the entire world, and that the entire world is [Brahman's] body. What is expressed by the word "thou" is the mode of being of the living being, which is nothing but Brahman. It is thus known that everything is comprised of Brahman. This is summarized with reference to a particular living being (Śvetaketu) by "you are that." (*Chāndogya* 6.8ff.)[7]

Śvetaketu himself is then a particular instance of the event that is the world coming forth from Brahman and continuing to be a spiritual-material reality expressive of God's self-manifestation. Every person is an instance of the reality that is originally and ultimately God. Later in the *Vedārthasaṃgraha* Rāmānuja again returns to the *Chāndogya* text, and emphasizes the presence of God in creation:

> The highest Brahman, whose wishes are always realized, wills, "May I have many modes" (cf. *Chāndogya* VI.2) ,and thus he divides himself up as the entire gross material form that holds subtly within it the entirety of non-conscious beings, plus the host of conscious beings, all dissolved into himself. He then emits all the material beings from that subtle being, and enters them as the enjoyer, and thus brings into order the entire world by the material beings linked to one another and governed by conscious beings. He establishes all bodies in their many modes, by being their highest self.[8]

To see any individual thing or person in the world is to see the body, the soul animating the body, and the Lord within, who likewise animates the soul and body.[9]

The Lord is disposed to respond favorably to those who turn to him. He makes possible contemplation in which devotees take pleasure in patient and slowly maturing contemplation, as they attain near and nearer approximations of a direct vision of God:

> The supreme person is pleased with the actions prompted by devotion—remembering the Lord and offering praise ceaselessly, making acts of reverence, striving, chanting, hearing, reciting and meditating on the Lord's qualities, performing temple worship and acts of obeisance. Most compassionate, He offers His grace and destroys all the devotee's inner darkness. The supreme person is to be obtained only by devotion in the form of continuous meditation, which attains the status of most clear perception and which is ceaseless and unsurpassable, and which has no other motive (than love of God).[10]

The relationship of God and world is not vague for Rāmānuja, but a vivid, evident reality, and so the genealogical account of the world is enriched by vivid depictions of what God looks like.

A further contemplation in *Vedārthasaṃgraha* n. 198 shows God in considerable material detail, seeming as known through visualizations based in the contemplation of scriptural passages:

> The texts of the Vedas define the substantive nature of this Nārāyaṇa, the supreme Brahman, as infinite knowledge, infinite bliss, and infinite

purity. They also sing of His unsurpassed, perfect and countless holy attributes like knowledge, power, sovereignty, strength, vigor and radiance. They describe Him as one by whose will all other entities both sentient and non-sentient, are sustained in their very being and controlled in all their activities. Similarly, there are thousands of *śrutis* [revealed utterances] which describe Him as follows: His divine form is wholly agreeable and appropriate to Him. Many kinds of numberless and infinitely auspicious ornaments adorn Him, suiting Him eminently; He bears numberless, wondrous weapons, suited to His prowess. His divine consort is agreeable and suited to Him in Her essential nature, form, beauty, glory, sovereignty, compassion and unsurpassed greatness.[11]

In *Vedārthasaṃgraha* n. 220, amid a long list of quotations regarding the vision of God, Rāmānuja offers an even more vivid vision:

His luster is that of a fine mountain of molten gold. He has the splendor of a hundred thousand suns. His pure eyes have the beauty of the petals of a lotus, just as they unfold under the rays of the sun and crown their rich stalk that has sprung up in deep waters. His brows and forehead and nose are charming. His coral-like lips radiate a pure smile. His cheeks are tender and radiant, His neck lovely like a conch. His exquisitely tender earlobes almost touch His high shoulders. His arms are well-developed, round and long. His beautiful and roseate palms are adorned with fingers of the same hue. His waist is slender, chest broad. . . . He has captivated the minds of all by His surpassingly sublime beauty. . . . He is the supreme Brahman, the highest Self, Nārāyaṇa.[12]

This vision prompts great delight (*prīti*):

It is said that the means for the attainment of Brahman is superior devotion, which has the form of meditation which has acquired the vividness of clearest perception, and which is flawless and insurmountably pleasing, accomplished by establishment in devotion aided by one's performance of duties preceded by knowledge of the nature of reality in accord with scripture. The term "bhakti" indicates a particular kind of delight, and delight is a particular kind of cognition.[13]

The world is the place in which what is, what is known, and what is experienced all cohere in knowledge and delight; and all of this, of course, is grounded in the utterly gracious and uncompelled act of God in making the world. This freely shared enjoyment is *līlā*, and the world may be termed the "*līlāvibhūti*," the realm of God's gratuitous assistance to humans in every way, even to a complete and final bliss. All this is so and can be emphasized as such, even if at the end of the *Vedārthasaṃgraha*, Rāmānuja again cautions his readers that direct and literal vision of God is not possible in this life, even if an interior vision of God is real and possible. Quoting the Mahābhārata, he notes, "The Lord's form does not stand within the scope of seeing. No one sees him with his eyes. Only he whose self is integrated fully by bhakti and firm focus does see fully the proper form of knowledge."[14]

Because there is a created world, Rāmānuja's idealized devout practitioner sees more of God, more directly. This practical fruition is grounded in Rāmānuja's embodiment theology and creation cosmology. Accordingly, the emerging vision of God in a vivid representation of the intellectual and material complexity of God seen by the devotee reliably (begins to) show the devotee what God looks like, as if by direct perception.[15] But this is a matter of grace, divine gifts freely given, and not of any natural necessity: It is, that is to say, *līlā*. As we shall see, Aquinas and Palamas are challenged by the same quandary, how to interpret the world as the privileged place in which God becomes visible, yet without making God seem to be one more object available for observation. Indeed, this is why there is a world at all, as a kind of theater in which vision is possible. The world in its variety and materiality is the realm of manifest grace, divine graciousness proffered simply so that humans can come to see God. This gracious gift is, I suggest, the divine *līlā*, the world established as the *līlā vibhūti*.[16]

Rāmānuja insists that this vision is like perception, the materiality of the world made graciously to "reflect" the divine presence. Here we can turn to Rāmānuja's famous interpretation of meditation as a kind of seeing, near the start of his most famous work, the *Śrībhāṣya* commentary on the *Brahmasūtras*:[17]

> "Meditation" means steady remembrance, i.e., a continuity of steady remembrance, uninterrupted like the flow of oil; in agreement with the scriptural passage which declares steady remembrance to be the means of release, "steady meditation, on the attainment of remembrance all the ties are loosened" (*Chāndogya Upaniṣad* VII.26.2). Such remembrance is of the same form as seeing; for the passage quoted has the same purport as the following one, "The fetter of the heart is broken, all doubts are solved, and all the works of that person perish when he has been seen who is high and low" (*Muṇḍaka Upaniṣad* II.2.8).

> And this being so, we conclude that the passage "the Self is to be seen" teaches that "meditation" has the character of "seeing" or "intuition." And that remembrance has the character of "seeing" is due to the abundance of imagination in it. All this has been set forth at length by the Commentator,[18] who says, "Knowledge means meditation. Scripture uses the word in that sense." That is, in all Upaniṣads that knowledge which is enjoined as the means of final release is meditation. . . . Such remembrance has been declared to be of the character of "seeing," and this character of seeing consists in its possessing the form of perception. Remembrance thus acquires the form of perception and is the means of final release. . . . Hence, he who possesses remembrance, marked by the character of immediate presentation, and which itself is dear above all things since the object remembered is such; he, we say, is chosen by the highest Self, and by him the highest Self is gained.[19]

Meditation that reaches a vividness like that of perception, possible in a world that by divine design is disclosive of the divine source for all material as well as spiritual realities. According to Rāmānuja, God can be seen in this life, in a real but not literal manner, and this vision is a source of great pleasure. *This is what creation is for.* This is also, I suggest, a way of making precise what Rāmānuja and his tradition think about creation, as the site for mutual divine-human vision, the pleasure of that vision, and thus, in the sense of gracious, free exchange that is a kind of delight, and it seems fair to describe this whole drama as *līlā*, the gracious creator manifesting the divine self in a delightful form.

There is just one more piece to be filled in, before I turn to the comparative part of this essay, by a reading of Thomas Aquinas and Gregory Palamas. The Rāmānuja tradition also characterizes the created world as an act of compassion, intended to free beings from the suffering caused by their accumulation of good and bad karma. The *Viśiṣṭādvaita Kośa* cited earlier speaks about creation as a matter of compassionate *līlā* in the course of another objection and response cited from the Rāmānuja tradition:

> [Thesis:] *The creation of the world is simply a matter of līlā* [*līlārthaṃ jagatsṛṣṭiḥ*]
>
> [Objection:] But if it is said that the Lord emits the world simply as a matter of *līlā*, this would contradict the statement that He performs the emitting of the world and the giving of liberation because of his compassion.

> [We reply:] The primary intent of *līlā* itself is to ward off the suffering of others. A king, compassionate regarding the case of the hunchback dwarf, the person afflicted with respiratory affliction, etc., gives out food and milk as if he is playing (*krīḍati*).[20] Thus too, (the lord's) *līlā* in the form of emitting the world occurs only as infused with compassion. The *līlās* performed by the Lord must therefore be meditated on as serving no purpose but the uplift of those taking refuge. They are nothing but the fruits of compassion.[21]

*Līlā* is purposeful, the Lord's *līlārtha* creation is an act of compassion. The world is the place where the burning off of karma is possible, and on this level, creation is a sign of God's determination to help beings in trouble, by giving them times and places for purification. This is the true *līlā*, gracious intervention on behalf of those in need. But if so, we cannot avoid also admitting that we are quite far removed from the ordinary connotations of "*līlā* as play."

Within this frame of the contemplative possibility of an experience of God in the world, such as is both interior and palpable to the senses, we can better appreciate the divine action of entering *into* the world, a world that is already a manifestation of the divine person's creative power. The Lord graciously enters the world by way of divine descents (*avatāras*) and consecrated temple presences (*arcā*). In the times of *avatāra*, and in temples, God can be seen in concrete particularity, and experienced by the senses, in ways that are superlatively pleasing to the senses. That God can be seen in the world in a concrete and specific *avatāra* form is clearly indicated in Rāmānuja's introduction to the *Bhagavad Gītā*. There Rāmānuja makes clear that the possibility of encounter with the Lord among humans is *the* reason for God's coming into the world:

> Under the pretext of removing the burden of the earth, but really for the purpose of becoming the place of refuge for ourselves and others, He descended to the earth and made Himself visible to the eyes of all those born human. He performed divine deeds of a sort which ravished the minds and eyes of everyone, both the high and the low.[22]

The fourteenth-century theologian Vedānta Deśika, one of the great thinkers in the lineage of Rāmānuja, amplifies the statement I have just quoted:

> The general nature of divine descent and its purpose have already been shown. But now he makes some specifications related to the topic, by

> saying "under the pretext of removing the burden of the earth," etc. Descending to support the earth is merely a pretext. Becoming refuge for all is the clear intent. Destroying evil-doers is the corollary of a greater purpose, the protection of the good.[23]

The greater purpose is the accessibility of the divine person to human eyes:

> Due to bountiful accessibility toward humans as a cowherd, He who is hard to grasp even by the most pure minds of great yogis, became visible even to the fleshly eyes of humans who do not respect the differences between the forbidden and what is not forbidden. This is the meaning. . . . The goal of His coming down and becoming the object of human eyes is not merely that He be worshipped, but also that He be experienced.[24]

Creation, in its diversity, is a place where God can be present, seen in material form, and enjoyed. By divine descent, God then appears within that world, and acts within it, so that humans and other conscious beings might experience God with their five senses.

As we have already seen with respect to *Vedārthasaṃgraha* nn. 198 and 220, by "vision of God" Rāmānuja has in mind placid and beautiful forms of God, which show divine accessibility, please the eye, and draw people close. Consider this passage which he inserts, without any apparent exegetic need for it, at *Bhagavad Gītā* 9.34, "Your mind focused upon me, devoted to me, sacrificing to me, pay obeisance to me. Thus having focused yourself, you will come to me, on me intent":

> "Your mind focused on Me"—Without interruption, like a smooth flow of oil, have your mind intent upon Me the lord of all, antagonistic to all that is evil and focused on what is auspicious, omniscient, whose wishes are always realized, the sole cause of the entire universe, the supreme Brahman, the supreme Person; who has slender radiant eyes like lotus petals; who has the complexion of a clear blue cloud; whose shining luster is like that of a thousand suns simultaneously risen; the great ocean of the nectar of loveliness; with four arms, fine and solid; wearing a brilliant yellow raiment, a flawless crown, fish-shaped ear-rings, garlands, bracelets and bangles, etc.; the ocean of boundless mercy, affability, beauty, sweetness, majesty, magnanimity and tender affection; the refuge of all without exception and without regard to their differences, the ruler of all.[25]

It is probable that Rāmānuja is here envisioning familiar temple images of the Lord as well as those inscribed in purāṇic texts. *Arcā* temple presences are more efficacious even than *avatāras* which include memories of *līlā* in ancient times, since every person in every age can simply walk into a temple and worship the real presence of the Lord there. The graciousness of the Lord's presence in the world is further intensified in temple, as nothing but structures of *līlā*.

The whole passage ends with a reinforcement of the need for an ongoing meditative praxis that is a duty but also a delight: "Meditating on the multitudes of My qualities which are exceedingly pleasing to you and offering me every day this worship, as defined, you will attain Me alone."[26] This attainment is a manner of vision that once begun is completed only in the utter clarity of vision that occurs after death. It is key to remember that this vision is not simply a matter of the work or play of the imagination. In the meditative praxis, what is encountered is a real form of the Lord, who is endowed with a material body as well as a spiritual reality, and that form can begin to be glimpsed in this world.[27]

Thus far I have shown how, according to Rāmānuja's panentheism, all conscious and non-conscious beings are distinct manifestations of the original divine person. Even in their undeniable differences from God and from one other, they are still reflective of the unitary divine source. That reflectiveness is embodied grace, which I am arguing is the most apt meaning of *līlā* for Rāmānuja. The outward dynamism of creation, however extended over time and space, remains in continuity with the original perfect One who God is. God, the one enduring source of all, extends the divine in time and space, making God's own self accessible in matter. Nature, *avatāras*, and temple presences are all instances of the divine *līlā*, God gracing the world with divine presence.[28]

## A Comparison: Creation and Vision of God according to Thomas Aquinas and Gregory Palamas

Once we understand *līlā* as grace, it ceases to be a merely pleasing yet still exotic term, and its resonances with the language of grace in other traditions become evident. To show this, and to deepen our understanding of līlā as grace, I turn now to the Christian tradition, in order to show an analogous understanding of the world as the site of God's sheerly graced intervention on behalf of humanity, and thus, in terms of this essay, as the realm of what might be termed "a Christian *līlā*" or even a *līlāvibhūti*.

Here, in lieu of a much lengthier exposition of Christian theology, I rely on Hans Boersma's *Seeing God: The Beatific Vision in Christian Tradition*, and in particular on Chapter 5: "Transfiguration and *Vision* in Thomas Aquinas and Gregory Palamas." These are well-chosen figures, since Aquinas (1225–1274) is a foremost systematic theologian in Christianity's Latin West, and Palamas (1296–1359) a leading Greek contemplative theologian in the East. Reading them side by side, alert to similarities and differences, Boersma considers the problem of seeing God in the world, throughout Christian tradition. He emphasizes the importance of a sacramental encounter with God in the created world. Boersma notes how certain objectivist scientific models have stripped the world of its sacramentality and made the very idea of seeing God in the world implausible:

> The [modern] rejection of a sacramental teleology—the belief that there is an inherent link between this-worldly things (including humans) and their final end—meant a break between the appearances of things and their purposes. Put differently, the seventeenth-century experimental sciences discarded the Christian assumption of an inherent (sacramental) link between the sensible thing and its final goal. . . . Modernity has ended up denying the very notion that the purpose of a thing is given with its nature. This rendered the loss of the notion of the beatific *vision* all but inevitable. Since all purposes or ends are now humanly "constructed" rather than inherent in nature itself, many consider it outlandish to look for such ends beyond the *pleasures* that the material world affords.[29]

By contrast, a sacramental understanding of the vision of God—espoused in different ways by Aquinas and Palamas—resists any rupture between appearance and purpose. Even sense objects are possessed of a finality pointing toward vision of God:

> A sacramental ontology closely links nature and the supernatural, earthly and heavenly realities, reason and faith, Old Testament Scriptures and Gospel truth. In each of these doublets, the former participates in the latter, and the latter is really (or sacramentally) present within the former. A sacramental ontology treats the first item in each of the pairs as the sacrament (*sacramentum*), and the latter as the reality (*res*). (Boersma, *Seeing God*, 10)

Accordingly, the world must be honored as possessed of its own integrity, and thereby able to speak of the reality of God. The sacramental opens up times and spaces in which the otherwise impossible God-human encounter becomes possible. This is, I suggest, the realm of grace—the *līlā* of God in this world.

In particular, Boersma looks to the Transfiguration of Jesus recorded in the Synoptic Gospels as a site for inquiring further into whether and how this-worldly experience can be conceived of as a sacramental possibility contributory to an actual vision of God. Boersma assesses how far Aquinas and Palamas can agree on some meaningful sense of a vision of God in Christian tradition, without a too lax view that would make a complete seeing of God possible here and now, or a too harsh view that would rule it out altogether. Boersma suggests that they agree on the importance of the Gospel Transfiguration scene as *a* or even *the* theophany "of God's presence in the world" (133); Christ's divinity is manifest in that moment, and the kingdom of God is made vividly present to the three apostles there.

Accordingly, both theologians propose "a sacramental reading of the transfiguration." The radiance of the transfigured Christ shines from his humanity, and not just by a momentary visitation of the external light of divinity. Accordingly, both see the transfiguration as "a pledge—an initial realization—of the eschatological kingdom" that is now sacramentally present to the disciples' eyes. More boldly than Aquinas, Palamas holds that the human "vision of the theophanic appearance of God in Christ progresses eternally, so that it will simply be deepened in the hereafter," and "by eternal progress into the life of God" (161–162). For Palamas, this vision of God in the world, as imperfect as it may be, "requires at least a supernatural transformation of the bodily eyes" (142), even if it is only with our "inner eyes" that we actually see God (148). Palamas maintains that "although the disciples never attained to the divine essence itself, the Spirit's transformation of the disciples' eyes and mind allowed them to look directly at the eternal light of God's glory and so participate in the divine energies" (150). In a modest contrast, Aquinas insists that with their human eyes the apostles saw the glory of Christ's divinity, "with natural eyes in a corporeal mode" (149–150). Yet the common ground shared by Aquinas and Palamas is crucial:

> Both [Aquinas and Palamas] were convinced that the kingdom of God is truly revealed and really present on the mount of transfiguration, and as a result both regarded the clarity or the light of Christ's transfigured body as the very presence of the glory of the eschaton. . . . According to

> Aquinas, the glory of the transfiguration was transient, and it was less perfect than the glory of the resurrection bodies will be. In Palamas's view [e.g., in Sermons on the Transfiguration], the fullness of the kingdom has not yet arrived, and the disciples' *vision* of the Taboric light was an experience that will be eternally deepened by their eternal progress into the life of God. (155)

The Transfiguration, now taken to be more than a one-time event, shows that "the vision of God is an integral part of Christian mystical experience" (158), a paradigm for the transformation by which a person is "made gradually more and more God-like by deification" (158).[30]

A Christian theologian considering the vision of God in this world has to explain the delicate balance between nature and beyond-nature, between the world and body as fleshly veils and as sacramental media of divine light showing the reality of God. How to think of the world, which is not-God, as a medium of encountering God? To what extent is the world a realm of grace—or, in terms of this essay, the enactment of the divine *līlā* as grace manifest in material reality?

Rossum suggests that Aquinas's view on creation would have been easier to formulate, had Aquinas, as Frederick Copleston put it, "adopted some form of pantheism."[31] Easier, I propose, would be the embrace of a form of panentheism, by which the world is dependent, entirely within the reality of God, even if God, sovereign and pure, does not depend on the world. This is close, of course, to Rāmānuja's views, considered earlier.[32]

Both Aquinas and Palamas—though Palamas the more boldly—are seeking a way of speaking of the beatific vision as beginning in this life, mediated constructively by the things of this world, the Christian doctrine of creation ex nihilo and their determination to avoid pantheism notwithstanding. We have seen how Rāmānuja also points out a particular way to connect vision and bliss. The idea of the beatific vision resonates with the same dynamic—vision and pleasure deeply interconnected—even if the conception of creation are not identical (and need not be so). Indeed, Rāmānuja's admittedly different metaphysics and narrative of God's relation to the world does not clash with Christian views. We are not barred from reading Rāmānuja, Aquinas, and Palamas together with respect to the world and the vision of God.

Palamas in particular echoes Rāmānuja's spirit in this reading of the Transfiguration:

> Thus, while He was praying, He became radiant and revealed this ineffable light in an indescribable way to the chosen disciples in the presence of the most excellent of the prophets, that He might show us that it is prayer which procures this blessed vision, and we might learn that this brilliance comes about and shines forth when we draw near to God through the virtues, and our minds are united with Him. It is given to all who unceasingly reach up towards God by means of perfect good works and fervent prayer, and is visible to them. Everything about the blessed divine nature is truly beautiful and desirable, and is visible only to those whose minds have been purified. Anyone who gazes at its brilliant rays and its graces, partakes of it to some extent, as though his own face were touched by dazzling light. That is why Moses' countenance was glorified when he spoke with God (Exod. 34:29).[33]

God's self-revelation, human purification and ascent, the longed-for vision of divine beauty and the attainment of beatitude—all these are in harmony, as Rāmānuja too proposed. This vision of God, impossible as it may be even as it is given to some humans possessed of human eyes, is parallel, I suggest, to Rāmānuja's conception of the world as the freely graced realm in which God chooses to be visible to humans who wish to see God. This gracious visibility of God is, in other words, the *līlā* of a God freely entered into and remaining in the world.

At the end of Palamas's next homily, also on the Transfiguration, we find this passage:

> Let us look with our inner eyes at this great spectacle, our nature, which dwells for all eternity with the immaterial fire of the divinity. And let us take off the coats of skins (cf. Genesis 3:21), the earthy and carnal ways of thinking, in which we were clothed because of our transgression, and stand on holy ground (cf. Exodus 3:5), each one of us hallowing our own ground by means of virtue and reaching up to God. In this way we shall have boldness when God comes in light, and as we run to Him, we shall be enlightened, and, once illumined, shall live forever in the glory of the one brightness in three Suns, now and forever and unto the ages of ages. Amen.[34]

For Palamas as for Rāmānuja the world exists in order that the divine self-manifestation can have its time and place. The world is a theater of purification wherein believers become ready, in time and yet only by grace, for Palamas, to see more of the divine light that shines always in Christ.

In sum, there are sufficient connections that can clarify issues of deep concern for Christian theologians who wish to continue Boersma's work in sorting out the topics of the vision of God and beatitude as beginning in this material world. My proposal is that this further work, even as it builds on Boersma's solid foundations, can and should be interreligiously grounded, and that *līlā* will be a key connecting concept, illumining the world in terms of created grace. There is a salutary conversation to be had among such theologians around the world, in many places and many centuries, who are able to affirm the importance of the created world as intimately disclosive of God, even while resisting the temptation to idolize material things and reduce the divine mystery to an object of the senses.

If this essay has succeeded in opening up such a conversation, then we ought not to be surprised that attention to Rāmānuja today can help the heirs of Aquinas and Palamas explain how it is that the world is not a barrier, but the site of a temporal-spatial pedagogy that furthers the quest to see God by a vision beginning now but reaching its climax only after the ending of this life. And for the sake of this extended conversation, *līlā as grace* stands forth as a productive point of contact.

## Līlā as Grace

In the preceding pages I have thought about "creation," "vision," "beatific vision," and "divine compassion" together, so as to show how such words and the realities to which they refer together disclose the operation of grace in the world, a world that itself is the site of grace. That grace is an act of freedom. There need not be a world; God need not manifest the divine self in the world; humans need not expect ever to be able to see God present in material, sacramental forms; the deepest desire of humans need not be fulfilled, since finitude and the obscurations of sin need not give way to luminous vision and beatitude. But the darkness does give away, the world is an effective site of divine grace, freely given; the vision does occur. This is what the *līlā* is really about, for Rāmānuja and more widely across interreligious borders. "*Līlā*" marks off a free and unpredicted set of possibilities, God's freely given gift of self that enables humans to receive the gift, opening into immense pleasure in encounter with the divine person. As such, *līlā* then characterizes creation as a graced site, a sheer gift, a time and place of immense and increasing delight, all because God, in unlimited divine freedom, chooses to allow the world to be radiant in this way.

If we translate "*līlā*" as "grace," the complexity of the latter, an English word richly evocative of conversations in the Latin and Greek Christian literature, is then all the more resonant with the complexity of the former. *Līlā* is suggestive not only of "play," but more fruitfully of "grace"—uncreated grace, created grace, actual grace, grace as knowledge, grace as bliss, grace as free encounter with God. There is no need to rule out other, more common understandings—*līlā* as "sport," "play," and "playfulness"—but as Lipner points out, the presumption that the word "*līlā*" ought immediately be possessed of intimations appropriate to the English word "play" narrows too much our understanding of *līlā*, a rich term that has more and more efficacious meanings in a world charged with divine grace.

## Bibliography


Boersma, Hans. *Seeing God: The Beatific Vision in Christian Tradition*. Grand Rapids, MI: William B. Eerdmans, 2018.

Carman, John B. *The Theology of Rāmānuja*. New Haven, CT: Yale University Press, 1973.

Clooney, Francis X. "The Drama of Panentheism in Śaṭakōpan's *Tiruvāymoli*." In *Panentheism across the World's Traditions*, edited by Loriliai Biernacki and Philip Clayton. 123–141. Oxford University Press, 2014.

Clooney, Francis X. "Finding God in All Things: Some Catholic and Hindu Insights." In *Western Jesuit Scholars in India: Tracing Their Paths, Reassessing Their Goals*, 260–274. Leiden: Brill, 2020.

Clooney, Francis X. *Seeing through Texts: Doing Theology among the Śrīvaiṣṇavas of South India*. Albany: State University of New York Press, 1996.

Lipner, Julius. "A God at Play? Reexamining the Concept of *Līlā* in Hindu Philosophy and Theology." *International Journal of Hindu Studies* 26 (2022): 283–326.

Lott, Eric. *God and the Universe in the Vedāntic Theology of Rāmānuja: A Study in His Use of the Self-Body Analogy*. Madras: Ramanuja Research Society, 1976.

Palamas, Gregory. *The Homilies*. Translated by Christopher Veniamin. Waymart, PA: Mount Thabor Publications, 2009.

Rāmānuja. *Śrī Rāmānuja Gītābhāṣya*. Translated by Swami Adidevananda. Mylapore: Sri Ramakrishna Math, 1991.

Rāmānuja. *The Śrīmad Gītābhāṣya with the Tātparyacandrikā of Vedānta Deśika*. Edited by Uttamur Viraraghavacharya. Ubhayavedāntagranthamālā, 1972.

Rāmānuja. *The Brahmasūtraśrībhāṣya with the Śrutaprakāśikā of Sudarśanasūri*. Madras: Visishtadvaita Pracharini Sabha, 1989.

Rāmānuja. *The Vedārthasaṃgraha*. Translated by S. S. Raghavachar. Mysore: Sri Ramakrishna Ashrama, 1956.

Rāmānuja. *Commentary on the Vedānta Sūtras* [*Brahmasūtras*]. Sacred Books of the East, volume 48. Translated by Georg Thibaut. Oxford: Oxford University Press, 1904.

*The Upaniṣads*. Translated by Patrick Olivelle. New York: Oxford University Press, 1996.

Joost van Rossum. "Deification in Palamas and Aquinas," *St. Vladimir's Theological Quarterly* 47, no. 3–4 (2003): 365–82.

*Viśiṣṭādvaita Kośa*, volume 8. Edited by Bhashyam Swami. Melcote: Academy of Sanskrit Research, 2008.

## Notes

1. Julius Lipner, "A God at Play? Reexamining the Concept of *Līlā* in Hindu Philosophy and Theology," *International Journal of Hindu Studies* 26 (2022): 283–326.
2. Sucharita Adluri, "*Līlā* and Divine Mercy in the *Hundred Verses to Compassion* of Vedānta Deśika," in this volume.
3. Rāmānuja, *Vedārtha Saṃgraha* (*Summary of the Meaning of the Veda*), on the right interpretation of the Upaniṣads and the right use of them for theological understanding and spiritual practice; the *Gītā Bhāṣya (Commentary on the Bhagavad Gītā); the Śrī Bhāṣya* (*Auspicious Commentary on the Brahma Sūtras*); the *Vedānta Dīpā* and *Vedānta Sāra* (respectively, the *Light of Vedānta* and the *Essence of Vedānta*, summaries of Rāmānuja's reading of Vedānta in the *Brahma Sūtras*); the *Gadyatraya* (three prose prayers of surrender to Nārāyaṇa with the Goddess Śrī): surrender as an interior act, in the *Śaraṇāgatigadya*; at the great Śrīraṅgam temple, in the *Śrīraṅgagadya*; and in heaven, in the *Śrīvaikuṇṭagadya*; and finally, the *Nityam* (the *Manual of Daily Worship*).
4. *Viśiṣṭādvaitakośa*, vol. 8, ed. Bhashyam Swami (Melcote: Academy of Sanskrit Research, 2008), 140–141. This commentarial passage, though not marked as such in the *Kośa*, is drawn from the commentary on the *Śrībhāṣya* by Sudarśanasūri, page 4 in the Sanskrit edition I have used/
5. *Chāndogya Upaniṣad* 6.2.1–4. In *The Upaniṣads*, trans. Patrick Olivelle (New York: Oxford University Press, 1996). Adapted slightly from the Olivelle translation, 247.
6. *Vedārthasaṃgraha*, Raghavachar, n. 9 , page 11. Throughout, paragraph numbers are to the Raghavachar translation, although I have modified his translation in small ways.
7. *Vedārthasaṃgraha*, trans. Raghavachar, n. 12, page 15.
8. *Vedārthasaṃgraha*, trans. Raghavachar, n. 236, pages 183–184.
9. In *God and the Universe in the Vedāntic Theology of Rāmānuja: A Study in His Use of the Self-Body Analogy* (Madras: Ramanuja Research Society, 1976) Eric Lott notes that "(in Rāmānuja) *there is a real 'communication'* between the Infinite Lord and his finite creation in a way similar to that of self and body. Brahman is not qualitatively isolated from, or discontinuous with, the relativities of the creature. However, this participation is not by virtue of innate similarity, *but rather by virtue of the imparted and infused presence of Brahman in the creature*" (148–149).
10. *Vedārthasaṃgraha*, trans. Raghavachar, n. 126, page 98.
11. *Vedārthasaṃgraha*, trans. Raghavachar, n. 198, page 159.
12. *Vedārthasaṃgraha*, trans. Raghavachar, n. 220, pages 172–173.
13. *Vedārthasaṃgraha*, trans. Raghavachar, n. 238, page 185.
14. *Vedārthasaṃgraha*, trans. Raghavachar, n. 252, page 192. As we shall see, Aquinas and Palamas surely agree that one cannot merely look upon God in this finite world. But still, the world is the graced location where one can attain clearer and clearer vision of the Lord, by grace and over a long purification process.

15. It is interesting then to see how Rāmānuja's disciples, and the lineage of their disciples, use the language of increasing clarity of vision to explain the life journey of Nammāḻvār, (ca, ninth century), the greatest of the Tamil saints. Commentators following in the footsteps of Rāmānuja interpreted his four poetic works as a poetic unfolding of the saint's desire for and journey toward an ever more intense vision of God. (See my *Seeing through Texts: Doing Theology among the Śrīvaiṣṇavas of South India* [Albany: State University of New York Press, 1996].) *Tiruvāymoḻi*, which in turn is the foremost of the Āḻvār's works, charts in its one hundred songs the saint's purificatory progress toward direct vision of God, by the approach to direct spiritual perception (*pratyakṣasamānākāra darśana*), which is marked by the ascending gradations of superior devotion, superior knowledge, supreme devotion (*para bhakti, para jñāna, parama bhakti*)—or, more simply as clear, clearer, and clearest vision (*viśada, viśadatara, viśadatama darśana*). They thus echo the language of gradual clarification employed by Rāmānuja, now employed to map the spiritual path as showcased in the life of the saint. See Clooney, *Seeing through Texts*, 139–154, and, for related developments in the post-Rāmānuja tradition, Adluri's essay, "*Līlā* and Divine Mercy in the *Hundred Verses to Compassion*," in this volume.
16. On *līlāvibhūti*, see John B. Carman, *The Theology of Rāmānuja* (New Haven, CT: Yale University Press, 1973), 140–146. Lipner also comments on the cosmological senses of *līlā*: "Both expressions of *līlā*, that of the heavenly court and that of the phenomenal realm, demonstrate a nexus of differentiated being in their manifestation, namely, the circle of attendants present, the joint worship of the devotees, and the other paraphernalia of devotional acknowledgment, as well as the graciousness and powerful outreach of the Lord; they are not mere 'sport' or 'play' or a 'pastime' in the conventional sense. God in Hindu tradition is not a joker, an irresponsible gamester. Quite the contrary. If one wishes to use these terms as unnuanced translations of *līlā* in this context, one risks substantial misunderstanding of what is meant by devotion to Kṛṣṇa" (Julius Lipner, "A God at Play? Reexamining the Concept of *Līlā* in Hindu Philosophy and Theology," *International Journal of Hindu Studies* 26 [2022]: 319).
17. The *Brahmasūtras* of Bādārayaṇa (ca. sixth century) is a work of 550 short aphorisms which constitute a masterwork that is generative of many layers of commentary.
18. Identity uncertain.
19. *Śrībhāṣya* I.1.1. Sanskrit pages 56–60; I have used, with some modifications, Thibaut's translation, pages 14–16.
20. See Lipner on the distinction between *līlā*, *krīḍā*, and related words.
21. Excerpted in the *Viśiṣṭādvaita Kośa* VIII, page 141, from a text entitled the *Sampradāya Vibhāga* (*Distinctions in the Tradition*). On a fuller consideration of the relationship between *līlā* and *kṛpā* (compassion), see Adluri's essay, "*Līlā* and Divine Mercy in the *Hundred Verses to Compassion*," in this volume.
22. *Gītābhāṣya* in Rāmānuja, *The Śrīmad Gītābhāṣya with the Tātparyacandrikā of Vedānta Deśika*, ed. Uttamur Viraraghavacharya (Ubhayavedāntagranthamālā, 1972), 11. My translation. See *Bhagavad Gītā* 4.4–11 for a classic characterization of divine descent as the gracious action of the supreme deity. For an excellent overview of the importance of Rāmānuja's introduction to the *Gītā*, see Carman, *The Theology of Rāmānuja*, 77–81.

23. *Tātparycandrikā* commentary on the *Gītābhāṣya*, Sanskrit 11. My translation.
24. *Tātparycandrikā* commentary on the *Gītābhāṣya*, Sanskrit 11.
25. I have used, with some adaptation, the Adidevananda translation; see Rāmānuja. *Śrī Rāmānuja Gītābhāṣya*, trans. Swami Adidevananda (Mylapore: Sri Ramakrishna Math, 1991), 322–323.
26. My translation.
27. See also Clooney, "The Drama of Panentheism in Śaṭakōpan's *Tiruvāymoḷi*," in *Panentheism across the World's Traditions*, ed. Loriliai Biernacki and Philip Clayton (Oxford University Press, 2014), 123–141, for further comment on this form of meditative insight, and parallels in the Ignatian contemplative tradition.
28. As mentioned earlier, Sucharita Adluri's essay in this volume goes beyond where I thus leave off, exploring in the writings of Vedānta Deśika, the later Rāmānuja school ācārya, how *līlā* is closely related to compassion and mercy (*dayā*): "In Deśika's hymn, *līlā* and *dayā* reflect the polarity of supreme transcendence and supreme accessibility respectively. Always connected, their interaction is explored as they complement each other, but never separating in the context of cosmic activities including human redemption through divine grace" (Sucharita Adluri, "*Līlā* and Divine Mercy in the *Hundred Verses to Compassion* of Vedānta Deśika," in this volume).
29. Hans Boersma, *Seeing God: The Beatific Vision in Christian Tradition* (Grand Rapids, MI: William B. Eerdmans, 2018), 21–22. Boersma's Chapter 5: "Transfiguration and *Vision* in Thomas Aquinas and Gregory Palamas." Further quotations are cited parenthetically in the text.
30. Quoting Richard Hayes.
31. Joost van Rossum, "Deification in Palamas and Aquinas," *St. Vladimir's Theological Quarterly* 47, no. 3–4 (2003): 377.
32. See Clooney, "The Drama of Panentheism in Śaṭakōpaṉ's *Tiruvāymoli*."
33. Gregory Palamas, Homily 34, in *The Homilies*. Translated by Christopher Veniamin. (Waymart, PA: Mount Thabor Publications, 2009), n. 10, pp. 270–271.
34. Palamas, Homily 35, n. 18, p. 281.

# 5 *Līlā* and Divine Mercy in the *Hundred Verses to Compassion* of Vedānta Deśika

*Sucharita Adluri*

*Līlā* in Hindu traditions is a multifaceted concept serving several theological functions, as essays in this volume amply illustrate.[1] Attentive to a recent exhaustive analysis by J. J. Lipner on the polysemic nature of *līlā*, this chapter traces the understanding of this concept in the context of the Śrīvaiṣṇava tradition of South India.[2] Undergirded by Viśiṣṭādvaita Vedānta, the Śrīvaiṣṇava imagination of *līlā* expands its primary denotation as spontaneous divine creative activity that is unmotivated, unnecessary, effortless, and responsible, to envision it instead as an instrument for liberation, intimately connected with divine compassion/mercy.[3] The first section of the chapter examines the ways in which the synthesizer of Viśiṣṭādvaita Vedānta, Rāmānuja (eleventh–twelfth century CE) discusses *līlā* in the context of divine grace (*dayā/krpā/karuṇā/anukaṃpā*).[4] The second part of the essay explores how an important post-Rāmānuja Vedāntin, Vedānta Deśika (thirteenth–fourteenth century CE), in his *Dayāśataka* (*Hundred Verses to Compassion*), elaborates further on the subduing effect of divine compassion (*dayā*) on *līlā*. For Deśika, *līlā* cannot be envisioned without divine mercy.

## Rāmānuja on Līlā and Divine Mercy

An important source on the concept of *līlā* in Vedānta is found in the *Brahmasūtra* of Bādarāyaṇa (~ 100 CE) in the section on the purpose of creation (2.1.32–36). Rāmānuja's commentary on these sūtras presents the Viśiṣṭādvaita view of Brahman's/Viṣṇu's creative causality.[5]

> For one whose desires (*kāma*) are all fulfilled, who is perfect, sport alone (*līlaiva*) is the sole purpose (*prayojana*) in the creation of the world

> composed of sentience and insentience in manifold, diverse modifications, due to his own will (*svasaṃkalpa*). . . . Just as in the world it is seen that a king who is full of valor, boldness, courage and who rules over the world, even the seven terrestrial regions, begins to play with balls for the purpose of sport alone.[6]

The example of a great king, who is in want of nothing, but still engages in sport for sheer pleasure and joy is proffered to deny the objection that Brahman has a motive for personal gain in bringing about creation. Though presented as an expression of divine will (*satyasaṃkalpa*), there is no personal purpose (*prayojana*) or end goal (*artha*) in creative activity.[7]

A second objection and its clarification are also addressed here and that is the charge that as the world is full of suffering, Brahman is culpable in the painful experiences of beings. Rāmānuja argues that the inequality in suffering during all phases of creation, both creation and dissolution, is not due to God's lack of mercy, but is dependent on the accrued past karmas of the respective individual selves. Inequity of suffering among beings is not due to Viṣṇu.

> Even if he (the Lord) is understood as the presider (over matter), because he is perfect, has endless and eminent bliss, is blameless and stainless, there is no motive that in the conditions of creation and dissolution, he produces inequality, from which it follows that he lacks compassion (*nirdayā*). For this reason, the error is the same in both cases (of considering the Lord as responsible for inequality of suffering in creation or in dissolution).[8]

> For one who is perfect, it is possible to create in sport. . . . And because it is only the karma of the individual selves that establishes the individual conditions to produce inequality.[9]

What is essential to note here is that first, the assumption that any activity in the world is for the purpose of a specific goal, and divine activity lacking this is defined as play.[10] Second, the vicissitudes of *saṃsāra* are solely due to past individual actions. The context of the *Brahmasūtra* circumscribes the discussion to the exploration of why a being who is self-sufficient and has all his desires fulfilled manages to create.[11] This rather mechanical explanation of *līlā*, when juxtaposed with other Viśiṣṭādvaita doctrines such as Viṣṇu's intense desire to commune with his devotees, creates a need for further elaboration of its connection to divine mercy and an understanding of *līlā* as ultimately existing for the welfare of beings.

We turn to other discussions of divine nature in Rāmānuja's writings for elaborations on *līlā*. One such context is that of Viṣṇu's originative causality, which for him is closely tied to the framework of the body-self ontology (*śarīraśarīribhāva*).[12] While other Vedāntins affirm Brahman as the cause of the world, Rāmānuja furthers this argument by defining causality as an aspect of the essential nature of Brahman (*brahmasvarūpaviśeṣa*) as he is the cause of creation as a whole (*aviśeṣaṇakāraṇa*).[13] That is, God, composed of matter and individual selves as his body, his modes, is together the cause as a whole of the manifestation of the universe. Creation is simply a change in the condition of his modes, but this impetus for alteration is itself because of his innate nature of a self-fulfilled being. Existence both in its manifest and unmanifest form is called the realm of God's *līlā* (*līlāvibhūti*).[14] This is a different type of metaphysics of the unfolding of creation than what is found for instance in Caitanya Vaiṣṇavism, where the impetus of divine fullness is to proceed from the transcendent unity to the visible plurality of creation that renders *līlā* as a dynamic process. This topic is explored in Jessica Frazier's essay in this volume.[15]

Coming back to Śrīvaiṣṇavism, for Rāmānuja, a body is something that is completely dependent on another entity and has no independent existence without this relationship.[16] Such dependency of creatures on the supreme being necessitates a divine response of compassion. In addition to the complete control that God exerts on the individual selves due to their dependence, as the all-merciful Lord, he also makes sure that these selves can commune with him and gain salvation.[17] There are two ways in which Rāmānuja discusses *līlā* depending on the context. First, *līlā* is simply a mechanical process of divine self-expression. Second, there is a component of divine mercy to *līlā*. Rāmānuja's descriptions of divine nature mention one or the other, but sometimes weave both perspectives together. In the following illustration, as a first example, the aspect of *līlā* as simply divine self-expression is highlighted:

> That Lord Puruṣottama, who has attained all desires, is all-knowing, the Lord over of all, who wills the truth, commenced in sport (*līlā*) according to his own magnanimity. Having laid down the knowledge of the two-fold karma that these actions are proper, these are not, having assigned equally to all individual selves, bodies and senses fit to accept their karmas and he gave them power over them (bodies etc.). Having revealed the scriptures which teach his decrees, having entered (into the self), as

> its inner self for the purpose of its (of the self) realization, he remains controlling them as permitted. However, they, the individual selves who have their senses and bodies given by him and power over them (self and bodies) given by him and which are supported by him, by themselves choose actions, according to their desires, in the form that is meritorious or demeritorious. Thereafter, having known the one who acts in a meritorious way and follows his commandments, he bestows them with dharma, artha, kāma, mokṣa and those who go against his decrees, he associates them with (that which is) contrary to those.[18]

Divine sport is not simply creation and dissolution, but a whole set of other events that accompany it, such as initiating the coming together of individual selves with material bodies in accordance with past karma. The revelation of scripture, which is important in the successful fulfillment of the goals of life, which he metes out, namely, righteousness (*dharma*), wealth (*artha*), pleasure (*kāma*), and liberation (*mokṣa*). This, however, does not mention divine compassion explicitly.

Elsewhere, Rāmānuja stresses the divine merciful nature in discussions of *līlā*. God who cannot bear to see individual souls repeatedly enter *saṃsāra* comes to their aid when they take refuge in him. This is an illustration of *līlā*'s close ties to divine mercy.

> In the beginning, at the time of creation, He, the lord, the lord of all created beings, beheld all beings, helpless on account of contact proceeding from time immemorial with non-intelligent matter excluded from the distinctions of name and form, dissolved within Himself, unfit to realize the objects of human pursuit and almost inanimate. He, the supremely merciful [one], through a desire to redeem them, placed them in the state of creation along with sacrifices with a view to [their] performance in the form of his worship. And he said thus—"by this sacrifice, may you multiply, that is, effect your increase and prosperity. Let this sacrifice yield you the desire called liberation which is the highest end of the life as also other desires which are in conformity with it."[19]

In contrast to the earlier descriptions of *līlā*, here the element of divine compassion is underscored. It is because of divine mercy and through *līlā* that the individual self can achieve its own perfection.

An addition to such cosmic activities of world-building and shaping, is the concept of incarnation (*avatāra*), which is also considered divine play. God descends periodically to enforce righteousness. For Rāmānuja however, divine incarnations are not just sport but play a significant role in human redemption and salvation.[20]

> To bless his worshippers, the Divine Lord who is all-merciful makes this same aforementioned natural form of his assume, in accordance with his own desire, the configurations of gods, men, etc., so that it may have that appearance which is suited to the understanding of those worshippers.
>
> The principal object of accomplishment (of incarnation) is nothing other than their protection. But the destruction of evildoers is an object of secondary importance because that is possible for him even by merely willing it.[21]

Here we see a merciful God at work, who tailors his manifestations to the sensibilities of his devotees. Moreover, the cause for such manifestations is not to unburden earth from the demonic who subjugate it. Indeed, he can attend to unrighteousness without incarnating. The reason is his desire to commune with those who have taken refuge in him. In his commentary on *Brahmasūtra* 2.2.3, Rāmānuja defines divine mercy as the inability to tolerate (*asahiṣṇutā*) the suffering of others without regard for one's own being (*svārthanirapekṣā*).[22] God seeks to increase the happiness of beings to the highest degree by subduing their karmic residue that prevents them from gaining emancipation.[23] Indeed, it is discussions such as these that lead Clooney to argue that the enactment of *līlā* is an enactment of grace in the writings of Rāmānuja.[24]

In the many descriptions of the auspicious qualities of Brahman, Rāmānuja invariably includes divine compassion/mercy. For instance, in his *Śaraṇāgatigadya*, extolling the auspicious qualities of the Lord, he says:

> You are an ocean of a multitude of streams of auspicious qualities that are immeasurable, natural to you, unlimited, superior, such as knowledge, strength, sovereignty, courage, radiance, graciousness (*sauśīlya*), motherly affection (*vātsalya*), gentleness (*mārdava*), sincerity, affection (*sauhārda*), equanimity (*sāmya*), compassion (*kāruṇya*), sweetness (*mādhurya*), earnestness, generosity (*audārya*), amiableness (*cāturya*), constancy, courage, valor. (4.3)[25]

Due to qualities, such as motherly affection, compassion, graciousness, and so on, the impulse to engage in *līlā* includes divine compassion, which is completely in the service of the welfare of beings.[26] The following example is once again an illustration of *līlā* and divine mercy working together as was the case with incarnations.

> In sport you create, maintain, destroy, the entire world, which forms the place of enjoyment, the instrument of enjoyment and a place for enjoyers, with varied and wonderful objects of enjoyment that are comprised of matter, individual selves, and time, whose essential attribute is to be subservient to you, and whose manifestation and existence follows your own will.
>
> O' ocean of beauty, sovereignty, motherly affection, graciousness, and immeasurable compassion; you are the refuge of the whole world without any distinctions/partiality, an ocean of solely motherly tenderness depending on which he is the remover of the suffering of the devoted. (4.10)[27]

For Rāmānuja, therefore, the creative act is not simply play, it works in conjunction with other divine characteristics that are innate to the supreme being, such as divine mercy, and he does not see a contradiction in this. Carman notes that

> Rāmānuja usually distinguishes between the creative action of God, for His sport (*līlā*) and His redemptive action which in general is to aid or benefit (*upakārāya*) the universe and specifically is to provide a refuge for all in the universe.[28]

These are two aspects of divine nature we see illustrated in the above excerpts from Rāmānuja's writings. For him, *līlā* and divine compassion are interconnected, but he does not elaborate on this relationship, though sometimes he emphasizes one without the other and in other instances mentions them together. In the next section, we see that Deśika explores this interaction between *līlā* and divine compassion more fully as a variety of cosmic scenarios are explored. In some cases, compassion subordinates *līlā* and in others they can strike a delicate balance influencing each other to different degrees. What is indelible for Deśika is that *līlā* cannot be considered apart from *dayā*, whereby the former's activities are rendered beneficial for human salvation.

## Vedānta Deśika on *Līlā* and Divine Mercy

Although he is one of the most important theologians, post-Rāmānuja, Vedānta Deśika (thirteenth-fourteenth centuries CE) was also a logician, poet, and dramatist who was endowed with the title of *kavitarkikasiṃha*, "a lion among poets and logicians/philosophers."[29] In addition to his prose commentaries, his poems in three languages, Sanskrit, Tamil, and Prakrit, blend the philosophy of Vedānta with the ecstatic devotional poetry of the Āḻvār saints.[30] This section addresses divine compassion/grace/mercy (*dayā*) in his Sanskrit poem the *Dayāśataka* (*Hundred Verses to Compassion*).[31] Its 108 verses are composed in praise of Viṣṇu as Lord Venkateśvara or Śrīnivāsa, the iconic form worshiped on Tirumala hill or Vṛṣagiri/Vṛṣācala, an important pilgrimage site in South India.[32] Taking refuge (*prapatti*) in the Lord's mercy is the main theme of the hymn; however, its discussion of divine sport is instructive and adds much needed nuance to our understanding of the concept of *līlā* in Śrīvaiṣṇavism.[33]

Though only a few passages in the *Hundred Verses* mention the term *līlā*, the verses that address divine activities that come under its purview are all declared as interconnected with god's mercy.

> O' Compassion, subject to you, the sports of the Lord of Vṛṣagiri are for the welfare of the entire world and nothing else.[34] (88ab)

*Līlā* is not simply joyous, divine self-expression. Because of the influence of compassion (*dayā*), it specifically functions for the welfare of beings, the goal of which is liberation from *saṃsāra*. Although we do find mention of the beginnings of such a view in the writings of Rāmānuja, here God's mercy engages with *līlā* in a way not seen in his writings. For one, it is subordinated to compassion. Deśika also explores divine mercy as all-encompassing and as surpassing all other qualities of Viṣṇu. We begin with a general characterization of divine compassion in the poem and then address its relationship to *līlā*.

## DEFINING DAYĀ

Personified as a goddess, the divine attribute of *dayā* is identified as the earthly abode of Viṣṇu who manifests as Lord Venkateśvara in the pilgrimage town of Tirumala Tirupati/Vṛṣagiri. Deśika writes,

> I take refuge in that hill, which like hardened sugar is formed from the flowing essence of the juice of sugarcane, that is Śrīnivāsa's compassion. (1)

The iconic (arca) image of Viṣṇu is one of the five forms of the deity reflecting his supreme accessibility.[35] He graciously condescends to take his place in regional temples, Tirumala being one among them, which are extolled by the Āḻvārs and are important in the expression of Śrīvaiṣṇava religiosity.[36] Deśika stresses the accessibility of God's compassion that takes many forms, one static and sturdy as the hill itself, on which he has chosen to reside so as to be close to his devotees. In yet another way, Dayā is the "flowing essence" of Viṣṇu's mercy reaching out to those who are helpless and wretched. For instance,

> O' Compassion, even if I run away from you, under the imagined pretext of the sport of the Lord of Vṛṣaśaila, you are fit to cast the strong net of his qualities (of the Lord), knowing the places/paths of beings, you extend it over an animal like myself here. (95)

Though the metaphor here is one of solidity as she takes the form of a hunter's net, the fact that she is aware of the places where such helpless beings are to be found and seeks them out to save them illustrates her fluid nature. In this passage, the phrase "sport of the lord" refers to the Lord as a hunter, who in sport, traps his prey with the strong net composed of divine qualities, which include mercy, and brings one such as the poet back onto the right path. *Dayā* here is the motivator. Though *līlā* is the pretext, it is she who skillfully saves beings who are in need of spiritual care.

Personified as a goddess, divine compassion does not have an independent existence as she is an attribute of Viṣṇu. This creates a theologically plausible space for the poet to explore the limits of divine compassion. As an innate divine quality, she does not supersede the Lord, but the personification allows Deśika a different kind of meditation on the divine quality and its experience. Hopkins notes that

> Deśika's theology as expressed in the form of poetry is decidedly (and appropriately) more fluid than in his purely discursive doctrinal prose works. . . . [It] creates a rich symbolic and aesthetic space where the doctrine and theological precept of the philosopher (the tarka and the tārkika) meet the imagined experience (anubhava) of the poet (kavi).[37]

So, it may seem in some passages that Dayā subordinates Viṣṇu himself. However, Deśika does intermittently throughout the poem remind us that she is an attribute of the Lord (14, 17–18, 93). This also illuminates the lack of a neat distinction between the quality of compassion and the possessor of the quality, that is Viṣṇu. For example,

> O' Compassion, sprung from the feet of the Lord of Vṛṣācala and rising toward the leafy shade around his face, you bend for those who take refuge, the branches that are his gracious glances, so that its fruits may be easily reached with their hands. (19)

She is firmly rooted in the Lord's feet and rises to offer her shade to the divine face. In this sense she is completely dependent on the Lord. But note also that her boughs are the glances of the Lord himself, suggesting an interweaving between her and Viṣṇu. Is the Lord the tree or is this a reference to her? Nevertheless, for those who surrender, she makes accessible the fruits that are the four main pursuits of life—righteousness (*dharma*), wealth (*artha*), pleasure (*kāma*), and liberation (*mokṣa*).

The fact that Dayā is an innate quality of the Lord means that her activities are also congruent with divine will. Deśika illustrates this in the following verse.

> O' Compassion, just like the coolness of water, you form the essential attribute (svabhāvabhūta) of the Lord of Vṛṣagiri You take his violent glances at the commencement of the dance of dissolution and turn them into those of a gentle dance. (23)

Dayā is innate to Viṣṇu just as the quality of coolness is innate to water. So, when she softens the violence of his terrible gaze such as it is when it is operative during dissolution and she transmutes his gazes into gentle glances, she does not operate independently. Deśika explores the limits of God's compassion, without necessarily subordinating Him to his attribute.

Another way in which Dayā's actions are congruent with the will of Viṣṇu is that Deśika equates her with divine volition.

> O' Compassion you are the controller of the manifestation and stability of existence composed of matter and individual selves; you are the desire (icchā) of the Lord.

> You carry all his other qualities that are inadequate, in being the bearer of the responsibility of the wretched, and how skillfully, you set your sights on me! (71)

The term *icchā* as wish/desire is divine will and volition and is connected to the term *satyasaṃkalpa*, one who wills the truth or one who has the will for the real.[38] In the *Vedārthasaṃgraha*, Rāmānuja says that *satyasaṃkalpa* means that creation is dependent on his volition or will.[39] This suggests that Dayā's functions complement divine intention in the context of *līlā*. Indeed, when other divine qualities are not influenced by compassion, they are inadequate in that they are not helpful for wretched beings such as the poet.

Deśika extols Dayā's immense influence over the other divine qualities in several passages. For example,

> I recognize Compassion, who has the Lord of Vṛṣagiri under her sway, who comes of her own accord, preceded by the light of the highest knowledge, and with qualities such as strength etc. as her attendants. (11)

This is a reference to the divine qualities denoted by the epithet "bhagavān" such as knowledge (*jñāna*), strength (*bala*), sovereignty (*aiśvarya*), courage (*vīrya*), power (*śakti*) and brilliance (*tejas*), which are enumerated in a subsequent verse. These are, according to Rāmānuja, the qualities of the divine essential nature.[40] For Deśika, knowledge or the Lord's omniscience precedes to light the way for Dayā, while the rest support her in her endeavors.

Not only is Dayā superior to the divine essential attributes but she also has an influence over numerous other qualities when they may be detrimental to human welfare. This was suggested in verse 71 above, as well.

> The chief qualities of the householder of Vṛṣagiri such as knowledge, strength, sovereignty, courage, power, will become faults, if ever there was absence of you, O' Compassion. (15)

Only through divine mercy do the other attributes of God even qualify as auspicious qualities (*kalyāṇaguṇa*), without it they are merely defects. But does this mean that Viṣṇu, characterized as completely flawless is in possession of faults? One way to understand this is that they act as faults from the point of view of beings. For instance, because of qualities such as knowledge, the omniscient God acts as an impartial divine judge in evaluating human actions that may be less than meritorious. But through the influence of Dayā, they may be overlooked.[41] In this way, divine qualities such as knowledge would work against human frailties. This echoes Rāmānuja's views of God through his compassion subduing or forgetting the demerits from accrued karma. However, through the influence of Dayā, in whom the poet has taken refuge, these very attributes become helpful for beings rather than simply critical of human transgressions.[42] Not only is she the attribute of significance, elsewhere, the poet says, "a single drop of compassion is 'two times double' the essential nature (svarūpa) of the Lord of Vṛṣagiri" (61). In other words, one drop of compassion is four times greater than God's essential nature, which is itself infinite. In this sense she is the most superior of all divine qualities.

> In fact, so powerful is Dayā that she inundates and encompasses Viṣṇu himself. O Great Goddess Compassion, when you inundate even the lofty Lord of Vṛṣagiri, my sinking transgressions will have no hand of support that attempts to rescue them. (13)

If Dayā submerges the Lord himself, the sins of the poet do not stand a chance. This absolution of one's sins, which are spiritual obstacles, can then empower beings in their quest for liberation. Continuing in this vein, Deśika subordinates even the Lord's anger to her.

> The infinite rage (pratigha) of the lord of Vṛṣācala which uproots the enemies of those who bow down to him, like weeds in a field of sprouting grain, approaches you as your servant (kiṃkara). (24)

Dayā can temper divine wrath, and this is yet another way in which she protects and nurtures beings who surrender to her. While Brahman as Viṣṇu possesses myriad auspicious qualities, Deśika singles out compassion as the most important. If Dayā is all powerful over the other attributes of God and is the most important of the essential qualities of Viṣṇu except knowledge (*jñāna*), then what effect does she have on his *līlā*? The next section explores Dayā's relationship with *līlā* and illustrates that activities such as creation-dissolution and incarnations generally attributed to *līlā* include Dayā as their relationship is articulated in various ways.

## DAYĀ, *LĪLĀ*, CREATION, AND INCARNATION

Two activities included in the discussion of *līlā* are the creation and dissolution of the world and the various descents. We saw earlier that the former is subordinated to compassion (88ab). Here, Deśika elaborates further.

> It is said—"he is the expert who in sport (*līlā*) accomplishes the production, sustenance and dissolution of the world and is the open door that

> is the sole means to liberation"—both these acts are dependent on you, O' Compassion, and because of you the Lord of Vṛṣaśikhara is the object of praise in such brilliant terms. (68)

In addition to creation and sustenance, liberation is also mentioned as an aspect of *līlā*. This is addressed in the next section. For now, we discuss the coming into being of existence as a result of *līlā* and its connection to divine compassion. Though it appears that Viṣṇu is renowned for creating wondrous worlds in joyful self-expression, it is in fact Dayā to whom he owes this reputation, as *līlā* is dependent on Dayā. The understanding of creation as mechanistic self-expression of a self-fulfilled being, which is what we see in the Vedānta discussion of creation in *Brahmasūtra* 2.1.32–36, is far different from creation as also including divine mercy.

Other aspects of creation discussed under the context of *līlā* are also reimagined as coming under the purview of compassion.

> O' compassion of the Lord of Vṛṣagiri, having witnessed during the deluge, sentient beings as unmodified insentience, with complete disregard for complex manifestation, you connect the senses with bodies. (17)

Rāmānuja in his description of *līlā* that was mentioned earlier, accords to it the motive for initiating the conjunction between individual selves and respective physical forms that are commensurate with their past karma.[43] Here, Deśika claims it is in fact the role of divine mercy. Compassion, who is unable to bear the almost insentient state of existence of the individual selves right after creation, brings together the senses and bodies so that they may experience the world. Just as divine *līlā* had no personal purpose or end-goal for the Lord, so too is his mercy. The description here of compassion as an attribute of Viṣṇu preserves his originative causal nature. However, Deśika examines its dynamics a little more closely and finds both *līlā* and Dayā are at play. It is Dayā through *līlā* that is the divine activator.

The second important cosmic activity associated with *līlā* is that of divine incarnations. To unburden earth and to establish righteousness (*dharma*) when unrighteousness (*adharma*) runs rampant, Viṣṇu descends periodically. Deśika devotes verses 82–90 specifically to the ten incarnations, and Dayā, not *līlā*, is the main operative in these manifestations.

> The Lord of Vṛṣabhaśikhara, due to his various descents, which he pretends (apadeśa) are due to his own *līlā*, gains disrespect among weak-minded people.
>
> But with instruction from you, he immediately grants in mercy his manifestations . . . for those engaged in taking refuge in him. (35)

*Līlā* is once again subordinated to Dayā since the former is just a divine pretense (*apadeśa*). The idea of pretense occurs in discussions on incarnations in Rāmānuja's writings also. For example, in his introduction to the commentary on the *Bhagavadgītā*, he says that "under the pretext (*apadeśa*) of incarnating to ease the burden of earth, but for the purpose of making himself the accessible object of refuge for even us, he incarnated."[44] Deśika goes further to declare that the rationale for why the supreme being desires to be accessible is his mercy. Divine descents are due to compassion and not solely due to *līlā*. So even though the Lord is slighted by his enemies for his many curious descents, he does not hesitate to do so again and again at the behest of Dayā.

Not only does she instigate his incarnations, but she is also ever present during these manifestations:

> O' Goddess, you reside in the heart of the Lord of Vṛṣagiri and assist him in all his descents, you are served by forgiveness (kṣamā) and remove all imperfections; you are the mother of the world. (72)

This is also a different characterization of incarnation from incarnation as divine sport. Even as God acts in *līlā*, compassion is ever-present. The presence of Compassion assisted by forgiveness, as a maternal nurturer, "mother of the world," evokes a context of tenderness and affection. These descents are not only instigated by divine mercy but are also under her constant influence. Even in the case of those manifestations that do not immediately suggest a compassionate nature, she is ever-present. For instance, even the incarnation of Narasiṃha, the ferocious man-lion who descends to save his devotee, Prahlāda, the son of the demon Hiraṇyakaśipu. Deśika writes that though the Lord's rage was conveyed through the mighty form of Narasiṃha, Dayā could be seen in her full form in his lotus-like eyes as He suckled the boy (84). The motherly affection (*vātsalya*) of the Lord is compassion, which works hand in hand with divine rage. While the wrathful aspect of this man-lion incarnation is meant to dispense divine justice in sport, Dayā is present and active. At the very least, sport and divine mercy work together.

Not only does Dayā actively participate in manifestations by residing in the heart of Viṣṇu, but yet in another way.

> O' Compassion, having created the various worlds for their prosperity, by you is the commencement of their thinking and seeing, you yourself seeing that enter the body of the Lord of Vṛṣācala,
>
> which has assumed the forms of the fish and the tortoise, and which are full of marvelous, varied qualities and are strangers to all kinds of faults. (82)

As she enters God's incarnated bodies, they become instruments of his own mercy. Rooted in both his heart (72) and his body, Viṣṇu cannot escape from his own innate compassionate nature. For instance, Deśika says that seeing the earth submerged, Compassion lifts the earth with the tusk (of the Lord), during the boar incarnation (83). In the case of both creation and sustenance of the world by means of descents, the relationship between Dayā and *līlā* is underscored contrary to the characterization of *līlā* as a lone actor. In addition to such cosmic activities Dayā's involvement with *līlā* is also considerable in the liberation of beings, which is discussed next.

## DAYĀ, *LĪLĀ*, AND LIBERATION

At the beginning of the last section, we saw that Deśika accords activities generally considered as *līlā*, such as creation, maintenance of the world, and dissolution to Dayā (68). He also declares that Viṣṇu is the sole means to liberation and that both these activities (creation and liberation) are due to divine mercy. Subsequent to the examination of the interaction between *līlā* and Dayā in the context of creation and so on, in this section, we explore the role of divine compassion and play in facilitating human salvation. Although divine sportive descents as discussed in the last section facilitate the communing between God and his devotees, thereby enabling freedom from the cycle of birth and rebirth, there are other ways in which the overall process toward liberation of beings is implicit in divine *līlā*, due to divine mercy. Dayā nudges the individual self toward liberation, and she once again undergirds activities that qualify as *līlā*, such as revelation of texts, spiritual teachers to convey the right spiritual message, the enjoining of various dharmic activities, and the proper expiation of sin. For Deśika, Dayā and *līlā* are linked and work toward human redemption; we examine each of these in turn.

In the pursuit of the path to liberation, one of the most important tools available to man is scripture as revealed by Viṣṇu. Deśika clarifies Dayā's involvement:

> To people who are immersed, in the always eternal sea of worldly existence and which results in their drowning,
>
> you order that the Lord of Vṛṣagiri extend his hand, as scripture, which is the essence of wisdom, it is auspicious, faultless, eternal, and composed of an intrinsically great part that is the root, with branches. (46)

The Lord reveals scripture, the Veda, that is sturdy at its root and extends into various branches (*śākhā*) of knowledge, at the behest of Dayā. The extent of her influence is such that "in her absence the lord sportingly compiles the false philosophies that deceive the enemies of his devotees" (47). For Deśika, uninfluenced by Dayā, the Lord in sport deceives those who are against his devotees in a reference to the anti-Vedic philosophies such as *sāṃkhya* and Buddhism. These schools of thought lead the enemies of those who take refuge in Viṣṇu, spiritually astray. We saw such influence of Dayā on other divine qualities and even *līlā* in verses 15 and 71. Affected by compassion, other divine attributes are much more amenable to overlooking human frailties than if they functioned on their own. Instead of working alongside divine justice they succumb to the forgiving nature of Dayā. The same type of relationship is evident here. *Līlā* by itself dispenses divine justice, automatically meting out punishment to enemies by misleading them with false knowledge. The fact that divine compassion subordinates *līlā* suggests a certain tension between the two, which will be further addressed below.

Deśika declares that all scripture, including Veda and texts that elaborate its meaning, are accessible due to Dayā's insistence, and as such her role is significant in the liberation of beings. Dayā also impels the descent of God as Kṛṣṇa, not so much to unburden earth, but primarily to explain and clarify the meaning of the Vedas:

> O' Compassion, you caused the Lord of Lakṣmī to descend under the pretense of removing the unbearable burden of earth who was exhausted from bearing the enemies of God.

> But in fact, it was to dispel the blindness due to the darkness, by making him sing for the learned in the world, the *Gītā* that is the auspicious lamp in the palace of the Vedas. (89)

The darkness of minds due to ignorance, stunting the salvific progress of beings, is neutralized by a second revelation, the important text of the *Bhagavadgītā*. This scripture, which is the essence of Vedic truths, makes known with lucidity the path to liberation. All of this is possible due to the machinations of Dayā and not simply *līlā*.

In addition to scripture, Deśika observes that divine mercy makes possible the various spiritual teachers (*ācārya*) of the Śrīvaiṣṇava tradition. Two of the formulators of Viśiṣṭādvaita Vedānta are taken up for special mention, and others are implied, as intermediaries through which Dayā reaches out to beings.

> O' Compassion, the artist/creator of movable and immovable beings, dwelling in Vṛṣācala, with brushes dipped in you, with those he painted/created brilliant minds beginning with Rāmānuja, Yāmuna etc. They teach "there is no goal that is helpful than unburdening sorrows on you." (59)

God sporting as an artist, paints to life both movable and immovable things and brings into existence the virtuous minds that teach the best way to salvation. The divine brush is smeared with paint that Deśika identifies as Dayā. In this way, the minds of the foremost teachers of this tradition are embodied forms of divine compassion. According to them, the most foolproof way to one's liberation and overcoming one's past sins is to take refuge in Dayā.

In addition to initiating the revelation of various scriptures and facilitating a lineage of spiritual guides, Dayā is also effective in influencing divine justice. At the beginning of this chapter, we discussed how the supreme being, in *līlā*, is the omniscient overseer of the workings of karma.[45]

> He impartially metes out justice based on actions of beings. Deśika finds compassion playing a significant role in minimizing the effects of divine justice.

> He exists subject to none; he is dependent on those who bow down to him. The Lord of Vṛṣagiri, though all-seeing,

> does not regard their mistakes, showing dependence on you, with boldness you break his rules, diverting yourself. (63)

Compassion influences the degree to which divine justice is dispensed. Because of her influence, God exhibits qualities that do not seem innate. He who is independent becomes completely dependent on those who take refuge in him. In this way, though omniscient, he forgives their mistakes, and Dayā herself sports, making Viṣṇu other than the impartial divine judge that he is. This is illustrated succinctly in this next passage.

> If beings surrender, she even transmutes, sportively, divine rage toward those who were previously enemies of the Lord.
>
> O' Compassion, the will of the Lord of Vṛṣagiri deprived of freedom, by your sportive acts, destroyed the foes of the ocean, the fetters of dharma of the angry sage, and that which was meant for killing alone, injured just one eye of Kakāsura. In this way (through you), the Lord brings forth a course of punishment, that is in fact beneficial to beings. (64)

These three mythological examples are all taken from the epic *Rāmāyaṇa*, and illustrate that because of Dayā, the Lord can forgive even former enemies, transmuting punishment resulting from the workings of divine justice into a kind of divine gift. The first example is of Varuṇa, the god of the ocean, who Rāma, the incarnation of Viṣṇu, propitiates to seek help in constructing a bridge to Lanka, to rescue his wife Sītā, held captive on the island.[46] As he finds the ocean unresponsive to his prayers, Rāma shoots flaming arrows to scorch the waters. Seeing this, the god of the ocean takes refuge immediately in Rāma and is pardoned. However, since his arrows once released cannot be recalled, they are instead redirected at the foes of the god of the oceans. What was intended as a punishment turns out to be a gift in disguise due to Dayā, who quickly dissipates the Lord's rage.

The second example is of the Sage Paraśurāma, who, considering Rāma a charlatan, challenges him to string and shoot a powerful bow.[47] The young prince successfully draws the bow and requests a target of the sage. Realizing immediately that Rāma is indeed a manifestation of Viṣṇu, Paraśurāma surrenders. However, the arrow that had been drawn must be released, and so it is aimed at his good deeds instead. Those very meritorious deeds of the sage had resulted in his arrogance that initially blinds him to the divine identity of Rāma. This is an example of even a righteous (dhārmic) life becoming an impediment to liberation.

The third example is the story of Kākāsura, the demon who in the form of a crow pecks away at Sītā's bosom. Rāma seeing this, hurls a blade of grass as a weapon at the crow.[48] It flees but the arrow follows him all over the universe. Realizing his mistake, the demon takes refuge in Rāma and is immediately forgiven. However, once again the arrow of divine justice cannot be recalled and so it takes out only one of the crow's eyes, though his life is spared. The idea conveyed is that even those who err, when they take refuge in the lord, through Dayā, have their punishment transformed into the gift of divine grace.[49]

It is for these reasons that Deśika turns to Compassion in hopes of attaining the Lord's favor, so that he may achieve liberation.

> O' Compassion of the Lord of Vṛṣagiri, even though I know of the action that is enjoined (in scripture), I pursue the path familiar to Vṛtra etc.
>
> Such being my affliction, you please assuage/calm the sportive punishment of the Lord. (93)

In the context of *līlā*, divine justice metes out punishment based on the refusal of beings to follow righteousness. Dayā, however, can soften the harshness of these punishments though they be justified, bringing the wretched back onto the right spiritual path. Knowing full well what is enjoined on him by scripture, Deśika still finds himself straying from the right path. He compares his transgressions to such prominent evildoers as Vṛtra, the demon subdued by the god Indra with the aid of Viṣṇu.[50] However, he takes refuge in the compassion of the Lord in hopes that this will lessen the divine repercussions for his wayward actions. Why? Because Dayā is the last resort for the most heinous of sinners, and surrender to her is itself a kind of expiation of prior transgressions.

> O' Compassion of the Lord of Vṛṣagiri, the wise know you as the tree granting all desires for the wretched people,
>
> you are the foremost atonement for those who have committed wrong and are the one who helps cross over saṃsāra. (14)

Deśika compares the Lord's compassion to a wish-fulfilling tree.[51] Though it may seem like he is suggesting that she is indiscriminate in her allocation of grace, taking refuge in her is itself a kind of expiation. It is in this way that she assists beings in crossing over *saṃsāra*, but without calling into question the impartial nature of justice that is meted out in *līlā*.[52] Ultimately, the Lord is partial to Dayā's actions and for this reason also the poet surrenders to her.

> O' Mother Compassion, there is nothing other than this, for me to ask of you. Bestow
>
> your grace (prasāda) on me, so that in this way, the Lord who loves Vṛṣagiri attaches
>
> great value to me. Make Mukunda, grant me the experience of liberation here itself. (100)

The last resort for one who is beyond redemption is to take refuge in Dayā, whose maternal affection assuages divine rage, allowing a return onto the path leading to freedom.

Thus far we have examined how Deśika reimagines activities generally attributed to *līlā* such as creation, incarnations, and salvation as enabled by Dayā, illustrating that *līlā* does not operate autonomously and is always envisioned together with compassion. In the examples above, Dayā influences *līlā*. Dayā also subordinates *līlā*, thereby creating a tension between them, as noted earlier (64). How are we to understand these passages that seem to delight in articulating Dayā and *līlā* as directing different outcomes? In two of his other writings Deśika provides context that clarifies his views on their relationship.

In the first canto of the *Yādavābhyudaya*, a poetic rendition of the life of Kṛṣṇa, Deśika says that the Lord as the painter paints with a brush identified as *līlā* and the paint itself is *dayā* or *kṛpā*:[53]

> The possessor of Śrī himself, all-pervading, with the brush of līlā and smeared
>
> with mercy (kṛpā) paints upon himself, the whole world, which he alone births.[54] (9)

We saw in an earlier verse that Deśika envisions compassion as the paint that brings the Śrīvaiṣṇava teachers to life (59). Here, the brush is equated with *līlā*, and the paint with *dayā*. In a sense, *līlā* and *dayā* are two sides of the same coin. One cannot be considered without the other. For Deśika, both *līlā* and *dayā* are at work in a complementary manner, though the degree to which they affect each other can be different.[55]

In his play, the *Saṃkalpasūryodaya*, Deśika presents yet another permutation of the relationship between *līlā* and *dayā*, as divine consorts of the Lord, whom he tries to please equally to maintain marital peace.[56]

> The Lord, subservient to Līlā and Dayā, that have equitable disposition/ability create strife reciprocally.

> (The Lord) rushes in and lifts us based on good deeds, anywhere, (even those) that are altogether unseen, just as a worm etches out letters (in wood).[57]

As co-wives, they are both equal and yet distinct in their cosmic function, and the Lord works to please them both. That is, he rushes to secure the well-being of the soul for the smallest of acts of merit. In this way he pleases both *Līlā* and *Dayā*. *Līlā* is satisfied that the Lord does not dispense his grace without merit, and *Dayā* is gratified that the Lord has bestowed mercy. The commentator notes that "the will of Līlā is that "I will make this living being," and the will of Dayā is "I will liberate this being."[58] In this case, *Līlā* is illustrative of the supreme being as the divine judge meting out rewards and punishments, and *Dayā* is evocative of God as the merciful savior. But both of them coexist, somewhat. A comparison is made to a worm unconsciously carving letters by boring into wood in the same way as God instinctively secures the well-being of the soul. In the first illustration from his play, Deśika understands *Līlā* and *Dayā* working in concert, while in the latter example, they have their respective domains and may even compete, but nevertheless, they exist together.

The paradoxical harmony between God as the supreme, transcendent moral sovereign and God who desires to commune with and uplift the individual selves is a constant refrain in Śrīvaiṣṇava theology and is referred to as God's supremacy (*paratva*) and his accessibility (*saulabhya*).[59] Deśika explores *līlā* and *dayā* as aligned along these two poles. Carman, writing on divine polarity, notes that

> The relationship between attributes of these two types is not always however, a simple conjunction, an "and." In certain crucial passages it is more like a "yet nevertheless also." . . . Sometimes the distinction seems to be between two halves that complement each other harmoniously, but at other times this distinction though never becoming a separation, does indicate a certain tension between the two poles in the Divine nature.[60]

In Deśika's hymn, *līlā* and *dayā* reflect the polarity of supreme transcendence and supreme accessibility respectively. Always connected, their interaction is explored as they complement each other, but never separating in the context of cosmic activities that include human redemption through divine mercy.

We began with Rāmānuja's understanding that *līlā* is not simply creation, as divine self-expression, but that such activities must include compassion. Deśika expands on the workings of divine mercy and its interaction with *līlā*. Though the *Hundred Verses* is a meditation on taking refuge in the divine compassion of Viṣṇu, the detail on the workings of both compassion and *līlā* mentioned in many of its passages highlight their interdependence and confirm that in Śrīvaiṣṇavism one cannot be envisioned without the other. What this suggests is that divine creative activity is not solely the joyous self-expression of a being who neither desires nor lacks nothing, but necessarily concerns human salvation as a goal. Moreover, through his *līlā* the divine being is not simply the upholder of the law of karma, as divine compassion accomplishes considerably more than this. Ultimately, *līlā* is divine activity through which grace is freely given, as Clooney notes in this volume.[61]

## Bibliography


Adluri, S. *Textual Authority in Classical Indian Thought: Rāmānuja and the Viṣṇu Purāṇa*. Hindu Studies Series. Oxon: Routledge, 2015.

Balasubramanyam, T. K. *Vedānta Deśika's Yādavābhyudayam with the Commentary of Appaya Dīkiṣita*. Vol I. Srirangam: Sri Vani Vila Press, 1907.

van Buitenen, J. A. B. *Rāmānuja's Vedārthasaṃgraha: Introduction, Critical Edition and Annotated Translation*. Pune: Deccan College Postgraduate and Research Institute, 1992.

Carman, J. B. *The Theology of Rāmānuja: An Essay in Interreligious Understanding*. New Haven, CT: Yale University Press, 1974.

Clooney, F. X. "Rāmānuja and the Meaning of Krishna's Descent and Embodiment on This Earth." In *Krishna: A Sourcebook*, edited by Edwin F. Bryant, 329–356. Oxford: Oxford University Press, 2007.

Clooney, F. X. "Rāmānuja's Nityagrantham ("Manual of Daily Worship"): A Translation." *International Journal of Hindu Studies* 24 (2020): 345–380.

Clooney, F. X. "Rāmānuja's Eleventh-Century Hindu Theology." In *The Cambridge Companion to Religious Experience*, edited by Paul K Moser and Chad Meister, 208–238. Cambridge: Cambridge University Press, 2020.

Clooney, F. X., with Hugh Nicholson. "Vedānta Deśika's Īśvarapariccheda ("Definition of the Lord") and the Hindu Argument about Ultimate Reality." In *Ultimate Realities: A Volume in Comparative Religious Ideas Project*, edited by Robert C. Neville, 95–124. Albany: State University of New York Press. 2001.

Doniger, W. *The Rig Veda*. London: Penguin Classics, 2005.

Goldman, R. P., and Sally Sutherland Goldman, eds. and trans. *The Rāmāyaṇa of Vālmīki*. 7 vols. Princeton, NJ: Princeton University Press, 1990–2018.

Hardy, F. "The Philosopher as Poet—A Study of Vedānta Deśika's Dehalīśaśtuti." *Journal of Indian Philosophy* 7 (1979): 277–325.

Hopkins, S. P. "Sanskrit from Tamil Nadu: At Play in the Forests of the Lord: The Gopalavimshati of Vedantadeshika." In *Krishna: A Sourcebook*, edited by E. F. Bryant, 285–306. Oxford: Oxford University Press, 2007.

Hopkins, S. P. *Singing the Body of God: The Hymns of Vedānta Deśika in Their South Indian Tradition*. New Delhi: Oxford University Press, 2003.

Krishnamacharya, V. *Saṃkalpasūryodaya of Śrī Venkaṭanātha with the Commentaries Prabhāvilasa and Prabhāvali*. 2 vols. Srirangam: Sri Vani Vilas Press, 1917.

Lipner, J. J. *The Face of Truth: A Study of Meaning and Metaphysics in the Vedāntic Theology of Rāmānuja*. Albany: State University of New York Press, 1986.

Lipner, J. J. "A God at Play? Reexamining the Concept of Līlā in Hindu Philosophy and Theology." *International Journal of Hindu Studies* 26 (2022): 283–326.

Mumme, P. Y. *The Śrīvaiṣṇava Theological Debate: Maṇavāḷmāmuni and Vedānta Deśika*. Banglore: Navbharath Enterprises, 2009.

Narayana, S. *Ramanuja's Gadyatrayam with Śrutaprakāśikābhāṣya of Sudarśanasūri and Rahasyarakṣā of Vedānta Deśika*. Melkote: Academy of Sanskrit Research, 2014.

Narayanan, V. "Arcāvatāra: On Earth as He is in Heaven." In *Gods of Flesh, Gods of Stone*, edited by J. P. Waghorne and N. Cutler with V. Narayanan, 53–68. New York: Columbia University Press, 1998.

Narayanan, V. "The Realm of Play and the Sacred Stage." In *The Gods at Play*, edited by William Sax. New York: Oxford University Press. 1995

Ramaswamy Ayyangar, D. *Dayāśatakam of Vedānta Deśika*. Translation with commentary. Tirupati: Tirumala Tirupati Devasthanams, 1961.

Rangacharya, M., and M. B. Varadaraja Aiyangar. *The Vedāntasūtras with the Śrībhāṣya of Rāmānujācārya*. 3 vols. New Delhi: Munshiram Manoharlal Publishers, 2002.

Sadhale, G. S. *The Bhagavadgītā with Eleven Commentaries*. 3 vols. New Delhi: Parimal Publications, 1985.

Sampatkumaran, M. R. *The Gītābhāṣya of Rāmānuja*. Tirupati: Tirumala Tirupathi Devasthanams, 1985.

Sax, W. S., ed. *The Gods at Play: Līlā in South Asia*. New York: Oxford University Press, 1995.

Singh, S. *Vedānta Deśika: His Life, Works and Philosophy. A Study*. Varanasi: Chaukhamba Amarabharati Prakashan, 2008.

Viraraghavacarya, U. *Rāmānuja's Commentary Śrībhāṣya with Its Gloss Śrutaprakāśikā of Sudarśanasūri*. 2 vols. Ubhaya Vedanta Granthamala. Chennai: Sri Uttamur Viraraghavacarya Centenary Trust, 2002.

Viraraghavacarya, U. Vedanta Desika's *Adhikaraṇasārāvali with Two Commentaries Adhikaraṇa Cintāmaṇi and Sārārtha Ratnaprabha*. Madras: Sri Nilayam Printers, 1974.

Young, K. K. *Beloved Places: The Correlation of Topology and Topography in the Śrīvaiṣṇava Tradition of South India*. Montreal: McGill University, 1978.

## Notes

1. Francis X. Clooney, SJ, "Creation, Vision, Bliss: *Līlā* as Grace according to Rāmānuja, with Reference Also to Thomas Aquinas and Gregory Palamas," and Rachel Fell McDermott, "What Does It Mean for the Goddess to Play? *Līlā* (or Its Absence) in the Śākta Traditions," in this volume. For additional articles on various conceptions of divine sport in Hindu traditions, see W. S. Sax, ed. *The Gods at Play: Līlā in South Asia* (New York: Oxford University Press, 1995).

2. For discussion on Rāmānuja's understanding of *līlā* see J. J. Lipner, "A God at Play? Reexamining the Concept of Līlā in Hindu Philosophy and Theology," *International Journal of Hindu Studies* 26 (2022): 293–298.
3. The terms "play" and "sport" used to translate *līlā* in this essay, refer specifically to its definition within Viśiṣṭādvaita as creative activity that is "responsible," "without motive," "spontaneous," and "effortless" (Lipner, "A God at Play?" 293, 294, 296).
4. Rāmānuja's writings include the *Vedārthasaṃgraha*, a summary of the teachings of the Upaniṣads, the commentary on the *Brahmasūtras* and *Bhagavadgītā*, the *Śrībhāṣya* and the *Bhagavadgītābhāṣya* respectively, and devotional texts the *Gadyatraya* and the *Nityagrantha* (J. B. Carman, *The Theology of Rāmānuja: An Essay in Interreligious Understanding.* [New Haven, CT: Yale University Press, 1974], 49–64; F. X. Clooney, "Rāmānuja's Eleventh-Century Hindu Theology," in *The Cambridge Companion to Religious Experience*, ed. Paul K Moser and Chad Meister [Cambridge: Cambridge University Press, 2020], 208–238).
5. I use the terms Brahman, Viṣṇu, and God interchangeably as that is the Śrīvaiṣṇava understanding.
6. All translations are my own unless otherwise indicated. U. Viraraghavacarya, *Rāmānuja's Commentary Śrībhāṣya with Its Gloss Śrutaprakāśikā of Sudarśanasūri* (Ubhaya Vedanta Granthamala. Chennai: Sri Uttamur Viraraghavacarya Centenary Trust, 2002), vol. 2, ŚBh 2.1.33, p. 272.
7. For more on the concepts of divine desire and divine will see J. J. Lipner, *The Face of Truth: A Study of Meaning and Metaphysics in the Vedāntic Theology of Rāmānuja* (Albany: State University of New York Press. 1986), 90–91.
8. Viraraghavacharya, *Rāmānuja's Commentary Śrībhāṣya*, vol. 2, ŚBh 2.2.2, p. 281, lines 5–9.
9. Viraraghavacharya, *Rāmānuja's Commentary Śrībhāṣya*, vol. 2, ŚBh 2.2.2, p. 281, lines 9–11.
10. A distinction is made between competitive and noncompetitive sport (Lipner, *The Face of Truth*, 92–93, and Lipner, "A God at Play?").
11. Even Deśika in his partially extant commentary on the *Brahmasūtras*, the *Adhikaraṇasārāvali*, does not add more than what Rāmānuja has said (U. Viraraghavacharya, Vedanta Desika's *Adhikaraṇasārāvali with Two Commentaries Adhikaraṇa Cintāmaṇi and Sārārtha Ratnaprabha* [Madras: Sri Nilayam Printers, 1974], 308–309).
12. For more on the self-body relationship see Lipner, *The Face of Truth*, 79–98; Carman, *The Theology of Rāmānuja*, 124–133.
13. S. Adluri, *Textual Authority in Classical Indian Thought: Rāmānuja and the Viṣṇu Purāṇa*, Hindu Studies Series (Oxon: Routledge, 2015), 25–39.
14. This term was not utilized by Rāmānuja himself, however it gains prominence in later Śrīvaiṣṇava theology (Carman, *The Theology of Rāmānuja*, 140, 143).
15. Jessica Frazier, "The Metaphysics of Emotion: Divine Play in Caitanya Vaiṣṇava Philosophy," in this volume.
16. For a discussion on how Rāmānuja conceives of the body see Lipner, *The Face of* Truth, 132.
17. Carman, *The Theology of Rāmānuja*, 186.

18. Viraraghavacharya, *Rāmānuja's Commentary Śrībhāṣya*, vol. 2, ŚBh 2.2.3, p. 282, line 10–p. 283, line 3.
19. Translation from M. R. Sampatkumaran, *The Gītābhāṣya of Rāmānuja* (Tirupati: Tirumala Tirupathi Devasthanams, 1985), BhGBh 3.10, p. 75.
20. For more on Rāmānuja on incarnations of Viṣṇu see F. X. Clooney, "Rāmānuja and the Meaning of Krishna's Descent and Embodiment on This Earth," in *Krishna: A Sourcebook*, ed. Edwin F. Bryant (Oxford: Oxford University Press, 2007), 329–356.
21. Translation from M. Rangacharya, and M. B. Varadaraja Aiyangar, *The Vedāntasūtras with the Śrībhāṣya of Rāmānujācārya* (New Delhi: Munshiram Manoharlal Publishers, 2002), vol. 1, ŚBh 1.1.21 p. 307.
22. Viraraghavacharya, *Rāmānuja's Commentary Śrībhāṣya*, vol. 2, ŚBh 2.2.3, p. 283, line 4.
23. Viraraghavacharya, *Rāmānuja's Commentary Śrībhāṣya*, vol. 2, ŚBh 2.2.3, p. 284, lines 2–4. Also Carman, *The Theology of Rāmānuja*, 189.
24. Clooney, "Creation, Vision, Bliss," in this volume.
25. S. Narayana, *Ramanuja's Gadyatrayam with Śrutaprakāśikābhāṣya of Sudarśanasūri and Rahasyarakṣā of Vedānta Deśika* (Melkote: Academy of Sanskrit Research, 2014), 32–36.
26. For an analysis of these divine characteristics see Carman, *The Theology of Rāmānuja*, 190–198.
27. Narayana, *Ramanuja's Gadyatrayam*, 48–49, 53–55.
28. Carman, *The Theology of Rāmānuja*, 187.
29. S. P. Hopkins, *Singing the Body of God: The Hymns of Vedānta Deśika in Their South Indian Tradition* (New Delhi: Oxford University Press, 2003), 7. On the life and writings of Vedānta Deśika see Hopkins, *Singing the Body of God*, and S. Singh, *Vedānta Deśika: His Life, Works and Philosophy. A Study* (Varanasi: Chaukhamba Amarabharati Prakashan, 2008). For more on Deśika's theology of God see F. X. Clooney, with Hugh Nicholson. "Vedānta Deśika's Īśvarapariccheda ("Definition of the Lord") and the Hindu Argument about Ultimate Reality," in *Ultimate Realities: A Volume in Comparative Religious Ideas Project*, ed. Robert C. Neville (Albany: State University of New York Press. 2001), 95–124.
30. For a recent publication on the Tamil grounding in Rāmānuja's writings, see Clooney "Rāmānuja's Eleventh-Century Hindu Theology," 212–214. On Deśika and the Tamil tradition in Sanskrit, see Hopkins, *Singing the Body of God*, 169–170, and F. Hardy, "The Philosopher as Poet—A Study of Vedānta Deśika's Dehalīśaśtuti," *Journal of Indian Philosophy* 7 (1979): 277–325.
31. From here on, referred to as the *Hundred Verses.*
32. Also known as Vṛṣagiri, Bull among mountains or Bull Mountain. For important pilgrimage sites in Śrīvaiṣṇavism and their significance see K. K. Young, *Beloved Places: The Correlation of Topology and Topography in the Śrīvaiṣṇava Tradition of South India* (Montreal: McGill University, 1978).
33. For a discussion on differences in Śrīvaiṣṇava theology of the poets and the commentators, see Hopkins, *Singing the Body of God*, 41–47.
34. The verse goes on to reference Balarāma, the brother of Kṛṣṇa and the incarnation of the primordial serpent, Ādiśeṣa, over whom Viṣṇu reposes in his heaven, Vaikuṇṭha. As such, he is considered as the secondary incarnation of Viṣṇu. Balarāma is offered

as an example of divine manifestation who, on the one hand, routs several notable demons, but due to intoxication is blind to the transgressions of those who take refuge in him, on the other hand. Both Paraśurāma, another partial incarnation of Viṣṇu, and Balarāma are problematic when it comes to illustrating the *dayā* of the Lord (D. Ramaswamy Ayyangar, *Dayāśatakam of Vedānta Deśika*, translation with commentary [Tirupati: Tirumala Tirupati Devasthanams, 1961],159–160; 164–165).

35. V. Narayanan, "Arcāvatāra: On Earth as He is in Heaven," in *Gods of Flesh, Gods of Stone*, ed. J. P. Waghorne and N. Cutler with V. Narayanan (New York: Columbia University Press, 1998), 53–68.
36. Young, *Beloved Places*.
37. Hopkins, *Singing the Body of God*, 170.
38. Carman, *The Theology of Rāmānuja*, 169–170, Lipner, *The Face of Truth*, 90–91.
39. J. A. B. van Buitenen, *Rāmānuja's Vedārthasaṃgraha: Introduction, Critical Edition and Annotated Translation* (Pune: Deccan College Postgraduate and Research Institute, 1992), 288.
40. Carman, *The Theology of Rāmānuja*, 88–91.
41. The theological controversy over divine mercy and autonomy for human salvation is of significance in the ultimate split of the Śrīvaiṣṇava tradition in the seventeenth century into the Teṉkalai and Vaṭakalai schools. For more on this see P. Y. Mumme, *The Śrīvaiṣṇava Theological Debate: Maṇavāḷmāmuni and Vedānta Deśika* (Banglore: Navbharath Enterprises, 2009), 187–224.
42. Ramaswamy Ayyangar, *Dayāśatakam of Vedānta Deśika*, 16.
43. Frazier, "The Metaphysics of Emotion."
44. G. S. Sadhale, *The Bhagavadgītā with Eleven Commentaries* (New Delhi: Parimal Publications, 1985), vol. 1, pg. 6, lines12–13.
45. Frazier, "The Metaphysics of Emotion."
46. R. P. Goldman and Sally Suterland Goldman, eds. and trans., *The Rāmāyaṇa of Vālmīki*, 7 vols. (Princeton, NJ: Princeton University Press. 2017), vol. 6, sarga 13–15.
47. Goldman and Goldman, *The Rāmāyaṇa of Vālmīki*, vol. 1, sarga 74–75.
48. Goldman and Goldman, *The Rāmāyaṇa of Vālmīki*, vol. 5, sarga 68ff.
49. Ramaswamy Ayyangar, *Dayāśatakam of Vedānta Deśika*, 105–107.
50. W. Doniger, *The Rig Veda* (London: Penguin Classics, 2005), 148ff.
51. The original, known as Kalpavṛkṣa, emerged during the churning of the ocean, and is transplanted to Indra's heaven, whereas the tree of Dayā is available to all beings everywhere.
52. Mumme notes that in his doctrinal works Deśika does not advocate divine forgiveness without proper expiation. Citing some of the verses from this poem, she finds some of the characterizations of divine compassion by Deśika to be dramatic exaggerations and that he is declaring that God simply absolves one of sins without proper expiation. If turning to Dayā is itself a kind of expiation, then the absolving of one's sins without atonement is not what is suggested here (*The Śrīvaiṣṇava Theological Debate*, 211ff).
53. S. Singh, *Vedānta Deśika: His Life, Works and Philosophy. A Study* (Varanasi: Chaukhamba Amarabharati Prakashan, 2008), 472–480; S. P. Hopkin, "Sanskrit from Tamil Nadu: At Play in the Forests of the Lord: The Gopalavimshati of Vedantadeshika,"

in *Krishna: A Sourcebook*, ed. E. F. Bryant (Oxford: Oxford University Press, 2007), 290–291.

54. T. K. Balasubramanyam, *Vedānta Deśika's Yādavābhyudayam with the Commentary of Appaya Dīkiṣita*, vol. 1 (Srirangam: Sri Vani Vila Press, 1907), 12.
55. Ramaswamy Ayyangar, however finds Dayā to be superior. Elaborating on the metaphor of the Lord as the painter, he says that while *līlā* is the brush, *dayā* as the paint remains in the painting, whereas there is no direct presence of the brush. He says that this indicates that *dayā* has more shaping power than *līlā* in creation. *Dayāśatakam of Vedānta Deśika*, 94.
56. Singh, *Vedānta Deśika*, 464–471.
57. V. Krishnamacharya, *Saṃkalpasūryodaya of Śrī Venkaṭanātha with the Commentaries Prabhāvilasa and Prabhāvali* (Srirangam: Sri Vani Vilas Press, 1917), 1:138–139.
58. Krishnamacharya, *Saṃkalpasūryodaya of Śrī Venkaṭanātha*, 1:138, lines 1–3.
59. Carman, *The Theology of Rāmānuja*, 79–87.
60. Carman, *The Theology of Rāmānuja*, 87.
61. Though his conclusion is in reference to the writings of Rāmānuja, as this essay illustrates, it is equally applicable to later Śrīvaiṣṇava theologians such as Deśika, who elaborate on their predecessor's theology. See Clooney, "Creation, Vision, Bliss" in this volume.

# 6 What Does It Mean for the Goddess to Play?

## *LĪLĀ* (OR ITS ABSENCE) IN THE ŚĀKTA TRADITIONS

*Rachel Fell McDermott*

### Where Is the *Līlā* in Śakti?

It's a funny thing, but the concept of "*līlā*" hardly ever comes up in studies of the Hindu Goddess. I have bookshelves of such volumes, and in writing this chapter I have pulled every single one from the shelf and checked its index. The indices skip from Lalita, Lanka, Laws of Manu, or Liberation, right over to *linga*, but no "l-i-l" words are present at all. Introductory stalwarts such as David Kinsley's *Hindu Goddesses* (1985), Narendranath Bhattacharya's *History of the Śākta Religion* (2nd ed., 1996), the series of essays in Hawley and Wulff's edited volume, *Devī: Goddesses of India* (1996), or Tracy Pintchman's *The Rise of the Goddess in the Hindu Tradition* (1994)—none of these discusses the concept of "play" or "sport"—either for "the" Goddess or for any individual goddesses. Indeed, the Goddess tradition has no one like Krishna the butter thief;[1] no parallel to Krishna's *rāslīlā* dance; no specific earthly site, like Braj, or Vrindavan, conceived as the counterpart of the heavenly Vaikuntha;[2] and no sustained theological discussion of the Goddess's *līlā* as a manifestation of the divine nature. As David Kinsley notes, "No Hindu deity expresses this [unconditioned, completely spontaneous free] aspect of the divine better than Kṛṣṇa."[3]

The Śākta traditions center on independent, powerful goddesses who are not subservient to male gods. For instance, the goddess Durgā in her various forms (Ambikā, Jagaddhātrī, Nandā Devī, Vaiṣṇo Devī, and Vindhyavāsinī), Kālī and her more dread forms Bhadrakālī and Cāmuṇḍā, Śītalā the smallpox goddess, Manasā the snake goddess, and a host of potent "village goddesses," or *āmmans*, whose provenance is supreme over their own locales.

What is far more important than *līlā* to these Śākta conceptions of the divine, something we find plentifully represented in books on goddesses, are the notions of *prakṛti, māyā, moha*, and *śakti*—the Goddess as bewitching nature, illusion, or pure potency. As Prakṛti, she infatuates the Sāmkhyan Puruṣa into joining with her in creation; or she performs the deluding function of the Vedāntic Brahman, who is only seemingly veiled in multiplicity; or she plunges the soul into apparent ignorance, or *avidyā*. Whether an ontological claim (Brahman somehow cloaks Itself in illusion) or a soteriological description of the state of the soul (we are subject to ignorance and illusion), the overall message is serious, not playful: Illusion must, if at all possible, be overcome by seeking the grace of liberation by the very One who enmeshes us. She gives, and removes, illusion. In this sense, the Hindu goddess traditions of India are less concerned with a Deus Ludens than a Dea Deludens.[4]

The Purāṇas and Tantras form a massive storehouse of thinking about the philosophical import of Goddess figures, particularly Śiva's consort in one of her multitudinous forms. Śiva and Śakti are associated in Purāṇic stories about their conjugal and domestic lives; their love-making is so engrossing that the world is in danger of browning down and blacking out. Sometimes they compete in an earth-threatening, *taṇḍava* dance contest (which Śiva usually wins).[5] In Tantric texts one of them teaches the other, and Tantric meditation prescriptions portray the two making love with abandon in the aspirant's *sahasrāra*, the highest *cakra* of the *kuṇḍalinī* system in the head. Sometimes, as in Śrīkaṇṭha's Viśiṣṭa Śivādvaita, the relationship between Śiva and Śakti is said to be *līlā*.[6]

The point here is that the Goddess in the Śākta tradition is creative, energetic, erotic, delusory, and ultimately redemptive. These activities can be generally understood as her inexplicable *līlā*, although this term is rarely appended as explanatory. Let me give three examples of the way in which one might visualize the Goddess at play—or, as is better in this tradition, at illusion.

The first is the earliest and most famous of the Sanskrit texts on the Goddess—still today read and utilized ritually all over India—the sixth-century "Devī-Māhātmya" section of the *Mārkaṇḍeya Purāṇa*—also called the *Caṇḍī*.[7] This contains a frame story about two dejected men, a king and a merchant, both of whom listen to three stories about the Goddess and then become her devotees. In the first story, essentially borrowed from the Vaiṣṇava tradition,[8] the Goddess is called Yoginidrā, or

Mahāmāyā, and the male gods importune her to leave Viṣṇu so that he can wake up and kill two demons who are threatening Brahmā.

In the next two stories, the Goddess, as Ambikā or Caṇḍikā, kills the buffalo demon Mahiṣa and then the brother-demons Śumbha and Niśumbha. For these salvific deeds she is praised in three hymns, where her epithets include Mahāvidyā (the Great Ignorance), Mahāmāyā (the Great Illusion), Mahāmedhā (the Great Insight), and Mahāsurī (the Great Demoness).[9] Although *līlā* as a term is not part of any epithet, "play" does enter the description of her battle prowess, for she is said to break the enemy's weapons "as if in play, showering down her own weapons and arms . . . [yet] appear[ing] unruffled."[10] Like the beautiful seventh-century Pallava-era sculpture of the Goddess who acts, even in battle, with casual calm, the "play" of the Goddess of the "Devī-Māhātmya" demonstrates a power that exudes effortlessly from an inexhaustible source. Although slaying demons and rescuing the world is deadly serious, she does it as if in sport. Of course, one can also say that the adolescent Krishna trounces his demon adversaries in play (think of his dance on the heads of Kāliya, the serpent infesting the Yamuna).[11] But somehow the Vaiṣṇava stories are told with more indulgence, less fear.

My second example is the eighteenth–nineteenth-century Bengali devotional poetry tradition. There are two main streams to this, one alive, the other somewhat moribund. The living stream is bhakti poetry to Kālī, called Śyāmā Saṅgīt, or Songs to Śyāmā, the Black One. In general, these are short poems of intimacy—of praise, petition, and intimate mocking of the Goddess, such as a mother might receive from her petulant child. These began to be composed in the mid-eighteenth century, and are a vibrant, robust tradition of Śākta composition in Bengali. When not praised or importuned for salvation, the Goddess is chided for her behavior (what other mother is as stingy as you?) and her looks (what sort of a mother wears a necklace of the cut heads of other mother's children, or lies on Daddy?). Among such poems is an entire subgenre centered on Kālī the magician's daughter, the deluder, the player of her devotees' lives. I give two examples, both from the late eighteenth or early nineteenth centuries. The first is by Ramprasād Sen (1718–1775):

What's the fault of the poor mind?
Śyāmā, You're the magician's daughter;
it dances as You make it dance.
You are action, virtue, and vice;

I've figured out Your secret.
Ma, You are earth, You are water;
You make fruit
ripen on the tree.
You are power, You are devotion;
You are even liberation,
says Śiva.
You are suffering; You are happiness;
so it's written in the *Caṇḍī*.

Prasād says,
The thread of attachment
is spun by action's wheel.
Crazy Kālī and crazy Śiva
bind souls with it
and make them play.[12]

The second poem is by Kamalākānta Bhaṭṭācārya (1769–1820):

Ever-blissful Kālī,
Bewitcher of the Destructive Lord,
Mother—
for your own amusement
You dance
clapping Your hands.

You with the moon on Your forehead,
really You are primordial, eternal, void.
When there was no world, Mother,
Where did You get that garland of skulls?

You alone are the operator,
we Your instruments, moving as You direct.
Where You place us, we stand;
the words You give us, we speak.

Restless Kamalākānta says, rebukingly:
You grabbed Your sword, All-Destroyer,
and now You've cut down evil *and* good.[13]

Here the mention of the Goddess's bewitching power has an edge to it; the playfulness of Kālī's *māyā* may produce some delight in the devotee, but the overarching emotion expressed is awe, and perhaps even resentment at being played with.[14]

My third example also comes from Bengal, from the worship of Śītalā, the erstwhile Smallpox (and now Skin Disease) Goddess. In "A Theology of the Repulsive: The Myth of the Goddess Śītalā," Edward C. Dimock Jr. investigates how one should understand what is locally called the "*līlā*" of the Goddess, when she "sweeps through villages and cities, like fire leaving one house unscathed to destroy the next, searing with her fevers good people and bad without distinction." Whether one derives *līlā* from the word to lick, as in waves of flame playing lightly over what it burns, or from the Prakrit word for "grace," a smallpox epidemic is the play of Śītalā, and while acknowledging her grace in the visitation, one nevertheless prays for her to withdraw.[15] She is both the afflicter and the means of salvation.

I have thought a lot about why the Śākta tradition is so *līlā*-less. Could it be because Krishna and the Goddess are so different? I mentioned above that there is a second, less prominent stream of bhakti poetry to the Goddess in Bengal, and in this set of poems the Goddess is Umā, a girl, the daughter of Menakā and Girirāj, who is married to the hemp-smoking, indigent, elderly, disreputable bridegroom, Lord Śiva. She lives with him, inaccessible, in Kailasa. Once a year, the yearning parents see their daughter when for a mere three days she is allowed to come home to Bengal for the autumnal Navarātrī holiday. The poems of welcoming and lamenting that form this poetic genre are said by scholars of Bengali literature to be heavily influenced by the Bengali Vaiṣṇava *padābalī* that pre-dated them in the region; however, what the Śākta composers borrowed was not *līlā*, but *viraha*. In other words, there is a divine child, but not a theology of play. Umā is said to be miserable with her aged, homeless husband, and nothing she does in the story bespeaks the carefree abandon of unmotivated joy.

There is one exception in Bengali literature to this stark absence of the playful child or adolescent, but it is not considered very accomplished and has hardly been imitated. Rāmprasād Sen wrote a short song cycle in which Umā is clearly modeled on Krishna: She takes over Krishna's association with cows, she plays the flute, and she performs his circle dance in the woods. A later poet even adds in Umā's taste for butter and cream.[16] In current literary contexts such poems are not sung or anthologized; they have no present life in the Goddess tradition. In another, much more prominent daughter-goddess tradition, that centered on Nandādevī in

Uttarakhand, the Goddess mirrors the sorrows of mothers and daughters who must part at the daughters' marriages. William Sax, who explored this tradition in some detail in the late 1980s, found little joy, abandon, and frolicking in the Nandādevī story.[17] While *prati-vātsalya bhāva*, or the attitude toward the divine in the form of a child, has been taken over by some Śākta traditions, Krishna's hilarity and playfulness have not.

Another way of thinking about this is to compare the *līlā-smaraṇa* meditation of the Gauḍīya Vaiṣṇavas, a "meditative technique of visualizing in the mind the *līlā* of Kṛṣṇa and his retinue of intimate companions in the enchanting land of Vraja,"[18] with the Śākta *dhyānas*, or meditative images of the Goddess Kālī standing on the battlefield or in the cremation grounds that take the aspirant through fear toward an acceptance of her death-dealing and -defeating power.[19] There is nothing playful about Kālī in this image, although—again—her delusive powers may be seen as divine trickery. The principal *rasa*, or aesthetic taste, she manifests is the terrible (one of her epithets is Bhayaṅkarī), although the bhaktas will say that she also expresses the *rasa* of compassion (*karuṇa*), and Tantric heroes, in a very dangerous and difficult stance, may approach her in an amorous (*śṛṅgāra*) fashion.

To sum up simplistically, whereas we do not find much *līlā* in the Goddess traditions of India, there is an emphasis on the *māyā* (ontological and soteriological, illusive and redemptive) of the divine feminine. She is usually depicted as an adult, a battle queen, an erotic partner, and a mother to devotees. Despite the fact that the Goddess offers liberation—and in this sense the Śākta poets and theologians come close to the Vaiṣṇava understandings of *līlā* as grace, compassion, and mercy, as shown in this volume by Clooney and Adluri—it is also abundantly true that if she plays with us, the consequences are serious.

## Where Is the Comfort in Līlā?

In the second half of this chapter, I want to take a side step and look at the topic of our volume from a pastoral perspective. What does the idea of a playful deity do for those who adhere to the theological worldview that encompasses that playfulness? For whom, and under what circumstances, is Deus Ludens—whether *līlā*-centric or *māyā*-centric—productive to think with? This is a genuine question, posed out of ignorance—but to me it is the most interesting question I personally can ask of the material. If Clifford Geertz is right, when he wrote in his famous essay about cultural symbols that in the face of the problem of suffering, the religious response is to formulate "an image of such a genuine order of the world which will account for, and even celebrate, the perceived ambiguities, puzzles, and paradoxes in human experience,"[20] then how does conceiving of a playful God help to bring order? In what follows I take some cues from practitioners and scholars of the Vaiṣṇava tradition, use these to muse about the issue from a Śākta perspective, and conclude with some stray thoughts about the question in a Christian context.[21]

In Indian theodical thinking, there is something called the "Līlā Solution" to the problem of evil: God cannot be blamed for allowing suffering, as, like a child, he is simply playing and expressing the unmotivated joy of his being. Arthur L. Herman, in his 1993 volume, *The Problem of Evil and Indian Thought*, claims that although this argument gets God off the hook, it is ultimately unsatisfying: Okay, so you are playing, and have no purposes or need. But why did you decide to play in the first place, or couldn't you have played better?[22] K. B. Ramakrishna Rao agrees in an article called "Suffering in Advaita Vedānta," "If it is said that all of these [problems and tragedies] form elements of an inscrutable game, a divine play (*līlā* as it is called), the theism which promulgates the solution reduces itself to a pathetic faith inspiring not hope, but committing eternally man's destiny and freedom to an unredeemable ransom."[23]

Even if one is not dismissive, like Herman and Rao, of the Līlā Solution as a philosophical concept, I would still like to know how a sufferer—say, someone who has just been told that she has advanced, inoperable cancer—might find it useful, comforting, or strengthening. I approached Vineet Chander, Coordinator for Hindu Life in the Chaplaincy Department at Princeton University, a man who has been at this job for several years and who, though Gauḍīya Vaiṣṇava in personal leaning, counsels Hindus of all varieties. Do you, or do you know of any pastoral counselors similar to yourself, I asked, who utilize the *līlā* aspect of the divine in counseling people who are facing some sort of personal crisis?

He responded that he had not found too much occasion to draw on this type of imagery in his own pastoral counseling. "Although Lila figures prominently in my own theology, I have been hesitant to go to it as a source of solace. I think this is partly due to the fact that, to do so effectively would require some shared vocabulary . . . and also a great deal of sensitivity and nuance (lest the person being ministered to feel that they are being told that God is an arbitrary or capricious entity, which is decidedly NOT the traditional Vaishnava understanding of Lila)." Practically, then, in most cases the risks that accompany the idea of "play" as applied to a soothing response to suffering may outweigh the potential benefits.

"Your question," he continued, "does remind me of an interesting (and endearing) story I heard when I visited a Pushti Marg Vaishnava Temple a few months ago. As you might know, this lineage (founded by Sri Vallabhacharya Mahaprabhu) emphasizes a 'radical' meditation on God as [a] playful child and envisages our worship to be in the mood of a surrogate parent tending to that child. . . .

"Once a very devoted Vaishnavi had a tragedy in which unexpectedly her two sons both died. She was despondent and inconsolable, and finally went to see her Guru. The guru, knowing her to be a stalwart and advanced practitioner, was a bit surprised at her grief, and lightly chided her. He told her, 'Hey, ma. Why are you lamenting so much like a common materialist? Did you forget the teachings of Mahaprabhu? Did you forget that you have a third son? Thakurji [the deity of Krishna as a small child] is still there, you still have one lala [darling son] in your home.' She replied, 'Yes, Maharaj, I know that I have one Lala at home. I am lamenting that my Lala has lost his two favorite playmates.' . . . I think in some tellings of the story," Vineet commented, "the Guru falls at the woman's feet and declares her to be the real learned master."[24] What I take from this story is that for a playful God to be a solace, *līlā* has to be squarely central to the theological framework of the devotee. It must antedate the crisis.

Vineet and I also discussed whether *līlā* might better be thought of as an explanation for suffering after the fact, as a sort of second-order meditation on what had occurred when the immediacy of the problem had passed. He concurred, and narrated another story.

"A few years ago, I led a study group that met for a few weeks and looked at a collection of Vallabha's teachings on refuge. . . . This group . . . was somewhat unique, in that (inadvertently) three-fourths of the participants were older folks from a substance abuse recovery background. Most of them were several decades sober, and in fact served as leaders and mentors in the recovery world. Along the way, they (re)discovered spirituality as the core and foundation of their approach to recovery and overcoming addiction. Anyway, they resonated with the Pushti Marg approach so naturally and profoundly that it was astounding. I could see that the teachings about taking refuge and trusting in the Lila of the Divine Beloved were deeply touching their hearts and aligning with their own lived experience. So, considering this study group a sort of 'second-order' pastoral experience, I would say that the play of God definitely does have a role to play in healing and affirming people."[25]

In this context I would also like to mention Jessica Frazier's sensitive comments on Rādhā's experience of acute and unending pain at Krishna's abandonment of the *gopīs* after he goes to Mathura. In her book, *Reality, Religion, and Passion: Indian and Western Approaches in Hans-Georg Gadamer and Rūpa Gosvāmi*, in a section called "The Theodicy of Suffering,"[26] she builds on the insights of Rūpa Gosvāmi, most of whose literary works focus on the period after Krishna has left Vrindavan and when there is no hope, for Rādhā, of escaping her pain of *viraha*. Although Rūpa's audience knows that her pain will eventually become an otherworldly bliss, Rādhā does not care about such. "This is a metaphysical vision of lila as a painful type of play," and the devotee, explains Frazier, must "abandon spectatorial distance and follow Rādhā's example by entering into that hopeless, and wholly absorbed, situation."[27] Meditating on the *līlā*-playing God, in this case, leads to profound sorrow, and precisely because of this, I imagine, Rādhā's experience of divine play might offer, if not an explanation, comfort—in the sense of providing a model for how to react—in acute suffering.

What is central, by contrast, to the Śākta tradition—what, in other words, might arise from this tradition to help worshippers in times of agony—is the philosophical claim of the Goddess's coincidence and transcendence of opposites, which are beyond understanding. Whether it is Durgā or one of her multiforms riding a tiger or lion and striding into battle with demons, her hands wielding weapons while she smiles beatifically; or Kālī, clad in dismembered body parts of her victims and yet showing "fear not" and boon-bestowing gestures with her hands; or Śītalā, covered in small-pox pustules at the same time as she promises release from them, all are icons of the totality of life and death.

Devotees who can see through their pain to the unity of the Goddess find it easier to handle their suffering. The famed Bengali saint and devotee of Kālī, Ramakrishna (1836–1886), died slowly and extremely painfully of throat cancer in the last two years of his life. "It was revealed to me in a vision that during my last days I should have to live on pudding. During my present illness my wife was one day feeding me with pudding. I burst into tears and said, 'Is this my living on pudding near the end, and so painfully?'"[28] And yet, when asked by the future Swami Vivekananda to pray to the Goddess for his own recovery, Ramakrishna reported: "I said to her, 'Mother, I cannot swallow food because of my pain.

Make it possible for me to eat a little.' She pointed you all out to me and said, 'What? You are eating through all those mouths. Isn't that so?' I was ashamed and could not utter another word."[29] He saw that Kālī was all, a view consistent with a Śāktādvaita philosophy. This is not a celebration of the Magician's daughter, but it is a profound acceptance of her.

My mentor and friend, Dr. Minati Kar, also modeled to me how a committed Śākta might handle death. When dying from jaw cancer in 2014, after much of the jaw on one side had been removed, leaving her with a disfigured face and the inability to eat normal food, she wrote to me and said that she did not think of Kālī as having sent the illness to her. Instead, she spoke of the comfort given her by the Compassionate Mother, and said that she had found mercy in the Karālavadanā—the horrible-faced Goddess.

The idea that all, including suffering, grief, and loss, *is* the Goddess, or her illusion, *can* therefore provide comfort and strength. But I suspect that a Hindu chaplain would need to tread carefully in putting this forward in a counseling session. "Your pain is part of the delusory nature of the Goddess" may not help in a situation of immediate crisis—although it could later, upon reflection. What might help is to follow the example of someone who has lived with that all-encompassing Goddess, like a Ramakrishna or a Minati.

Given the Goddess's potency, urging a devotee to pray to her for strength or healing may resonate better with the resources of the Śākta tradition; after all, the Goddess is known for being a demon-killer, for putting things right. In the Bengali *Rāmāyaṇa* she is said to have aided Rāma in his battle with Rāvaṇa;[30] in the "Devī-Māhātmya" she restores the king Suratha's kingdom and gives liberation to the merchant Samādhi;[31] and, closer to our own times, she was adopted as a symbol of rebellion in the Indian Independence Movement from the 1920s on.[32] The "Father of Kālī Studies" in North America, scholar David Kinsley (1939–2000), found the image of Durgā slaying demons to be very helpful as he battled cancer cells in his body.

While Śāktas do not have a concept of a Śākta heaven, like the Vaiṣṇava Vaikuntha, to which devotees may hope to go after death, and while they do not, like the Christian believer, have a suffering God on whom they can pattern their own anguished perseverance, or like the Vaiṣṇava, have a suffering Rādhā who may be seen as a model for living with pain, they can lean upon the strong arm of the Goddess and rely upon the pioneers of their Śākta tradition who have shown how to love and accept her in all her paradoxical kindness. As such, they, like most religious people, may veer away from attributing "responsibility" to the playful or *māyā*-filled deity—at least initially—and focus instead on deriving strength to cope.

Before closing, I want to ruminate on "the God who Plays" in the Christian tradition. Several essays in this volume address playfulness and creativity from a number of Western philosophical and ludic traditions, but as far as I am aware, there are not too many theological texts that take up this theme on behalf of the specific Christian believer. There are a few exceptions, however. Jürgen Moltmann, in his 1972 *Theology of Play*, writes of creation as meaningful but not necessary to God, and as such creation is "God's play, a play of his groundless and inscrutable wisdom. It is the realm in which God displays his glory."[33] Robert E. Neale, in his 1964 doctoral thesis, "Play and the Sacred: Toward a Theory of Religion as Play," and more recently Brian Edgar's 2017 *The God Who Plays: A Playful Approach to Theology and Spirituality*, both consider that the appropriate response of the believer to the idea of God at play[34] is to approach life as an adventure that contains chance, risk, and pain. The aim of the Christian, therefore, should be to delight in this adventure, to see how it will end, just as Jesus did on the cross. "This form of playing is a way of bringing a new reality into the present," says Edgar.[35] Here again one copes by following the example of someone who adopted the right attitude toward God's playful creation.

Despite these few indications and hints, I do not think that God the player is often commended for Christian meditation in times of suffering and pain. Jesus himself apparently loved children and praised their play, guilelessness, and innocence, but the life of Jesus as it has come down to us has almost nothing of the playfulness of the Vaiṣṇava Krishna or the illusory magic of the Goddess. In normative Christian theologies, I suspect that the Līlā Solution to the problem of evil would at best be parried into a Mystery solution, where God's purposes are veiled but must be accepted.

A final thought about the Christian Deus Ludens. There is a noncanonical form of Jesus that first appears in the apocryphal second-century Acts of John, when Jesus commands his disciples to form a circle around him and intone "Amen" as he dances and sings a hymn. It is likely that the idea of Jesus' life and suffering as a dance formed the subject of medieval Mystery Plays. A more modern version of this is the popular Christian hymn, "I am the Lord of the Dance," composed by English songwriter Sydney Carter (1915–2004) in 1963 but sung to an American Shaker song, "Simple Gifts." Carter explained that he got the idea partly from looking at a statue of the dancing Śiva Naṭarāja on his desk.[36] A rendition of the song produced by a group called LordSong is complemented by images drawn by Indian Christian artist-theologians, the most famous being Jyoti Sahi (b. 1944). The choice of Indian artists' work to accompany Carter's "Lord of the Dance" is extremely evocative, I think. Seeing Jesus dancing in a fashion similar to Krishna on Kāliya, or Śiva's dance of creation and destruction; and seeing paintings of his holding sufferers when he dances, makes me think that a Christian in pain might take comfort from Jesus' own self-abandoning joy in the midst of pain. I do not know, but I find it suggestive.

## Five Concluding Thoughts

I conclude with five thoughts, derived from my own playing with the theme of this volume. First, while the Śākta tradition does not celebrate "play" in the same manner as the Vaiṣṇava, it does emphasize the illusory nature of the divine, which, in terms of solving the problem of evil, is just as challenging and elusive: The Goddess's delusory activities may perhaps result in a compassionate gift of liberation, but an acceptance of that gift requires deep faith. Second, insofar as thinking of the divine as a player, or as a magician, "works" for a believer in his or her immediate situation of suffering, it is because the themes of play or illusion are central to the religious worldview of the believer. Third, even if such images are part of the tradition in question, the *līlā* explanation may provide comfort at a later stage of healing, when the devotee can step back and take a larger view. Fourth, even when *līlā* or *māyā* is grasped for solace in the immediate moments of pain, what may provide relief is not the fact of God in play or the Goddess as magical operator but the model of a prior devotee who lived in and with that play or magic. Fifth, as Vineet Chander's story of the recovery group, or my own attraction to the dancing Jesus, shows, there is no predicting what will comfort whom when.

The Goddess brings the world and our souls into being, into play; she plays with us; and she plays for keeps—that is, she does not abandon us. How we live with this belief is the Śākta theological challenge.

## Bibliography


*Ancient Indian Tradition & Mythology: The Linga-Purana*. Translated by a board of scholars and edited by J. L. Shastri. Vol. 6, pts. 1 and 2. Delhi: Motilal Banarsidass, 1973.

Coburn, Thomas B. *Devī-Māhātmya: The Crystallization of the Goddess Tradition*. Delhi: Motilal Banarsidass, 1985.

Coburn, Thomas B. *Encountering the Goddess: A Translation of the Devī-Māhātmya and a Study of Its Interpretation*. Albany: State University of New York Press, 1991.

Dimock, Edward C., Jr. "A Theology of the Repulsive: The Myth of the Goddess Śītalā." In *The Divine Consort: Rādhā and the Goddesses of India*, edited by John Stratton Hawley and Donna Marie Wulff, 184–203. Berkeley: Graduate Theological Union, 1982.

Edgar, Brian. *The God Who Plays: A Playful Approach to Theology and Spirituality*. Eugene, OR: Cascade Books, 2017.

Frazier, Jessica. *Reality, Religion, and Passion: Indian and Western Approaches in Hans-Georg Gadamer and Rūpa Gosvāmi*. Lanham, MD: Lexington Books, 2009.

Geertz, Clifford. "Religion as a Cultural System." In *The Interpretation of Cultures: Selected Essays*, 87–125. New York: Basic Books, 1973.

Hawley, John Stratton Hawley. *Krishna, the Butter Thief*. Princeton, NJ: Princeton University Press, 1983.

Herman, Arthur L. *The Problem of Evil and Indian Thought*. 2nd ed. 1976. Delhi: Motilal Banarsidass, 1993.

Kinsley, David R. *The Sword and the Flute: Kālī and Kṛṣṇa: Dark Visions of the Terrible and the Sublime in Hindu Mythology*. Berkeley: University of California Press, 1975.

Kumar, Pushpendra. *The Principles of Śakti*. Delhi: Eastern Bookliners, 1986.

M (Mahendra Nath Gupta). *The Gospel of Sri Ramakrishna*. Translated by Swami Nikhilananda. Abridged edition. New York: Ramakrishna-Vivekananda Center, 1970.

McDermott, Rachel Fell. "Evil, Motherhood, and the Hindu Goddess Kālī." In *Deliver Us From Evil*, ed. David M. Eckel and Bradley L. Herling. New York: Continuum, 2008. 44–56.

McDermott, Rachel Fell. *Revelry, Rivalry, and Longing for the Goddesses of Bengal: The Fortunes of Hindu Festivals*. New York: Columbia University Press, 2011.

McDermott, Rachel Fell. "Śākta Theological Foundations for Hindu Chaplaincy: How Does the Goddess Help Us Handle Pain and Suffering?" In *Hindu Approaches to Spiritual Care*, edited by Vineet Chander and Lucinder Mosher, 115–122. London: Jessica Kingsley Publishers, 2019.

McDermott, Rachel Fell. *Singing to the Goddess: Poems to Kālī and Umā from Bengal*. New York: Oxford University Press, 2001.

Moltmann, Jürgen. *Theology of Play*. Translated by Reinhard Ulrich. New York: Harper & Row, 1972.

Neale, Robert E. *Play and the Sacred: Toward a Theory of Religion as Play*. 1964. New York: Union Theological Seminary, 1973.

*Rāmāyaṇa Kṛttibās Biracita*. Edited by Harakṛṣṇa Mukhopādhyāy. Kolkata: Sahitya Samsad, 1957.

Rao, K. B. Ramakrishna. "Suffering in Advaita Vedānta." In *Suffering: Indian Perspectives*, edited by Kapil N. Tiwari. Delhi: Motilal Banarsidass, 1986.

Verma, Archana. *Performance and Culture: Narrative, Image and Enactment in India*. Cambridge: Cambridge University Press, 2011.

## Notes

I am grateful to members of the workshop on "Deus Ludens" at the University of Cambridge on January 12, 2019, for helpful comments on this essay.

1. John Stratton Hawley, *Krishna, the Butter Thief* (Princeton, NJ: Princeton University Press, 1983).
2. "The wheel of life and death does not revolve in Kṛṣṇa's heaven. It has permanently stopped to revel in life alone, entranced, as it were, by Kṛṣṇa's bewitching presence." In David R. Kinsley, *The Sword and the Flute: Kālī and Kṛṣṇa: Dark Visions of the Terrible and the Sublime in Hindu Mythology* (Berkeley: University of California Press, 1975), 32.
3. Kinsley, *The Sword and the Flute*, 74.
4. The Latin *ludo/ludere* means to sport, to play, and to play or toy with. It is not far from the last definition to *delude/deludere*, which means to delude. I find it interesting that in Latin, both *līlā* and *māyā* therefore come from the same root.
5. See *Linga Purana* 1:106.25–28, in *Ancient Indian Tradition & Mythology: The Linga-Purana*, translated by a board of scholars and edited by J.L. Shastri, vol. 6, pts. 1 and 2 (Delhi: Motilal Banarsidass, 1973), 6, pt. 2: 581, and Archana Verma, *Performance and Culture: Narrative, Image and Enactment in India* (Cambridge: Cambridge University Press, 2011), 12–28.
6. *Śrīkaṇṭha Bhāṣya* 1.9.10; 1.3.40, edited by R. Chaudhry, as cited in Pushpendra Kumar, *The Principles of Śakti* (Delhi: Eastern Book liners, 1986), 110. Śrīkaṇṭha's thirteenth-century commentary is the best Śaiva commentary on the *Brahmasūtra kārikās*.
7. Two classical studies of the "Devī-Māhātmya" remain crucial for entry into the study of this text: Thomas B. Coburn, *Devī-Māhātmya: The Crystallization of the Goddess Tradition* (Delhi: Motilal Banarsidass, 1985), and *Encountering the Goddess: A Translation of the Devī-Māhātmya and a Study of Its Interpretation* (Albany: State University of New York Press, 1991).
8. See Coburn, *Encountering the Goddess*, 1.34–1.78, pp. 35–39.
9. See "Devi-Māhātmya," 1.58, in Coburn, *Encountering the Goddess*, p. 37.
10. "Devī-Māhātmya," 2.49, in Coburn, *Encountering the Goddess*, p. 43. See also 8.30, p. 65, and 8.62 p. 67. "As if in play," or "delighting in play," is Coburn's rendition of *līlayā*.
11. Kinsley, *The Sword and the Flute*, 75.
12. Rachel Fell McDermott, trans. *Singing to the Goddess; Poems to Kālī and Umā from Bengal* (New York: Oxford University Press, 2001), 48.
13. McDermott, *Singing to the Goddess*, 50.
14. Malcolm McLean, in his "At the Whim of the Goddess: The Līlā of the Goddess in Bengal Śāktism," in *The Gods at Play: Līlā in South Asia*, ed. William S. Sax (New York: Oxford University Press, 1995), 87–96, makes a similar argument but with different examples.

15. Edward C. Dimock Jr., "A Theology of the Repulsive: The Myth of the Goddess Śītalā," in *The Divine Consort: Rādhā and the Goddesses of India* (Berkeley: Graduate Theological Union, 1982), 184.
16. See Rachel Fell McDermott, *Mother of My Heart, Daughter of My Dreams: Kālī and Umā in the Devotional Poetry of Bengal* (New York: Oxford University Press, 2001), 200–201.
17. William S. Sax, *Mountain Goddess: Gender and Politics in a Himalayan Village* (New York: Oxford University Press, 1991).
18. David L. Haberman, *Acting as a Way of Salvation: A Study of Rāgānugā Bhakti Sādhana* (New York: Oxford University Press, 1988), 16.
19. The *dhyānas* of the Goddess are discussed in more detail in Rachel Fell McDermott, "The 'Orientalist' Kālī: A Tantric Icon Comes Alive," in *Revelry, Rivalry, and Longing for the Goddesses of Bengal: The Fortunes of Hindu Festivals* (New York: Columbia University Press, 2011), 161–182.
20. Clifford Geertz, "Religion as a Cultural System," in *The Interpretation of Cultures: Selected Essays* (New York: Basic Books, 1973), 108.
21. This section of my chapter builds on two former publications on related topics: "Evil, Motherhood, and the Hindu Goddess Kālī," in *Deliver Us from Evil*, ed. David M. Eckel and Bradley L. Herling (New York: Continuum, 2008), 44–56; and "Śākta Theological Foundations for Hindu Chaplaincy: How Does the Goddess Help Us Handle Pain and Suffering?" in *Hindu Approaches to Spiritual Care*, ed. Vineet Chander and Lucinder Mosher (London: Jessica Kingsley Publishers, 2019), 115–122.
22. Arthur L. Herman, *The Problem of Evil and Indian Thought*, 2nd ed. (1976; Delhi: Motilal Banarsidass, 1993), 267–271.
23. K. B. Ramakrishna Rao, "Suffering in Advaita Vedānta," *in Suffering: Indian Perspectives*, ed. Kapil N. Tiwari (Delhi: Motilal Banarsidass, 1986), 192.
24. Vineet Chander, email correspondence, December 13, 2018. Quoted with permission.
25. Vineet Chander, email correspondence, December 14, 2018. Quoted with permission.
26. Jessica Frazier, *Reality, Religion, and Passion: Indian and Western Approaches in Hans-Georg Gadamer and Rūpa Gosvāmi* (Lanham, MD: Lexington Books, 2009), 208–212.
27. Frazier, *Reality, Religion, and Passion*, 212.
28. *The Gospel of Sri Ramakrishna*, trans. Swami Nikhilananda, abridged edition (New York: Ramakrishna-Vivekananda Center, 1970), 473, in the diary entry for Wednesday, December 23, 1884.
29. *The Gospel of Sri Ramakrishna*, introduction, 110. "M," or Mahendranath Datta, also reports that Ramakrishna told him that his illness "is the will of the Divine Mother. This is how she is sporting through his body." *The Gospel of Sri Ramakrishna*, 515; diary entry for Thursday, April 22, 1886.
30. See *Rāmāyaṇa Kṛttibās Biracita*, ed. Harakṛṣṇa Mukhopādhyāy (Kolkata: Sahitya Samsad, 1957), 384–385.
31. 13.5–17, in Coburn, *Encountering the Goddess*, 83–84.
32. For examples, see Rachel Fell McDermott, *Revelry, Rivalry, and Longing for the Goddesses of Bengal: The Fortunes of Hindu Festivals* (New York: Columbia University Press, 2011), 64–68.
33. Jürgen Moltmann, *Theology of Play*, trans. Reinhard Ulrich (New York: Harper & Row, 1972), 17.

34. Robert E. Neale, *Play and the Sacred: Toward a Theory of Religion as Play* (1964; New York: Union Theological Seminary, 1973); and Brian Edgar, *The God Who Plays: A Playful Approach to Theology and Spirituality* (Eugene, OR: Cascade Books, 2017).
35. Edgar, *The God Who Plays*, 23.
36. Obituary in *The Telegraph*, 16 March 2004. Online version, accessed 1/2/19.

PART III

# Some Aesthetic and Dramatic Dimensions of *Līlā*

# 7 "You have made me endless, such is thy pleasure"

## THE *LĪLĀ* OF LOVE IN THE METAPHYSICAL POETRY OF RABINDRANATH TAGORE

*Ankur Barua*

In various strands of premodern Hindu devotional poetry, the dialectic of the absence of God and the presence of God is worked out with a rich array of symbolic tools, narrative styles, and ritual expressions. The dialectic, which emerges from scriptural texts such as the *Upaniṣads* (ca. 600 BCE), the *Bhagavad-gītā* (ca. 200 CE), and the *Bhāgavata-purāṇa* (ca. 1000 CE), is shaped by two opposing strands. First, because *Brahman*, the divine reality, is universally present in, and indeed constitutes, every finite reality, *Brahman* is supremely accessible to the human person. To find *Brahman* one does not have to travel to the outermost reaches of the distant galaxies—one turns inward, meditatively or ecstatically, to the interiority of one's spiritual depth (*ātman*). In the characteristic Vedantic vocabularies of Vaiṣṇava devotion (*bhakti*), the supremely personal *Brahman*, Kṛṣṇa, who is the transcendental governor of the cycles of transmigration (*saṃsāra*), is simultaneously accessible to the devotees (*bhakta*)—whether as their little child throwing a tantrum, their mischievous friend grazing cows, or their bewitchingly beautiful lover dancing with them. Second, however, human beings, who are marked by various kinds of worldly privations, cannot encapsulate or comprehend the plenitude of *Brahman*. Thus, throughout Vaiṣṇava devotional literature, we find repeated reminders that the seemingly human Kṛṣṇa is not just another child, not just another friend, and not just another lover.

These reminders are often phrased with the language of *līlā*—we may translate this polyvalent Sanskrit term as "structured spontaneity." From the perspective of Vaiṣṇava Vedānta, *līlā* provides a helpful conceptual pathway to avoid two types of viewpoints regarding divine action. On the one hand, the sovereign Lord is not under any compulsion, whether internal or external—so, the production of the world is not impelled by the chain of logical necessity that inflexibly runs through these two premises, "2 + 2 = 4" and "4 > 3," to their conclusion "2 + 2 > 4." We need an idiom which highlights not conceptual necessitation but existential spontaneity, malleability, and fluidity. On the other hand, however, the Lord does not produce the world as a flippant gesture or unreflective event—this world-directed dynamism is said to be informed by consideration of the accumulated *karma* of embodied selves. The world cannot bind the transcendental Lord, yet the Lord may take delight in a type of voluntary binding to the human devotee—the motifs of *līlā* provide a conceptual space in which we may articulate this paradox of the Lord's "structured spontaneity." In other words, the language of *līlā* makes possible an audacious theological claim—the Lord who has no need whatsoever somehow needs our loving response.

In this chapter, we will explore some expressions of these motifs in the devotional songs of Rabindranath Tagore (1861–1941) who skillfully intermarried premodern Sanskritic and vernacular Bengali idioms in speaking of God with the languages of longing, desolation, separation, joyfulness, love, and fulfillment. Tagore composed around two thousand and two hundred songs, which are collected in a standard compilation titled *Gītabitān*. Of these songs, six hundred and seventeen are placed in the genre of devotional worship (*pūjā*), which articulate themes such as the quest for God, God as the true telos of all human striving, the incomparable sweetness of God who remains hidden in the human heart, the unbearable agony of feeling separated or distant from God, God's enlivening power in the world-weary individual who awakens to see the world bathed in joy, and so on. The symbolic fire of these songs alternately breathes through the tormented anguish of the devotee who feels deserted by God and the gentle peace of the devotee who feels reassured that God's omnipresent embrace yet extends to all finite reality. Across different songs, and at times across different verses within the same song, the poet inhabits oscillating spirals of pain and consolation, despair and hope, and restlessness and equipoise. The multiple iterations of these spirals in Tagore's songs embody one key truth—even though God remains intimately bound up with the world at all times, through a bondage that God undertakes voluntarily, God cannot be domesticated by the world's finitude.

Our discussion will unfold in three stages. We begin with an outline of the theo-logical conundrum that Tagore inherited from premodern

Vedantic Hindu cosmologies of grappling with the ungraspable God and comprehending the incomprehensible God—a riddle that is *dis*solved in these cosmologies with the idiom of God's joyful manifestation in and through the world. We then delineate some contours of Tagore's distinctive patterns of religiosity which are woven with contemplative threads from the *Upaniṣads* and devotional threads from Bengali Vaiṣṇava milieus. In the light of these introductory sketches, we will offer readings of some of his devotional songs where the interplay between the human self and the divine self becomes a dynamic locus of the world's unfurling. The relation between God and the world is shaped by the sinuous circuits of radiant love along which God seeks out and waits on the free response of individuals. This deity-devotee affinity is envisioned in Tagore's songs through two lenses which are perspectivally distinct and yet ontologically interrelated in the manner of a Möbius band. From one vantage point, God remains supremely sovereign over the world in and through which human beings are pursuing their devotional trajectories on their return to God. From another vantage point, however, the metaphysically complete God who lacks nothing delightfully participates in patterns of devotional reciprocity with the devotee—indeed, even "kenotically" waits on the devotee for their participatory (re)turn to the unfolding cosmic joy.

This dual perspective is embodied in the declaration in the title of this chapter, which is also the very first sentence in the first poem in the *Gitanjali*, the collection of poems for which Tagore received the Nobel Prize in literature in 1913. Crucially, the Bengali poem from which this poem is translated has the term *līlā*—which Tagore renders, with a somewhat Victorian flourish, as "pleasure." The term defies straightforward translation into English—its meanings range across "play," "sport," "charm," "beauty," and so on.[1] Such is the nature of God's *līlā*, Tagore suggests through this declaration, that God delights in making us what we can never become if we are left to our own devices—a companion of God lovingly reveling in and contributing to God's ongoing manifestation. Without this divine pleasure, God too would not be *God*—thus, the God who lacks nothing yet waits for our devotional response. As we will see, it is this existential location of the devotee—who, from within sorrowful conditions of finitude, becomes interleaved with God's undiluted bliss—that constitutes the devotee's agony and the devotee's ecstasy.

## The Poignant Presence of Absence

The theological puzzle that is articulated in many of Tagore's devotional songs has textual antecedents in certain verses from the three scriptural corpora noted earlier—the *Upaniṣads*, the *Bhagavad-gītā*, and the *Bhāgavata-purāṇa*. A *locus classicus* of many Vedantic speculations about how the supreme originative source is indivisibly expressed through the divisible world is a set of declarations in the *Chāndogya Upaniṣad*: "In the beginning, my dear, this was Being alone [*sad eva*], one only without a second. Some people say 'in the beginning this was non-being alone [*asad eva*], one only, without a second. From that non-being, being was produced'. But how, indeed, my dear, could it be thus? . . . On the contrary, my dear, in the beginning this was being alone, one only, without a second. It thought, May I be many [*bahu syām*], may I grow forth."[2] In other words, being *qua* being remains utterly one, even as it manifests itself through the world of multiplicity. More precisely, the unicity of being is not antagonistic to, but is accommodative of, the multiplicity of beings. This interweaving of the notions of God's transcendence and God's immanence is articulated tersely in a verse from the *Śvetāśvatara Upaniṣad* which declares that the supreme reality, which is other (*para*) to the world of time and the root from which the world proceeds (*parivartate*), is seated within one's true self (*ātmastha*).[3] Once again, the metaphysical perfection of the divine reality is not tainted by the imperfect world which it supports at all times as its transcendental substratum.

Some of these ontological paradoxes are cast in more distinctively devotional molds in the *Bhagavad-gītā* and the *Bhāgavata-purāṇa*, where the motifs of God's sovereignty and God's accessibility are intricately interwoven with each other. In the eleventh chapter of the *Bhagavad-gītā*, Kṛṣṇa reveals to Arjuna the majestic splendor of his infinite cosmic form, in which Arjuna sees the whole world with all its beings, and Arjuna is struck with fear and bewilderment. Arjuna asks for forgiveness for having presumptuously addressed him as "Kṛṣṇa," "Yādava," and "friend"—unaware of Kṛṣṇa's majesty, whether out of negligence or affection, Arjuna had engaged with Kṛṣṇa disrespectfully, while playing, resting, sitting, and eating (11:41–42). When Arjuna is terrified after witnessing Kṛṣṇa's horrific (*ghora*) form, Kṛṣṇa resumes his gentle (*saumya*) human form to which Arjuna is accustomed (11:49–51).[4] In other words, the human charioteer with whom Arjuna may have engaged in playful banter is, in truth, the divine reality who is the beginning, the middle, and the end of all things—so, the sense that he may have overstepped the bounds of acceptable behavior vis-à-vis God fills Arjuna with trepidation. In the deity-devotee relationship, then, certain bounds do exist, but they may be temporarily suspended by the deity precisely for imparting spiritual insight to the devotee.

This "accommodation" of the deity to the finitude of the devotee is highlighted even more dramatically in the famous narrative from the *Bhāgavata-purāṇa* (10.8.32–45) where Yaśodā tells her infant Kṛṣṇa that his playmates have complained that he has eaten some earth, and is then struck with awe when on peering into his tiny mouth, she sees worlds upon worlds enfolded into its finitude. More specifically, we learn that Yaśodā sees entities such as the sky, islands and oceans, the wind, the fire, the moon and the stars, and so on—along with herself (*sahātmānam*). That is, in this vision of fractal-like reality in which each part is encompassed by and replicated in the whole, not only does her infant microcosmically embody macrocosmic expanses but he also contains her who is gazing at him. Bewildered by what she is seeing, she decides to surrender herself at his feet, considering him to be her refuge (*gati*), when Kṛṣṇa, through his cosmic power, makes her forget the vision, so that she again takes her infant on her lap with maternal affection (*sneha*). This narrative ends with the remark that the supreme reality, whose glories are recited in the three Vedas, the *Upaniṣads*, and other treatises, was regarded by Yaśodā simply as her son (*ātmaja*).[5]

This theme of the finite world as a "fitting" habitation of the infinite reality is further elaborated in five chapters in the tenth book of the *Bhāgavata-purāṇa* (29–33) through the paradigmatic narrative of Kṛṣṇa and the cowherd women (*gopī*). One evening in autumn, when the charming full moon has risen in the sky, Kṛṣṇa begins to play on his flute. So enthralling are the notes of the flute that the cowherd women leave behind their domestic chores and run to the middle of the forest to be with him. They praise him with song, and he responds with his own singing, and takes them to the riverbank suffused with breezes carrying the fragrance of the white lotus. Some of them become filled with pride in thinking that they possess Kṛṣṇa, and suddenly Kṛṣṇa disappears, plunging them into grief.[6] Wracked with pain, they begin to look for Kṛṣṇa everywhere. This agonized quest, during which they discern vivid signs of Kṛṣṇa's absence everywhere, is followed by their reunion with Kṛṣṇa and their rejoicing when Kṛṣṇa joins them in a circle dance (*rāsa līlā*). Highlighting this oscillation of presence and absence, Graham Schweig argues that Kṛṣṇa disguises, through his cosmic power (*māyā*), his majesty and sovereignty (*aiśvarya*), and allows worldly individuals to be related to him with intimacy and sweetness (*mādhurya*). Thus, we find in the chapters of the *rāsa līlā* that the cowherd women alternate between expressing their sense of wonder at Kṛṣṇa's supremacy and their sense of intimacy with him as their beloved.[7]

At the heart of these alternations lies the acute pain of separation (*viraha*) from the divine, and this theme is worked out extensively in the Vaiṣṇava theological traditions as a soteriological means of attaining the divine presence. The argument works as follows: If God is present to us, we might mistakenly think that we possess or control God, and thus even become oblivious to the divine presence in our midst. However, when God disappears from our vision, so excruciatingly painful is this absence to the devotees that they single-mindedly focus their existential core on the absent God, and on the absent God alone. Thus, the *Bhāgavata-purāṇa* (10.29.10–11) states, regarding the women who could not join Kṛṣṇa, that "[the *karma*] from their impious deeds was destroyed by the intense and intolerable pain of separation from their lover, and their auspicious deeds were diminished by the complete fulfilment resulting from the intimate contact with [Kṛṣṇa] that they obtained through meditation. Their bondage was destroyed, and they immediately left their bodies made of the [worldly] *guṇas*."[8] In other words, their lives are broken by the weight of the wound of love, and precisely in that brokenness, which de-familiarizes them from their worldly absorption, lies their liberation from mortal coils. Thus, somewhat paradoxically, the absence of God is soteriologically more powerful than the presence of God in drawing devotees nearer to God—in presence, the complacent devotee may be filled with egocentric satisfaction, but in absence, the grief-struck devotee may become wholeheartedly riveted on God in the spiritual alchemy of love.

One implication of this paradox is that in the case of the supreme devotees of Kṛṣṇa, the more intimately they feel Kṛṣṇa's presence, the more painfully they become aware of Kṛṣṇa's absence, and the more agonizingly they are torn apart by the pain of Kṛṣṇa's absence, the deeper they can move toward the hidden radiance of Kṛṣṇa's presence. They aspire to contain Kṛṣṇa within their earthly habitations, and yet this is a spiritual hunger that cannot be satisfied in worldly circumstances, for the infinite cannot be definitively encapsulated within the bounds of the finite. Thus, the revealed Kṛṣṇa is also the hidden Kṛṣṇa, as much as the hidden Kṛṣṇa carries the soteriological potentiality of moving toward the revealed

Kṛṣṇa. The supremely personal Kṛṣṇa engages in a spiraling dance of absence-in-presence and presence-in-absence with the devotees—in modes of divine presence he makes his devotees aware of his infinitude, which they cannot humanly grasp, so that they apprehend the divine absence. Thus, to push the paradox to its breaking point, in Kṛṣṇa's divine dance with his devotees, Kṛṣṇa's presence *is* Kṛṣṇa's absence.

Now, why does Kṛṣṇa involve, according to these Vaiṣṇava narratives, his human devotees in such cosmic circuits of hide-and-seek, sometimes appearing to them in the mode of a child, friend, and lover, and at other times suddenly disappearing? We have already noted one answer—because the infinite cannot be comprehensively domesticated by the finite human mind, every self-revealing of Kṛṣṇa is simultaneously a self-veiling. We are drawn into the orbit of God by the spiritual gravity of love, then we are de-centered from ourselves when we mistakenly think that we have finally arrived, and then we are drawn even deeper toward God, in continually iterative spirals. Suppose, however, we push this question a step backward to the cosmic "why?": Why does Kṛṣṇa bother at all—in the first place—to generate and participate in these whorls within whorls? Kṛṣṇa could have remained blissfully satisfied in the perfection of his divine being without descending as an *avatāra* to the conditions of human finitude. And yet God is not a distantly detached divinity—such is the power of devotional love (*bhakti*) that God is said to become bound to the devotees. Thus, the *Bhāgavata-purāṇa* (11.2.55) states that the supreme devotees are they whose heart the divine reality does not abandon, for the divine feet are bound to these devotees with ropes of love (*praṇaya*).[9]

In these theo-logical contexts, the motif of *līlā* enables the Vaiṣṇava Vedānta traditions to articulate the claim that when God "condescends" to become bound to humanity, such adaptation to human conditions is a mark not of God's powerlessness but of God's love. These traditions often draw on an aphorism in the *Brahma-sūtra* (2.1.33) that suggests that *Brahman*'s production of the world is to be seen as an unnecessitated expression of the divine delight (*līlā*). Commenting on this aphorism, the Vedantic theologian Rāmānuja argues that the Lord Viṣṇu-Nārāyaṇa is ever self-satisfied (*ātma-tṛpta*) in that the Lord has no desires that are unattained. However, the Lord may delightfully undertake a certain activity not because the Lord stands to gain something from it that was lacking earlier but simply because the Lord finds it inherently delectable. For Rāmānuja, the production of the world is precisely such an activity, namely, the Lord's *līlā*. The only motive that drives the Lord to the production, sustenance, and dissolution of multiple world-orders is *līlā*, which is not impelled by any necessitarian logic. To emphasize this point, Rāmānuja gives the example of a great king who indulges himself in a game of balls not because he wishes to attain anything (he has already conquered the world) but entirely as a sport.[10]

In other words, God's *līlā* betokens a superabundant "excess" that pulsates throughout the finite world riddled with suffering, fragmentation, and limitation. This premodern scriptural motif continues to animate certain contemporary forms of devotional practice in the Braj region of northern India. John Hawley argues that the *rāsa līlās* which are performed there by human actors emphasize the anti-structural dimensions of the supreme divinity who communes with mere cowherds in a land where everything is turned "upside down," and who even becomes sold into the hands of his devotees. Sermons associated with the *līlās* of the young Kṛṣṇa as a butter thief highlight the fact that the land is ruled over by a divinity who is mad (*lavār*) and has freely given up his position of authority in the eternal heaven of Vaikuṇṭha.[11] Crucially, this thievery of Kṛṣṇa, through which he captivates the hearts of his devotees and establishes a bond with them, is depicted as the highest form of theft. This theological reversal is based on a difference between ordinary (*laukika*) theft and the transcendental (*alaukika*) thievery of Kṛṣṇa—whereas human beings steal things belonging to others because of a lack, and if necessary, with force, thereby generating *karmic* demerit, Kṛṣṇa is the transcendental plenitude who lacks nothing. Through his "thievery," Kṛṣṇa only increases love (*prema*) in his devotees, and produces merit (*puṇya*) and auspiciousness (*maṅgal*).[12] Thus, Hawley notes that the *līlās* alternate between elements of Kṛṣṇa's transcendental lordship and Kṛṣṇa's lowly status as a human being, and this oscillation blurs "the distinction between the two levels, running together the human and the divine, conflating amusement and exaltation."[13] So, drawing on Tyler's discussion, we may say that Kṛṣṇa is the superlatively mischievous "trickster" who invites us to become "holy fools" in whose existence a transactional calculus based on egoistic subjectivities becomes effaced by a relationality of human-divine love.

Let us step back from the fine-grained details of these scriptural universes and their contemporary ritual expressions, and draw out one central aspect of the concept of *līlā*. The everyday world that we routinely inhabit and through whose matrices we pursue our needs is structured by a "more-than" dimension, so that the heart of reality is constituted not by a privation but by a fullness. While this divine plenitude or *līlā* of love is not subject to any worldly constraints, it steadily works within and through them, drawing us away from our egocentric dispositions. As we have seen, Kṛṣṇa's *līlā* is not a flippant or nonchalant exercise—through his *līlā*, Kṛṣṇa is engaged in the "serious play" of turning individuals away from their world-immersion and leading them to become more intensely intoxicated with divine love. What is more, the sovereign Kṛṣṇa of bewitching beauty becomes willingly bound to the existential densities of human contexts, whether as a friend, a lover, or an infant. Thus, at the intersection of freedom and necessity, Kṛṣṇa's *līlā* of love is a form of "structured spontaneity"—Kṛṣṇa joyfully inhabits the structures of the world, which are to Kṛṣṇa not a limiting fetter but a locus of spontaneity.

## Tagore's Quests for the Divine Beloved

Tagore creatively reworked these Vaiṣṇava themes into his poems and songs, even if the divinity is usually not named *as* Kṛṣṇa. While some of the clearest resonances of Vaiṣṇava devotional lyrics in Tagore's writings are present in the English *Gitanjali*, with its rich poetic imageries of the quest (*abhisār*) of the individual toward the divine reality, the love between the bride and the bridegroom, the painful torment of separation (*biraha*) of the devotee from the beloved, and so on, Tagore does not mention Vaiṣṇava doctrines or statements. However, Vaiṣṇava conceptual and experiential materials would have been mediated to him along multiple channels from his Bengali religious landscapes. Some women in the Tagore family were devout Vaiṣṇavas and during Tagore's childhood, congregational singing (*kīrtan*) was performed in the Jorasanko house in Calcutta.[14]

Certain Vaiṣṇava inheritances resonate through his expression of wonder at the loving accessibility of God who becomes bound to devotees and his reflections on the centrality of love on the journey to God. Thus, around the age of twenty-two, he wrote a song in which the cowherd children ask Yaśodā to let them take Kṛṣṇa to the fields where they graze cattle. Reflecting on this song later, Tagore writes that these children want to play with Kṛṣṇa, because they wish to see the infinite reality bedecked in beautiful form, and not simply apprehend its majesty (*aiśvarya*).[15] Highlighting the interplay between the human lover and the divine lover, Tagore writes that God cannot stay away from us and indeed serves us in the manner of a mother who serves her child. God could have announced the world with great pomp and fanfare, and yet God seeks to charm us through various means and draw us out to love the world.[16] This dialectic between the notions of the divine as transcendentally sovereign and as supremely accessible is evident in the different terms Tagore uses for God in the songs in the *Gītabitān*, such as *tribhūbaneśvar* ("Lord of the three worlds"), *bhava śaraṇa* ("protector of the world"), *biśvanāth* ("Lord of the world"), *sudūr* ("the distant"), *āmār mānab-janma-tarīr mājhi* ("the helmsman of my life's boat"), *biśva-pitā* ("Father of the universe"), *jībana-nāth* ("Lord of life"), *sakal kājer kājī* ("the agent of all agents"), *rājār rājā* ("the king of kings"), *sajani* ("sweetheart"), *antaratar* ("the intimate"), *prāṇer prāṇ* ("life of my life"), *bandhu mora* ("my friend"), and so on.[17]

In this context, it is important to note that Tagore's religious standpoints defy any straightforward characterization in terms of the standard Vedantic labels such as Advaita, Viśiṣṭādvaita, Dvaita, and so on.[18] At several places in his prose writings, Tagore opposes some of the monastic and ascetic forms of Hindu spirituality, which are often associated with Advaita, but he is equally opposed to certain ecstatic modes of devotional love located in Vaiṣṇava Vedānta worldviews. Tagore's relationship with the cosmologies of Vaiṣṇavism is, therefore, somewhat ambivalent.[19] On the one hand, he argues that Vaiṣṇava forms of self-absorptive ecstasy draw devotees away from active engagement with the world. On the other hand, he skillfully reconfigures the classical Vaiṣṇava motif of a *līlā* of love between the divine lover and the human beloved. This ambivalence is reflected in some of the songs we will discuss in the next section—Tagore does not explicitly refer to Kṛṣṇa, even when it is clear that his song is a variation on the Vaiṣṇava motif of the divine reality who, in a cosmic *līlā*, becomes willingly bound or subservient to the devotee. The transcendental God woos the devotees, and humbly waits on them to return their own love to God.

This theme of the "excess" of God's love is highlighted in Tagore's autobiographical comment that if there is any religious teaching (*dharmatattva*) in his writings, it is that the consciousness of *dharma* is the realization of the relationship of complete love (*paripūrṇa premer*) between the finite self and the supreme self. From one perspective, there is duality, separation, and bondage in this love, and from another perspective, there is nonduality, union, and liberation (*mukti*).[20] The path of love takes away the sense of duality between human beings and the divine reality, whom they learn to discern as the innermost reality in their worldly lives. When we think that God lives in some remote heavenly realm, God becomes a frightening (*bhaẏaṅkar*) reality, and then we resort to various intermediaries to placate this fearsome God. However, when we know God to be our innermost (*antaratar*) reality, all our fear dissolves and we seek to be united with God through the bond of love (*premer yoge*).[21] This spiritual power of love, even more strongly than that of knowledge, draws people together and leads them to the purity of devotion which is not encumbered by scriptural diktats, ceremonial ritualism, and sacerdotal hierarchies. People cannot regard all beings as rooted in the self (*ātmabaṯ*) unless they can activate the highest power of the self, namely, love, and when they do so, the lover of humanity (*mānab-premik*) gains the supreme self in the midst of all human beings.[22] In love, we give ourselves to others freely without making any transactional calculations (*hisāb*) and those who receive love too should not be concerned about their eligibility (*yogyatā*) for it.[23]

The devotional love, then, which Tagore speaks of is characterized by a meditative gravitas as well as a sweet intensity—it keeps the beloved as its center and irradiates its blessedness and sweetness toward everyone in the world.[24] The non-institutionalized pattern of *līlā* that Tagore articulates in his numerous songs was deeply influenced by the folk simplicity and the capacious viewpoints of the itinerant minstrels known as the Bauls. Within the human person, according to the Bauls, lies the "person of the heart" who is beyond all social hierarchies and cultural conventions. Tagore creatively assimilated various aspects of the songs of the Bauls such as their melodies and their imageries, and wove into his poems and songs the Baul themes of the maddening quest for the divine reality in response to the call of the flute, the presence of the eternal reality in the innermost recesses of the heart, the vanity of worldly possessions, the security provided by the divine boatman who takes individuals across the river of the world, and so on.[25] Thus, he writes that the Vaiṣṇava teachings that God's love becomes perfected through our response of love and we are the "complement" of the divine lover are articulated by the Bauls in a way that is "full of the dignified beauty of truth, which shuns all tinsels of ornament."[26] The Bauls experience the divine companionship, and they respond, through their joys and their sorrows, to the divine flute-player who inbreathes love into them.[27]

Tagore's essay "Great and Small" (*Choṭo o Baṛo*, 1913) highlights three central motifs relating to Baul spirituality—the enfoldment of the human heart by the divine heart, the limitlessness of the spirit which cannot be confined to institutionalized systems, and the presence of the divine reality in the individual. He writes that according to the Jewish scriptures, God has created humanity in the divine image (*pratirūp*)—God has generated human beings through an interior self-giving, and this is why we experience in everything a someone who is greater than ourselves (*āpnār ceẏe baṛo ekṭi kāke anubhab*). At certain moments, we get to know the unknown reality beyond limits as present within the bounds of limits, and our heart thirsts restlessly to make the infinite our own (*āmār karte pārbār janye prāṇer byākulatā*). Thus, the Baul sings: "Oh, where shall I find the person of my heart?" The true source of this thirst is the divine reality—by maddening human beings, the divine reality sends them out and does not let them slumber motionlessly. And yet, in referring to the infinite (*asīm*) as the divine father, and in calling out to the infinite with homely terms (*gharer ḍāke*), we are not mistaken, for the divine is not hidden far away but suffuses our homes in every way (*sakal rakam karei bharechen*).[28]

In short, Tagore's Vaiṣṇava-shaped *līlā* nimbly treads a middle path between austere world-renunciation of all affiliations of love, which he rejects, and ecstatic self-forgetfulness in enmeshments of love, which too he rejects. Rather, participation in the *līlā* of God's love should lead individuals to become integrated within themselves and to enact this self-integration in bonds of mutuality with the world. Therefore, just as God does not remain enclosed in a cosmic aloofness but surrenders Godself to human devotees, human beings too should step out of the egoistic encirclements of their everyday lives and find themselves, along the path of love, in and through the other. By thus envisioning everywhere the divine beloved, who has chosen us as partners in the cosmic drama of an unfolding *līlā*, we begin to develop a deep love for all. These themes recur throughout Tagore's meditations in Bengali on the *Upaniṣads* which strike the distinctly Vaiṣṇava notes of the primacy of love on the spiritual path and the voluntary subservience of the deity to the devotee.

Tagore often articulates the motif of the cosmic congruence or harmony (*sāmañjasya*) between the finite self and the divine self in the *līlā* of love where the human devotee and the divine lover are bound together. This nexus of human-divine love is the dynamic locus where worldly dualities become interrelated poles of a deeper unity. Although from a logical perspective, duality (*dvaita*) and nonduality (*advaita*) are opposed to each other, they are yet reconciled on the plane of love, which requires unity as well as duality.[29] Again, in love, loss and gain are not opposed but are congruent—we give ourselves joyfully to the beloved and this self-renunciation itself is our supreme gain. The nature of love also indicates that the divine reality has both personal (*saguṇa*) and impersonal (*nirguṇa*) aspects, for there can be no love without an "I" (*āmi*) just as there can be no love unless the egoistic "I" is abandoned.[30] Therefore, our individuality is not utterly illusory—it is, in fact, an aspect of the *līlā* of love that God has given us a sense of otherness through which the ongoing *līlā* of separation and union is possible. If we seek to become united with the divine reality, we have to become completely independent (*sampūrṇa svādhīn*), since there can be genuine relationality (*ādān pradān*) only between those who are independent. There can be no servility on the path of love—servants can approach the divine reality in the public hall to express their worldly concerns, but they cannot enter the hall for special audiences which is meant for those who have surrendered everything in love.[31]

For individuals whose love is thus perfected, their loves are not satisfied (*tṛpta*) within the ambit of worldly affections—rather, they seek the most intimately beloved reality (*priẏatam*).[32] The supreme self has chosen our inner self and the marriage of the two has been accomplished, so that we are engaged in the infinite *līlā* of love where we continue to find the supreme self in diverse ways through our joys and sorrows. If we as the bride (*badhū*) know that the world is of her lord (*svāmīr saṃsār*) and an expression of her lord's joy, it does not torment us any longer. Instead, we find the bridegroom, who is the eternally attained (*ciraprāptake*), in diverse ways through the circuitous paths of union and separation (*biched-milaner madhye diẏe*).[33] Thus, the divine reality is not a distant monarch but is our co-player who waits on us even when we might remain indifferent to the offer of friendship. Tagore marvels at the astonishing mystery that the divine who is complete bliss diversifies the *līlā* of joy precisely through the incomplete world.[34] If God were simply the monarch of the world, God would have been intensely alone (*eklā*), but impelled by love (*premer jore*), God has renounced absolute sovereignty (*ekādhipatya*) and descended to the "I" as a friend.[35] While the natural world is the domain (*kṣetra*) where God's power (*śakti*) operates, the individual self is the domain where God's love (*prem*) operates.[36]

Tagore's emphasis on the irreducibility of human individuality in the divine *līlā* is clearly articulated in his statement that if there is one thing that is not part of the divine treasure and is uniquely ours, it is our will (*icchā*) which we can truly offer to God. Thus, God is engaged in an astonishing *līlā* with us—God has given us the wealth of our will and stands waiting for us to offer to God our own will.[37] Through the polarities of finding and losing proceeds the supreme *līlā* of our innermost beloved (*antaratam priyatam*) in the abode of the "I" (*āmi-niketanei*).[38] Indeed, it is part of God's *līlā* that God allows us to lose what lies extremely near to us—while the divine is more natural to us than our processes of inhalation and exhalation, we lose the divine so that we are able to find the divine again.[39] However, so that we become capable of giving to God, we have to collect certain objects through the exercise of our own powers and invest these objects with distinctive qualities (*biśeṣatva*). Such a form of energetic construction presupposes a lively "I" which makes our very own certain aspects of the world. Therefore, just as a father lovingly allows his children to win at play, God too admits defeat before us who are without any intrinsic powers, and allows us to think of our worldly activities as our own victories. Without this relegation of divine power, the finite self would not be able to join in the play of joy (*ānander khelāẏ*) and the play of creation (*sṛṣṭir khelāẏ*).[40]

In elaborating this paradox of the sovereign ruler of the universe who voluntarily undergoes a form of self-abasement before human devotees, Tagore quotes the poet Jñānadāsa (ca. 1600 CE) who says to God that he wishes to share with God the divine pain of separation (*biraha-bedanā*):

> I am your loving wife [*premer patnī*]
> What shame do I have, o Lord!
> Make me feel all your pain [*tomār sakal byathār byathī āmāẏ karo*],
>     night and day.
> If there is no sleep in your eyes
> Why should I remain asleep!
> The world is your vast home
> I too am dissolved in that world.[41]

Tagore also quotes an English poet, Edmond Holmes (1850–1936), writing that we hear in the idioms of people from other lands echoes of the audacity (*spardhā*) with which Hindu texts on devotional love (*bhakti*) declare that the desire of the infinite (*ananter icchā*) stands waiting for us at the door of our own desire:

> Thou hast need of thy meanest creature;
> thou hast need of what once was thine:
> The thirst that consumes my spirit
> is the thirst of thy heart for mine.[42]

Indeed, for Tagore, without the free response of human beings, the divine love itself would remain incomplete. Tagore writes that the desire of the divine for us is infinite and is expressed in natural beauty, and issues a call (*ḍāk*) to us to move toward the infinite ocean of the divine heart. We were within the divine heart but have become separated from it, and the divine heart is calling us to return along the path of suffering so that the heart-to-heart union of God and humanity can be completed. Because of the presence of this cosmic pain of separation in the infinite (*ei ekṭi birahabedanā ananter madhye raẏeche*), such a pain of separation is also present in us. We have emerged from the divine heart and when we return after countless ages to the divine heart, we are included in a heart-vibration (*hṛṯ-spandan*) of the infinite reality.[43] Commenting on a song by Vidyāpati (ca. 1400 CE), Tagore writes that though we have not fully attained the Lord, the Lord is yet present to us in our separation (*biraha*). The Lord is, in fact, with us at the beginning of this separation, at its end, and also in the in-between, while playing a plaintive (*karuṇ*) tune on the flute.[44]

However, even though the "I" is the site of human-divine interplay, its egoistic absorption has to be effaced so that the cosmic interrelationalities can be perfectly enacted. We often remain immersed in our temporal possessions, so that we do not perceive the divine reality patiently calling out to us from all sides. Through our volitional independence there emerges untruth, injustice, sin, and impurity, for God has willingly moved away from us to some extent (*ekṭu sare giẏechen*). Just as a mother walks alongside her child who is learning to walk without holding on to the child, God too stays with us and yet is not with us in the domain of our exercise of free choice (*icchār kṣetraṭukute tini āchen, athaca nei*). When devotees are able to dissolve their egoistic attachments and freely align their own will with the divine will (*icchā*), the divine joy is completely expressed in them.[45] In another place, Tagore says that the omnipresent God has given us the entitlement (*adhikār*) to invite God to our homes as our guest (*atithi*). Yet we rarely invite God as our friend (*bandhu*) and instead we keep God waiting at the door. Thus, God sits outside the house with face covered, thinking: "Let's see whether I am called."[46]

However, when individuals perfect their love for the divine reality, joy, beauty, and harmony are made manifest in the world. The indescribable form (*anirbacanīẏa rūp*) of this expression is the form of love, where joys and sorrows are both beautiful, renunciation and enjoyment are both holy (*pabitra*), and loss and gain are both fulfilling. This love brings together in an intense sweetness (*prabal mādhurye*) the near and the far, and relatives and strangers (*ātmīẏake ebaṃ parke*). The infinite then appears as intimately near to us—as father, friend, husband, sharer of our joys and sorrows, and the person of our heart (*maner mānuṣ*). So, Tagore writes, it is not merely the case that there is a place (*sthān*) for us within the divine reality, for there is also a place for the divine reality within us—if the divine is our lover (*premikā*), we are also a lover of the divine.[47]

## A Sonic Theology of Loss and Recovery

Against the conceptual backdrops sketched in the previous two sections, I now explore how the *līlā* of love is elaborated in some of Tagore's devotional songs. I begin with the first song of the English *Gitanjali*—this is a clear articulation of the paradox of God "accommodating" Godself to human conditions. God, who is endless, wishes to engage in *līlā* with a human devotee, and for this *līlā* to be endless, God has to endlessly empty the devotee and revitalize the devotee. Thus, every emptying is a prelude to a self-restoration which itself is oriented to another emptying. At the end of one iteration of the *līlā*, we only stand at the threshold of another iteration—thus, God's *līlā* is not over, and the poet declares: "I only continue to seek."

The next two songs, 2. and 3., articulate the motif of God's self-abasement before the devotee. There may indeed be many accomplished maestros in the divine court, and yet God wishes to hear the singing of a devotee, even if the devotee is only an amateur who sings in solitude with faltering notes. The God of limitless wealth is not satisfied with simply possessing this transcendental plenitude—indeed, God becomes a beggar to receive this plenitude, bit by bit, from the hands of the devotee. The "upside-down" pattern of this interaction—the transcendental source of everything has become impoverished and the destitute devotee has become resourceful—is so ludicrous that the whole world erupts in laughter.

Next, song 4., which happens to be one of the most well-known of Tagore's songs, is a clear articulation of the motif of God's "condescension" to the heart of the devotee. In a declaration of theological audacity, the poet says that without the devotee, God's love would remain unfulfilled. As song 5. indicates, the fulfillment of God's life takes place precisely through the life of the devotee—by giving Godself to the devotee, God beholds the unfurling of divine life *in* the devotee. Whereas mother

Yaśodā sees herself in her God-infant's mouth, in a theological reversal, here God wishes to hear God-inspired songs through the ears of the human composer.

In the next two songs—6. and 7.—the poet's mood shifts from joyfulness at God's presence to anguish at God's absence. The pain of separation too is, in truth, a divine gift, for it keeps the heart continually oriented toward the divine fullness. The mise-en-scène of songs 7. and 8. is the darkness of the desolate night—in the first, the poet has the assurance of God's presence amid the deepening gloom, but in the second, the poet laments the absence of the divine flute-player who had come knocking at the door when he was asleep. Thus, while 7. ends on a note of quiet confidence ("You walked in secret with me on my path"), at the end of 8. the poet inhabits the tentativeness of an unanswered question ("Will you find the one whom you sent away from your home?").

The next five songs—10. to 14.—are different variations on the theme of progressive attunement to God's love. God arrives with a fiery thunder, decentering the heart from its circle of egoistic concerns and reorienting it toward God. This recalibration is a painful purgation, but as the human-divine *līlā* progresses, the devotee becomes rooted and stabilized in God's perfect love. The tangle of egoism becomes incinerated in radiant love, and the divine song begins to resound through the innermost heart and the whole world.

1. You have made me endless, such is your *līlā*—
Emptying me, you have again filled me with new life.
On so many hills and so many river shores
You have roamed carrying this little flute,
Playing again and again so many notes
To whom can I ever tell?
At your immortal touch, my little heart
Loses itself in supreme joy and breaks out in song.
Filling up only my little fist
You give to me day and night
Countless ages pass and you are not finished
I only continue to seek.[48]

2. You came down from the seat of your throne—
Pausing, you stood at the door of my lonely home, Lord.
Sitting by myself, I was singing my own song
The tune caught your ear, you came down—

Pausing, you stood at the door of my lonely home, Lord.
At your court there is so much singing, there are so many masters—
This amateur's song came alive today in your love!
A piteous tune was struck in the midst of the world-melody,
You came down with a garland of honour in your hands—
Pausing, you stood at the door of my lonely home, Lord.[49]

3. Infinite is your wealth, yet you are not satisfied with that
You wish to take it from my hands, bit by bit.
Giving away your jewels you have made me rich—
Now you come calling at my door, the door that is kept shut.
You would make me the giver [*dātā*], and you would become the
beggar [*bhikkhu*]—
The whole world is delirious with laughter.
You do not stay on that chariot, you have come down to the dusty path—
You will walk with me through all the ages.[50]

4. Thus is your joy with me
This is why you have come down to me—
Without me, o Lord of the three worlds,
Your love would have been in vain.
With me you have started this fair,
Delight plays in my heart,
Your own will takes varied forms
And ripples through my life.
Thus you, the king of kings,
Roam through my heart in captivating attire,
Lord, you are ever awake.
Thus, o Lord, you have come to me
Your love is in the love of the devotee's heart [*bhaktaprāṇer preme*]
There your form, in the union of the two
Is expressed in its fullness.[51]

5. O my Lord, filling up my body and life
What nectar [*amṛt*] is it that you wish to drink?
This picture of your world in my eyes
You seek to observe, my poet,
Silently dwelling in my enchanted ears
You wish to hear your own songs.
Your creation composes in my mind

Your own varied forms.
Your love, o Lord, mingles with them
And awakens all my songs—
You gaze on me in your sweet delight [*madhur rase*]
By giving yourself unto me as a gift![52]

6. At the end of the night, who has brought to me in secret
The jewel of your pain of separation [*biraha-bedanā-mānikkhāni*]
I will keep in my heart that gift of sorrow—
So that I do not lose it in the complicated tasks of the day,
Let it sway in my heart, overcoming all worry.
This eternal sorrow will be my eternal treasure,
And will be fulfilled in my final worship.
Let it glow in secret in the dense darkness
of the night filled with dreams when I am bewildered
For that is your silent call unto me.[53]

7. Across this space of separation [*biraher antarāle*] between you and me
How many more bridges do I build—with tunes and melodies.
Yet a sorrow strikes in secret in my heart—
Call out to me to serve you this time at the hour of dusk.
I stay away from the world in the inner quarters of the heart,
My mind is enveloped by webs of dreamy thought.
Joys and sorrows are mine alone and that burden grows heavy,
May I be able to surrender them on the tray of true worship.[54]

8. You have held me with both hands in the darkness.
When did you come, o Lord, with soft footsteps?
I thought I had lost you, the Lord of my life [*jīban-svāmī*]—
I know tonight that you will not lose me.
That night when I put out the light with my own hands
You shone your north star [*dhruba-tārā*] brightly in the darkness.
When I finished walking along your path, I saw
You walked in secret with me on my path.[55]

9. My heart, when you did not wake up,
The companion of your heart [*maner mānuṣ*] came to the door.
Hearing the sound of his going away, you woke up—
You woke up in the darkness.
Lying on the ground on your sari's end, you spend the night alone,

His flute sounds in the darkness, but you do not see him.
The one whom you let pass by, can your eyes find that one?
Setting out now on the road,
Will you find the one whom you sent away from your home?[56]

10. The pain was indeed terrible when you were tuning the strings—
Play the *bīṇā*, make me forget all sorrowful things.
What had remained hidden in your mind all these days
Let me hear it today on my strings.
Do not delay any longer, the lamp is going out.
The night waits at the door, listening.
The tune that you set to star after star, in a never-ending stream of fire,
Play out your eagerness [*byākulatā*] in my heart with that tune.[57]

11. From where does it strike, alas, this torment of love
[*prema-bedanā*]!
Slowly and slowly, I think, my friend comes
To the darkened courtyard of my heart.
Cast aside all your poverty [*dainya*]
Wake up in joy, my heart.
Light all your lamps, light them—
Call out eagerly, "Come, my dearest [*priyatam*]."[58]

12. Today I will exchange my pride with your garland.
At the closing of the night let me end the story of tears.
I have thrown away to the wayside my hard heart,
Your feet will give it a sweet touch that melts stone.
I had darkness around me but you pulled it away,
Your love came as fire and illuminated it.
That "I" [*āmi*] was to me the most valuable thing,
I have exhausted it in bedecking your ceremonial tray.[59]

13. You played different tunes on your flute in the day—
Your songs touched my heart, but you remained far away.
I ask wayfarers, "Who is playing on this flute?"—
They confuse me with different names, and I go to many doors.
Now the sky is dimmed, the tired day closes its eye—
If you send me back to the roads, I will die in a futile search.
Leave the outside world and lay a seat for yourself inside—
Come and play your flute in my soul's inner home [*prāṇer
antaḥpure*].[60]

14. When I was blind,
Time passed by in games of happiness [*sukher khelāẏ*], but I did not find joy [*ānanda*].
I set up walls around the playhouse, I was lost in my own fancies,
When you came into the house, breaking the foundations, my bondage ended.
Games of happiness do not delight me any more, I have found joy.
My terrible [*bhīṣaṇ*] Lord, my destroyer [*rudra*], my little sleep has gone—
With sharp pain you set anew my rhythms.
The day you came in a fiery dress and took away all I had
That day I become whole, all my conflicts [*dvanda*] were dispelled.
Beyond sorrow and happiness, I have found you, true joy.[61]

## Conclusion

Across these fourteen songs, we hear different voices of God's *līlā* rippling through Tagore's religious cosmos. They alternately employ the languages of lament and delight, losing and finding, and hoping expectantly and receiving consolation. At times, the poet is enraptured by the divine presence which suffuses the filigrees of his mortal being, while at other times, the poet is distraught in the dark night of the soul when the divine absence pervades the world.

Placing these songs in the *longue durée* of Vedantic Hindu theological worldviews, we see how deeply saturated they are by symbolisms, narratives, and experientialities drawn from texts such as the *Upaniṣads*, the *Bhagavad-gītā*, and the *Bhāgavata-purāṇa*. The "I" is on the pathway of progressive purification in the crucibles of God's fiery love so that it can respond spontaneously to, and participate in, the call of divine love. This is why the "I" is caught in spirals of absence and presence—it *is* what it needs to be (namely, the individual who possesses the volitional independence to turn toward or away from God) and it is *not* yet what it should become (namely, the individual whose volitional delight is to always turn toward God). Each "I" is the dynamic site of the *līlā* of love, and when it overcomes its egocentric opacity and walks along the pathway of selfless transparency, it may become interleaved into a cosmic tapestry through which the divine love courses freely. This primordial *līlā* was not initiated by any finite being—indeed, God is its source, basis, and telos. It is from God's superabundant "excess" or "structured spontaneity" that mediates freedom and necessity that the *līlā* simultaneously unfolds through human densities and surpasses them. Divine *līlā* is the cosmological template for quotidian enactments of human *līlā*—thus, the effortless virtuosity with which a pianist may play Rachmaninov would have been generated by years, even decades, of methodical and painstaking practice.

These themes are concisely articulated by Tagore in a meditation from 1910 where he outlines the identity-in-difference and the difference-in-identity between the "I" and God. God does not seek to erase the "I," which is the abode of worldly conflicts (*dvanda-niketan*), for it is the existential space through which God's love is expressed. God draws out the "I" from, and God draws the "I" toward, the eternal heart. In a moment of infinite separation, God makes the "I" other than God, and in a moment of infinite love, God makes it God's own. Thus, no matter how insignificant (*kṣudra*) a particular "I" might be, if this "I" were to be lost, all cosmic calculations would become destabilized.[62]

In this sense, God's *līlā* is the "eternal now"—at every moment, the world passes away and is constantly renewed so that the *līlā* may proceed unimpeded in the "I," through all its agonies and joyfulness. This is the note on which we will end our explorations with another song from Tagore.

The treasure of my heart—
I lose you, moment to moment
Only so that I will find you again.
You move away from my sight
Only so that you will appear before me, again.
Indeed you are not veiled from me
You are mine for all times
You become immersed in a moment's *līlā*.
When I set out in frantic search of you
My heart trembles in fear
Waves of love break over me.
You are endless—
Thus you empty yourself by donning the garment of emptiness
My tears of separation touch your smile.[63]

## Bibliography

Beck, G. L. "Song: Two Braj Bhāṣā Versions of the *Rāsa-Līlā Pancādhyāyī* and Their Musical Performance in Vaisnava Worship." In *The Bhāgavata Purāṇa: Sacred Text and Living Tradition*, ed. R.M. Gupta and K.R. Valpey. New York: Columbia University Press, 2013.

Bhatt, S. R. *Studies in Rāmānuja Vedānta*, New Delhi: Heritage Publishers, 1975.
Bryant, E. F., trans. *Krishna: The Beautiful Legend of God*. London: Penguin Books, 2003.
Chaudhuri, A. *On Tagore: Reading the Poet Today*. Oxford: Peter Lang, 2013.
Chunkapura, J. *The God of Rabindranath Tagore: A Study of the Evolution of His Understanding of God*. Kolkata: Visva-Bharati, 2002.
Dimock, E. C. "Rabindranath Tagore—'The Greatest of the Bāuls of Bengal.'" *Journal of Asian Studies* 19 (1959): 33–51.
Ghosh, B. *Dharmapathik Rabīndranāth*, Calcutta: Bookland, 1969.
Haberman, D. L. *Acting as Way of Salvation: A Study of Rāgānugā Bhakti Sādhana*. New York: Oxford University Press, 1988.
Hawley, J. S. *Krishna, The Butter Thief*. Princeton, NJ: Princeton University Press, 1983.
Kapoor, O. B. L. *The Philosophy and Religion of Śrī Caitanya*. New Delhi: Munshiram Manoharlal Publishers, 2008.
O'Connell, J. T. "Tracing Vaishnava Strains in Tagore." *Journal of Hindu Studies* 4, no. 2 (2011): 144–164.
Radhakrishnan, S. *Bhagavadgītā*. London: George Allen & Unwin, 1948.
Radhakrishnan, S. *The Principal Upaniṣads*. London: George Allen & Unwin, 1953.
Ray, B. G. *The Philosophy of Rabindranath Tagore*. Calcutta: Progressive Publishers, 1970.
Schweig, G. *Dance of Divine Love: India's Classic Sacred Love Story: The Rasa Lila of Krishna*. Princeton, NJ: Princeton University Press, 2018.
Tagare, G. V., trans. *Bhāgavata-purāṇa*. Delhi: Motilal Banarsidass, 1955.
Tagore, R. *Creative Unity*. London: Macmillan, 1922.
Tagore, R. *Gītabitān*. Calcutta: Visva-Bharati, 1931.
Tagore, R. *Jīban-smṛti*. Calcutta: Adi Brahmo Press, 1912.
Tagore, R. *Rabīndra Racanābalī*. 27 vols. Calcutta: Visva-Bharati, 1965–1971.
Thibaut, George. *The Vedānta-Sūtras: With the Commentary by Rāmānuja*. Delhi: Motilal Banarsidas, 1971. Radhakrishnan, S. *Bhagavadgītā* (London: George Allen & Unwin Ltd, 1948).

## Notes

1. D. L. Haberman, *Acting as Way of Salvation: A Study of Rāgānugā Bhakti Sādhana* (New York: Oxford University Press, 1988); O. B.L. Kapoor, *The Philosophy and Religion of Śrī Caitanya* (New Delhi: Munshiram Manoharlal Publishers, 2008); G. L. Beck, "Song: Two Braj Bhāṣā Versions of the *Rāsa-Līlā Pancādhyāyī* and Their Musical Performance in Vaisnava Worship," in *The Bhāgavata Purāṇa: Sacred Text and Living Tradition*, ed. R. M. Gupta and K. R. Valpey (New York: Columbia University Press, 2013), 181–201; J. S. Hawley, *Krishna, The Butter Thief* (Princeton, NJ: Princeton University Press, 1983).
2. S. Radhakrishnan, *The Principal Upaniṣads* (London: George Allen & Unwin, 1953), 448–449.
3. Radhakrishnan, *Upaniṣads*, 745.
4. S. Radhakrishnan, *Bhagavadgītā* (London: George Allen & Unwin, 1948), 284–88.
5. G. V. Tagare, trans., *Bhāgavata-purāṇa* (Delhi: Motilal Banarsidass, 1955), 1302–1303.
6. Tagare, *Bhāgavata-purāṇa*, 1431–1442.
7. G. Schweig, *Dance of Divine Love: India's Classic Sacred Love Story: The Rasa Lila of Krishna* (Princeton, NJ: Princeton University Press, 2018), 135–136.

8. E. F. Bryant, trans., *Krishna: The Beautiful Legend of God* (London: Penguin Books, 2003), 126.
9. G. V. Tagare, trans., *Bhāgavata-purāṇa* (Delhi: Motilal Banarsidass, 1955), 1902.
10. George Thibaut, *The Vedānta-Sūtras: With the Commentary by Rāmānuja* (Delhi: Motilal Banarsidas, 1971), 477; S. R. Bhatt, *Studies in Rāmānuja Vedānta* (New Delhi: Heritage Publishers, 1975), 99.
11. Hawley, *Krishna, The Butter Thief*, 272–273.
12. Hawley, *Krishna, The Butter Thief*, 230–231.
13. Hawley, *Krishna, The Butter Thief*, 269–270.
14. J. T. O'Connell, "Tracing Vaishnava Strains in Tagore," *Journal of Hindu Studies* 4, no. 2 (2011): 148.
15. R. Tagore, *Jīban-smṛti* (Calcutta: Adi Brahmo Press, 1912), 171–172.
16. R. Tagore, *Rabīndra Racanābalī*, 27 vols. (Calcutta: Visva-Bharati, 1965–1971), 13: 470–471.
17. J. Chunkapura, *The God of Rabindranath Tagore: A Study of the Evolution of his Understanding of God* (Kolkata: Visva-Bharati, 2002), 130–132.
18. B. Ghosh, *Dharmapathik Rabīndranāth* (Calcutta: Bookland, 1969); B. G. Ray, *The Philosophy of Rabindranath Tagore* (Calcutta: Progressive Publishers, 1970).
19. A. Chaudhuri, *On Tagore: Reading the Poet Today* (Oxford: Peter Lang), 8–9.
20. Tagore, *Rabīndra Racanābalī*, vol. 27, 238.
21. Tagore, *Rabīndra Racanābalī*, vol. 26, 566–567.
22. Tagore, *Rabīndra Racanābalī*, vol. 26, 470.
23. Tagore, *Rabīndra Racanābalī*, vol. 27, 209.
24. Tagore, *Rabīndra Racanābalī*, vol. 5, 514.
25. E. C. Dimock, "Rabindranath Tagore—'The Greatest of the Bāuls of Bengal,'" *Journal of Asian Studies* 19 (1959), 33–51.
26. R. Tagore, *Creative Unity* (London: Macmillan, 1922), 84–85.
27. R. Tagore, *Creative Unity*, 87.
28. Tagore, *Rabīndra Racanābalī*, vol. 5, 449–450.
29. Tagore, *Rabīndra Racanābalī*, vol. 13, 467.
30. Tagore, *Rabīndra Racanābalī*, vol. 13, 468–469.
31. Tagore, *Rabīndra Racanābalī*, vol. 13, 465–467.
32. Tagore, *Rabīndra Racanābalī*, vol. 13, 395.
33. Tagore, *Rabīndra Racanābalī*, vol. 14, 336–337.
34. Tagore, *Rabīndra Racanābalī*, vol. 13, 532.
35. Tagore, *Rabīndra Racanābalī*, vol. 13, 518.
36. Tagore, *Rabīndra Racanābalī*, vol. 13, 532.
37. Tagore, *Rabīndra Racanābalī*, vol. 13, 521.
38. Tagore, *Rabīndra Racanābalī*, vol. 13, 515.
39. Tagore, *Rabīndra Racanābalī*, vol.14, 490–491.
40. Tagore, *Rabīndra Racanābalī*, vol. 14, 377–378.
41. Tagore, *Rabīndra Racanābalī*, vol. 16, 369–370.
42. Tagore, *Rabīndra Racanābalī*, vol. 16, 368.
43. Tagore, *Rabīndra Racanābalī*, vol. 16, 369.
44. Tagore, *Rabīndra Racanābalī*, vol. 15, 473–474.

45. Tagore, *Rabīndra Racanābalī*, vol. 16, 367–368.
46. Tagore, *Rabīndra Racanābalī*, vol. 16, 504–505.
47. Tagore, *Rabīndra Racanābalī*, vol. 16, 372.
48. R. Tagore, *Gītabitān* (Calcutta: Visva-Bharati, 1931), 28.
49. Tagore, *Gītabitān*, 124.
50. Tagore, *Gītabitān*, 37–38.
51. Tagore, *Gītabitān*, 123–124.
52. Tagore, *Gītabitān*, 40.
53. Tagore, *Gītabitān*, 62.
54. Tagore, *Gītabitān*, 62.
55. Tagore, *Gītabitān*, 39.
56. Tagore, *Gītabitān*, 216–217.
57. Tagore, *Gītabitān*, 93.
58. Tagore, *Gītabitān*, 173–74.
59. Tagore, *Gītabitān*, 30–31.
60. Tagore, *Gītabitān*, 237.
61. Tagore, *Gītabitān*, 218.
62. Tagore, *Rabīndra Racanābalī*, vol. 15, 509–510.
63. Tagore, *Gītabitān*, 24–25.

# 8 The Metaphysics of Emotion

## DIVINE PLAY IN CAITANYA VAIṢṆAVA PHILOSOPHY

*Jessica Frazier*

Is Being itself a thing of value wherever and insofar as it is the case? Or is it simply the value-neutral proliferation of things, or even a negative phenomenon that increases worldly suffering—as many soteriological traditions suggest when they encourage mortals to abandon the embodied realm? The question applies questions of value to ontology, asking whether it is better for there to be a world of manifold forms in active relation, escalating ever-new thoughts and emotions, than for there to be unchanging, simple Being, or none at all. In short, do we feel that more is better, where Being is concerned? In this chapter I show how the concept of *līlā*, in addition to being a theology of grace and a practice of spiritual participation, expresses key insights into the natural creativity, artistic sophistication, and dramatic value of existence itself.

The doctrine of divine play in the early modern Caitanya Vaiṣṇava school of Vedānta explores this metaphysical puzzle. In a culture where some people valued pure, unchanging, undivided, and abstract existence (e.g., the Advaita school), and some even preferred "emptiness" (Madhyamaka Buddhists), the Bhedābheda Vedānta school celebrated the divine as a fundamental reality full of active powers that naturally lead it to flow into the world, and transform into infinite new forms from which are emergently generated ever-new levels of reality. In terms that Douglas Hedley applies to Plotinus in the present volume, they were committed to "the playful spontaneity of the first principle." Yet they also saw it in terms of its upbuilding creativity of emotionally powerful, sophisticated high-order phenomena like persons, relationships, passions, and arts.

Across more than two millennia from the *Chāndogya Upaniṣad* through to early modern Vedānta, we see various accounts of why the fundamental reality creatively evolves in this way. The divine Krishna's dance, musical skill, and pastoral love stories were a visceral expression of this: Why should the deity play, rather than sit in still contemplation like meditative Śiva? As the twelfth-century Vedāntic theologian Rāmānuja put it, why should a king who enjoys all pleasures and rules the whole realm, seek to match his wits against a ball-game? (See Sucharita Adluri's chapter in the present volume.) Alternatively, to borrow the Caitanya Vaiṣṇava analogy, why would one enact a powerfully passionate drama . . . rather than merely a peaceful withdrawal into stillness where there is no risk, no suffering?

Many of the Vedāntic schools of Indian thought answered this question in a somewhat apologetic way, since they recognized that however positive divine play is, it is nevertheless ultimately responsible for the sufferings of the world as well as the misdeeds of we free-willed creatures. Thus the Viśiṣṭādvaita tradition discussed by Adluri and Clooney in the present volume emphasized that play goes along with divine grace, which mitigates the negative effects of ignorant and contrarian souls. As Clooney notes, for Viśiṣṭādvaita, seeing the divine via its embodied worldly form can only happen "by grace and over a long purification process," and with the caveat that ultimately "God cannot be seen with the physical eyes." Further, we should beware of thinking that the creation in all its forms and dramas flows "of necessity" from the divine nature; it is a contingent expression that could, presumably *not* have happened. The magical play of the Goddess, which McDermott discusses in her chapter, has the divine appear almost incorrigibly cruel for binding souls with the thread of worldly attachment and making them dance—even though we are also provided with the advice needed to advance toward liberation. Even Tagore, as Barua shows, was both celebratory of divine presence and also solicitous that the divine not become "domesticated by the world's finitude." But compared with those approaches, the Acintya Bhedābheda Vedānta theology of the Caitanya Vaiṣṇavas seems least apologetic for divine creation, and most willing to place the creative sophisticated scintillatingly dramatic artfulness that the world demonstrates at the heart of the divine nature—asserting that aesthetic enjoyment (*hlādinī*) is an essential power (*svarūpa śakti*) inalienable from the divine nature, and its products exist eternally.

Philosophically, this school took the theological question of why the divine plays to be linked to more strictly metaphysical ones: Does existence per se or in increased diversity and sophistication of forms have innate value? Is reality essentially the same at all levels—whether as something basic like a mere space-time framework or mass of particles, or as something more ontologically developed like an organism, consciousness, personality, or complex artistic feeling? Is reality structured as a hierarchy of Being, with greater complexity, creative capacity, and value as we ascend through emergent levels? Alternatively, we may think that entities seem to diminish in quality or significance as they depart from their underlying ground—so that objects, systems, and even consciousness are less than pure existence in a timeless, changeless, and simple state. This view was held by those who favored the idea of an abstract (*nirguṇa*), unqualified (*nirviśeṣa*), simple (*advaita*), and pure (*śuddha*) form of Being.

As the philosopher J. G. Arapura once noted, the fork in views about the value of contingent beings relative to their ultimate ontological ground was central to debates in Hinduism's school of Vedānta.[1] It prefigures debates in modern metaphysics about whether we should view the world in terms of a hierarchical stratification of reality with more and less fundamental levels,[2] and whether apparently second order phenomena are "ontologically innocent" or "ontologically loaded" additions to the book of the world.[3] These questions were linked to Indian discussion of whether the world should be seen as a real transformation (*pariṇāma*) of the divine into something different, or merely a manifestation (*vyakti*) of its innately "full" (*pūrṇa*) generative power (*śakti*), or a diminishing lower level (*vyāvahārika*) form of reality, downgraded to the merely apparent (*māyā*), seeming (*ābhāsa*) or limited (*upādhi*) existence. The dialectic of views can be seen as a centuries-long grappling with this question of the value of Being.

This question is also of interest to philosophers of the divine nature, who seek to understand what the act of world-creation tells us about the divine. So too, it is a problem for theodicy, which must weigh up the value that making the world might have had in the first place, against the disvalue of creating suffering, cruelty, and finitude. In medieval Europe divine creativity and its motivations led Aquinas to reason that God must have creative power as a defining feature of his essence.[4] So too, we will see that the Bhedābheda tradition invoked creative power and the aesthetic responses it enables to justify *divine creation* with its bittersweet legacy of minds, lives, relations, art, and emotion.

## The Philosophy of Dramatic Divinity

Hindu theological debates about the divine nature and the value (or not) of human life were caught up in the dialectic between schools like Advaita Vedānta, which saw empirical reality as something unreal and of little value, and schools like Bhedābheda Vedānta, which saw empirical reality as a natural outpouring, manifestation, or transformation (a *sṛṣṭi*, *vyakti*, or *pariṇāma*) of the divine ground itself. A particularly mature version of Bhedābheda's affirmative position was advanced by the sixteenth-century Caitanya Vaiṣṇava school of Vedānta; it combined metaphysics, theology, and aesthetics to depict the divine as naturally disposed to create a world in which the most intense and sophisticated emotions can emerge. The school saw divine activity not merely as *play*, but as *drama* that should be rich in melodramatic zest.

According to their distinctive doctrine of Acintya Bhedābeda Vedānta ("inconceivable difference-in-non-difference"), the divine possesses infinite powers that naturally manifest in the many types of beings, the relations they instantiate, the conscious minds that perceive it all, and the aesthetic feelings invoked by it all in those very minds. As they put it, the divine is the enjoyer, the object of enjoyment, and the joy all in one dialectically complex package. Indeed, its essential nature was said to be bliss that is naturally active like the flickering of a fire.

Rūpa Gosvāmī (1489–1564) gave theological interpretations of the poetic literature that described the God Kṛṣṇa's incarnate life among mortals, portraying the divine life as a play of passions meant to rouse the devotee until they are "split in two, swayed by anger, now by love"[5] at the thought of God's provocatively delightful nature. Kṛṣṇa creates the world through immanent causation, manifests all of its contents, and participates in it as a personal deity and an incarnate protagonist. But rather than incarnating for the purpose of sacrifice, he incarnates in order to heighten emotion. Flowing from this rationale, "The Absolute then is an eternal love affair between God and himself . . . played out forever with all its humour and tenderness, frenzy and abandon."[6] The divine nature is manifested in the pleasing geometry of Krishna's dance, the arabesques of vines and wantonly unraveled saris that ornament the pastoral setting of his incarnation; the literature describing the divine play amplifies this through analogy, rhythm, and alliteration, all manifesting the creative, evocative divine nature.

In Rūpa Gosvāmī's literature God seems mutable, complex, and passible. Where we may expect divinity to be defined by its freedom, instead it prefers "commitment in love"—not only for its followers but also for itself.[7] Kṛṣṇa is emotionally enmired in the complex world of his own making, so deeply moved at the thought of a lost love that he becomes filled with longing for what is in truth a manifestation of his own nature; he is transfixed by his own worldly creation,[8] and experiences sufferings as great as the "mighty mountain Meru," fevers that make one seek the shelter of death.[9] In short, Rūpa's *dramatic* account challenges the usual depiction of divine play as a pleasantly ludic form of exalted leisure. Instead, there is risk and danger, pain and passion. In this he charted a middle way between the pastoral narratives of early medieval texts like the *Bhāgavata Purāṇa*, and the fiercely psychological drama of later medieval poems like the *Gītāgovinda*. This is a fundamental reality best expressed in a world of emotional intensities.

Here, as in the Western traditions of *Deus Ludens*, divine play can seem to contradict divine attributes of *immutability, eternity* (in the sense of being outside of time), *sovereignty* (not being dependent on anything), and *simplicity* (in the sense of having no internal divisions). In what follows, I consider the way this school contributed its own nuance to Bhedābheda Vedānta's affirmation of worldly being.[10] This school added the views that (a) naturally active potencies are at the heart of reality; (b) if reality involves a hierarchy of emergent levels of existence (e.g., time and space, particles, aggregates and patterns, matter, life, relations, consciousness, ideas, and emotions), then there is reason to accord most value to the higher levels; (c) the most complex, intense, comprehensive emotions must have a particularly high value.

To borrow terms from modern Western philosophy of religion, these views produced a "theology that understands God's creativity as constituting, supporting and proliferating the capacities of the world of creation" in accord with the "internal self-realization" of the fundamental reality that grounds the cosmos.[11] The idea that intensely dramatic forms of existence most deeply reflect the divine nature, echoes the Caitanya Vaiṣṇava view that being is *consciousness,* dialectically entailing the structures of affective response. On this account, the divine *must* express itself relationally,[12] in a "self-referral play" *as* and *in* the world.[13] In the sections below I look more closely at two specific pillars of this philosophy of divine play. These are the idea of the divine as (a) possessed of intrinsic powers (*śaktis*) that naturally tend toward full expression (*pūrṇatva*) and (b) generating or manifesting (*vyañjana, vyakti*) a world of emotional values via the narrative complexity these powers create.

## Bhedābheda and the Richness of Reality

The Bhedābheda tradition of Vedāntic nondualism offered the most robustly *realist* account of the world that was willing to admit transformation and complexity in the ultimate divine ground of things. It bears some similarities to the thought of Spinoza.[14] One early source of the notion of *Brahman*, the ontological ground, medium, and sufficient material, efficient, and formal cause of the world, may have been the original meaning of the word as "a power of being, known in the phenomenon of growth, expansion . . . the hidden power of being behind all beings, behind being itself."[15] In the ca. 800 BCE sixth chapter of the *Chāndogya Upaniṣad* (from which the Bhedābheda tradition took its key motif of a self-proliferating god), the generation of the cosmos is attributed to a divine wish to pro-create (*pra-ja*) and become many.[16] In the slightly later *Kena Upaniṣad,* the potencies that move the natural world—fire, wind, and the chief of the gods—are ultimately attributed to the one divine being, Brahman. The *Śvetāśvatara Upaniṣad* speaks of the divine as a person rich in potencies (*śaktis*) with many heads, hands, and feet, looking out through every being, and possessing a magical power of illusion-making.[17] It undertakes the work of creation and draws it back again over and over, joining itself with the realities and with time repeatedly. Yet all this takes place without motivation or cause (*kāṃya* or *kāraṇa*) but with diverse intrinsic potencies (*śaktir vividhaiva . . . svābhāvikī*).[18]

The *Śvetāśvatara Upaniṣad* helped to initiate a *powers-rich* conception of the divine as creative ground of Being. It was taken up in the *Bhagavad Gītā*'s influential image of Kṛṣṇa as a divine source with infinite qualities and capacities, constantly creating and dissolving the world. Early medieval Purāṇas such as the *Bhāgavata Purāṇa* gave new expression to this idea.[19] Telling the story of Kṛṣṇa's manifest life as an *avatāra*, it set up a complex range of kinds and levels of essential-energies (*ātma-śakti*), action-energies (*kriya-śakti*), primal-energies (*pūra-śakti*), and even destructive energies (*bibhrat-śakti*) possessed by a divinity who could grasp and deploy them (*gṛhīta, aśritya*) through its central agency.[20] The resulting vision was of a complex God that possessed a lively, playful, multifaceted agency at the very heart of its being. The result was a multilevel cosmology constituted from different kinds of being interacting in different ways—but all situated *within* the divine nature and its manifestation. The divine powers or *śaktis* played a metaphysically essential role as "an intermediary force" of creation.[21]

The *Viṣṇu Purāṇa* added new detail to the divine architecture. The Upaniṣadic division of the divine into being, consciousness and bliss (*sat-cit-ānanda*), was reframed as a division into capacities for entities, consciousness, and enjoyment (the *sandhinī, saṃvit, and hlādinī śaktis*).[22]

All of this had to be part of the divine being, waiting to emerge, for the influence of the *satkāryavāda* doctrine of causality, holding that substrates contain their future developments *in potentio*, meaning that these texts were inclined to see sources as containing whatever they produce. Yet with all its affirmation of divine activity, this text was reluctant to associate God with the ambiguous dramas of the world; it proclaimed to God that "enjoyment, being, and awareness are one in You, the site of all things. [But] the cause of mixed pleasure and pain is not in you."[23] A theological challenge was born, and subsequent Vedāntic thinkers wrestled with the problem of whether the things of the world taint the divine nature.

These cosmogonic powers were developed into a metaphysical explanation for the world in the systematic treatises of medieval Vedānta. The great idealist monist Śaṃkara argued that the consistency and coherence of all things as they develop over time shows that there is a unified causal basis for all reality at work beneath things, dictating their entangled development into ever-new forms.[24] Although Śaṃkara himself was loath to admit the implication that the divine is mutable, puissant, and creative, thinkers in more realist branches of the tradition embraced this implication. Some used language of arising (*utpatti*), material and efficient causes (*karaṇa*), and coming to be (*saṃbhu-*),[25] rather than the terminology of powers (*śaktis*), but the implication was the same. The world we know is shaped by a coherent power that dictates both unity and diversity.

Reality as we know it is thus naturally "full," as some texts put it. A Vedic description of creation of the cosmos declared that "it raises the full from the full, pouring out the full with the full,"[26] and this theme was taken up in the earliest of the Upaniṣads which similarly observed:

> The world there is full; The world here is full;
> fullness from fullness proceeds.
> After taking fully from the full, It still remains completely full.[27]

This verse emphasized that the originating ground of the cosmos is able to furnish existence to new things without apparently being depleted. This means that not only is it naturally creative, but it is also inexhaustibly creative. The text uses the analogy of space as something that does not seem to be limited in extent, and later thinkers used the analogy of fire that can spark ever new infinitely expandable fires without depletion. But play is also just such a thing: art, story, and (in theory) love and joy are not exhausted in use, but can overflow beyond the individual and inspire others.

## Pūrṇa Śakti: The Fullness of Divine Power

This conception of the divine was active instead of immutable, full instead of pure, and complex instead of simple—although opinions varied on whether to characterize the relation between the world and its source as one of aspects (*aṃśas*), qualities (*viśeṣas*), arrangements or manifestations (*vyūhas*), capacities (*śaktis*), or analytic subdivisions (*upādhis*) of the underlying ground. It was well expressed in the classic Bhedābheda positions of thinkers such as Bhartṛprapañca, Yādavaprakāśa, Nimbarka, and Śrīnivāsa, who, like Spinoza in Europe, derived the divine nature from philosophical understanding of the "unified causation that flows from the foundational level" of reality. The reality we see is like waves upon a divine ocean or branches of blossom grown from a divine seed.

But as the Bhedābheda tradition developed, its thinkers more explicitly emphasized that the divine, as immanent cause of all reality, must possess "spiritual spontaneity and . . . creative urge."[28] The strongly devotional sixteenth-century branch of Bhedābheda called the Caitanya Vaiṣṇava school rejected substantial analogies for the divine nature and instead adopted *processual* ones: a fire flickering and spreading naturally, and a sun infinitely reflected in mirror after mirror.[29] Further, uncle and nephew theologians of the Caitanya Vaiṣṇava school, Rūpa and Jīva Gosvāmī (1513–1596), introduced a fresh twist to the old idea of plenipotent divinity. They insisted that powers were not only *natural* to the divine, but also most naturally *active in use* rather than sitting latent *in potentio.*[30] The *satkārya* doctrine of the Sāṃkhya school had affirmed that prime matter is rich in potentialities but regarded their latent, unactivated state as most fundamental. By contrast, the Caitanya Vaiṣṇavas used the idea of an *upādhi*, or a partial delimitation of something, to depict the divine powers as something that may provisionally *appear* dimmed, but always in truth exist in a state of fulfilled activation within the divine being. It is not God that restrains itself, but consciousnesses within God that sometimes suffer a veiled perception of the whole. Rūpa Gosvāmī developed this point in his *Laghubhāgavatāmṛta* (LBA), a text that sought to defend the superiority of the incarnate, active Kṛṣṇa over the abstract, passive conception of the divine as *Brahman*, or even the creator-God Viṣṇu.[31] For Rūpa, Kṛṣṇa as *Bhāgavan* or "the Lord" was the magnificently plenipotent, complete, truest manifestation of the divine in its infinite play of powers. He possesses multiple capacities,[32] and it is merely their pattern of activation that creates the appearance of individuated dynamic beings, so that "manifestation or non-manifestation of power is the cause of variegation."[33]

To explain this metaphysically, Rūpa contrasted the *upādhi* or *limited* state of powers with their actualized *pūrṇa* or *full* state, crucially claiming that the most active state was the true one.[34] There are degrees of realization of the divine nature: "'Partial-ness' (*aṃśatvam*) is displaying only ever a small portion of the powers, and fullness is clearly displaying the distinct powers."[35] Kṛṣṇa as highest, original, and complete divinity "manifests the complete powers" of the divine (*akhila-śaktīnāṃ prākaṭyaṃ*),[36] and represents its highest and fullest state (*parāvasthaś ca sampūrṇāvasthaḥ*),[37] which is characterized by "displaying clearly the distinct powers."[38] Rūpa thus reconfigures earlier part-whole, property-substrate, or mode-object conceptions of the divine nature in terms of a new model of full and occluded powers. Merging the idea of the divine as constantly fully active in all its potentialities, with the idea of divine being as timeless peaceful perfection, was challenging—but the result was a sense that at the ultimate level divine play and embodiment are a timeless "potentiality that is eternally actualised."[39]

As Rūpa's nephew Jīva Gosvāmin put it, the divine possesses its intrinsic capacities (*svarūpa-śaktimān*) in the same way that the moon possesses all its native brightness in an unclouded sky.[40] In such a state it is unlimited.[41] It is partly in this sense that Caitanya Vaiṣṇavas considered the divine nature to be inconceivable (*acintya*): It has infinite powers always activated in apparently contradictory ways so that, in God, it is both night and day, cold and warm, enamored and disdainful, man and woman.[42] At the ultimate level play is less an activity than a complex structure of rich form and meaning.

## *Vyakti Rasa*: The Emergence of Emotion

It is tempting to leave things at that: Play is the rich creative structure of the divine being, just as it is fire's nature to burn and shine, and light's to illuminate that on which it falls. But to appreciate the divine attribute of "fullness" revealed by Hindu theologies of play, we should lastly consider the metaphysical role of *emergence* in the world's creativity, and the curious ontological status of *emotion*. India was well aware of the phenomenon of emergence, where in special cases things generate strange new phenomena that depend on all the subsidiary parts, but exhibit novel features. We can see this in the way that the parts of the body make consciousness, the mechanisms of mind enable reasoning, spices create a new distinctive flavor, and words create meaning—all images used in Indian classical sources. The world thus acts as a cauldron of "developmental causality,"[43] a kind of upbuilding creativity that rises from the most basic forms of Being to more ontologically sophisticated ones. Each "adds" ontologically to the lower levels by introducing novel qualities that were not previously present. It is a multilevel world that emerges from the divine nature.

This is reflected by the different classifications of creative powers that the Caitanya Vaiṣṇavas attributed to the divine, including material, consciousness, and affectivity-creating powers.[44] Indeed, the former of these powers enables the actualization of the latter, since matter forms a base for mind, and mind for concepts, art, and emotional response. Rūpa drew on dramaturgical theory to model this process in the case of the arising of the highest emotion: love.[45] Settings, characters, and their actions and motivations are all necessary to create affective response, which responds to and in a sense unites them all in a new phenomenon. Rūpa writes that the divine nature supports different qualities in the way that milk forms a foundation for different flavors,[46] borrowing an analogy long associated with the emergence of emotion out of the concrete apparatus of artworks.[47] Rūpa's well-known aesthetic work the *Bhaktirasāmṛtasindhu* (BRS), and his specialist devotional manual, the *Ujjvala Nīlamāṇī*, both focus on the practical cultivation of emotion rather than the philosophy of the divine nature. In the *Bhaktirasāmṛtasindhu* Rūpa reiterates the idea of a divinity manifesting different degrees of its native fullness[48] and explains that the passionate emotion reveals the "pure luminous quality of the [divine] self" in its full state of play.[49] Thus, the transient phenomena of dramatic emotion are understood by the Caitanya Vaiṣṇava philosophers as expressions of an "eternally existent transphenomenal reality."[50] Wulff has written that "the absolute for Rūpa is not a metaphysical principle, but an emotion";[51] we might rather say that it is both.

The emergence of the divine powers in the higher-order phenomenon that is dramatic emotion was emphasized by the eighteenth-century Caitanya Vaiṣṇava thinker Baladeva Vidyābhuṣaṇa (ca. 1700–1793). He cites the *Śvetāśvatara* and *Taittirīya Upaniṣads*[52] to confirm that creative powers are fully inherent in the divine nature, so that it is "all of one essence—yet it scintillates with many colours, like the feathers of a peacock."[53] He also reinforced divine simplicity by explaining that there is no separation (*bheda*) between the divine being and its attributes, and specifically no separation between the blissful *character* of the divine and its actual *identity* as bliss, nor between the world and the Lord of the world.[54] Baladeva was at pains to emphasize that the divine powers are not merely contingent acts limited to the physical cosmos. Passionate emotion shows us the divine as "self-enjoying, self-enamoured"[55] within "'erotic sentiment' that spreads within the created world, amplified by those who respond to it with enlightened devotional appreciation."[56] Passion for the divine is "a special form of *śuddha sattva*, pure luminous being, that participates in Kṛṣṇa's essential nature (*svarūpa*) as a manifestation of the *mahāśakti*" and so "the love for Kṛṣṇa that arises in the heart of the [devotee] is the spontaneous expression of Kṛṣṇa's own blissful nature."[57] For Baladeva, emotional responses to the world are some of the most evolved forms of divine play. Each case in which someone feels a deep response to reality is a case in which something at the emergent heights of existence loves the divine "root of its existence." Effects love their causes, and actions their agencies, in the same way that "the branch cannot but love the tree, nor the rays of the moon their lord, the moon."[58]

Since all of this must ultimately be attributed to the divine nature, Baladeva argues that this shows us God as an artist:

> The world shows wonderful construction and design, and it is impossible for unintelligent matter, to have produced this wonderful universe, without the direct action of an intelligent agent. No one has ever seen a beautiful palace constructed by the fortuitous coming together of bricks.[59]

For these thinkers, divine play must be *dramatic*: It entails complexity and emergence, histories and hopes, and passions. Indeed, the more complex, the more passionate, the more overarching our understanding and response, the better. This is a slightly different conception of ludic activity from Śiva's lovemaking or Kṛṣṇa's dance, for it must be richly melodramatic to achieve its truest expression. Accordingly, the devotional arts of India have often remained full of baroque ornamentation and visceral emotion, and their metaphysical framework is easy to miss among the sighs, swoons, and artistic flourishes. Yet these dramatic pieces literally instantiate the complex emergent creative nature of the divine. The realist theology of Bhedābheda took a radical stand against the more pessimistic culture of aversion to suffering that we often see in illusionist Advaita and Buddhism. It takes the creation of more, and more developed existence as an intrinsic good.

In this light, it recalls Christian theologies such as Arthur Peacocke's, which affirmed that reality unfolds as an "emergent monism" uniting the whole course of reality's complex development.[60] Here the divine intentionally makes a world in which the things are made themselves makers of new things. This view goes some way toward dissolving the distinction between divine and natural causation, resulting in a "theistic naturalism" that builds "complex systems" into the divine plan. Divine play is supported by a powers-based ontology that draws evidence from causation of all kinds; efficient causation that sparks forth activity and development, teleological causation that artistically plans and designs the whole of the world's plot, and even material causation of a substance (*sat*) or foundation (*adhiṣṭḥāna*) that transforms itself into new forms for purely aesthetic reasons. Being is shaped by an inspiring playwright who makes the set, the characters, and the audience as well as the story. This implies something like a "powers holism"[61] in which the whole range of fundamental powers generating the world exist entangled together in an *autopoietic* nature evident in "non-uniform continuous creation."[62] Thus, the intensities of aesthetic value that we see around us are veins that reach down to the very heart of things.

Importantly, here, the paradigm of creation shifts from purposeless "play" to artistic vision. Instead of being "creation without a why" as McGinn puts it in the present volume, the whole pattern of divine play exists timelessly *in* the divine nature. In a sense, a total gestalt shift of perspective is meant to arise from the Caitanya Vaiṣṇavas' project of fully working out the implications of divine play. The divine attributes are changed:[63] From seeing the divine as a mere person or superintending agent, we see it as something more than a person that is naturally creative rather than deliberatively designing, something that is both the artist and the art, creating a kind of goodness more aligned with an artist's great insight and power to move, than an always-pleasant person. The world is also changed: We see things all around us as "the ultimate ground immanently unfolding before our eyes" and providing "a window into God's soul."[64] When we become one of the spectators of the divine drama, our pleasure at viewing reality gives us a taste of that fundamental power that drives the world.

## Bibliography

Arapura, J. G. "Some Special Characteristics of Sat (Being) in Advaita Vedānta." In *The Question of Being: East-West Perspectives*, edited by Mervyn Sprung. University Park: Pennsylvania State University Press, 1978.

Audi, Paul. "A Clarification and Defense of the Notion of Grounding." In *Metaphysical Grounding: Understanding the Structure of Reality*, edited by F. Correia and B. Schnieder, 101–121. Cambridge: Cambridge University Press, 2012.

*Baladeva's Brahma Sūtra Bhāṣya. The Vedānta Sūtras of Bādarāyaṇa with the Commentary of Baladeva.* Translated and edited by Rai Bahadur Srisa Chandra Vasu. New Delhi: Munshiram Manoharlal, 1912.

Bennett, Karen. "Construction Area (No Hard Hat Required)." *Philosophical Studies* 154, no. 1 (2011): 79–104.

Bennett, Karen. *Making Things Up*. Oxford: Oxford University Press, 2017.

Bernstein, S. "Could a Middle Level Be the Most Fundamental?" *Philosophical Studies* 178, no. 4 (2020). https://doi.org/10.1007/s11098-020-01484-1.

Bhāgavata Purāṇa. Edited by J. L. Sastri. *Bhāgavata Purāṇa with the Sanskrit Commentary Bhāvārthabodhinī of Śrīdhara Svāmin*. Delhi: Motilal Banarsidass, 1983.

Bhaktirasāmṛtasindhu. Haberman trans. *Bhaktirasāmṛtasindhu of Rūpa Gosvāmin*, Delhi: Motilal Banarsidass, 2003.

Bliss, Ricki Leigh. "Viciousness and Circles of Ground." *Metaphilosophy*, 45, no. 2 (2014): 245–256.

Chakrabarti, Arindam. "Play, Pleasure, Pain: Ownerless Emotions in Rasa Aesthetics." In *Project of History in Indian Science, Philosophy, and Culture*, edited by Amiya Dev, 15:189–202. New Delhi: Centre for Studies in Civilisations, 2009.

Chatterjee, Amita. "Power and Śakti: A Comparative Study." *Journal of Hindu Studies* 15, no. 3 (1987): 209–230.

De, Sushil Kumar. *Early History of the Vaisnava Faith and Movement in Bengal: From Sanskrit and Bengali Sources.* Calcutta: Firma KLN Private, 1986.

Frazier, Jessica. "The Destiny of Phenomenology: Gadamer on Value, Globalism, and the Growth of Being." *Heythrop Journal* 64, no. 2 (2023): 215–226. https://doi.org/10.1111/heyj.14188.

Frazier, Jessica. "Monism in Indian Philosophy: The Coherence, Complexity, and Connectivity of Reality in Śaṃkara's Arguments for Brahman." *Religious Studies* 58, no.1 (2022): 17–33. doi:10.1017/S0034412522000117.

Frazier, Jessica. "Omnipresence as Ultimate Ground: Power and Oervasion in Śrīnivāsa's Medieval Indian Philosophy." In *The Oxford Handook of Omnipresence*, edited by Anna Marmodoro, Ben Page, and Damiano Migliorini. Oxford: Oxford University Press, 2025.

Frazier, Jessica. *Reality, Religion and Passion: Indian and Western Approaches in Hans-Georg Gadamer and Rūpa Gosvāmī.* Lanham, MD.: Rowman and Littlefield, 2008.

Frazier, Jessica. "Roots of Reality: The Philosophy of Foundations in the Monisms of Spinoza and Śrīnivāsa." In *Panentheism in Indian and Western Thought*, edited by Benedikt Göcke and Swami Medhananda. Routledge, 2023.

Frazier, Jessica. "What Kind of 'God' Do Hindu Arguments for the Divine Show? Five Novel Divine Attributes of Brahman." *Sophia: International Journal of Philosophy and Traditions* 63 (2024): 471–495. https://doi.org/10.1007/s11841-024-01036-8.

Frazier, Jessica. "The 'World Soul' in India: Complex Causality and Artful Emergence in 'Śakti' Vedānta." In *The World Soul*, edited by James Wilberding, 100–123. Oxford: Oxford University Press, 2021.

Gosvāmī, Rūpa. *Mystic Poetry: Rūpa Gosvāmin's Uddhava Sandeśa and Haṃsadūta.* Translated by Jan Brzezinski. San Rafael, CA.: Mandala Publishing, 1999.

Gosvāmī, Rūpa. *Vidagha Mādhava.* Edited by Bhavadatta Shastri. Bombay: Nirnaya Sagar Press, 1937.

Gregersen, Niels. "Autopoiesis: Less Than Self-Constitution, More Than Self-Organisation: Reply to Gilkey, McClelland and Deltete, and Brun." *Zygon* 34, no. 1 (1999): 117–138.

Gregersen, Niels. "The Idea of Creation and the Theory of Autopoietic Processes." *Zygon* 33, no. 1 (1998): 333–367.

Gupta, Ravi. *The Caitanya Vaiṣṇava Vedānta of Jīva Gosvāmī: When Knowledge Meets Devotion.* Abingdon: Routledge, 2007.

Haberman, David. *The Bhaktirasāmṛtasindhu of Rūpa Gosvāmī.* Delhi: Motilal Banarsidass/Indira Gandhi Centre for the Arts, 2003.

Holdrege, Barbara. *Bhakti and Embodiment: Fashioning Divine Bodies and Devotional Bodies in Ksrna Bhakti.* Abingdon: Routledge, 2015.

Kapoor, O. B. L. *The Gosvamis of Vrndavana.* Caracas: Sarasvati Jayasri Classics, 1995.

Kinsley, David. *The Sword and the Flute: Dark Visions of the Terrible and the Sublime in Hindu Mythology,* Berkeley: University of California Press,1975.

Koslicki, Kathrin. "Varieties of Ontological Dependence." In *Metaphysical Grounding: Understanding the Structure of Reality,* edited by Fabrice Correia and Benjamin Schnieder, 186–213. Cambridge: Cambridge University Press, 2012.

Kretzmann, Norman. *The Metaphysics of Creation: Aquinas's Natural Theology in Summa Contra Gentiles II.* Oxford: Oxford University Press, 2001.

Lāghubhāgavatāmṛtam, HH Bhānu Swāṃī. *Lāghu-Bhāgavatāmṛtam* with Commentary by Śrīlā Baladeva Vidyābhuṣaṇa. Chennai: Sri Vaikunta Enterprises, 2007.

Lutjeharms, Rembert. "An Ocean of Emotion: Rasa and Religious Experience in Early Caitanya Vaiṣṇava Thought." In *Caitanya Vaiṣṇava Philosophy: Tradition, Reason and Devotion,* edited by Ravi Gupta, 175–230. Farnham: Ashgate, 2014.

Marmodoro, Anna, ed. *The Metaphysics of Powers: Their Grounding and Their Manifestations.* Abingdon: Routledge, 2010.

Nelson, Lance. "The Ontology of Bhakti: Devotion as Paramapurusartha in Gaudiya Vaisnavism and Madhusudana Sarasvati." *Journal of Indian Philosophy* 32 (2004): 345–392.

Nicholson, Andrew. *Unifying Hinduism: Philosophy and Identity in Indian Intellectual History.* New York: Columbia University Press, 2010.

Peacocke, Arthur. "Complexity, Emergence, and Divine Creativity." In *From Complexity to Life: On the Emergence of Life and Meaning,* edited by Niels Gregersen. Oxford: Oxford University Press, 2003.

Pollock, Sheldon. "Bhoja's Śṛṇgāra Prakāśa and the Problem of Rasa: A Historical Introduction and Annotated Translation." In *Asiatische Studien* 70, no. 2 (1998): 117–192. Bern: Peter Lang.

Pollock, Sheldon. *The Rasa Reader: Classical Indian Aesthetics*. New York: Columbia University Press, 2016.

Pollock, Sheldon. "Vyakti and the History of Rasa." *Journal of Rasthriya Sanskrit Sansthan* 6 (2012): 232–253.

Pollock, Sheldon. "What Was Bhaṭṭa Nāyaka Saying? The Hermeneutic Transformation of Indian Aesthetics." In *Epic and Argument in Sanskrit Literary History: Essays in Honor of Robert P. Goldman*, edited by Sheldon Pollock, 143–184. Delhi: Manohar, 2010.

Schaffer, Jonathan. "Grounding in the Image of Causation." *Philosophical Studies* 173, no. 1 (2016): 49.

Schaffer, Jonathan. "On What Grounds What." In *Metametaphysics*, edited by David Manley, David Chalmers, and Ryan Wasserman, 347–383. New York: Oxford University Press, 2009.

Schaffer, Jonathan. "What Not to Multiply without Necessity." *Australasian Journal of Philosophy* 93, no. 4 (2014): 644–664.

Sheridan, Daniel. *The Advaitic Theism of the Bhāgavata Purāṇa*. Delhi: Motilal Banarsidass, 1986.

Srinivasacari, P. N. *The Philosophy of Bhedābheda*. Chennai: Adyar Library, 1950.

van Inwagen, P. *Material Beings*. Ithaca, NY: Cornell University Press, 1995.

Vasu, Rai Bahadur Srisa Chandra Vasu. *The Vedānta Sūtras of Bādarāyaṇa with the Commentary of Baladeva*. New Delhi: Munshiram Manoharlal, 1912.

Wulff, Donna Marie. "A Sanskrit Portrait: Radha in the Plays of Rupa Gosvami." In *The Divine Consort: Radha and the Goddesses of India*, edited by J. S. Hawley and D. M. Wulff. Boston: Beacon Press, 1982.

## Notes

1. J. G. Arapura, "Some Special Characteristics of Sat (Being) in Advaita Vedānta," in *The Question of Being: East-West Perspectives*, ed. Mervyn Sprung (University Park: Pennsylvania State University Press 1978), 113.
2. See reasons for advocating a hierarchy in Kathryn Koslicki, "Varieties of Ontological Dependence," in *Metaphysical Grounding: Understanding the Structure of Reality*, ed. F. Correia and B. Schnieder (Cambridge: Cambridge University Press, 2012), 186–213; Paul Audi, "A Clarification and Defense of the Notion of Grounding," in *Metaphysical Grounding: Understanding the Structure of Reality*, ed. F. Correia and B. Schnieder (Cambridge: Cambridge University Press, 2012), 101–121; Jonathan Schaffer, "On What Grounds What," in *Metametaphysics*, ed. David Manley, David Chalmers, and Ryan Wasserman (New York: Oxford University Press, 2009), 347–383; Jonathan Schaffer, "Grounding in the Image of Causation," *Philosophical Studies* 173, no. 1 (2016): 49; Karen Bennett, "Construction Area (No Hard Hat Required)," *Philosophical Studies* 154, no. 1 (2011): 79–104; Karen Bennett, *Making Things Up* (Oxford: Oxford University Press, 2017); as well as revisionist conceptions of grounding in Ricki Leigh

Bliss, "Viciousness and Circles of Ground," *Metaphilosophy* 45, no. 2 (2014): 245–256; S. Bernstein, "Could a Middle Level Be the Most Fundamental?" *Philosophical Studies* (2020), https://doi.org/10.1007/s11098-020-01484-1, and elsewhere.

3. E.g., P. van Inwagen, *Material Beings* (Ithaca, NY: Cornell University Press, 1995).
4. See *Summa Contra Gentiles* books 1 and 2, which elaborate the steps by which creation proceeds "from God to everything else," as Kretzmann puts it in his commentary (Norman Kretzmann, *The Metaphysics of Creation: Aquinas's Natural Theology in Summa Contra Gentiles II* [Oxford: Oxford University Press, 2001]). Here, as in the Indian philosophical theology we will look at, powers are seen to be intrinsic to the divine nature and inseparable from their actualization in divine activity; "God's creativity involves no movement or change."
5. *Vidagha Mādhava* (VM), 4.51. Rūpa Gosvāmī, *Vidagdha Mādhava*, edited by Bhavadatta Shastri. Bombay: Nirnaya Sagar Press, 1937.
6. David Kinsley, *The Sword and the Flute: Dark Visions of the Terrible and the Sublime in Hindu Mythology* (Berkeley: University of California Press, 1975), 70–71.
7. Donna Marie Wulff, "A Sanskrit Portrait: Radha in the Plays of Rupa Gosvami," in *The Divine Consort: Radha and the Goddesses of India*, ed. J. S. Hawley and D. M. Wulff (Boston: Beacon Press, 1982), 33.
8. Uddhava Sandeśa 2. Rūpa Gosvāmī, *Mystic Poetry: Rūpa Gosvāmin's Uddhava Sandeśa and Haṃsadūta*, trans. Jan Brzezinski (San Rafael, CA.: Mandala Publishing, 1999).
9. Uddhava Sandeśa 9. Rūpa Gosvāmī, *Mystic Poetry: Rūpa Gosvāmin's Uddhava Sandeśa and Haṃsadūta*, trans. Jan Brzezinski (San Rafael, CA.: Mandala Publishing, 1999).
10. The philosophical theology of divine play shaped by the Gosvāmī family and its associates has received attention from a series of scholars (e.g., Sushil Kumar De, *Early History of the Vaisnava Faith and Movement in Bengal: From Sanskrit and Bengali Sources* (Calcutta: Firma KLN Private Ltd, 1986); Lance Nelson, "The Ontology of Bhakti: Devotion as Paramapurusartha in Gaudiya Vaisnavism and Madhusudana Sarasvati," *Journal of Indian Philosophy* 32 (2004): 345–392; Ravi Gupta, *The Caitanya Vaiṣṇava Vedānta of Jīva Gosvāmī: When Knowledge Meets Devotion* (Abingdon: Routledge, 2007); Barbara Holdrege, *Bhakti and Embodiment: Fashioning Divine Bodies and Devotional Bodies in Ksrna Bhakti* (Abingdon: Routledge, 2015; Jessica Frazier, *Reality, Religion and Passion: Indian and Western Approaches in Hans-Georg Gadamer and Rūpa Gosvāmī* (Lanham, MD.: Rowman and Littlefield, 2008).
11. Niels Gregersen, "Autopoiesis: Less Than Self-Constitution, More Than Self-Organisation; Reply to Gilkey, McClelland and Deltete, and Brun," *Zygon* 34, no. 1 (1999): 118.
12. See Frazier, *Reality, Religion, and Passion.*
13. Holdrege, *Bhakti and Embodiment*, 32.
14. See Jessica Frazier, "Roots of Reality: The Philosophy of Foundations in the Monisms of Spinoza and Śrīnivāsa," in *Panentheism in Indian and Western Thought*, ed. Benedikt Göcke and Swami Medhananda (Routledge, 2023) comparing the thought of Spinoza and Śrīnivāsa.
15. Arapura, "Some Special Characteristics of Sat (Being) in Advaita Vedānta," 113.
16. *Chāndogya Upaniṣad* 6.2.3.

17. See *Śvetāśvatara Upaniṣad* (ŚU) 4.1, 3.14, and 4.10.
18. ŚU 6.3, 8.
19. Where the classical Vedānta of the Upaniṣads tended to affirm the traditionally "transcendent" qualities of immutability and simplicity, the Purāṇic Vedānta advocated a "tantric-style bipolar monism" (Nelson, "The Ontology of Bhakti, 359). Rāmānuja used the same cultural sources to produce a theology similarly committed to affirming the value of divine internal variation, in his case conceived in terms of aspects, qualifications, and qualities (*aṃśas, viśeṣas* and *guṇas*), rather than energetic capacities or *śaktis*.
20. E.g., *Bhāgavata Purāṇa* (BP) 2.4.6–7, 2.5.4–5, 3.6.2.
21. Daniel Sheridan, *The Advaitic Theism of the Bhāgavata Purāṇa* (Delhi: Motilal Banarsidass, 1986), 31.
22. *Viṣṇu Purāṇa* (VP) 1.12.69.
23. hlādinī-sandhinī-saṃvit tvayy eka sarva-saṃsthitau| hlāda-tapā-kari miśra tvayi no guṇa-varjita|| (*Viṣṇu Purāṇa* 1.12.69).
24. See Jessica Frazier, "Monism in Indian Philosophy: The Coherence, Complexity, and Connectivity of Reality in Śaṃkara's Arguments for Brahman," *Religious Studies* 58, no. 1 (2022): 17–33.
25. See Śaṃkara's *Brahma Sūtra Bhāṣya* 2.2.18–19.
26. *Atharva Veda* 10.8.29: pūrṇāt pūrṇaṃ ud acati pūrṇaṃ pūrṇena sicyate|.
27. *Bṛhadāraṇyaka Upaniṣad* 5.1.1: pūrṇam adaḥ pūrṇam idaṃ pūrṇāt pūrṇam udacyate| pūrṇasya pūrṇam ādāya pūrṇam evāvaśiṣyate|.
28. P. N. Srinivasacari, *The Philosophy of Bhedābheda* (Chennai: Adyar Library, 1950), 22.
29. The images of a sun extending its rays and of a fire with many subsidiary flames, have a long history before being taken up by the Gosvāmis (see De, *Early History of the Vaisnava Faith and Movement in Bengal*, 225–227; Gupta, *The Caitanya Vaiṣṇava Vedānta of Jīva Gosvāmī*, 39–45; Holdrege, *Bhakti and Embodiment*, 33–35).
30. Nelson linked the idea that divine *śaktis* are subject to a natural *need* to be fulfilled, to a "tantric-style bipolar monism" that was already implicit in the texts, rooted in the *śakti* doctrine's historical connotations of the union of the male and female aspects of divinity (Nelson, "The Ontology of Bhakti, 359).
31. Much of the *Laghubhāgavatāmṛtam* (LBA) is taken up with the arrangement of the order of *aṃśas* or aspects of the divine powers—his arguments for the doctrine of multiple *śaktis* is given as a digression (LBA 5.120) from that larger exposition of Kṛṣṇa as the source creator, and avatars as his "parts." The subsequent discussion of Kṛṣṇa's superiority is often focused on exegetic tasks of reinterpreting statements about Viṣṇu, Narāyana, Vasudeva, and others in such a way that they affirm the supremacy of Kṛṣṇa.
32. LBA 5.120.
33. *śakter vyaktis tathāvyakta tāratamasya kāraṇam*; LBA 5.90.
34. Rūpa also hints that this full-*śakti* nature of the divine explains some of the more counterintuitive activities represented in stories about Kṛṣṇa, involving passibility and worldly interaction (LBA 5.117–8). He also implies that their distinct separate natures are not real, but are only differentiated by one's level of meditation or awareness (*dhyāna-bhedāt*).
35. aṃśatvaṃ nāma śaktimān sadālpāṃśa-prakāśitā| pūrṇatvaṃ ca svacchayaiva nānā-śakti-prakāśitā|| śaktir aiśvarya-mādhurya-kṛpa-tejo-mukhā guṇāḥ śakter vyaktis tathāvyaktis tāratamyasya kāraṇam|| (LBA 5.89–91)

36. LBA 5.87–8.
37. LBA 5.10.
38. *pūrṇatvaṃ ca svacchayaiva nānāśakti prakāśitā*; LBA 5.89.
39. O. B. L. Kapoor, *The Gosvamis of Vrndavana* (Caracas: Sarasvati Jayasri Classics, 1995), 2.
40. *Tattva Sandarbha* (TS) 31.1.
41. *nirupādhi*; TS 30.3.
42. *acintyānanta-śaktitaḥ*; LBA 5.93.
43. Jessica Frazier, "The 'World Soul' in India: Complex Causality and Artful Emergence in 'Śakti' Vedānta," in *The World Soul*, ed. James Wilberding (Oxford: Oxford University Press, 2021), 100–123.
44. sandhinī, saṃvit, and hlādinī śaktis
45. To his theological works, Jīva Gosvāmī added not only works on the aesthetics of devotional love (in his *Priti-sandarbha*, *Durgama Sangamaṇi* commentary on the *Bhaktirasāmṛtasindhu* and *Locana Rochani* commentary on the *Ujjvala Nīlamāṇī*, and his *Rasāmṛtasesa* development of Viśvanāṭha Kaviraja's *Sahitya Darpani*), but also drew on grammatical theory as a broader intellectual support for his Vedānta in the *Harinamāmṛta-vyakaraṇa*, *Sūtra malika* and *Dhatu saṇgraha*. The tradition of Kṛṣṇaite rasa-aesthetics, having flourished in the poetry of Orissans such as Jayadeva and Caṇḍidas, was apparently taught by Rāmānanda Rāya to Caitanya and developed into formal aesthetic discourse by Kavikarṇapūra.
46. *yathā rūpa-rasādīnām guṇānām āśrayaḥ sadā*; LBA 5.201–202.
47. See Pollock's 2012 account of emotional manifestation in Indian aesthetics (Sheldon Pollock, "Vyakti and the History of Rasa," *Journal of Rasthriya Sanskrit Sansthan* 6 [2012]: 232–253). Jīva Gosvāmī also cites the spice analogy in TS 2.5.80 and 2.5.92; *mahāśakti-vilāsātmābhāvo 'cintyas-varūpa-bhāk*.
48. hariḥ pūrṇatamaḥ pūrṇataraḥ pūrṇa iti tredhā . . . prakāśitākhilaguṇaḥ smṛtaḥ pūrṇatamo budhaiḥ | asarvavyañjakaḥ pūrṇataraḥ pūrṇo 'lpadarśakaḥ ||BRS Eastern 1.221–222.
49. *Bhaktirasāmṛtasindhu* (BRS), 2.5.3 *śuddha-sattva-viśeṣātma*.
50. Nelson, "The Ontology of Bhakti."
51. Wulff, "A Sanskrit Portrait," 41.
52. See Baladeva Vidyābhūṣaṇa's Brahma Sūtra Bhāṣya (BBSB) 3.3.39 and 3.3.37 respectively.
53. Baladeva Vidyābhūṣaṇa's Brahma Sūtra Bhāṣya (BBSB) 3.3.36, in Rai Bahadur Srisa Chandra Vasu, *The Vedānta Sūtras of Bādarāyaṇa with the Commentary of Baladeva* (New Delhi: Munshiram Manoharlal, 1912), 564. All translations are from Vasu, *The Vedānta Sūtras of Bādarāyaṇa*.
54. BBSB 3.3.37 commentary, in Vasu, *The Vedānta Sūtras of Bādarāyaṇa*, 564.
55. BBSB 3.3.42, Vasu, *The Vedānta Sūtras of Bādarāyaṇa*, 572.
56. BBSB 3.3.41, Vasu, *The Vedānta Sūtras of Bādarāyaṇa*, 569–573.
57. Holdrege, *Bhakti and Embodiment*, 88.
58. BBSB 3.3.41, Vasu, *The Vedānta Sūtras of Bādarāyaṇa*, 571.
59. BBSB 3.3.42, Vasu, *The Vedānta Sūtras of Bādarāyaṇa*, 572.
60. Arthur Peacocke, "Complexity, Emergence, and Divine Creativity," in *From Complexity to Life: On the Emergence of Life and Meaning*, ed. Niels Gregersen (Oxford: Oxford University Press, 2003), 199.

61. Anna Marmodoro, ed., *The Metaphysics of Powers: Their Grounding and Their Manifestations* (Abingdon: Routledge, 2010), 5.
62. Gregersen, "Autopoiesis: Less Than Self-Constitution, More Than Self-Organisation."
63. See Jessica Frazier, "What Kind of 'God' Do Hindu Arguments for the Divine Show? Five Novel Divine Attributes of Brahman," *Sophia: International Journal of Philosophy and Traditions* 63 (2024): 471–495, on the way that certain core Vedāntic arguments for the divine imply a shift in five common divine attributes.
64. See Jessica Frazier, "Omnipresence as Ultimate Ground: Power and Pervasion in Śrīnivāsa's Medieval Indian Philosophy," in *The Oxford Handbook of Omnipresence*, ed. Anna Marmodoro, Ben Page, and Damiano Migliorini (Oxford: Oxford University Press, 2025) on the implications of this Bhedābheda conception of omnipresence.

# 9 The Making of the Sacred City

## *LĪLĀ* AS GOD'S VIOLENCE IN A TAMIL ŚAIVA *TALAPURĀṆAM*

*Srilata Raman*

It is extremely difficult to establish at which point the specifically Tamil genre of these works known as the *talapurāṇams* (which are in the tradition of the Sanskrit *māhātmya* works on the significance of sacred sites and often appended to the major Sanskrit *purāṇas*), emerged. In the extant literature we do not have any such work prior to the thirteenth and fourteenth centuries.[1] This changes dramatically a few centuries later, with a proliferation of this literature between the sixteenth and eighteenth centuries.[2] David Shulman points out that the efflorescence of these texts begins in the sixteenth century and could be plausibly linked to the establishment of the important Śaiva Siddhānta *maṭhas* and their scholarly communities, in the midst of which these works were composed.[3] The *talapurāṇam* of Śaiva persuasion that is the subject matter of this chapter is the extremely well-known and popular *Tiruviḷaiyāṭaṟpurāṇam (TVP)*, composed possibly around the seventeenth century by Parañcōtimuṉivar. By looking at how this work narrativizes the *līlā* of Śiva we gain a sense of how a specific genre of Tamil religious literature narrativized *līlā* as the sometimes violent activity of the gods in creating sacred cities, manifest in their interaction with humans, and in their decisive intervention in sustaining the earth's sacred geography.

### Śiva's Creation of Madurai in the *Tiruviḷaiyāṭaṟpurāṇam*

Before I turn to Śiva's *līlā* it would be necessary to consider the many connotations of this word, its Tamil counterpart—*viḷaiyāṭal* or *viḷaiyāṭṭu*—and what is meant when this word is used in the context of Tamil Śaivism in the *Tiruviḷaiyāṭaṟpurāṇam* (*TVP*). In the few references we have earlier to Śiva's *viḷaiyāṭal* in the Tamil devotional poetry of the

*Tēvāram* and the *Tiruvācakam* (whose dates might be placed between the sixth and ninth centuries and which constitute the first eight books of the *Tirumuṟai* the word can best be translated as "activities," as when Śiva's different forms enable his *viḷaiyāṭṭu* (*Tirumuṟai*, 2.83.9) or even as his "dance," as when he dances in the graveyard (*Tirumuṟai* 3.21.3 and 3.104.4). At the very beginning of the *TVP* the poet Parañcōtimuṉivar, in listing the topics of his composition in verse 26, tells us that one of the topics is "the sixty-four divine *viḷaiyāṭṭu* of the deity" (*anta mūrtti aruḷviḷaiyāṭṭ eṭṭeṭṭu*).[4] In other words, as Julius Lipner has pointed out, if we carefully contextualize the word *līlā* we find that, rather than simply translating it as play, sport, or game, we might need to understand it in its specific contexts.[5] And if we do so specifically in the context of Śiva's behavior in the *TVP*, it is best understood as his creative activity that might be inscrutable but is not random, that it is, in fact, a working out of his specific intentions either directly or indirectly, through his prompting of human agents who carry out his wishes, and that it is activity that sometimes leads to the creation of new worlds and new cities. To this extent I prefer to speak of Śiva's *viḷaiyāṭal* as his "deed" rather than play or game, in the *TVP*, even while it is clearly analogous to the word *līlā*. Further, in examining how god acts or performs his deed, this essay suggests that intertwined with his actions, at least, in many cases, is a violence that tends to be rationalized, underestimated, or overlooked either by traditional exegesis or by contemporary scholarship on it, obfuscated by the idea of *līlā* as sport, play, or game, and the benign connotations of these words. But what is required to understand the complexity of *līlā/tiruviḷaiyāṭal* is to ask how it functions, its rationale within its world, and its repercussions for those who are affected by it, and to recognize that in certain narrative contexts *līlā* is a far from benign activity, and might well be described as inherently violent in how it functions.[6]

The Tamil literary evidence shows us that a certain list of Śiva's divine activities already existed well before it came to be put down in its most popular version in the *TVP*. Kamil Zvelebil[7] points out that the *TVP* version was long preceded by a listing of Śiva's deeds in Tamil religious literature,[8] with these deeds gradually coalescing into sixty-four by the time the *TVP* was composed. In fact, the references to many of these deeds evolved in the *Tirumuṟai* and then in the eleventh- to twelfth-century work, the *Kallāṭam*. In the *Kallāṭam* thirty-one of those *viḷaiyāṭal* listed in the *TVP* are already given,[9] even while the text speaks of sixty-four deeds.

Following this, the major work which dealt with all the sixty-four deeds, and which undoubtedly was the model for the *TVP*, was composed possibly in the fifteenth century by Perumpaṟṟapuliyūr Nampi and was the first *Tiruviḷaiyāṭaṟpurāṇam*. This was popularly read and cited well into the seventeenth century before it came to be decisively replaced by the growing popularity of Parañcōtimuṉivar's *TVP*.[10]

The TVP, structurally, follows a pattern that comes to be the standard for the *talapurāṇam* works. As summarized by Shulman, the text usually begins with invocations to deities, to the saints of the Śaiva canon, to one's own guru, and so on.[11] This is followed by the *avaiyaṭakkam*, which gives a synopsis of the entire *purāṇa*. "Inevitably, there will be one or more cantos singing highly conventionalized descriptions of the beauties of the town or village in which the shrine is located (*tirunakaracurukkam*), the river that flows through or the sacred tank within the walls of the shrine (*tīrttavicēṭam*), the region as whole (*tirunāṭṭuccurukkam*), and perhaps a central image worshipped in the temple (*mūrttivicēṭam*)."[12] This might be considered the introductory part of the *purāṇa*, after which Śiva's deeds start to be described.

In the *TVP* the stories of Śiva's interventions on earth are closely intertwined with the fortunes and mythical origins and deeds of the royal dynasty of the Pāṇṭiya kings, whose royal seat was the city of Madurai (Maturai). The text braids the legends regarding the Pāṇṭiyas with the history of Tamil devotional Śaivism and its instantiation as the religious tradition of the city through the myths of the Śaivite Goddess Mīnākṣī/Mīnāṭcī the Pāṇṭiya princess, and celebrates her marriage to Śiva as Sundareśvara/Cuntarēcuvarar in the city precincts. Nevertheless, several of the episodes in the *TVP* deal with Śiva's direct interventions in its existence and its continued flourishing. Thus, even before Mīnāṭcī is born and before many of Śiva's other exploits, the city has to come into being. This happens in the very first book of the *TVP* in *The Section on Madurai* (*Maturaikkāṇṭam*).

At the very beginning of the first book the poet states that the *TVP* was composed to speak of the greatness of the city of Madurai, its sacred centre or river (*tīrtam*) and its God (*mūrtti*) as well as the sixty-four deeds of God.[13] This is followed by sixty verses on the greatness of the Pāṇṭiya land (*tirunāṭṭucciṟappu*)—a standard feature in a work that also seeks to belong to the belles lettres genre of *kāppiyam* and not just the story of a sacred site; 109 verses on the greatness of the city (*tirunakaracciṟappu*); 7 verses on a description of Śiva's abode, the Kailāśa mountain; and

25 verses about the context in which this work is composed. After this the *TVP* focuses on the significance of this place (*talavicēṭam*) in 23 verses, the sacred river pond, which Śiva himself creates at this spot in 36 verses, and in 37 verses praises Śiva as Cōmacuntarar, establishing himself in this spot as the *liṅga*. These sections might be regarded as a prelude to the *TVP*'s main subject matter, which are the 64 deeds of Śiva, proper. Following this prelude there is a summary of all 64 deeds in a short section of 15 verses, after which the episodes that narrate the deeds begin. The first two episodes have been well summarized by William Harman as follows:

> In the first of the Sacred Games, "The Chapter in which Indra's Sin is Effaced," we find the god Indra in a difficult position. A series of misfortunes has forced him into the unenviable predicament of having to kill a Brahmin. . . . Indra seeks out advice from Bṛhaspati, preceptor of the gods, about how he can be rid of this sin. He is advised to find his purification in the world of humans. When he descends to earth and wanders there, he discovers that passing through a particular area, a forest of cadampa oak trees, brings unexpectedly the sense of purification he has sought. On closer inspection, Indra discovers that the source of his purification is a miraculous Śiva *liṅga* of incomparable beauty, shaded by a clump of cadampa oaks. Beside the beautiful *liṅga* is a golden lily pond in which Indra bathes and from which he takes golden lilies to decorate the *liṅga*. Indra then pledges to return to this spot every year at full-moon time in the month of Citrā (April–May) to worship in thanksgiving for the purification he has thus received.
>
> In the second sacred game, "The Chapter in Which the Curse on the White Elephant is Effaced," we have a similar situation. Indra's mount, his glorious white elephant named Airāvata, is cursed by a particularly powerful sage . . . and Airāvata will become a wild elephant who must wander the earth for 100 years. After a hundred years of wandering as a wild, black elephant on earth, Airāvata passes through the cadampa oak forest in which the Golden Lily Pond and the Śiva *liṅga* are located. He bathes in the pond and is immediately transformed to his earlier, white, domesticated self.[14]

I have cited these two sacred deeds at some length because they precede the episode which is the focus of this chapter—where the city of Madurai comes to be built, and because the episodes illustrate a very important point, which is that Śiva's presence has been established at this site in the oak grove, the site is sanctified, and that Śiva has acted to help the gods and the animals, the elephant, through his *līlā,* perhaps even before human habitation.

Nevertheless, Śiva's active intervention in human affairs in this region begins in the third episode of the *TVP,* which consists of 47 verses. The poet begins the episode by explaining that he will speak, to the extent of his limited knowledge, of how the vast, *kaṭampa* oak forest (mentioned in the previous episodes) becomes the ancient town of Madurai (*kaṭampa māvaṉa mutunakaram āṉavāṟu*).[15] To the east of the forest lies the city of Maṇavūr, ruled over by the Pāṇṭiya King Kulacēkara (v. 472) where there lives a trader who is also a pious Śaivite (v. 473). Once this trader, Taṉañcayaṉ, goes west on business and on his return comes back home via the forest (v. 474). As darkness descends, he sees Śiva there and seating himself in front of the temple of the god, he starts to worship him (*caṭayavaṉ kōyiliṉ ñāṅkar tāṉ amarnt arucaṉai ceyvāṉ* (v. 480). Śiva appears to reward the merchant with a vision of him. The latter is overjoyed, falls at his feet, and then, once this encounter is over, sets out to return to his home. Immediately upon arrival Taṉañcayaṉ goes to have an audience with the Pāṇṭiya King and speaks of the wondrous vision he had in the *kaṭampa* forest (v. 483). The account that Taṉañcayaṉ gives of his experience is somewhat interestingly more nuanced than what the previous verses laid out. Thus, he now speaks of catching sight of a chariot (*vimāṉam*) with a *śivaliṅga* on top of it (v. 484). The gods were crowded around the deity, he says, and worshipped him that entire night. I myself, he says, then took leave of him and returned to the city (v. 485). Śiva now takes matters into hand himself. A Cittar/Siddha comes in the dreams of the king that very night (*cittarāyt tōṉṟiṉār kaṉavil)* (v. 487). The Siddha tells the king to destroy the forest and create a beautiful city in its place (*kāṭ akaḻnt aṇinakar kāṇka*). The king lies sleepless in bed that whole night (*viṭiyum vēlai kaṇviḻittaṉaṉ*) (v. 488). The next day he calls his counsellors and sages, narrates the dream to them, and then sets out westward after conferring with them (v. 489). He enters the great forest, immerses himself in the pond there with its golden lotuses, and then taking the feet of Śiva seated there on his golden chariot, placing them on his own head, he worships him (v. 490).

The Pāṇṭiya King now starts to praise the deity's mercifulness and accessibility in the three subsequent verses that narrate how Śiva made himself available to those on earth. The king is overcome with emotion and stands there, with tears rolling down his face (v. 495). The counsellors, acting on the king's commands, fan out in different directions bringing those skilled in trades who destroy the large forest and construct the beautiful city in its place (v. 496). Dark complexioned men, carrying axes and sickles, they come forward to cut down the forest (v. 497). The next verse lyrically describes the din that ensues from this act of destruction. The bees buzz around in agitation, the trees are cowed, there is the steady noise of cutting, there are the noises made by the men working, and then the crash of the trees as they fall down. All this cacophony, the poet tells us, is as loud as thunder coming down from the clouds and filling the space (v. 498). The falling of the cut trees, their branches filled with flowers dripping honey, is like the falling down of war elephants, their tusks broken, felled in battle (v. 499). The act of destruction disperses the inhabitants of the forest—bees move away swiftly to other landscapes, the birds head for camphor forests, and other wild beasts, like lesser kings who move aside for a greater, leave to take shelter in nearby mountains and forests (v. 500). The clearing of the forest, the poet tells us now, is far from a bad thing—the wood cutters are like those wise ones whose hearts have uprooted darkness and let light in. They are like those who have cut the roots of transmigration itself, full of compassion, devoid of attachment, who have reached the feet of Śiva (v. 501). Once the forest is cleared, the king confers with his ministers about how to plan and build the city (v. 502). At this juncture, the Siddha who appeared in the king's dream, comes once more before him (v. 503). The king welcomes him and gives him a place to stay (v. 504). We now become privy to information that was not given before—the Siddha had previously introduced the king to the sacred scriptures, the main revelatory text (*ātinūl*) as well as others based on it (*vaḻinūl*). He advises the king to build houses, pavilions, and towers that are based on the rules encoded in these works, and then he vanishes (v. 505). The next verse tells us, finally, who this Siddha really is—he is Civaparañcōtiyār. This could be one of the Śaivite poet-saints, also known more famously as Ciṟuttoṇṭar, already sanctified in the twelfth-century hagiography the *Periyapurāṇam*, or it could be an allusion by the poet to his own name.

That which is first built is the main shrine of the temple complex that will be at the very centre of the city of Madurai. It consists, we are told, of a lotus pavilion (*patuma maṇṭapam*), then the hall which is immediately in front of the innermost shrine, the *aruttamaṇṭapam*, the shrine room where the god who wears the crescent moon resides, and within it a throne with six legs. There is also a dance hall, a pearl-studded hall where festivities occur, a sacrificial enclosure, and the temple kitchen beside it, as well as shrines of the lesser deities surrounding the main shrine (v. 507). To the right of the main shrine is that of the Goddess. And this sacred centre is surrounded by walls, with flags reaching up to the sky. There are white mansions and fortified constructions, all built according to the guidelines laid down in the texts (v. 508). The magnificence of the city, its painted shops, halls with trees surrounded by a raised platform, processional streets festooned with strings of pearls—these and other magnificent buildings and paths are found in this city (v. 509). The streets are segregated into those of the priests, the royals, traders, and agriculturists. There are stalls for the domestic animals, schools, and feeding houses for those who come in search of food (v. 510). Waterbodies such as wells and ponds are created, and these together with the parks and flower gardens make the city beautiful.

The king establishes his own palace in the northeastern corner of the city and then thinks about what he might do both to purify and sanctify the city (v. 511). Knowing the king's wishes, Śiva himself spills the nectar from the moon in his hair. That nectar turns the entire city into a blissful place, similar to that bliss experienced by those who attain the liberation of uniting with Śiva. It purifies the entire city, and by making it sweet—*maturam*—the city came to bear the name Madurai, says the poet (v. 512). The guardian deities of the city, protecting the four directions, are listed in the next verse—to the east Cāttaṉār, to the south the eight mothers or the Saptamātṛkās, to the west Tirumāl/Viṣṇu, and to the north the dark Goddess (v. 513). The king brings over those learned in both the Vedas and the Āgamas as well as Ādiśaiva priests from Kāśī to do the rituals in the temple of Śiva (v. 514). The king caused the city to prosper, with all its peoples abiding in right conduct, with the Vedic and the Śaiva ways flourishing, such that it was like an embossed *tilaka*, mark of beauty, on this green earth surrounded by the seas (v. 515), says the *TVP*. The king lives in the city worshipping the god three times a day without fail and ruling righteously (v. 516). Then, the king, once he has a child which is like the dawning sun, leaves his abode, goes to the temple and falling at the feet of the Lord, circumambulates him, attains bliss and that state of union and not of union (*oṉṟiy oṉṟā nilai*) with God (v. 517), which is the highest state of liberation in the Tamil Śaiva Siddhānta.[16]

When the poet, Parañcōtimuṉivar, came to write about the city, described as a utopian space in the *TVP*, we can already assume that he had earlier literary models that occupied themselves with the magnificence of this ancient place. Two of the most famous of these can be pointed out, which undoubtedly would have influenced his own poetic vision. The earlier is the *Maturaikāñci*, one of the long poems of 800 lines in the *Caṅkam* literature called the "Ten Idylls," or *Pattupāṭṭu*, composed in the first centuries of the first millennium. The work, by the poet Māṅkuṭi Marutaṉār, praises the Pāṇṭiya King Neṭuñceḻiyaṉ, his prowess in battle, and Madurai as the city that reflects his splendour. The poem tells us about a fortified city with tall walls and high mansions. An entire section describes the market with the flower, food, and areca nut sellers. The twilight celebrations are described, when offerings are made to Śiva, described as the axe-bearer (*maḻuvāḷ neṭiyōṉ*), who created all the five elements, as well as great sacrificial offerings (*uyar pali*) to other fierce gods. But, in this poetic composition we also see that Śiva is not the only deity who is the focus of the religious life of the city. Immediately after referring to his worship the *Maturaikāñci* speaks of the young women who worship at another shrine, to those learned in the Vedas in their allotted residences, which look like mountains that have been dug out, and to the beautiful monasteries of the Jains, the *cāvakar/śrāvakas*. The poem also celebrates the revelries of warriors who celebrate the birthday of Tirumāl/Viṣṇu. It speaks of the *vēlaṉ* who is possessed and worships Murukaṉ, while women dance the *kuravai* dance. The poem splendidly follows the doings in the city from twilight through the different times of the night and ends at dawn when the city's inhabitants wake up to another hectic day. This is the city, of which the poet says, "This is the city of Madurai, of widespread fame and renown, its beauty such that even the gods from the divine worlds come to see it" (*puttēḷ ulakam kavuṉik kāṇvara mikkup pukaḻ eytiya perum peyar maturai*). The picture we have from the *Maturaikāñci* is of a splendid, cosmopolitan city with a thriving trade with other parts of the world, where Śiva is one of the many Brahmanical gods worshipped and where Buddhists and Jains also thrive.

The second work that could well have been even more influential, as far as the *TVP* is concerned, was perhaps composed around the fifth century CE. This is the *Cilappatikāram* of Iḷaṅkō Aṭikaḷ, which has justifiably been called an epic, literary masterpiece of Classical Tamil literature. The *Cilappatikāram* also has an entire section on Madurai, named identically, *Maturaikkāṇṭam*, or *The Book of Madurai*, which is the second book of the epic. It is the book in which the story that propels the plot, the marriage of Kōvalaṉ and Kaṇṇaki, ends in calamity for the Pāṇṭiya king, for his citizens, and for the city itself.

*The Book of Madurai* begins with tribute paid to the Arhat, the enlightened Jain being worshipped by a central character in the plot, the wise Jain nun Kavunti who accompanies Kaṇṇaki and Kōvalaṉ to the Pāṇṭiya lands. Very early on they are told about the greatness and fame of the Pāṇṭiya king by a brahman they meet who also gives them detailed instructions on various paths that would lead them to Madurai. He eloquently describes how the very south wind that blows from Madurai is redolent with all kind of fragrances and adds, in R. Parthasarathy's superb English translation of the epic, "Therefore, that ancient prosperous city isn't very far from here."[17] Further on in the very next canto we have our first detailed description of the city:

> In groves on the outskirts of the city, in gardens
> Flooded with water, in fields ripe
> With crops, was the clamor of birds
> That had arisen from sleep. At daybreak, the sun
> Adored by the entire world, opened
> The petals of the red roses in the pond,
> Woke up the people of immortal Madurai
> Of the Pāṇṭiyaṉ who wielded the sword and made
> The heads of his foes tremble. The roar
> Of the morning drums, the echo
> Of the pure, white conches sounded in unison
> From the temple of Śiva with an eye on his forehead,
> The temple of Viṣṇu with the eagle-banner,
> The temple of Balarāma who brandished the plow
> As a weapon, the temple of Murukaṉ with the cock-banner,
> The temples of the arhats who expound dharma,
> And the palace of the victorious king.[18]

Much like in *Maturaikāñci,* the canto tells us about the beautiful women who inhabit the city, the trade from all over that leads to its exceptional prosperity, the wide streets, the elegant mansions, the markets where wares are sold that attest to its cosmopolitanism, and the different neighbourhoods—those of the cloth merchants, those of the grain merchants, and so on—that are to be found in it. Thus, between the two works just discussed, we have a poetic creation of an ideal and utopian city. There is much we learn about how Madurai was conceptualized in these examples of the earliest literature on it. It is intimately linked with the lineage of the royal house of the Pāṇṭiyas and, in that sense, it serves almost as a spatial validation of Pāṇṭiya claims to greatness. The city spaces are laid out in a geometrically harmonious fashion, and it is seen as a fortified settlement, due to the ever-present threat of war, which the king both invites and faces. The ideal city is also a military garrison of sorts, housing warriors and war elephants and horses, all of which are required for battle. The city's utopian qualities are reflected in its citizenry—it houses beautiful women and elegant courtesans accomplished in the many musical arts. It looks outward confidently onto the world—through its wealth generated by trade and the rich wares in its marketplaces. Above all, it is not specifically religious, in that it is not dominated by one religion. Both texts speak of the many gods of the city and their adherents—worshippers of Śiva, Viṣṇu, Murukaṉ, the War Goddess Koṟṟavai, the Jain Arhat, and the Buddha, all have their place in it and their places of worship. In that sense, though it is full of temples and sacred places, one does not have the impression that the city itself is sacralized. Taking this image of the utopian city, Parañcōtimuṉivar does something different with it—he sacralizes it and, simultaneously creates a new civic order, turning it into a creation of Śiva with the latter as both its creator and its preeminent deity. By doing so, he also establishes as the main religious paradigm of the city a monotheism that has a significant impact on its destiny and that of its citizens.

Let us now return to the episode of its emergence in the *TVP* and what it further tells us about the creation of Madurai and what Śiva wants. The city emerges not on a barren plain but out of the destruction of a beautiful forest of white *kaṭampa* oaks. This forest has been described in idyllic terms in a previous section of the *TVP*, and it worthwhile recollecting what was said there about it. This is in the story of the first deed of Śiva, referred to in Harman above, where Śiva rids Indra of his sins. Indra enters the *kaṭampa* forest during his peregrinations in search of purification and expiation for the sin of brahmanicide. Here Parañcōtimuṉivar gives us the following description of the life of the forest:

> Unschooled monkeys plunge into the waterfalls,
> take the gems thrown up by the flowing waters,
> place them on the rocks,
> pour water over them,
> pluck flowers, garland them, give them fruits,
> and worship.
> In a watering hole

two elephants drink,
drawing water with their trunks,
feeding each other.
Tigers give and nourish fawns with their milk,
to still the pangs of hunger. (v. 414)[19]

The image we have here is of an animal world that seems to be, almost innately, both devout and nurturing. The monkeys behave as devotees of Śiva. They treat the gems retrieved from the waterfall as if they were Śiva *liṅga*s, worshipping them in the appropriate manner. The elephants take care of each other solicitously. By depicting the tiger feeding the fawns with its own milk, treating them as it would its own cubs instead of as its natural prey, the poet is attempting to show an animal world that is uniquely different because it is a world where there is no predator and prey but only mutual support and compassion—this magical forest is the way it is because the animals inhabit Śiva's realm, they are in his immediate vicinity and reflect his innate compassion as well. This image of a mutually sustaining animal world is further reinforced in the next verse.

Crawling baby snakes
lie in open spaces in the heat and suffer.
The King of Birds
stretches out his radiant wings
and spreads shade.
The silly monkeys nearby exclaim,
"the bird is suffering."
"Oh no" they say kindly.
They gather the water droplets the waterfall drips
with the conch shell pots
and pour it over him
with their black hands. (v. 415)[20]

In this verse we again see a natural yet ethical world—the King of the Birds is the eagle, Garuḍa, who would normally prey upon the hapless baby snakes exposed to him in the heat. Instead, he protects them and tries to alleviate their suffering by providing shade with his wings. The monkeys, in turn, are both silly and kind enough to assume that it is he who also needs protection from the heat, and they gather waters to pour over him to keep him cool.

Finally, there is a third verse that continues to reiterate these themes:

Hooded snakes throw up gems,
as if to light the marriage hall of peacocks,
their legs as green as tender *nocci* leaves,
as they mate with peahens.
In the great, cool forest
the young cuckoos with their broad wings
sing "Om" raucously,
and baby birds repeated the five sacred syllables loudly.
The bush myna with its round eyes delighted there,
As if hearing the wise words of the teacher. (v. 416)[21]

Here, the description of life in the forest reaches its climax, as it were, in a Śaivite celebration. There is the marriage of the peacock and the peahen, and the snakes regurgitate gems from their bellies to illuminate the marriage place. The cuckoos chant "Om" and the baby birds constantly repeat the *pañcākṣara* mantra of Śaiva, *namaḥ śivāya*, at which the mynas delight as if listening to the discourse of their guru. The forest here is not a wild, untamed, and dangerous place. Rather, it is portrayed as a place which frames the deity who resides there and is completely attuned to a devotional ethos. The animals and birds have abandoned their natural traits of being predator and prey but have turned, instead, into protector and the protected, mirroring the ideal relationship of Śiva to his devotees. The behavior of the animals is, in some way, even more perfect than that of humans because it is not learned but instinctive. The poet emphasizes that the monkeys are unschooled; they lack *kalvi* or learning, and they are even stupid or silly, *maṭam*. Yet they know what to do without being taught—they perform worship to stones every day as if the latter were *liṅga*s, and they rush to aid the eagle even when it doesn't need their help. The entire forest is but a theatre for the performance of Śaiva devotion, resounding with the bird calls of "Om" and the repetition of the mantra that guarantees liberation to the lay devotee—the *pañcākṣara*.

Nevertheless, it is this pious and harmonious forest which is completely destroyed in the very next chapter of the *TVP*, in order to build the city of Madurai. The *TVP* eloquently, in verses of the third deed, as we saw above, describes this destruction. There is the dreadful noise of the cutting down of the forest, a cacophony as loud as thunder. When the trees fall, it is a sight as tragic as the death of war elephants that are killed in battle. The poet also tells us that all the wildlife that till then inhabited the forest is rendered homeless and migrates to other groves. Yet inasmuch as the destruction has been ordered by Śiva himself, it is made explicit that it is for the right reasons and is necessary and proper. Let us recollect that it is Śiva who appears as a Siddha in the dream of the Pāṇṭiya king and tells him that he must get rid of the forest and build a beautiful city in its place. The king begins this task by entering the forest and first worshipping the god there, thus inaugurating the destruction of the forest through the auspicious act of worship. Nevertheless, we cannot ignore the environmental destruction that follows or cease to recollect that, along with the forest, its pious and peaceful inhabitants will either be driven away or perish. What are we to make of Śiva's *līlā*, which seems to unleash such wanton destruction?

The erasing of the *kaṭampa* forest inevitably reminds us of another famous destruction of a forest in South Asian religious, epic literature. This is the burning of the Khāṇḍava forest that happens at the end of the first book, the *Ādiparvan*, of the *Mahābhārata*. "The *Ādiparvan* of the *Mahābhārata* concludes with a passage in which Kṛṣṇa and Arjuna aid Agni (the god of fire) in the destruction of a vast tract of forest richly populated with animals and other living beings. Not only do Kṛṣṇa and Arjuna help Agni devour the great forest and its inhabitants, but they do so eagerly and joyfully, and with excessive force."[22] As Christopher Framarin points out, the description of the destruction of the forest and the accompanying distress of the animals is particularly gruesome and many times more so than in the passages above from the *TVP*.[23] Thus:

> The two tiger[-like] men stood at both sides of the forest on chariots [and] undertook a great slaughter of creatures in every direction. Indeed, anywhere creatures of the Khāṇḍava forest were seen fleeing, the two heroes trapped [them] right there. [The creatures] saw no opening, due to the quick speed of the two chariots. . . . As the Khāṇḍava was burning, creatures by the thousands flew upwards in the ten directions, howling frightful screams. Countless were burnt in one place, multitudes were burnt in another, broken, scattered, confused, eyes cracking. [Some] having embraced [their] sons, others [their] fathers [and] mothers, unable to abandon [each]other out of affection, went to death. Others sprang up by the thousands with distorted faces, whirling here and there [and] fell into the fire again. All over the ground, creatures were seen perishing.[24]

Framarin suggests that this deeply painful description of the burning of the forest has not really been dealt with in any satisfactory way by many scholars of the *Mahābhārata*. They are either content with simply referring to it and passing over it in negative, descriptive terms or, as in the case of J. A. B. van Buitenen, we have the explanation that the forest had to be burned in order for the Pāṇḍavas to found their own kingdom on the Khāṇḍava plateau that is gifted to them.[25] Thus, it becomes a device in pushing forward the narrative plot. Framarin himself takes a different approach to the episode even while he rejects a contemporary positionality on the episode as one which might see it as an anti-environmental narrative. Rather his primary conclusion, based on some of Biardeau's earlier observations, is that "these problems can be avoided, however, if the burning of the Khāṇḍava Forest is also understood mythically, specifically in terms of the myth of *pralaya*—the periodic dissolution of the material universe."[26] Framarin later adds that such a destruction is a "destroying of the universe not out of scorn or indifference, but out of amoral necessity."[27] What all these explanations do, including Framarin's, is to ignore or deflect the fact of divine violence and thus, as Adi Ophir points out in his 2023 study of divine violence,[28] they concentrate on the "moral and religious framework, which asks 'why' without asking "how."[29] And if we ask "how" instead of "why" in the case of the destruction of the *kaṭampa* forest in the *TVP*, we are led to an answer that deconstructs *līlā* as the unfolding of god's violence, that functions in this case through his unequivocal directions to those who have sworn fealty to him, such as the Pāṇṭiya king, to carry out his instructions without questioning them. Here, *līlā* becomes the manifestation of the relationship of monotheism, sealed by an unquestioning monotheistic loyalty between his peoples, on the one hand, and the deity, on the other.

From this perspective the destruction of the *kaṭampa* forest is, indeed, an environmentally destructive act, displacing its nonhuman inhabitants who are valued less than the humans, for whom they must make way. Therefore, bees and birds that once lived in the forest must go much like lesser kings make way for the greater. The woodcutters are not being destructive but are like those who cleave through darkness to let in light and wisdom. The city that will rise in that cleared space will be built according to sacred geometry, as laid down in the scriptures. The first building to be constructed is the shrine to Śiva with many halls around it, and the shrine of the Goddess adjacent to it. Then, the shrines of other deities are constructed. Śiva, therefore, takes up residence in this space that he has decreed for himself. He makes the decision to move from the wilderness, from nature, to the domesticated and civilized space of the city, where he will eventually wed the Pāṇṭiya princess and enter into the divine marriage. Thus, he settles down, as it were, with his entourage, in this city. The king's residence itself is only built after this, and orients itself toward this sacred core. Finally, in this episode, Śiva purifies and consecrates the city with the nectar from the crescent moon on his head—rendering it both sweet and auspicious and, thereby, giving it its name, Madurai.

But, as Harman has shown, Śiva's involvement and work with Madurai does not stop with this episode. Many of the old architectural features of the city—other temples, temple tanks, and the river Vaikai that runs through it—are also linked to Śiva's *līlā*, in other episodes. Further, the mythologization is also extended to the natural topography and not just the buildings of the city. Certain granite hills that surround the city are given names that link them with specific episodes in the *TVP*. Thus, Harman, concludes: "The landscape in and around Madurai is thus a sacred geography: prominent mountains, rivers, and bathing tanks are attributed to the gracious acts of Śiva. . . . Topographical features become the vehicle by which a sacred history is communicated to devotees. These features are reminders of and testimonies to Śiva's involvement in their past and, perhaps more important, in their present experience in the world."[30]

Yet when we return once more to Śiva's creation of Madurai, we are struck by how this *līlā* seems to encompass both destruction and creation—how Madurai is not possible to be imagined without an inaugural story of violence, without the destruction of the oak forest that preceded it. And Madurai, precisely because of its great beauty, its prosperity, and its cosmopolitanism, seems to have invited the destruction that engendered it more than once. Already in the *Cilappatikāram* the city comes to be destroyed by fire, lit by the terrible wrath of a wronged woman, Kaṇṇaki. This destruction of Madurai is described as one which is unimpeded because it metes out justice:

> The four demigods spoke:
> "We have known
> That the day the king's justice fails
> This city will be devoured by fire. Since this is right,
> Is it not proper that we should leave?
> The four guardian deities quit their regions
> Long before the heroic woman wrenched off her breast.
> There was excitement in the grain merchants' street,
> The chariot street festooned with banners,

And the four streets of the four castes
As on the day a fire raged in the Kāṇḍava forest.
The flames spared the homes of the virtuous
But destroyed those of the wicked."[31]

In contrast to this righteous fire which must be allowed to consume Madurai the second book of the *TVP* called *Kūṭalkāṇṭam* speaks of why Madurai's other name, *Kūṭal* or *Gathering/Junction* came about because of its preservation from near destruction due to Śiva's merciful protection. This sacred deed is a continuation of the previous one, where Varuṇa, the god of the seas, has been humiliated already by Śiva, who had the ocean which the former had sent to drown Madurai swallowed up by nine, gigantic clouds that he unleashes from his bound-up hair. This is the eighteenth *tiruviḷaiyāṭal* and the final one of the first book of the *TVP*, the *Maturaikkāṇṭam*. Varuṇa is deeply humiliated by this and seeks further revenge. The backdrop to the nineteenth deed consists of 26 verses, with which the second book opens. Verse 1310 tells us that Varuṇa did not seem to understand Śiva's dance (*āṭal*) in his role as the Lord of Madurai (*naḷirpuṉaṉ maturai mūtūr nāyakaṉ āṭaṟaṉṉai teḷikilaṉ*). Thus, Varuṇa summons his seven clouds again to drink up the waters, pour down rain, and to destroy Madurai completely. The clouds pour forth a deluge that resounds in all directions, causing mountains to burst apart and the Meru mountain itself to bend down (v. 1311). All the sacred geographical landscape in severely stressed by Varuṇa's wrath. The destruction resembles the coming of the final, cosmic deluge, "Like the sound of the sphere of the cosmic egg shattering at the end of the world" (*ūḻināḷ veṭikkum aṇṭakaṭākattin olipōl*), says the *TVP*. The great snake that holds up the world, Ādiśeṣa himself, spills all the gems in his body and contracts. The elephants that bear the weight of the eight directions shudder in fear. Then, the flooding of Madurai begins (v. 1312).

Raindrops as large as white pumpkins pelt down, and streams of water cascade down, like strong, crystal columns (*tiraṇṭa tiṇ paḷikkut tūṇpōl oḷḷiya tārai cōra*). The stars in the sky and the fish of the sea both seem to meet through the coming together of the waters from sky and earth (v. 1313). The clouds hover over all moving and still things of the world and shroud it in an impenetrable darkness (*pārtta kaṇṇuḷaiyāvākap parant iruḷ kāṉṟavar aṉṟē*) (v. 1314). Strong winds blow, and the swiftly moving clouds surround Madurai. In the face of this calamity, the king Apiṭēca (Abhiśekha) Pāṇṭiyaṉ and his people fear that they are confronted by the end of the world (v. 1316). Nevertheless, the king is well aware of Śiva's deeds and how he had come once before to the rescue of Madurai and its inhabitants. He gathers his virtuous peoples and hurries to the temple of the god who arrives mounted on his buffalo. Seeing him, the king goes and falls at his feet (v. 1317). The king utters almost a formulaic prayer, seeking refuge. He praises Śiva's potency and his fearsome weapons and ends up asking the deity to alleviate the suffering of his people and to save all their lives (*eṅkaṇalluyir kāttal vēṇṭum*) (v. 1318). The *TVP* tells us, at this point, that there was a special bond between Śiva and the Pāṇṭiya kings and that he would always protect them. The god now looks at the four clouds he had unleashed before. He commands them to go to the four corners of the city and to bend themselves into four towers to protect the town and to drive away Varuṇa's clouds (v. 1319). They, obeying him, surround the city altogether in confluence—*kūṭal*—and, like strong pillars, they completely protect it (v. 1320). Within these protective towers the people of the city, counsellors to the king, and the king himself take shelter and feel as if immersed, not in the flood waters, but in an ocean of bliss that feels akin to taking shelter under Śiva's protective feet (v. 1321). The seven clouds of Varuṇa are broken up by the towers and rendered impotent, and Varuṇa himself is humbled (v. 1322). He is now liberated from both fear and shame and, instead, rejoices, accepts Śiva also as his deity and worships him. Such is the extent of his surrender that he now wears the appurtenances of a devout Śaivite—the sacred ash and the *rudrākṣa* beads and has done the rituals of worship. This nineteenth deed of Śiva ends with verse 26, where the *TVP* explains that because in it the four clouds of Śiva came together, Madurai is also known as Confluence/Junction or *kūṭal*. Thus, unlike in the *Cilappatikāram*, where Madurai is burned for being the site of injustice, here the city is saved and protected because its very existence has been guaranteed by Śiva himself. He brings it into being, and he is the ultimate guarantor of its continued existence.

When we speak about *līlā* as the playful activity of God, we inevitably think of the activities of Kṛṣṇa, and particularly either his mischievousness as the cowherd child who steals butter and vanquishes various enemies or his dance on the autumnal nights with the cowherd women, the *rāsalīlā*. Tracing the genealogy of the *rāsalīlā* in his unparalleled study, Friedhelm Hardy[32] shows us its evolution through Sanskrit *kāvya* literature and the epics, particularly the *Harivaṃśa*, which is affixed as an appendix to the *Mahābhārata* and, thereafter, its evolution via the

Classical Tamil *Caṅkam* literature to the poetry of the Vaiṣnavite Āḻvārs from between 500 and 900 CE. Among the Āḻvārs particular mention must be made of Peiryāḻvār's *Tirumoḻi*, which has a series of songs deeply loved within the devotional repertoire, that speak of the childhood games of baby Kṛṣṇa and the rituals he undergoes. Crucially, the Tamil literary corpus also has several allusions, from the earliest literature of the *Caṅkam*, to the close association between Kṛṣṇa/Viṣṇu and the Pāṇṭiya kings.[33] In the doctrinal Vaiṣṇava literature that builds itself on the Āḻvār devotional poetry, the literature of the Śrīvaiṣṇavas, we have the understanding of the entire cosmos as composed of the two different realms, or *vibhūtis* of Viṣṇu-Nārāyaṇa—there is the pure world, composed of pure matter, *śuddhasattva* called *nityavibhūti*, where Viṣṇu resides with those souls who have never been a part of the transmigratory cycle. There is the *līlāvibhūti* that is the world of humans and other beings, subject to transmigration and eventual dissolution, in which Viṣṇu acts. Thus, as the thirteenth- to fourteenth-century polymathic theologian of Śrīvaiṣṇava doctrines, Vedānta Deśika, explains it in the fourth chapter of his work *Rahastrayasāra*, God engages himself with the world merely for *līlā* and the world where he acts is called the *līlāvibhūti.*[34]

But it is clear that not just the Vaiṣṇavas, but also the Śaivas in the Tamil region constantly and imaginatively conceptualized Śiva's activity in the world also as a form of unfathomable engagement that tested his devotees. The *TVP* is, therefore, a fairly late iteration of this understanding of Śiva's engagement with his devotees, already comprehensively imagined in the twelfth-century hagiography, the *Periyapurāṇam*.

In the *TVP* Śiva's relationship with Madurai is constantly reinforced both by the city's origin story itself as well as by the imprint of his activities on its natural landscape, and finally, by the miracles he performs at regular intervals to demonstrate his link with it. Madurai thus becomes one of the 274 sacred sites that are linked to the presence of Śiva on earth, with most of them located in the Tamil country, according to the listing. And it comes into being for no fathomable reason but only because Śiva wills it, demanding that the Pāṇṭiya king clear the oak forest to create the city. Similarly, the city's imminent destruction through flooding only comes to pass because of a rivalrous play between the gods, Varuṇa and Śiva, where the inhabitants of Madurai become unwitting pawns. And their redemption only happens because of Śiva's intervention again—he rescues them through his miraculous powers, evoking both wonder and the promise of protection. In all this there is the premise of an inflexible, monotheistic relationship, between the god, worshipped as the one, supreme god, and his people. The enactment of this relationship of monotheism is Śiva's *līlā* or *tiruviḷaiyāṭal*. The relationship of monotheism contains, in its very premises, a potential for violence—a violence that is directed toward "others" whether nonhuman, as in the case of the destruction of the *kaṭampa* forest, or whether toward other gods, such as Varuṇa, who threaten Śiva's city. The sacred city of Madurai is the geographic space, resplendent, and also the visible reward, of this monotheism.

In the final analysis, Madurai is what is made of it. In the Tamil literary imagination, it has been the urban city, sumptuous and expansive and the home of many religious traditions and many gods. With the stories of the *TVP* it became, for the citizenry of Madurai, a place of monotheism and its attendant perils, in which the transcendent reality of Śiva is near at hand, through the places he has traversed and created and the deeds he has done. There is the secular city of everyday politics, traffic jams, and climatic uncertainties, but for those who are native to Madurai and, in their own imagery nourished by a civic order that relies on religious mythology and its interpretation, there is an internalized sacred topography. Madurai experienced and known in this way makes the secular city seem a pale, unreal shadow of the sacred one, characterized by the unfathomable eruptions of Śiva's deeds.

## Works Cited


Ambach, Malini, Jonas Buchholz, and Ute Hüsken, eds. *Temples, Texts, and Networks. South Indian Perspectives.* Heidelberg: Heidelberg Asian Studies Publishing, 2022.

Cāminātaiyar, U. Vē, ed. *Pattupāṭṭu mūlamum Maduraiyāciriyar pārattuvāci Nacciṉārkkiṉiyaruraiyum.* Ceṉṉai: Tirāviṭaratnākara Accukkūṭam, 1889.

Cāminātaiyar, U. Vē, ed. *Tiruvālavāyuṭaiyār Tiruviḷaiyātaṟpurāṇam.* Cellinakar Perumpaṟṟapuliyūr Nampi iyaṟṟiyatu. Ceṉṉai: Presidency Press, 1906.

Framarin, Christopher G. "Environmental Ethics and the *Mahābhārata*: The Case of the Burning of the Khāṇḍava Forest." *SOPHIA* 32 (2013): 185–204.

Hardy, Friedhelm. *Viraha Bhakti: The Early History of Kṛṣṇa Devotion in South India.* New Delhi: Oxford University Press, 1983.

Harman, William P. *The Sacred Marriage of a Hindu Goddess.* New Delhi: Motilal Banarsidass, 1992.

Lipner, Julius. "A God at Play? Re-examining the Concept of *Līlā* in Hindu Philosophy and Theology." *International Journal of Hindu Studies* 26 (2022): 282–326.

Nachimuthu, K. "A Survey of the Sthalapurāṇa Literature in Tamil." In *Temples, Texts, and Networks: South Indian Perspectives*, edited by Malini Ambach, Jonas Buchholz, and Ute Hüsken, 41–76. Heidelberg: Heidelberg Asian Studies Publishing, 2022.

Oberhammer, Gerhard. *Materialien zur Geschichte der Rāmānuja-Schule V. Zur Lehre von der ewigen vibhūti Gottes.* Vienna: Verlag der Ostrreichischen Akademie der Wissenschaften, 2000.

Ophir, Adi. M. *In the Beginning Was the State: Divine Violence in the Hebrew Bible.* New York: Fordham University Press, 2023.

Parañcōtimuṉivar. *Parañcōtimuṉivar aruḷiya Tiruviḷaiyāṭaṟpurāṇam. Mūlamum uraiyum.* Ceṉṉai: Cakuntalai Patippakam, 2017.

Parthasarathy. R. *The Cilappatikāram of Iḷaṅkō Aṭikaḷ.* New York: Columbia University Press, 1993.

Shulman, David. *Tamil Temple Myths: Sacrifice and Divine Marriage in the South Indian Śaiva Tradition.* Princeton, NJ: Princeton University Press, 1980.

Van Buitenen, J. A. B. *Mahābhārata: The Book of the Beginnings.* Chicago: University of Chicago Press, 1973.

Zvelebil, Kamil. *Lexicon of Tamil Literature.* Leiden: Brill, 1995.

## Notes

1. K. Nachimuthu, "A Survey of the Sthalapurāṇa Literature in Tamil," in *Temples, Texts, and Networks: South Indian Perspectives*, ed. Malini Ambach, Jonas Buchholz, and Ute Hüsken (Heidelberg: Heidelberg Asian Studies Publishing, 2022), 43.
2. Nachimuthu, "A Survey of the Sthalapurāṇa Literature," 44–45.
3. David Shulman, *Tamil Temple Myths: Sacrifice and Divine Marriage in the South Indian Śaiva Tradition* (Princeton, NJ: Princeton University Press, 1980), 32.
4. Parañcōtimuṉivar, *Parañcōtimuṉivar aruḷiya Tiruviḷaiyāṭaṟpurāṇa: Mūlamum uraiyum* (Ceṉṉai: Cakuntalai Patippakam, 2017), 24.
5. Julius Lipner, "A God at Play? Re-examining the Concept of *Līlā* in Hindu Philosophy and Theology," *International Journal of Hindu Studies* 26 (2022): 282–326.
6. I here take a definition of violence offered by Adi Ophir as useful for the purposes of this essay: "'Violence' will be understood here as the operation of any force that violates, harms, injures, dissociates, destroys, dismantles, uproots, or annihilates what is affected by it, whether targeted or not, whether that be bodies, psyches (through humiliation, insult, or denial of recognition), solid structures, or landscapes and entire environments where humans and other beings dwell" (Adi M. Ophir, *In the Beginning Was the State: Divine Violence in the Hebrew Bible* [New York: Fordham University Press, 2023], 25).
7. Kamil Zvelebil, *Lexicon of Tamil Literature* (Leiden: Brill, 1995), 695.
8. William P. Harman collates the evidence to show that one of the core stories of the text, the sacred marriage of a royal princess to a god, was probably in circulation on a pan-Indian scale much prior to the earliest literary evidence (*The Sacred Marriage of a Hindu Goddess* [New Delhi: Motilal Banarsidass, 1992], 28).
9. A list of the specific references to these deeds in both the *Tirumuṟai,* primarily in the *Tēvāram* and the *Tiruvācakam*, as well as in the *Kallāṭam*, has been given in U. Vē. Cāminātaiyar's 1906 edition of Perumpaṟṟapuliyūr Nampi's earlier *Tiruviḷaiyātaṟpurāṇam*. See pages 38–49 of this 1906 edition.
10. Cāminātaiyar (1906) tells us that Perumpaṟṟapuliyūr Nampi's text is quoted in the seventeenth-century Vīraśaiva author Cāntaliṅka Cuvāmikaḷ's *Kolaimaṟuttal*, attesting to its popularity.

11. Shulman, *Tamil Temple Myths*, 32–33.
12. Shulman, *Tamil Temple Myths*, 33.
13. Parañcōtimuṉivar, *Parañcōtimuṉivar aruḷiya Tiruviḷaiyāṭaṟpurāṇam: Mūlamum uraiyum* (Ceṉṉai: Cakuntalai Patippakam, 2017), 24, v. 26.
14. Harman, *The Sacred Marriage of a Hindu Goddess*, 33.
15. Parañcōtimuṉivar, *Parañcōtimuṉivar aruḷiya Tiruviḷaiyāṭaṟpurāṇam*, 244, 3.1.
16. This refers to a specific theological position in the Tamil Śaivasiddhānta referring to the final relationship in liberation between the soul and God—which is neither one of complete union nor of complete separation.
17. R. Parthasarathy, *The Cilappatikāram of Iḷaṅkō Aṭikaḷ* (New York: Columbia University Press, 1993), 136.
18. Parthasarathy, *The Cilappatikāram of Iḷaṅkō Aṭikaḷ*, 140.
19. Parañcōtimuṉivar, *Parañcōtimuṉivar aruḷiya Tiruviḷaiyāṭaṟpurāṇam*, 213:

*aruvipaṭin taruviyeṟi maṇiṇaṭuttup*
*pāṟaiyiliṭṭaruvi nīr tūyk*
*karuviralkoy talarcūṭṭk kaṉiyūṭṭi*
*vaḷipaṭuva kallā manti*
*oruturaiyil yāḷikari puḷaikkaimukan*
*toṉṟaṟ koṉṟūṭṭi yūṭṭip*
*parukuvaṉa pulimulaippāl pulvāykkaṉ*
*ṟaruttiyiṭum pacinōy tīra.*

20. Parañcōtimuṉivar, *Parañcōtimuṉivar aruḷiya Tiruviḷaiyāṭaṟpurāṇam*, 214:

*neḷiyarāk kuraḷaiveyil veḷḷiṭaiyiṟ*
*kiṭantuyaṅki neḷiyap puḷḷē*
*ṟoḷiyaṟāc ciṟaivirittu niḻalparappap*
*paṟavai nōyuṟṟa tēkol*
*aḷiyavā yaccōveṉ ṟōtiyayaṉ*
*maṭamanti yaruvi yūṟṟun*
*tuḷiyanīr vaḷaittcumpiṉ mukanteṭuttuk*
*karuṅkaiyiṉār coriva mātō.*

21. Parañcōtimuṉivar, *Parañcōtimuṉivar aruḷiya Tiruviḷaiyāṭaṟpurāṇam*, 214–215:

*paṭavarava maṇiyīṉṟu noccipā cilaiyaṉṉa*
*paintāṇ maññai*
*peṭaitaḷuvi maṇañceyya maṇavaṟaiyil*
*viḷakkiṭuva peruntaṇkāṉat*
*taṭarciṟaimeṉ kuyilōmeṉ ṟārppamaṭak*
*kiḷḷaiyeḻut tataintu mōcait*
*toṭarpupeṟa vuccarippak kurumoḻikēṭ*
*ṭāṅkuvappa toṭikaṭ pūvai.*

22. Christopher G. Framarin, "Environmental Ethics and the *Mahābhārata*: The Case of the Burning of the Khāṇḍava Forest," *SOPHIA* 32 (2013): 186.
23. Framarin, "Environmental Ethos and the Mahābhārata."
24. Framarin, "Environmental Ethos and the Mahābhārata," 186–187.

25. J. A. B. van Buitenen, *Mahābhārata: The Book of the Beginnings* (Chicago: University of Chicago Press, 1973), 13.
26. Framarin, "Environmental Ethos and the Mahābhārata," 193.
27. Framarin, "Environmental Ethos and the Mahābhārata," 197.
28. Ophir, *In the Beginning was the State.*
29. Ophir, *In the Beginning was the State*, 2.
30. Harman, *The Sacred Marriage of a Hindu Goddess*, 35.
31. Parthasarathy, *The Cilappatikāram of Iḷaṅkō Aṭikaḷ*, 192–193.
32. Friedhelm Hardy, *Viraha Bhakti: The Early History of Kṛṣṇa Devotion in South India* (New Delhi: Oxford University Press, 1983).
33. Hardy, *Viraha Bhakti*, 155–156, 610–612.
34. For more on this, see chapters in this volume by Sucharita Adluri, "*Līlā* and Divine Mercy in the *Hundred Verses to Compassion* of Vedānta Deśika," and Francis X. Clooney, SJ, "Creation, Vision, Bliss: *Līlā* as Grace according to Rāmānuja, with Reference Also to Thomas Aquinas and Gregory Palamas."

PART IV

# Human Playfulness as Imitation of Divine *Līlā*

# 10 Looking to the Leader

## THE DIVINE DANCE IN NEOPLATONISM

*Stephen R. L. Clark*

### Dancing with Stars

When his friend and disciple Amelius asked Apollo where the soul of Plotinus (204–270 CE) had gone, so Porphyry tells us, the oracle responded that he had joined "the company of heaven" (*daimonia homeguris*), the children of God and all "the noblest of mankind," in "the dance of immortal love": "There the most blessed spirits have their birth and live a life filled full of festivity and joy; and this life lasts for ever, made blessed by the gods."[1]

It is possible that the oracle, or Amelius, had it in mind that Plotinus was now visibly a "fixed star," a point of light in the heavens beyond the planetary spheres. Imagining ourselves back into a pre-Copernican cosmos is perhaps an unnecessary effort, but we should not forget that this was the more likely attitude of our ancestors, to see the astronomical heavens as an ever-lasting, ever-renewed, image of something that they could also imagine, as it were, "from inside": We "must correct the orbits in the head which were corrupted at our birth" by aligning them, somehow, with the heavens.[2] And before abandoning that astronomical vision, it is worth noticing that the order described here is that of a joyful dance, rather than the military image coined by George Meredith to intimidate his Lucifer:

> Soaring through wider zones that pricked his scars
> With memory of the old revolt from Awe,
> He reach'd a middle height, and at the stars,
> Which are the brain of heaven, he look'd, and sank.
> Around the ancient track marched, rank on rank,
> The army of unalterable law.[3]

Both the fixed and planetary stars, to the pre-Copernican, pagan eye were dancing rather than marching. "We have the gods as fellow-dancers," and it is from the joy (*chara*) that is natural to the dance that we get the name "choruses."[4] The dance that Plotinus has in mind here is a round dance—though he also often refers to the dancing of individual pantomimes.

Another feature of the stars'-eye view that is still resonant is that it diminishes the felt weight of our present lives. Scipio's Dream—one of the seminal texts of Western thought—tells how in his dream ascent he saw

> stars which we never see from here below, and all the stars were vast far beyond what we have ever imagined. The least of them was that which, farthest from heaven, nearest to the earth, shone with a borrowed light. But the starry globes very far surpassed the earth in magnitude. The earth itself indeed looked to me so small as to make me ashamed of our empire, which was a mere point on its surface.[5]

And the earth itself was a mere blue dot—according to Ptolemy and Boethius, an infinitesimally small point in comparison with the breadth of heaven.[6] Nowadays we have mapped, or credible experts have mapped, the superclusters of galaxies all the way up to Laniakea ("immeasurable heaven," in Hawaiian) and Perseus-Pisces.[7] We have discovered, or credible experts have discovered, that *visible* matter is only a fraction even of the material cosmos, that most material is invisible. We are even prepared to imagine that the whole universe is only one realized possibility from indefinitely many versions of the aftermath of creation. But all these imaginings probably do little more, in practice, to put terrestrial life in perspective than Scipio's Dream long ago. We may feel small for a moment, but everyday concerns speedily overwhelm us.

But what did the ancients actually believe? Could Porphyry and his colleagues have believed that Plotinus had *become* a star? There is no suggestion that this would be a *new* star in the sky, nor yet that he had taken the place of some earlier astral intelligence. Rather it might be thought that he himself had always been a star, and that others, godlike men and women, had been too.[8] We have briefly, in this life, forgotten our real selves.

> Even before this coming to be we were there, men [that is, *anthropoi*, humans] who were different, and some of us even gods, pure souls and intellect united with the whole of reality; we were parts of the intelligi-

> ble, not marked off or cut off but belonging to the whole; and we are not cut off even now.[9]

Each soul stretches down from its origin in the Divine Intellect, entering the material world at the sidereal level, and sinking or traveling further as it wishes, or as it is compelled.[10] The most recalcitrant eventually stick their heads in the earth and live on as plants[11]—a point to which I shall return. Conversely, we can—perhaps—begin to climb back up.

> If a man is able to follow the spirit (*daimon*) which is above him, he comes to be himself above, living that spirit's life, and giving the pre-eminence to that better part of himself to which he is being led; and after that spirit he rises to another, until he reaches the heights. For the soul is many things, and all things, both the things above and the things below down to the limits of all life, and we are each one of us an intelligible universe, making contact with this lower world by the powers of soul below, but with the intelligible world by its powers above.[12]

However, the higher self is sometimes distinguished more completely from the lower, as a guardian *daimon*.

> He who is before the soul is more of a spirit (*daimonioteros*), or rather is a god, and a spirit is an imitation of a god, dependent on the god as man is on the spirit; for the being on whom man is dependent is not called a god.[13]

Porphyry records, on the contrary, that Plotinus's own guardian, evoked in a séance, turned out really to be a god[14]—though quite what was to be understood by this strange event is unexplained. Whether the soul of Plotinus was presumed to be an echo or image of that god, or else a distinct entity as it were *apprenticed* to the deity, may make a difference to the practice of a Plotinian spirituality, but it is not a question easily settled from the textual or other evidence.

One feature of Plotinus's account of the stars and the life they are presumed to live establishes a definite distinction at least between his life in late antiquity, from Lycopolis to Campania, and his sidereal being. Stars need not remember where they have been, nor anticipate where they are going[15]—and in living the life of stars (whether by analogy or in literal truth) we too need not remember anything from our merely mortal lives. At least if there is an essential identity between the composite soul-body that is our current life and the eternal being, it does not depend on the latter's *remembering* us. Lloyd Gerson's terminology, distinguishing the "endowed" and the "ideal" self, turns on just this puzzle.[16] Are they two or one? Have we forgotten the life we lived, and will we forget our present life when once we have returned? Or is it rather that the sidereal self, which is at least a little closer to the ideal self, is something always other than the empirical self here-now? That ambiguity—by analogy the question whether a butterfly (that is, in Greek, *psyche*) is the adult form of a caterpillar or else, as Aristotle supposed, a separate entity born from the egg-like chrysalis[17]—is one that I have addressed elsewhere.[18] And yet the stars we might or shall be, though they may not remember "being us," might still be instantly recognizable.

> For here below, too, we can know many things by the look in people's eyes when they are silent; but there [that is, when we see things in the light of the spirit] all their body is clear and pure and each is like an eye, and nothing is hidden or feigned, but before one speaks to another that other has seen and understood.[19]

Our present empirical selves hide what we truly are, both from our neighbors and ourselves.

> "Know Yourself" is said to those who because of their selves' multiplicity have the business of counting themselves up and learning that they do not know all the numbers and kinds of things they are, or do not know any one of them, nor what their ruling principle is, or by what they are themselves.[20]

Up aloft, the stars have each their particular spectral shape.

## Dancing Down Below

"There" we shall understand and recognize our friends as well as ourselves—but where, for Plotinus, is "There"? The astronomical story may not, after all, be what Plotinus himself intended. Other Platonists, of a more Hermetic disposition, may have thought in terms of an "astral vehicle," a chariot to carry us back aloft to a literal heaven, past the planetary spheres.[21] But Plotinus expressly denies the need of this.

> What then is our way of escape, and how are we to find it? We shall put out to sea, as Odysseus did, from the witch Circe or Calypso—as the poet says (I think with a hidden meaning)—and was not content to stay though he had delights of the eyes and lived among much beauty of sense.

> Our country from which we came is there, our Father is there. How shall we travel to it, where is our way of escape? We cannot get there on foot; for our feet only carry us everywhere in this world, from one country to another. You must not get ready a carriage, either, or a boat. Let all these things go, and do not look. Shut your eyes, and change to and wake another way of seeing, which everyone has but few use.[22]

Our country, the home of our immortal being, is not up aloft—or at any rate the stars above are only *representations* or *reminders* of that home. We do not need to travel to it, since its very nature is non-local: It is not far away, since nothing real is far away. "Nothing is a long way off or far from anything else."[23] Our significance, after all, is not diminished by the vast expanse of space and time that modern research has uncovered, or that Scipio experienced. That expanse is an illusion.

It may be that Plotinus's friends and disciples really believed that he had been reunited with his own sidereal self, perhaps on the way to a complete disengagement from material reality. It is at least very likely that he (and they) employed an imaginative technique, of self-identification with the presumed life of stars, in the cause of self-transformation. But it is also likely that Plotinus thought it possible to join "the dance," or realize that we were already dancers, even in this life, and despite its obvious hazards. Even a tortoise, he jokingly remarks, could avoid being trampled on if it only managed to range itself with the movement of the dance.[24] And we can manage this (even the tortoise can manage this) if we look toward the leader of the chorus:

> It is like a choral dance: in the order of its singing the choir keeps round its *koruphaios* but may sometimes turn away so that he is out of their sight, but when it turns back to him it sings beautifully and is truly with him; so we are always around him—and if we were not, we should be totally dissolved and no longer exist—but not always turned towards him; but when we do look to him, then we are at our goal and at rest and do not sing out of tune as we truly dance our god-inspired dance around him.[25]

Armstrong and others translate *koruphaios* as the chorus's "conductor," but this has the wrong connotations: The head or leader of the chorus is not standing at the front of the stage with a baton. He is the leader of the dance, and of their singing. "If one takes away the leader," according to Demosthenes in an earlier century, "the rest of the chorus is done for."[26] The leader of the *real* chorus is Apollo, the god "who sits in the centre, on the navel of the earth, and is the interpreter of religion to all mankind"[27] and who—according to the oracle I cited earlier—summons the Muses to sing and dance in triumph in honor of his friend.[28] He is himself unmoving—or does he dance as well?

The image also appears in the work of Nicholas Cabasilas (1319–1392) many centuries later, by whatever obscure descent: Christ will one day return as a "beautiful choir master (*koruphaios*) in the midst of a beautiful choir" and will draw all creatures to himself in a great movement of ecstasy. "What a vision we will see at the Second Coming! An assembly of beautiful creatures, gods, surrounding God himself to form a crown around him who is supreme Beauty."[29]

So how are we to join in the dance? How are we to notice or follow the Lord of the Dance? What difference can we expect from doing or not doing this? Do we in fact have a choice? The dance is carrying on around us, and we are already dancing. In the dance or play of Nature differing, apparently opposed, movements all have a place.

> So, then, there are good men and wicked men, like the opposed movements of a dancer inspired by one and the same art; and we shall call one part of his performance "good" and another "wicked," and in this way it is a good performance (*kalōs echei*). But, then [so some will say], the wicked are no longer wicked. No, their being wicked is not done away with, only their being like that does not originate with themselves. . . . There is a place for every man, one to fit the good and one to fit the bad.[30]

Stepping outside the dance, it seems, will be impossible. Dramas need their villains too; the evil sounds of Tartarus enhance the whole; and "the public executioner, who is a scoundrel, does not make his well-governed city worse."[31] Even if we rail against the gods who allow such things, or against mindless destiny, it will only be "as if a poet in his plays wrote a part for an actor insulting and depreciating the author of the play"![32] Everything, we might conclude in Stoic mode, is only and exactly as it must and should be, and our only apparent liberty (if even this is possible) is whether or not to accept it, in our hearts.

> Lead me, Zeus and Destiny, wherever you have ordained for me. For I shall follow unflinching. But if I become bad and am unwilling, I shall follow none the less.[33]

Plotinus himself appears to allow a larger liberty,[34] but even this seems to amount to no more than playing the part allotted to us well or ill. Good actors may get a better part "next time," in their "next life" or maybe in another age of the world, when the same drama is reenacted with a different cast.[35] This seems to require us to play the part even of "villains" with appropriate good taste and sense—and maybe an anecdote from Lucian's defense of pantomime is a partial explanation. He tells how one pantomime (that is, a silent actor) was so involved in his characterization of Ajax that he struck the dancer portraying Odysseus with a flute snatched from the musician. This did not please those who understood the nature of pantomime. Lucian adds that

> the illiterate riffraff, who knew not good from bad, and had no idea of decency, regarded it as a supreme piece of acting; and the more intelligent part of the audience, realizing how things stood, concealed their disgust, and instead of reproaching the actor's folly by silence, smothered it under their plaudits; they saw only too clearly that it was not Ajax but the pantomime who was mad.[36]

The actor in question, once he had come to his senses, was mortified, and still more embarrassed "by the success of his rival, who, though a similar part had been written for him, played it with admirable judgement and discretion, and was complimented on his observance of decorum, and of the proper bounds of his art."

Is this enough? We have already, from outside the world, *selected* our own destinies—or so Plato tells us in "the myth of Er"[37]: however dire the result we must now play it out, within "the proper bounds of our art." How could there be a better material world than this?[38]

This is a rather more robust account of life than most of us can easily endure: We are more inclined to insist that some features of our lives here-now, and of the material universe, are *wrong*, and that our real duty must often be to protest, to abstain, to resist such evil doings, and not pretend that "we are only doing our jobs" (as those seem to be assigned by the relevant powers). "For we wrestle not against flesh and blood, but against principalities, against powers, against the rulers of the darkness of this world, against spiritual wickedness in heavenly places."[39] Plotinus was less certain—or rather he was certain, on the contrary, that we should not despise the Powers.

> Despising the universe and the gods in it and the other noble things is certainly not becoming good. Every wicked man, in former times too, was capable of despising the gods, and even if he was not altogether

> wicked before, when he despised them, he became so by this very fact, even if he was not wicked in everything else.[40]

If we condemn the God or gods who made us, how can we be much moved by the moral laws they impose? What we had thought were virtues or good deeds now turn out only to be devices to exacerbate our misery. And the less that we are bound by them, of course, the less good reason we have to condemn our makers.

There seem to be two possible interpretations of Plotinus's insistence that not even the planetary stars (by tradition, the helpful or unhelpful guardians of the way between the worlds) could intend any evil, and that we ourselves are not bound by astral necessity to do or to be evil.[41] Either the course of events is not actually evil, or it is not the fault of the powers. If it is not evil, then we are already dancing with the gods; if it is—or even if it is flawed—then there is something we need to do to join the dance, which will (presumably) make things better. We need to change the way we think, and so also the way we behave. We must think of what we do as *dancing.*

> What is the right way of living? Life must be lived as play. Playing certain games, making sacrifices, singing and dancing, and then a man will be able to propitiate the gods, and defend himself against his enemies and win in the contest.[42]

The point, or a related point, is made by Alan Watts: Life must be lived as *play,*[43] without troubling about the eventual outcome of our actions.

This is a flawed and fallen world—but not all the features to which we object are evil (that is, of a sort that any decent Maker would erase at whatever cost). What "ordinary nature normally finds terrible" are usually no more than children's bogies.[44] In the very next treatise that he wrote Plotinus added that "we should be spectators of murders, and all deaths, and takings and sacking of cities, as if they were on the stages of theatres."[45] That, after all, is how the gods will see them: "In this city [of the world] virtue is honoured and vice has its appropriate dishonour, and not merely the images of gods but gods themselves—[that is, presumably, the stars]—look down on us from above."[46] Such things are no more than children's games: "One must not take weeping and lamenting as evidence of the presence of evils, for children, too, weep and wail over things that are not evils."[47] If children are being bullied, the remedy must lie with them.[48] If professed adults are fearful or distressed or greedy, they must discipline their "inner child."

> If sometimes when he is concerned with other things an involuntary fear comes upon him before he has time to reflect, the wise man [in him] will come and drive it away and quiet the child in him which is stirred to a sort of distress, by threatening or reasoning; the threatening will be unemotional, as if the child was shocked into quietness just by a severe look. A man of this sort will not be unfriendly or unsympathetic; he will be like this to himself and in dealing with his own affairs: but he will render to his friends all that he renders to himself, and so will be the best of friends as well as [holding on to *Nous*] (*meta ton noun ekhein*).[49]

This must even apply to public catastrophes of a sort with which Plotinus, who served in the Roman army under Gordian and Philip the Arab, must have been well familiar.

> When men, mortal as they are, direct their weapons against each other, fighting in orderly ranks, doing what they do in sport in their war-dances (*purrichai*) their battles show that all human concerns are children's games, and tell us that deaths are nothing terrible, and that those who die in wars and battles anticipate only a little the death which comes in old age—they go away and come back quicker.[50]

But it is already implicit in the passages I have cited that acceptance is not *apathy*, in the usual modern sense. If we are to think of these things as if they were "children's games," we need still to remember that children can rightly be *serious* about their games, as Dominic White insists in "The Serious Subject of Play: Play in Dance and Music" in this volume: "Play is a serious matter for children," and also—in a way—for us! On the one hand, we are to understand that the Lord makes his rain to fall on the just and the unjust,[51] and the wicked as well as the virtuous draw water from the river.[52] We are not to be always finding fault with people or things or the material world itself. We are to "love our enemies" even while they are enemies.[53] On the other hand, there are proper responses to what happens, which will include the immediate urge to help or heal. That, after all, is what is involved in dancing. We are constantly being given *opportunities* to "give God glory," to let "the spirit" move us.

> The activity of life is an artistic activity, like the way in which one who is dancing is moving; for the dancer himself is like the life which is artistic in this way and his art moves him.[54]

The movement and music of the dance—both the sidereal and the terrestrial—depend on *harmonia*—but this does not mean quite what modern readers usually suppose. Plotinus is not recommending a "harmonious" performance, and implicitly chiding those who sound "inharmonious," discordant, notes. The point is rather to represent the full range of musical possibility, all the notes there are. The single voice to which all living creatures are contributing will sometimes sound, to us, a little raucous!

> If the parts are struck in a particular way, the speaking parts give out a corresponding sound, and others receive the blow in silence and make the movements which result from it; and from all the sounds and passive experiences and activities come a kind of single voice of the living creature, a single life and way of living.[55]

## Dancing Away Elsewhere

On the one hand, all of us are already dancing. On the other, we may need to be reminded of the fact, if we are really to *join* the dance rather than, absurdly, seek to subvert it. But we can still ask—especially if our untaught impulses seem so often, in retrospect, to lead to missing cues and being trampled—what figures we are reproducing in our dance, and how we might allow them a stronger presence in our lives here-now.

The Platonic answer depends on reckoning that there is a real and abiding beauty only fitfully and partially represented here. There is, that is, a fundamental "harmony"—but not the harmony that we now usually expect. *Harmonia* refers to the abstract system of notes in the octave, rather as Saussure could distinguish "langue" from "parole," the underlying system of implications and exclusions that constitute a language, from the particular speeches and conversations that "langue" makes possible. Different *harmoniai*, as the Dorian, Lydian, Mixolydian and so forth, arrange the intervals (tone and semitone) between successive notes of the octave differently. A total, systematizing account was offered by Aristides Quintilianus (himself very likely a follower of Plotinian Platonism),[56] in which those differing *harmoniai* can be conceived as a single cycle.[57] What seems to us a merely abstract system was rather, for Plotinus, at once an instance and an analogy of the eternal forms coherent in the divine Intellect. Soul—that is the World Soul and all the lesser souls together—make their selection from the realm of eternal possibility. This latter is the beauty to which all things, even the underlying stuff of worlds, are drawn, and the object of his own spiritual ascesis. But though he desires an understanding and appreciation of the real, eternal, relationships that constitute intellectual beauty, this is not to demean or ignore any beauties of the here and now. "How could there be a musician who sees the *harmonia* in the intelligible world [the world as it is properly understood] and will not be stirred when he hears [it] in sensible sounds?"[58]

> Despising the universe and the gods in it and the other noble things is certainly not becoming good. . . . For anyone who feels affection for anything at all shows kindness to all that is akin to the object of his affection, and to the children of the father that he loves. But every soul is a child of That Father. (II.9 [33].16, 1–3, 7–10)

The basic pattern of the material world is shaped by the World Soul to represent, spread out in time and space, the eternal order. Lesser souls have been enticed to share in the working, and have often (usually) lost themselves in the play. On the one hand we need to remember who we are. On the other, we may need—paradoxically—to forget ourselves (or at least the false image of ourselves we carry along with us). The World Soul works in silence, without any need of planning: "what comes into being is what [she] sees in [her] silence."[59] Hedley cites Sri Aurobindo to similar effect: "The world, as God has made it, is not a rigid exercise in logic but, like a strain of music, an infinite harmony of many diversities."[60] And this is also the ideal which we are offered. Most of us poor humans, in fact, must often struggle to think things through, and carefully plan our actions. Most of us pay more attention to our own *image* of our great achievements (or conversely our humiliating failures) than to the work itself. Those more in touch with the spirit need not think, and need not worry about their image any longer—any more than a great trained dancer needs to *think* exactly how to respond, or to worry about her reputation.

> The dancer's intention looks elsewhere; his limbs are affected in accordance with the dance and serve the dance, and help to make it perfect and complete; and the connoisseur of ballet [that is, the pantomime] can say

> that to fit a particular figure one limb is raised, and other bent together, one is hidden, another degraded; the dancer does not choose to make these movements for no reason, but each part of him as he performs the dance has its necessary position in the dancing of the whole body.[61]

This metaphor is adduced both to explain the varied movements of the material world through time, and to recommend a form of life to us—an unselfconsciousness that can respond exactly to whatever happens.

That is the recommendation—but how can we expect to follow it? It is after all the great, *trained*, dancer that exemplifies this pattern, not the struggling novice, nor yet the sort of pantomime that made a mess of Ajax. Certainly, for most of us, poor dancers and worse actors (whether dramatic or moral), it will be better to try to follow some explicit rules and reminders—beginning, perhaps, with the effort really to imagine that what we do to others may be done also to us.

> There is no accident in a man's becoming a slave, nor is he taken prisoner in war by chance, nor is outrage done on his body without due cause, but he was once the doer of that which he now suffers; and a man who made away with his mother will be made away with by a son when he has become a woman, and one who has raped a woman will be a woman in order to be raped.[62]

As an explanation for the horrors routinely inflicted on the apparently innocent this may be counterproductive (since the victims turn out, in some sense, to "deserve" their fate). But the Golden Rule (to treat others as we would wish ourselves to be treated) depends at least on the possibility that we might suffer, that we do suffer, just what we impose on others. "For with what judgment ye judge, ye shall be judged: and with what measure ye mete, it shall be measured to you again."[63] We may also need explicit rules to guard us against the error of supposing that just any "natural impulse" is the work of the Spirit: Plotinus, so Porphyry tells us, was enraged by Diophanes' attempt to justify a guru's right to sexual favors from his disciples[64]—a belief that has been all too common among twentieth-century gurus convinced of their own virtue.

*Nous*, so Plotinus insists, is King,

> But we too are kings (*basileuomen*), when we are in accord with it; we can be in accord with it in two ways, either by having something like its writing written in us like laws, or by being as if filled with it and able to see it and be aware of it as present.[65]

Even the former state, of having the laws written in our hearts, is far beyond most of us, who need the laws written firmly down in front of us: What is written in our hearts has a tendency to mutate without our notice. Only the latter state, being animated wholly by the Spirit, is really royal (and also really rare).

What relevant guidance does Plotinus offer? The Golden Rule is rarely enough by itself, granted our usual capacity for self-deception. There are explicit (and mostly negative) laws conveyed by the wise such as Minos, from conversation (perhaps) with the gods themselves.[66] These may not always be *verbal* reminders: We are often also moved by visible signs and symbols:

> The wise men of Egypt, I think, also understood this, either by scientific (*akribes*) or innate (*sumphute*) knowledge, and when they wished to signify something wisely, did not use the forms of letters which follow the order of words and propositions (*logoi* and *protaseis*) and imitate sounds and the enunciations of philosophical statements (*prophoras axiomaton*), but by drawing images and inscribing in their temples one particular image of each particular thing, they manifested the non-discursiveness of the intelligible world, that is, that every image is a kind of knowledge and wisdom and is a subject of statements, all together in one, and not discourse (*dianoesis*) or deliberation (*bouleusis*).[67]

There are judgments made by consensus—for the Many (unless they have been corrupted) are more likely to reach a right judgment than the few.[68] There are the helpful presences of our *internal* statues, however much they are covered with rust or mold,[69] and perhaps an occasional light sent down from heaven "so that [our] eyes could see out of the mournful darkness."[70]

What above all Plotinus recommends is to keep our eyes on the leader, the center. "Except for the point, the still point, there would be no dance, and there is only the dance," so T. S. Eliot assured us, taking *koruphaios* as the central, seated musician.[71] The solution offered by Hesychios the Priest (ca. eighth to ninth century)—and by Orthodox Christian tradition in general—was to invoke the name of Jesus constantly: "Whenever we are filled with evil thoughts, we should throw the invocation of our Lord Jesus Christ into their midst. Then, as experience has taught us, we shall see them instantly dispersed like smoke in the air."[72] This solution was not available to pagan Platonists, but they had some similar hopes of properly divine intervention.

> The guardian spirit of Socrates, possessing this sort of individual character, I mean one that is purificatory and productive of an undefiled life, and ranked under that power of Apollo which governs simply the whole of purification, restrains Socrates from relationship with the many and the life that extends towards multiplicity, leads him round to the inner portion of the soul and to activity undefiled by contact with the less perfect, and for this reason "never impels but ever deters him." For what else is "to deter" than to restrain him from the many activities that tend towards externals? . . . The guardian spirit is analogous to Apollo, being a follower of his, and Socrates' reason to Dionysos, since the intellect within us is a product of the power of this god.[73]

Both pagan and Christian appeals may be interpreted subjectively, as imaginative exercises to help control and consolidate our wandering souls, or else objectively, as real appeals to a really existent somewhat. On that a jobbing philosopher need express no view. Our task, as Plato and Plotinus knew, is only to carry on playing!

> Well, as this discussion has arisen among ourselves, there will be no risk in playing with our own ideas. Then are we now contemplating (*theoroumen*) as we play? Yes, we and all who play are doing this, or at any rate this is what they aspire to as they play.[74]

The Christian account is often nowadays interpreted simply as a suggestion that we take Jesus as an improbable moral model or ethical ideal: That is probably untrue both to the Christian tradition, and more certainly the pagan. Apollo has no character or history for us to imitate: The very name is only to indicate that the leader is "Not Many."[75] His figure stands in for the Unknowable One, and the attitude required of his devotees is a willingness to discard easy assumptions, and go up naked into the shrine.[76] His ways are very clearly not our ways. And the same may be true also of the Incarnate Word.

But the problem remains: "It does no good at all to say 'Look to God,' unless one also teaches how one is to look."[77] We are to avert our eyes from some things and concentrate on others—or rather on One Other—but what does that require? "The kingdom of heaven is like a merchant in search of fine pearls. When he found one very precious pearl, he went away and sold all he had and bought it."[78] There is something—Aristotle agreed—that is worth more than anything else we can value,[79] a form of life that identically *is* God.[80] Christians supposed that "the Word of God

Himself assumed humanity that we might become God."[81] Pagan Platonists believed that, in essence at least, we possibly already were. What in either case could that be like?

Is there a discernible difference between pagan and Christian values? This, certainly, is an often-repeated judgment.

> [Plotinus] would, of course, observe the vulgar decencies; it is just that they would be subsumed into something higher. One feels of Plotinus that he would have gladly helped an old lady across the road—but he might very well fail to notice her at all. And if she were squashed by a passing wagon, he would remain quite unmoved.[82]

Can this really be correct? Does Plotinus proffer, as J. M. Dillon suggests,[83] an "uncompromisingly self-centered and otherworldly" ethic, despite insisting that we should live by the god in each of us, that we should struggle to bring that god back "to the god in the all"?[84] Surely not.

> It does no good at all to say "Look to God," unless one also teaches how one is to look. . . . In reality it is virtue which goes before us to the goal and, when it comes to exist in the soul along with wisdom, shows God; but God, if you talk about him without true virtue, is only a name. Again, despising the universe and the gods in it and the other noble things is certainly not becoming good. . . . For anyone who feels affection for anything at all shows kindness to all that is akin to the object of his affection, and to the children of the father that he loves. But every soul is a child [specifically, a *daughter*] of That Father.[85]

Plotinus, after all, did *not* disregard old ladies, nor emperors, nor orphan children, even if he thought that there were higher and better goals than worldly health and success. He helped the children with their homework, swiftly identified a thieving slave (and so spared the rest from torture), was "gentle [*praos*], and at the disposal of all who had any acquaintance with him."[86] He spotted Porphyry's terminal depression and intervened to help him.[87]

But perhaps all this was at least of secondary importance? Is not the final phrase of *The Enneads* translated, at least since the days of the Cambridge Platonists, as "the flight of the alone to the Alone,"[88] so that our final salvation is in solitude? Thus Andrew Louth, speaking for many, contrasts the Plotinian goal with Augustine's conviction "that it is with others, in some kind of *societas*, that we are to seek God."[89] But this is a mistranslation: "*monos*," in this context, does not mean "solitary" but "pure": *Nous*—in this context meaning our own spiritual concentration—is "simplified into happiness (*haplotheis eis eupatheian*) by having its fill."[90] Seeking a literal *solitude* is, on the contrary, the very essence of the fall: "As if they were tired of being together, they each go to their own,"[91] and the inward turn that Plotinus recommends is actually a turn *toward* community. Phenomena, as they are present to us at a particular angle, suited to our sensory capacities and our emotional state, are what *divide* us from each other. Discovering the world we all inhabit and create requires us to put phenomena aside in favor of the ever-present reality: Even a merely *notional* acknowledgment of that real world is an advance, but our *real assent* is an awakening.

> Deductions have no power of persuasion. The heart is commonly reached, not through the reason, but through the imagination, by means of direct impressions, by the testimony of facts and events, by history, by description. Persons influence us, voices melt us, looks subdue us, deeds inflame us. Many a man will live and die upon a dogma: no man will be a martyr for a conclusion. A conclusion is but an opinion; it is not a thing which *is*, but which we are "*quite sure about*;" and it has often been observed, that we never say we are sure and certain without implying that we doubt. To say that a thing *must* be, is to admit that it *may not* be. No one, I say, will die for his own calculations: he dies for realities.[92]

That awakening, Plotinus says, may require us to be *woken up*.

> When we look outside that on which we depend we do not know that we are one, like faces which are many on the outside but have one head inside. But if someone is able to turn around, either by himself or having the good luck to have his hair pulled by Athena herself, he will see God and himself and the all. . . . He will stop marking himself off from all being and will come to all the All without going out anywhere.[93]

It was as true for Plotinus as for any orthodox Christian that

> Loving God most of all does not diminish our love for our brothers and sisters, but illumines it by helping us see that we love them rightly when we want for them what we want for ourselves, namely to be in God. When we love another person in charity, we love them as one who, like ourselves, can participate now in the divine life.[94]

Plotinus would not have limited that love to other *persons*: "Every soul is a child of the Father,"[95] even if it is only, here and now, we humans who have the dangerous privilege of *talking* about such things. But he would have agreed—he did agree—that we are to see and admire the real abiding selves that lie behind and above the passing show. What we ordinarily see and hear, from one particular perspective and with whatever passionate distortions, has only a derivative existence, as it were a painted corpse.[96] We only glimpse reality when we remember the real beings whose mere echoes and appearances normally distract us. We remember them when we remember our own compresence in the divine *Nous*, the sphere with many faces, "shining with living faces."[97] At the moment we see the real beauties on which all things depend "only in a mirror, darkly, but afterwards face to face."[98] Our salvation, for pagan and Christian alike, lies in the realization that our *real* selves are already and always There, in the dance of immortal love.[99]

## Bibliography

Aristotle. *De Partibus Animalium; De Historia Animalium; Politics; Nicomachean Ethics.*

Athanasius. *De Incarnatione.* Translated by Penelope Lawson. New York: St. Vladimir's Seminary Press, 1989.

Barker, Andrew, ed. *Greek Musical Writings,* vol. 1: *The Musician and His Art.* Cambridge: Cambridge University Press, 1984.

Barker, Andrew, ed. *Greek Musical Writings,* vol. 2: *Harmonic and Acoustic Theory.* Cambridge: Cambridge University Press, 1989.

Bellah, Robert N. *Religion in Human Evolution: From the Paleolithic to the Axial Age.* Cambridge, MA: Harvard University Press, 2011.

Boethius. *Consolation of Philosophy.* Translated by Victor Watts. London: Penguin Classics, 2003.

Cabasilas, Nicholas. *The Life in Christ.* Translated by Carmino de Catanzaro. New York: St. Vladimir's Seminary Press, 1974.

Cicero. *De Amicitia (on Friendship) and Scipio's Dream.* Translated by Andrew P. Peabody. 1884. Ithaca, NY: Cornell University Press, 2009.

Clark, Stephen R. L. *Plotinus: Myth, Metaphor and Philosophical Practice.* Chicago: University of Chicago Press, 2016.

Clark, Stephen R. L. "Souls, Stars and Shadows." In *Differences in Identity in Philosophy and Religion: A Cross-Cultural Approach,* edited by Sarah Flavel and Russell Re Manning, 7–20. London: Bloomsbury, 2020.

Copenhaver, Brian P. *Hermetica.* Cambridge: Cambridge University Press, 1992.

Dillon, J. M. "An ethic for the antique sage." In *The Cambridge Companion to Plotinus,* edited by Lloyd Gerson. Cambridge: Cambridge University Press, 1996.

Diogenes Laertius. *Lives of Eminent Philosophers.* Translated by R. D. Hicks. Loeb Classical Library. Cambridge, MA: Harvard University Press, 1989.

Dodds, E. R. *Missing Persons.* Oxford: Oxford University Press, 1977.

Eliot T. S. *Four Quartets; Burnt Norton.* 1944. London: Faber, 2001.

Evdokimov, Paul. *The Art of the Icon: A Theology of Beauty*, Translated by Steven Bigham. Pasadena, CA: Oakwood Publications, 2011.

Finamore, John. *Iamblichus and the Theory of the Vehicle of the Soul*. New York: Oxford University Press, 1985.

Gerson, Lloyd. *Plotinus*. London: Routledge, 1994.

Hornung, Erik. *Conceptions of God in Ancient Egypt: The One and the Many*. Translated by John Baines. Ithaca, NY: Cornell University Press, 1982.

Huizinga, Johan. *Homo Ludens: A Study of the Play Element in Culture*. 1938. Boston: Beacon Press, 1950.

Isar, Nicoletta, "ΧΟΡΌΣ: Dancing into the Sacred Space of Chora." *Byzantion* 75 (2005): 199–224.

Linforth, Ivan M. *The Arts of Orpheus*. Berkeley: University of California Press, 1941.

Long, A. A., and D. N. Sedley, eds. *Hellenistic Philosophers*. Cambridge: Cambridge University Press, 1987.

Louth, Andrew. "Augustine." In *The Study of Spirituality*, edited by Cheslyn Jones, Geoffrey Wainwright, and Edward Yarnold, 134–145.(London: SPCK, 1992).

Lucian. *Works*, vol. 2. Translated by A. M. Harmon. Loeb Classical Library. Cambridge, MA: Harvard University Press, 1989.

Macrobius. *Commentary on the Dream of Scipio*. Translated by William Harris Stahl. New York: Columbia University Press, 1952.

Mathiesen, T. J. *Apollo's Lyre*, Lincoln: University of Nebraska Press, 1999.

McCluskey, Stephen C. *Astronomies and Cultures in Early Medieval Europe*. Cambridge: Cambridge University Press, 2001.

Meredith, George. *Poems*. New York: Charles Scribner, 1907.

Mortley, Raoul. *Plotinus, Self and the World*. Cambridge: Cambridge University Press, 2013.

Naerebout, F. G. *Attractive Performances: Ancient Greek Dance—Three Preliminary Studies*. Amsterdam: J. C. Gieben, 1997.

Newman, John Henry. *Essay in Aid of a Grammar of Assent*. London: Longmans Green & Co., 1903.

Palmer, G. E. H., P. Sherrard, and Kallistos Ware, eds. *The Philokalia*, vol. 1. London: Faber, 1979.

Patrides, C. A., ed. *The Cambridge Platonists*, 1969. Cambridge: Cambridge University Press, 1980.

Plato, *Republic*; *Timaeus*; *Laws*.

Plotinus, *The Enneads*. Compiled by Porphyry. Translated by A. H. Armstrong. Loeb Classical Library. Cambridge, MA: Harvard University Press, 1966–1988.

Proclus. *Alcibiades I: A Translation and Commentary*. Translated by William O'Neill. The Hague: Nijhoff, 1965.

Smith, John. "The Excellency and Nobility of True Religion." 1660. In *The Cambridge Platonists*, edited by C. A. Patrides. 1969. Cambridge: Cambridge University Press, 1980,

Tully, R. Brent, Hélène Courtois, Yehuda Hoffman, and Daniel Pomarède. "The Laniakea Supercluster of Galaxies": *Nature* 513 (2014): 71–73.

Wadell, Paul, J. "Charity: How Friendship with God Unfolds in Love for Others." In *Virtues and Vices*, edited by Kevin Timpe and Craig Boyd, 369–389. Oxford: Oxford University Press, 2014.

Watts, Alan. *The Book on the Taboo against Knowing Who You Are*. 1996. London: Souvenir Press, 2011.

West, Martin L. *Ancient Music*. Oxford: Clarendon Press, 1992.

## Notes

1. Porphyry, *Life* 23.36f., after 22.54ff. All quotations from Porphyry's *Life* and from Plotinus are drawn from *The Enneads*, trans. A. H. Armstrong, Loeb Classical Library (Cambridge: Harvard University Press, 1966–1988), unless some variation is needed.
2. Plato, *Timaeus* 90d.
3. George Meredith, "Lucifer in Starlight" (1883), in *Poems* (New York: Charles Scribner, 1907), 185.
4. Plato, *Laws* 2.653: a false etymology. *Choros* is more probably derived from *chora*, place: F. G. Naerebout, *Attractive Performances: Ancient Greek Dance—Three Preliminary Studies* (Amsterdam: J. C. Gieben, 1997), 178. But the verbal association may still be real.
5. "Dream of Scipio": Cicero, *Republic*, bk. 6, ch. 3, trans. Andrew P. Peabody: http://ancienthistory.about.com/library/bl/bl_text_cic_scipiodream.htm. Cicero's text was repeated and amplified by Macrobius, *Commentary on the Dream of Scipio*, trans. William Harris Stahl (New York: Columbia University Press, 1952).
6. Boethius, *Consolatio*, 2p7.3–4, after Ptolemy *Almagest* 2.1; see Stephen C. McCluskey, *Astronomies and Cultures in Early Medieval Europe* (Cambridge: Cambridge University Press, 2001), 123.
7. See http://dx.doi.org/10.1038/nature13674: R. Brent Tully, Hélène Courtois, Yehuda Hoffman, and Daniel Pomarède, "The Laniakea Supercluster of Galaxies," *Nature* 513 (2014): 71–73.
8. *Ennead* III.4 [15].6.
9. *Ennead* VI.4 [22].14, 18ff.
10. *Ennead* IV.3 [27].17 for our souls' descent into the stars, and IV.4 [28].5 for the ascent. Note that it was an Egyptian opinion that the stars embodied the souls of the dead: Erik Hornung *Conceptions of God in Ancient Egypt: The One and the Many*, trans. John Baines (Ithaca, NY: Cornell University Press, 1982), 81.
11. *Ennead* V.2 [11].2, echoing the line of descent in Plato's *Timaeus* 91c (see also Aristotle, *De Partibus Animalium* 4.686a25ff).
12. *Ennead* III.4 [15].3.18–24.
13. *Ennead* VI.7 [38].6, 27–30.
14. *Life* 10.19–31.
15. *Ennead* IV.4 [28].8, 41ff.
16. Lloyd Gerson, *Plotinus* (London: Routledge, 1994), 141ff.; see also Raoul Mortley, *Plotinus, Self and the World* (Cambridge: Cambridge University Press, 2013), 19.
17. Aristotle, *De Historia Animalium* 5.551a3.
18. See my "Souls, Stars and Shadows," in *Differences in Identity in Philosophy and Religion: A Cross-Cultural Approach*, ed. Sarah Flavel and Russell Re Manning (London: Bloomsbury, 2020), 7–20. See Dante, *Purgatory*, 10.130: "O proud Christians, weary and wretched, who, infirm in the mind's vision, put your trust in downward steps: do you

not see that we are caterpillars, born to form the angelic butterfly, that flies to judgement without defence? Why does your mind soar to the heights, since you are defective insects, even as the caterpillar is, in which the form is lacking?": http://www.poetryintranslation.com/PITBR/Italian/DantPurg8to14.htm.

19. *Ennead* IV.3 [27].18, 19–24.
20. *Ennead* VI 7 [38].41, 22–26.
21. See John Finamore, *Iamblichus and the Theory of the Vehicle of the Soul* (New York: Oxford University Press, 1985).
22. *Ennead* I.6 [1].8, 16–28
23. *Ennead* IV.3 [27].11, 22–3.
24. *Ennead* II.9 [33].7, 36f.
25. *Ennead* VI.9 [9].8, 38ff.
26. Demosthenes, *Against Meidias* 60, cited by Martin L. West, *Ancient Music* (Oxford: Clarendon Press, 1992), 46, who goes on to report from other ancient sources that "he gave the lead and did his best to keep his fellows to the proper rhythm, which they managed better when there were more of them. . . . [His] place was in the middle, while at the edges there might be two or three who could not sing at all, and who kept mum."
27. Plato, *Republic* 4.427c.
28. "I call the Muses to raise their voices with me. . . . I, Phoebus of the thick hair (*Phoibos bathukhaites*), singing in the midst of them" (*Life* 22.16–22). "Thick hair" does not exactly convey the aesthetic or sacred meaning of the epithet!
29. Nicholas Cabasilas, *The Life in Christ*, trans, Carmino de Catanzaro (New York: St. Vladimir's Seminary Press, 1974) 136, 149, cited by Paul Evdokimov, *The Art of the Icon: A Theology of Beauty*, trans. Steven Bigham (Pasadena, CA: Oakwood Publications, 2011), Kindle 5731–2. See further Nicoletta Isar, "ΧΟΡΌΣ: Dancing into the Sacred Space of Chora," *Byzantion* 75 (2005): 199–224.
30. *Ennead* III.2 [47].17, 9–14, 22–4.
31. *Ennead* III.2 [47].17, 64–67, 86–9.
32. *Ennead* III.2 [47].16, 8–11.
33. Cleanthes, according to Epictetus, *Manual* 53 (SVF 1.527): A. A. Long & D. N. Sedley, eds., *Hellenistic 'sophers* (Cambridge: Cambridge University Press, 1987), vol. 1, 386 [62B].
34. See *Ennead* III.1 [3].4, 25–29.
35. *Ennead* III.2 [47].17, 42–53.
36. Lucian, 'On Pantomime," in *Works*, vol. 2., trans. A. M. Harmon, Loeb Classical Library (Cambridge, MA: Harvard University Press, 1989), 262–263.
37. Plato, *Republic* 10.618–20.
38. *Ennead* II.9 [33].4, 25–32.
39. Paul, Ephesians, 6.12.
40. *Ennead* II.9 [33].16, 1–5.
41. See *Ennead* III.1 [3].6, 11: "how could a wicked character be given by the stars, who are gods?"
42. Plato, *Laws* 7.796; cited from Johan Huizinga, *Homo Ludens: A Study of the Play Element in Culture* (1938; Boston: Beacon Press, 1950), 18–19, by Robert N. Bellah, *Reli-*

*gion in Human Evolution: From the Paleolithic to the Axial Age* (Cambridge, MA: Harvard University Press, 2011), 110.

43. Alan Watts, *The Book on the Taboo against Knowing Who You Are* (1996; London: Souvenir Press, 2011), 135 (and many other places on the web: for example, https://www.youtube.com/watch?v=29atSZKbmS4). Aristotle (as well as Plotinus) said much the same: the only sort of life worth living is one that does *not* depend on any exterior achievement.
44. *Ennead* I.4 [46].8, 23–24.
45. *Ennead* III.2 [47].15, 44–45.
46. I *Ennead* I.9 [33].9, 19ff.
47. *Ennead* III.2 [47].15, 61.
48. *Ennead* III.2 [47].8, 16–21.
49. *Ennead* I.4 [46].15, 17–25. Armstrong's translation, "as well as remaining intelligent," is misleading. *Nous* is not *intelligence*—and certainly not the sort of intelligence that the term mostly suggests to us (which is no more than cleverness). *Nous* is better, but perhaps still misleadingly, translated "Spirit."
50. *Ennead* III.2 [47].15, 33–40.
51. Matthew 5.45.
52. *Ennead* IV.4 [28].42, 15f.; see also IV.3 [27].16.
53. Watts, *The Book on the Taboo*; he suggests that "paradise," where "lion lies down with lamb," is the "off-stage level," where all parties recognize their interdependence, and the necessary condition for the "absolutely essential chivalry" that sets the limits on all warfare.
54. *Ennead* III.2 [47].16, 23–7.
55. *Ennead* III.3 [48].5, 8–13.
56. See T. J. Mathiesen, *Apollo's Lyre* (Lincoln: University of Nebraska Press, 1999), 521–582, who identifies passages that seem to depend on Porphyry's commentary on Ptolemy, and Andrew Barker, ed., *Greek Musical Writings*, vol. 2: *Harmonic and Acoustic Theory* (Cambridge: Cambridge University Press, 1989), 229–244. Porphyry tells us that Plotinus himself was well acquainted with musical theory: *Life* 14, 7–10.
57. See Andrew Barker, ed., *Greek Musical Writings*, vol. 1: *The Musician and His Art* (Cambridge: Cambridge University Press, 1984), 166: "The interval structure of any *harmonia* can be converted into that of its successor simply by removing the interval at the bottom of its series and replacing it at the top. . . . The sequence of *harmoniai* is cyclic." Or rather, it is eternal, and not sequential.
58. *Ennead* II.9 [33].16, 39–41.
59. *Ennead* III.8 [30].4. 5–6.
60. Douglas Hedley, "Play in East and West" in this volume, citing Aurobindo *Centenary Library Writings* (Pondicherry: All India Press, 1972), 16, 428.
61. *Ennead* IV.4 [28].33; see also VI.9 [9].38. Lucian remarks in his defense of pantomime that he "once heard someone hazard a remark, to the effect that the philosophy of Pantomime went still further [than modeling the control of passion, and care for beauty], and that in the *silence* of the characters a Pythagorean doctrine was shadowed forth" (Lucian, *Works*, 2:258–259).
62. *Ennead* III.2 [47].13, 11ff.

63. Matthew 7.2.
64. Porphyry, *Life* 15.7–17, after Plato, *Symposium* 218d.
65. *Ennead* V.3 [49].4.1–4. So also Philo, *Quod Omnis Probus Liber Sit* 3.20; *Works*, vol. 9, 21: "He who has God alone for his leader, he alone is free, though to my thinking he is also the leader of all others, having received the charge of earthly things from the great, the immortal King, whom he, the mortal, serves as viceroy"; see also Diogenes Laertius, *Lives* 7.122.
66. *Ennead* VI.9 [9].7
67. *Ennead* V.8 [31].6; see also IV.3 [27].11; *Asclepius* in Brian P. Copenhaver, *Hermetica* (Cambridge: Cambridge University Press, 1992), 37. See Erik Hornung, *Conceptions of God in Ancient Egypt: The One and the Many*, trans. John Baines (Ithaca, NY: Cornell University Press, 1982), 124: "The mixed form of their [the Egyptians'] gods is nothing other than a hieroglyph, a way of 'writing' not the name but the nature and function of the deity in question. The Egyptians do not hesitate to call hieroglyphs 'gods,' and even to equate individual signs in the script with particular gods; it is quite in keeping with their views to see images of the gods as signs in a metalanguage. As is true of every Egyptian hieroglyph, they are more than just ciphers or lifeless symbols; the god can inhabit them, his cult image will normally be in the same form, and his priests may assume his role by wearing animal masks."
68. *Ennead* VI.5 [23].10; see also Aristotle, *Politics* 3. 1281a42–b2. But compare *Ennead* IV.4 [28].17 for a more familiar judgment on the follies of an undisciplined assembly, whether in the soul or in the city.
69. *Ennead* I.6 [1].5, 43–58.
70. Porphyry, *Life* 22.35–39.
71. T. S. Eliot, *Four Quartets; Burnt Norton* (1944; London: Faber, 2001), 2, lines 21–22. *Burnt Norton* itself was first published in 1936. Eliot read Plotinus alongside E. R. Dodds in Oxford in 1915 (in J. A. Stewart's class): E. R. Dodds, *Missing Persons* (Oxford: Oxford University Press, 1977), 40. Dodds and Eliot were the only students to persevere with this supposedly "unexciting" class.
72. G. E. H. Palmer, P. Sherrard, and Kallistos Ware, eds. *The Philokalia*, vol.1 (London: Faber, 1979), 178–179.
73. Proclus, *Alcibiades*, 54–55 (83): Proclus, *Alcibiades I: A Translation and Commentary*, ed. William O'Neill (The Hague: Nijhoff, 1965). O'Neill further cites Proclus, *In Cratylum*, 100.27–101.3: "Apollo unifies the multitude and gathers it into one: he uniformly prepossesses every kind of purification, cleansing the whole heavens and birth and all intramundane forms of life; he separates individual souls from the crass layers of matter."
74. See Plato, *Republic* 7.537; Plotinus, *Ennead* III.8 [30].1: discussed by Douglas Hedley in "Play in East and West," in this volume.
75. According to Plutarch, *De Ei* 9.388e, the indestructible divinity that undergoes transformations is known as Apollo (that is, *a-polla*, not many) in the Conflagration, and as Dionysus (or cognate identities) when he is rent apart and distributed "into winds, water, earth, stars, plants and animals" (Ivan M. Linforth, *The Arts of Orpheus* (Berkeley: University of California Press, 1941), 317–318.
76. *Ennead* I.6 [1].7.

77. *Ennead* II.9 [33].15, 33.
78. Matthew 13.45–46.
79. Aristotle, *Nicomachean Ethics* 1.1097b16–21; 10.1176b30–1.
80. Aristotle, *Nicomachean Ethics* 10.1177b26–35; Aristotle, *Metaphysics* 12.1072b13f. Modern Aristotelian commentators generally prefer to ignore such passages, in favor of the working assumption that Aristotle meant only to praise the life of a decent bourgeois.
81. Athanasius, *De Incarnatione*, trans. Penelope Lawson (New York: St. Vladimir's Seminary Press, 1989), 54.3.
82. J. M. Dillon, "An Ethic for the Antique Sage," in *The Cambridge Companion to Plotinus*, ed. Lloyd Gerson (Cambridge: Cambridge University Press, 1996), 324.
83. Dillon, "An Ethic for the Antique Sage," 331.
84. Porphyry, *Life of Plotinus* 2.26–2 Dillon, "An Ethic for the Antique Sage," 7. That the god in each of us is one and the same, Plotinus says, is common doctrine (*Ennead* VI.5 [23].1, 2–4); see also Aristotle, *Nicomachean Ethics* 7.1153b32: "Everything has something divine in it."
85. *Ennead* II.9 [33].15, 33–16.10.
86. Porphyry, *Life of Plotinus*, 9.19–20.
87. Porphyry, *Life of Plotinus*, 11.12–20.
88. *Ennead* VI.9 [9].11; see John Smith, "The Excellency and Nobility of True Religion" (1660), chapter 6, in *The Cambridge Platonists*, ed. C.A. Patrides (1969; Cambridge: Cambridge University Press, 1980), 180.
89. Andrew Louth, "Augustine," in *The Study of Spirituality*, ed. Cheslyn Jones, Geoffrey Wainwright, & Edward Yarnold (London: SPCK, 1992), 137.
90. *Ennead* VI.7 [38].35.
91. *Ennead* IV.8 [6].4, 11f.
92. John Henry Newman, *Essay in Aid of a Grammar of Assent* (London: Longmans Green & Co., 1903), 92–93.
93. *Ennead* VI.5 [23].7, 9–10.
94. Paul J. Wadell, "Charity: How Friendship with God Unfolds in Love for Others," in *Virtues and Vices*, ed. Kevin Timpe and Craig Boyd (Oxford: Oxford University Press, 2014), 381.
95. *Ennead* II.9 [33].16, 10.
96. *Ennead* II.4 [12].5, 18.
97. *Ennead* VI.7 [38].15, 25.
98. Paul, 1 Corinthians 13.12.
99. *Ennead* IV. 7 [2].10; IV.8 [6].8.

# 11 *Serio Ludere!*

## DIVINE LESSONS FROM TRICKSTERS AND HOLY FOOLS

*Peter Tyler*

> The trickster cannot be exiled from the human species, although representatives of this or that establishment have tried, time and again, in the history of Western civilization to banish him/her/it for good. But always the trickster returns, in fact never leaves, a heterogeneous and androgynous beauty of a figure.
>
> —Stanley Diamond, "Jung contra Freud: What It Means to Be Funny"

Stanley Diamond's views, quoted in the epigraph,[1] encapsulate a (post-) modern view of that most elusive of figures—the trickster. Since Carl Jung's and Paul Radin's influential essays on the figure were written in the middle of the last century, he/she/it has continued to make an appearance in a diverse range of academic and non-academic sources.[2] In recent times sociologists and psychologists have speculated on the psychosocial role of the figure while culture and media theorists have traced the trickster's appearance in popular and classical film and literature. Within theological and religious studies on play, which concern us here, the figure has also been sighted. Some have noted the cross-cultural appearance of a trickster cutting (or perhaps, better, flying) across interdenominational boundaries and suggested that trickster archetypes can be found in most world religions. The purpose of this chapter is to assess one instance of this—the psycho-spiritual role of the trickster figure within Christianity—speculating as to what function such a figure might (if at all) perform and whether there is a place within Western Christianity, at least, for this most elusive of psychopomps. In assessing this claim, I shall also assess the role of *play* within the Christian tradition and, in particular, how the trickster, as psychopomp, performs, via play, the necessary transcendent function of the psyche in its relationship to the divine.[3] To this end the chapter argues that play/*līlā* is an essential element in the arsenal of the Divine Trickster as the tricksters undertake their transmutational work of bringing the Divine to human consciousness.

## A Note on Methodology: A Psycho-Spiritual Approach

Some years ago I completed the first part of a trilogy of books concerning the contemporary relationship between psychology and spirituality. In the first part, *The Pursuit of the Soul*, I investigated the origins of both Christianity and contemporary psychoanalysis by asking fundamental questions about the nature of the soul-*psyche* in both traditions.[4] I concluded this earlier book by suggesting that we approach discourse about the soul with a certain care. Because of the soul-psyche's gossamer-fine nature, the intellect will often have to take a back seat as we observe the movements of the soul by means of paradox, symbol, myth, the relational and the libidinal. Within the present chapter this practice is adopted. So, as well as examining the trickster/holy fool through theological, psychological, and historical lenses, I shall also draw on mythological and symbolic perspectives to examine this most elusive of phenomena.

## What Is the Trickster?

The classic modern exposition of the trickster and its psychological significance appeared in Carl Jung's commentary on Paul Radin's *Der Göttliche Schelm* (literally, the "Divine Rogue or Trickster") in 1954, which then appeared in English as a preface to the volume *The Trickster: A Study in American Indian Mythology* and reproduced in Jung's *Collected Works,* volume 9i. Radin's notion of the liminal figure in American mythology (often crystallizing around the figure of the coyote-trickster) inspired Jung to a wonderful flight of imagination as he evoked all the tricksters of the Western tradition beginning with Hermes/Mercurius and advancing through the medieval "feast of fools" via mythological figures such as Tom Thumb and Loki before resting with the great picaresque creations of early modern literature such as Don Quixote, Baron Munchausen, and characters such as Pulcinella (to which lineage can be added no end of modern trickster comedians). In Jung's typology it is evident that "all mythical figures correspond to inner psychic experiences and originally sprang from them"; it is therefore "not surprising to find certain phenomena in the field of parapsychology which remind us of the trickster."[5] In British terms the figure that comes to mind is Puck in William Shakespeare's *A Midsummer's Night's Dream*:

> You are that shrewd and knavish sprite
> Call'd Robin Goodfellow: are you not he
> That frights the maidens of the villagery;
> Skim milk, and sometimes labour in the quern,
> And bootless make the breathless housewife churn;
> And sometime make the drink to bear no barm;
> Mislead night-wanderers, laughing at their harm?
>
> (*A Midsummer's Night's Dream*, Act II, Scene 1)

The Warwickshire boy Shakespeare clearly knew the country lore around this sprite, and he appears in several guises throughout his work (e.g., Ariel, Sir John Falstaff). The role of the trickster in Jung's schema is thus as a manifestation of an atavistic layer of the unconscious lying close to the sources of the conscious: "He is obviously a 'psychologem,' an archetypal psychic structure of extreme antiquity. In his clearest manifestations he is a faithful reflection of an absolutely undifferentiated human consciousness, corresponding to a psyche that has hardly left the animal level."[6]

Such an earthed and earthing character has for Jung another element—the trickster also carries elements of the divine: "He is a fore-runner of the saviour, and like him, God, man and animal at once. He is both subhuman and superhuman, a bestial and divine being, whose chief and most alarming characteristic is his unconsciousness."[7] As the trickster works against the norms of conscious life he/she/it thus enables consciousness to touch that which is unconscious at both ends of the animal-human-divine spectrum: The unconscious animal aspect may appear as crude or atavistic; breaking the boundaries of conscious life also allows the trickster to manifest the hidden transcendent aspects of the self. Thus, the trickster is a "primitive 'cosmic' being of divine-animal nature, on the one hand superior to man because of his superhuman qualities, and on the other hand inferior to him because of his unreason and unconsciousness."[8] He is very much a "bridge creature," that bridges the animal-divine spectrum, sometimes missing out the human in his/her desire to bridge the two. Such a view of the role of the trickster is shared by Radin who is quoted by Jung with approval: "Viewed psychologically, it might be contended that the history of civilization is largely the account of the attempts of man to forget his transformation from an animal into a human being."[9] For Jung, as for Radin, the cloak of civilization merely lightly wraps a hard and persistent core of stubborn paganism, which, via figures such as the trickster, will jump back into civilized life at the touch of a cap's bell. Therefore, Jung concludes, "The trickster is a collective shadow figure, a summation of all the inferior traits of character in individuals" and as such can be a blessing to the individual as a component of the dynamic of *enantiodromia*, so central to Jung's psychological schema.[10]

## Critique of Jung

But we must ask ourselves, how legitimate is Jung's/Radin's analysis? In his excellent recent summary of sociological views of the phenomenon, William Hynes acknowledges one of the first problems with the Jung/Radin paradigm, namely, how legitimate is it to take an essentialist view of the phenomenon and, as Jung does, see it is as a cross-cultural phenomenon with an unvarying, or in Jung's description "archetypal," quality?[11] In contrast to Jung's view, several in Hynes's volume argue that the trickster is culturally specific, and cross-cultural comparisons are questionable.[12] The second argument raised against the Jungian stereotype is his continued reference to the trickster as a "primitive" or "regressive" figure. Again, this aspect of Jung's analysis seems increasingly questionable to our postcolonial eyes and raises issues as to who determines what is "primitive" and whether the category has academic legitimacy in the first place. To these two criticisms we can add another. As presented in the "classic" fashion above, Jung's Trickster is a combination of the "animal/primitive" and the "metaphysical/transcendent." I introduced the figure at the beginning of this chapter as a "psychopomp," and it is this aspect, in particular, I want to emphasize here. For whereas Jung would like to mix the two "primitive" and "psychopomp" elements of the trickster, in the present chapter I propose to separate the two elements. As I examine the nature of the psycho-spiritual role of the figure in a religion such as Christianity, I will concentrate on the latter, metaphysical, function at the expense of the former. Part of this arises at a certain squeamishness at Jung's/Radin's forensic descriptions of the "primitive," which, as I say, cannot but sound offensive in our present era, but also, more important, by mixing these two strands in creating the essentialist figure of the "trickster" I think that Jung creates a chimera that may not throw too much light on the psycho-spiritual role of the trickster. In this respect

I shall follow Hynes, who keeps a critical eye on the use to which the figure has been put by generations of scholars while wanting to rescue the figure from over-comparativist annihilation:

> We steer a course between those who see the trickster as so universal a figure that all tricksters speak with essentially the same voice and those who counsel that the tricksters belonging to individual societies are so cultural-specific that no two of them articulate similar messages.[13]

Such a curious figure, an amalgam of so many types, is thus difficult to "pin down" or "define." As Hynes continues: "To define (*de-finis*) is to draw borders around phenomena, and tricksters seem amazingly resistant to such capture, they are notorious border breakers!"[14] Within the term we can include the: "Anti-hero, Boundary Figure, Bungling Host, Clever Hero, Culture Hero, Confidence Trickster, Demiurge, Lord of the Animals, Numbskull, Old Man, Picaro, Buffoon, Selfish Deceiver, Swindler and Transformer."[15] It would be beyond the abilities of this chapter to do justice to all these aspects of the trickster phenomenon and, once we have shorn the trickster of its Jungian "primitive" elements, we are then left with the key elements of its psycho-spiritual role to contemplate here. In particular, in the rest of this chapter I concentrate on three key aspects of the figure in this role:

1. The one who inhabits two worlds. An essentially ambiguous figure who can hold the "coincidence of opposites" together.
2. The one who initiates transformation. For good or ill, the trickster is the one who initiates change in a system that has become paralyzed.
3. The one who plays. The trickster is at home among fun, play, and laughter and will use this to initiate change. In this respect the trickster takes its place as a key element of the work of the *Deus Ludens*.

In this respect the three elements reflect the theme of the present volume that assesses the role of play/*līlā* in theological context, in particular with respect to its manifestations across the Hindu and Christian religions. With this in mind, let us briefly look at each of these aspects in turn.

## BETWEEN TWO WORLDS

Following Jung's psychological exposition, we see that the trickster is thus essentially an unstable figure. In D. Aycock's words he/she/it "stands at the nexus of mortality and immortality, structure and anti-structure, the individual and society," or, in Jungian terms, between consciousness and unconsciousness.[16] The *avatāra* of Lord Viṣṇu in Hinduism comes to mind, Narasimha, who is neither man nor lion and kills the wicked Hiranyakasipu because "at that time, it was neither day nor night, but dawn; it was neither inside nor outside, but on a threshold; and his assailant was neither man nor beast, but both, a man-lion."[17] Just as Narasimha acquires the power to kill demons because of his ambiguous status, so the trickster often haunts the twilit world between life and death, good and evil, sacred and profane, dawn and dusk, reason and imagination; it is thence he/she/it derives power. The other mythic figure from world religions that comes to mind is the Islamic-Sufi figure of Khiḍr—the manifestation of Elijah often referred to in English as "The Green Man." In Sara Sviri's fascinating exposition of the figure, she notes that, like Narasimha, Khiḍr derives his significance from crossing the two realms of life and death, or, as she puts it: Khiḍr "is always there where the two planes meet. He is there, 'where the two seas meet,' the sea of life and the sea of death, the space-bound and the spaceless, the time-bound and the timeless."[18] This notion of Khiḍr as inhabiting the zone "where the two seas meet" derives, as Sviri makes clear, from the Quranic passage (Sūra 18:60–82), which recounts Moses's encounter with a mystical stranger who lives "on a green island abundant with lush vegetation in the heart of the sea."[19] In his encounter with Moses, Khiḍr is one step ahead as he revives those who are dead (including people and fish) in a way that even Moses cannot fathom. Giving her interpretation of this mysterious Quranic passage, Sviri stresses that "the mystical journey is *always* a search for this meeting point. This is one of the deep meanings of the 'union of opposites,' the *coincidentia oppositorum*."[20] This nicely encapsulates the psycho-spiritual role of the Trickster figure, one who changes night into day, death into life (and, of course, vice versa), for as Sviri reminds us, the trickster Khiḍr is "both the undertaker and the midwife."[21] In Hindu contexts Srilata Raman in her accompanying essay in this volume draws our attention to the role of Lord Śiva in acting as transcendent psychopomp in the creation of the city of Madurai in the modern Indian state of Tamil Nadu, where, to this day, "the secular city of everyday politics, traffic jams, and climatic uncertainties" is held in tension with "the sacred one, characterized by the eruptions of Śiva's play," his divine *līlā*.

## THE TRANSFORMER

Owing to their ability to shift between worlds, tricksters will often be agents of change, especially in a system that has become ossified and rigid. In psychological terms the change is often marked by the appearance in dreams of strange and unexpected figures, perhaps of ambiguous sexuality, but always with an aura of the numinous. In my work as a therapist I have often encountered this phenomenon where such a figure, often contra-sexual to the dreamer, will appear to initiate change or act as a guide to the "underworld." In Jewish terms the mysterious figure of Raphael accompanying Tobit comes to mind. In the Christian context we are reminded of the Holy Spirit in the Acts of the Apostles—changing shape from flame to wind to water and offering the early Christians the "gift of tongues" as they are transformed from rather timid Jewish traders, merchants, and artisans into the bold preachers who will proclaim the "good news." The impulsive and spontaneous powers of the trickster allow the recipients of such powers to break conventional boundaries and norms (cf. St. Peter's conversion to eat all animals depicted in Acts 10). In Hindu terms we are reminded by Ankur Barua in his accompanying essay in this volume of the role of Lord Kṛṣṇa, who, as the cowherd of Vraja, entices the village women, the *gopīs,* by the sound of his flute from their everyday household chores and domestic relationships to the ecstatic round-dances in the forest clearing under the autumn moon.

## PLAYING BEFORE GOD

One of the primary inspirations for this chapter was to ensure that this volume contained a psycho-spiritual account of the importance of play and laughter within the activity of the *Deus Ludens.* While acknowledging the important metaphysical and theological dimensions the discussion of play contains, I have aimed to sketch out the necessary psycho-spiritual function play performs as it reconnects the human conscious with that which is unconscious—both atavistically and spiritually. This is amply provided for by the accounts of the tricksters and their Christian cousins, the holy fools, to whom I shall turn shortly. Yet, as Hynes reminds us, we must remember "a Western cultural bias against allowing humor to represent serious and important cultural information"[22] with our common assumption that "if something is comical or entertaining, it cannot represent socially significant [or, we could add, religiously significant] material."[23] If nothing else, the trickster allows humor, laughter, and play to enter into the hallowed halls of theological discussion, for "the trickster's humor melds entertainment and education. We may laugh, but a deeper unfolding is at work. At one level the trickster bears the gift of laughter, but it is tied to another level, linked to another gift, one that enables insight and enlightenment."[24] In this respect certain mid-twentieth-century commentators wanted to recover the importance of play in social, philosophical, and even theological contexts. Most notable among these was the Dutch academic Johan Huizinga whose mid-century *Homo Ludens* had a lasting effect on the emergence of the nascent discipline of "play studies."[25] Like Hymes, Huizinga stressed the difficulty of categorizing play and how it eludes facile intellectual classification: "The *fun* of playing resists all analyses, all logical interpretation. As a concept it cannot be reduced to any other mental category. No other modern language known to me has the exact equivalent of the English 'fun.'"[26] However, Huizinga was at pains to distinguish his "play" or "fun" from the more tricksterish "folly"; for him play could not really embrace the more extreme liminal aspects of the latter:

> The category of the comic is certainly connected with folly in the highest and lowest sense of that word. Play, however, is not foolish. It lies outside the antithesis of wisdom and folly. The later Middle Ages tended to express the two cardinal moods of life—play and seriousness—somewhat imperfectly by opposing *folie* to sense, until Erasmus in his *Laus Stultitiae* showed the inadequacy of the contrast.[27]

The other important twentieth-century voice in the development of a Christian understanding of play was Hugo Rahner's; in his *Man at Play, or Did You Ever Practise Eutrapelia* Rahner wanted to use the writings of Thomas Aquinas and Aristotle to baptize a Christian sense of play and humor as a middle way between the fool and the dullard.[28] This he would do by promoting the idea of "the eutrapelos man" who "strikes the happy mean between the 'bomolochos,' the inveterate 'funny man,' the buffoon and the 'agrokos,' the humourless man who never as much as smiles."[29] Following Aquinas and Aristotle, Rahner argued that "unmitigated seriousness" reveals a lack of virtue on account of the fact that it "despises play."[30] Thus Rahner's "eutrapelic Christians" are able to stand between the two extremes of loutishness and priggishness, expressing a refined joy in the pleasure of the divine game on earth.[31]

However, from the psycho-spiritual perspective presented here, both of these influential accounts miss something of the wilder trickster energy that I have traced so far in this chapter. For, with respect to Huizinga and Rahner, the trickster figure does not always appear as an English gentleman out for fair play and a good game. The trickster, as liminal figure, transforms through the wilder and sometimes dangerous breaking of boundaries demanded from their altered perspective on the borderline of time and eternity, limit and boundlessness, life and death. In this respect the example from Hinduism cited earlier—Lord Kṛṣṇa's love games in Vraja, is a good example of the divine play that threatens social norms and pushes its adherents beyond the balance of staid routine and "normality."

Now that I have delineated these three essential psycho-spiritual aspects of the role of the trickster, it is important to state too what has been left out from the classic Jung-Radin archetype. I am aware that my analysis is open to criticism, but, as I explained earlier, as the purpose of the chapter is not to present a comprehensive overview of the figure in Christianity, I shall simply note these lacunae and suggest that other scholars may want to take the analysis further into these realms. They are three:

The first, and most obvious, exception is the exclusion of the essentially *animal* aspect of the trickster from my analysis here. Christianity's unease with the natural world is well documented, and it could be that the repression of this characteristic of the trickster figure is indicative of the wider malaise within the belief-system.[32] If this is the case, then we might, under our principles 1 and 2 above, expect any future emergent Christian tricksterism to reclaim once again the role of the animal and natural world. Hinduism, with which this volume dialogues, would perhaps not find such a problem here, and this would be worth exploring by future scholars of the religion, especially with regard to "animal deities" such as Lord Hanuman.

The second missing element is the *sexual*, and in particular the *phallocentrism* of so many trickster figures in other cultures from Hermes onward. Again, as with the animal side, from a psycho-spiritual viewpoint, this would seem to suggest a deeper psycho-spiritual unease with the sexual within the Christian psyche. The *rāsa līlā* of Lord Kṛṣṇa explored by Ankur Barua in his essay may suggest a Hindu counterweight to this sexual timidity within Christianity; however, again, I consider this a vast topic that I do not intend to engage with here but which may form a fruitful basis for a future study.

Finally, there is the role of the deliberate (and immoral) *deceiver*. Again, this element of tricksterism is played down in the Christian tradition, and in as far as it is represented in that tradition its manifestations might traditionally coalesce around a figure such as Judas. Recent renewals of interest in this figure might suggest that this aspect too of the faith is beginning to resurface.[33] As Barua points out in his essay in the present volume the young Kṛṣṇa engages in a form of "divine thievery," where a difference is established between "ordinary [*laukika*] theft and the transcendental [*alaukika*] thievery of Kṛṣṇa." An area I think that could form the basis of a future study but, again, far from the morality espoused in the Christian tradition.

Having isolated, then, the three tricksterist qualities of liminality, transformation, and play I conclude this chapter by applying them to two manifestations of tricksterism within the Christian tradition. The first instance of which, as indicated earlier, is that of the "Holy Fools."

## The Holy Fools

As with the trickster figure, much has been written in recent years of the fascinating figure of the "Holy Fool."[34] Foolishness, as St. Paul reminds us, lies at the heart of Christian discipleship: "We are fools for the sake of Christ, but you are wise in Christ" (1 Cor 4:10), for "God's foolishness" as shown through the power of the Crucifixion "is wiser than human wisdom, and God's weakness is stronger than human strength" (1 Cor 1:25). In the post-apostolic period one of the first, and most cited, sources referring to the Holy Fool in the Eastern tradition is Leontius of Neapolis's *The Life of Symeon the Fool*.[35] Recent commentators such as C. Johnson and D. Krueger have questioned the actual existence of Symeon as a person, but what is clear on re-reading the *Life of Symeon* is that the trope of the Holy Fool was a legitimate one for Leontius to adopt in the mid-seventh century.[36]

The figure of Holy Fool that Symeon portrayed in the *Life* has many of the classic characteristics of the trickster, especially the three highlighted in the preceding section, namely his liminality, transformative qualities, and capacity to play. Although several elements in the Symeon story reflect the prevailing tendency among the desert dwellers to offer challenging and sometimes eccentric examples to their followers, what is notable with Symeon's story is the deliberate desire to "mock the world."[37] Having received his call, Symeon enters the city of Emesa in

Turkey (pulling a dead dog on a lead) and proceeds to disrupt religious services by throwing walnuts at parishioners, dancing in the streets, and disobeying the rules of Lent by publicly eating meat during the sacred fast. This was accompanied by his befriending prostitutes and actors and visiting brothels and taverns (although, as we are told, he remained untouched by vice during these sojourns). By breaking taboos and transgressing social and sexual norms, Symeon, like the fellow "holy fool" often cited in the Eastern tradition, Andreas the Fool for Christ, displays extreme behavior that fits well into the classic "trickster" model of Jung or Radin that I cited at the outset. However, even though the tradition of holy foolery seems to have survived in the Eastern Orthodox tradition well into nineteenth-century Russia (as depicted in sources as diverse as the novels of Fyodor Dostoyevsky and Lev Tolstoy and Modest Mussorgsky's grand opera *Boris Godunov*), it nevertheless never seemed to have become a central part in Christian practices, remaining a marginal and somewhat eccentric aspect of Christian life. True to his marginality, the Orthodox "holy fool" seems to have more in common with the wild *fakirs* and *bauls* of South Asia as depicted by J. Frembgen in a recent study of the wild holy men and women in Northern Pakistan.[38] Like Symeon and Andreas, Frembgen's holy men and women have no respect for the boundaries and proprieties of everyday orthodoxy and clearly exist on the boundaries of organized religion.

Although all these figures are fascinating to study (and all the above studies are well worth reading) and present a challenge to normative approaches to Christian religious practice, it is clear that the life of the fool or fakir is a specialized and special calling that, if it is divinely inspired, is clearly given to only very few, and rarely at that.[39] In an earlier essay I questioned how far an extreme practice such as the Hindu notion of *sannyāsa* could be adapted, if at all, to mainstream Christian living.[40] In that essay I argued, following the example of various practitioners of Indian Christianity, that there was a place for such extreme forms of religious behavior within mainstream Christianity, but that in Christianity, as opposed to Hinduism, such "Christian *sannyasa*" could best flourish within the climate and precincts of a Christian ashram. In similar fashion, in the present chapter, having presented the phenomenon of tricksterism and explored the more extreme forms of its expression such as holy foolery (clearly only an option for a very limited number of present-day Christians, if such an option still exists), I would like to conclude the chapter by seeing if there could be an answer to the question I posed at the beginning of our study: "Is there a place for the trickster tradition within present-day Christianity, and if so, how would it look?" I aim to do that by citing a second example of tricksterism within the Christian tradition—the medieval tradition of the "Feast of Fools."

## Dancing in the Aisles: Reclaiming the Feast of Fools

One of the most memorable passages in Jung's essay on the Trickster with which we began is his description of the medieval "Feast of Fools." Taking his descriptions mainly from the seventeenth-century accounts of Du Cange, Jung uses the later reports of the phenomenon to press his case for the trickster as a "psychologem"—"obviously an archetypal psychic structure of extreme antiquity. In his clearer manifestations he is a faithful reflection of an undifferentiated human consciousness, corresponding to a psyche that has hardly left the animal level."[41] To make this argument he demonstrates a well-worn trope that the medieval "feast of fools," occurring in the days after Christmas and culminating on the Feast of the Circumcision (1 January) is a relic of the ancient Roman "Cervula" or "Cervulus" that "took place on the calends of January and was a kind of New Year's festival, at which people exchanged [gifts], dressed up as animals or old women and danced through the streets singing, to the applause of the populace."[42] The notion that the pre-Christian "Cervulus" persisted into the Christian Middle Ages and underlay the post-nativity festivals in medieval Christian Europe, especially France, is an abiding one and found in many commentators. As we can expect from Jung's prose here, he revels in the absurd situation and quotes Du Cange's late descriptions of the misrule with relish:

> In the very midst of divine service masqueraders with grotesque faces, disguised as women, lions, and mummers, performed their dances, sang indecent songs in the choir, ate their greasy food from a corner of the altar near the priest celebrating mass, got out their games of dice, burned a stinking incense made of old shoe leather, and ran and hopped about all over the church.[43]

Jung also embellishes his description with an account of the "Liturgy of the Ass" (*festum asinorum*), seemingly celebrated at Beauvais cathedral in memoriam of the flight of the Holy Family to Egypt on an ass and incorporating, according to Du Cange, quoted by Jung, a responsory for the congregation where after "each part (Introit, Kyrie, Gloria, etc.) of the high mass that followed, the whole congregation *brayed* [Jung's emphasis], that is, they all went "Y-a" like a donkey" and the whole service concluded so that "at the end of mass, instead of the words "Ite missa est," the priest shall bray three times, and instead of the words "Deo gratias," the congregation shall answer "Y-a" (*hinham*) three times.[44]

Amusing and intriguing though these accounts are (and Jung milks them for their entertainment value throughout), Max Harris, in his 2011 *Sacred Folly: A New History of the Feast of Fools*, has painstakingly combed through the French cathedral records to disentangle the reality of the *festum stultorum* from the layers of myth that have built up around it, especially in the hands of seventeenth-century writers such as Du Cange.[45] What he conclusively demonstrates is that, *pace* Jung, the *festum* did have a clear liturgical and theological purpose whose aims have been distorted by later attacks and especially the cartoonish exaggerations of the seventeenth- and eighteenth- century writers. The existence and occurrence of the *festum asinorum* as described by Du Cange is dubious in the extreme, and in his description of the 1 January *festum stultorum* Du Cange runs together descriptions from diverse sources, usually unsympathetic or hostile ones such as the Parisian masters who wrote a letter of condemnation in 1444. Peering through this liturgical fog, however, Harris is able to piece together an explanation for the practices so strongly libeled at a later date. What then was the purpose of the feast and how does it link to this chapter's pursuit of the psycho-spiritual role of the trickster in contemporary Christian setting?

As Harris points out, the first person to make explicit mention of the *festum stultorum* is John Beleth in his *Summa de ecclesiasticis officis* (1160–1164). In his description Beleth notes: "It is customary for archbishops and bishops to play with their subordinates in the cathedral close and even to indulge in a ball game."[46] What was this "ball game" and how did it relate to the *festum stultorum*? For authors such as Harris the "ball game" was almost certainly a form of liturgical dance that was performed in French medieval cathedrals, such as Auxerre, sometimes along the labyrinth inscribed into the nave:

> Early in the afternoon of Easter Sunday, the dean and as many as "a hundred" canons would gather at a paved stone labyrinth set into the floor at the west end of the nave. The newest member of the chapter carried a large leatherball. In 1412 the cathedral chapter ordered that the ball should be "smaller than usual, but too large to be grasped in one man's

hand, requiring two hands to stop it." It was, perhaps, the size of a soccer ball.[47]

Once assembled, the cathedral chapter would initiate the game-dance as described in a manuscript account of 1538:

> The dean began to sing antiphonally the appropriate Easter sequence, "Victimae paschali laudes"; then he took the ball with his left hand and danced the *tripudium* [dance] repeatedly in time to the music, while the others joined hands and danced the *chorea* [circle dance] around the labyrinth [*circa daedalum*]. While they danced, the dean would deliver the ball alternately to each and every one of the dancers, [who were] in the form of a garland [*serti in speciem*], and they would throw it back. There was sport, and the meter of the dance was set by the organ.[48]

No stinking leather-shoe incense, no clergy dressed as animals or old women and definitely no donkey-braying. The Auxerre dance-game (and evidence for others comes from Sens, Reims, Amiens, and Chartres) suggests a more stately measure that had a clear intention to reinstate the "Deus ludens" at the heart of the post-Easter liturgy.[49]

What are we to make of this? And how does it fit into the argument of this chapter? The first thing to note, as Harris reminds us, is that acceptable behavior in a medieval cathedral was probably quite different from what is the norm today. Whereas the altar and choir would have been set aside for liturgical functions, the saying of mass and the recital of the office, the nave could often serve more as a "people's space" and the situation of the game-dance there is congruent with the more democrat forms of devotional practice that would predominate in that space. Second, Harris argues that foisting pagan interpretations onto these medieval practices seems to over-theorize practices that can be given quite legitimate Christian interpretations (Christ as the rising sun represented in the ball, etc.). Recent scholars such as Dominic White have done just that. In his *Lost Knowledge of Christ* and more recent work including his chapter in the present volume, Fr. White explores how he has adapted the Auxerre dance-play for contemporary use and found that contemporary Christians and spiritual seekers have responded very positively to the incorporation of movement within the liturgical context:

> Many devout people complain of distractions in prayer, that all their lives whirl around in their heads when they sit still to pray. Perhaps if we brought back the movement of our bodies to prayer, we'd be able to be

> more still? . . . What might at first sight look like a pagan hangover is in fact the deepest teaching about angels/stars, one that we need to understand if the Angelic Dance is to become part of our lives.[50]

Might then the "divine dance" of the medieval feast of fools offer a path back for contemporary seekers to the origins of their faith in its divine milieu? Fr. White's essay in this volume certainly suggests that, and although, as we saw earlier, other religions such as Hinduism have the "divine circle dance" of Lord Kṛṣṇa, perhaps the time has come, as scholars such as White argue, for other religions such as Christianity to reclaim the role of divine play as an important psycho-spiritual part of their heritage too.

## The Divine Trickster: Conclusions

I began this chapter with Jung's and Radin's classic account of the trickster: He was depicted as the rollicking Lord of Misrule with all its jolly manifestations and given a psychological underpinning for its psychic manifestation according to Jung's own schema. Yet, as we saw, a problem remained with Jung's account. As stated at the beginning, this chapter particularly wanted to elaborate the role of the *divine* trickster from a psycho-spiritual perspective, for which Jung's schema gave little space. In one respect this should not surprise; Jung consistently failed to adopt theological categories when exploring human desire and motivation, and although fond of citing ecclesiastical examples (as we saw above), for him the theological can have (and must have) no life of its own independent of the psyche. For Jung the religions reflect these inward psychological schemas:

> If we consider, for example, the daemonic features exhibited by Yahweh in the Old Testament, we shall find in them not a few reminders of the unpredictable behaviour of the trickster, of these senseless orgies of destruction and his self-imposed sufferings.[51]

Which means that in areas such as the trickster Jung quite literally "misses a trick." In his desire to find a supposed hidden pagan root behind all that cannot be explained in, for example, medieval Christianity, he misses, as I have argued here, a theological or psycho-spiritual perspective that allows such seemingly eccentric practices to perform a legitimate function within the Body of Christ—the Church. Accordingly, to answer our initial questions as to how far, if at all, tricksterism could fit into contemporary Christianity, we sought to look elsewhere for inspiration and theological clarification.[52] The first candidate for exploration, the holy fool, was deemed too extreme and extraordinary to act as a containing vessel for more quotidian tricksterism within contemporary Christianity. However, the second tradition we examined, the ludic liturgies of the medieval "feast of fools," struck us as more promising. As we saw, they fulfilled the three Christian qualities of tricksterism as laid out earlier in the chapter (liminality, transformation, and play) while having good liturgical and theological precedent. The phenomenon of the return of the labyrinth and liturgical dance to contemporary liturgy (albeit in a somewhat piecemeal fashion) attests to the sense that the holy feast of fools *could* once again find a home within the more stately and somber quotidian liturgies of the church. In this respect, in response to the overriding question of the present volume, that is, what role does play/*līlā* have in current academic discussion of religion, we have, I think, clearly demonstrated that, as with other religions such as Hinduism, it *does* have a role within contemporary Christianity but one that will inevitably be circumscribed. In this respect, following Jung, for example, I have agreed that the ludic performs an important psycho-spiritual role, especially as acting as a gateway to the divine from the ordinary and mundane, much as Lord Kṛṣṇa summons the *gopīs* of Vraja from their everyday activities to the divine ecstasy of the *rāsa līlā*. However, this conclusion comes with a warning. If we accept, as Jung does, that the trickster plays an important psycho-spiritual role in our cultural and socioreligious milieu, we can regard the medieval liturgies and carnivals described in this chapter as acting as "escape valves" to release the trickster element within society and religion. If modern society has perhaps blocked such safety valves, how long will it be before a divine madness, or indeed frenzy, were to manifest itself within mainstream Christianity or society? Jung wrote much of his work on this subject shortly after the frenzy of Nazism had swept Europe; must we too be on our guard for an equally damaging manifestation of the "divine madness" if we do not pay serious attention to the divine trickster and its place in religion and society in our own troubled times?

This chapter has explored the role of the trickster through the lenses of Western psychology and the Christian tradition especially in relation to the "play of fools" that enables the earthly to reconnect to the Divine. As with other essays in this volume that explore the role of *līlā*/play in divine context, we are left with the tantalizing possibility that the divine foolishness of dance and play may ultimately recall that foolishness which St. Paul reminds us lies within us all, the Church and the Divine. The heart of the *deus ludens* that summons us to eternal *serio ludere*!

## Bibliography


Aycock, D. "The Mark of Cain." In *Structuralist Interpretations of Biblical Myth*, by E. Leach and D. Aycock, 120–127. Cambridge: Cambridge University Press, 1983.

Beidelman, T. "The Moral Imagination of the Kaguru: Some Thoughts on Tricksters, Translation, and Comparative Analysis." In *Mythical Trickster Figures: Contours, Context and Criticisms*, edited by William J. Hynes, and William G. Doty, 174–192. Tuscaloosa: University of Alabama Press, 2009.

Diamond, S. "Jung contra Freud: What It Means to Be Funny." In *C. G. Jung and the Humanities: Toward a Hermeneutics of Culture*, edited by K. Barnaby and P. D'Acierno, 67–75. London: Routledge, 1990.

Du Cange, C. *Glossarium ad scriptores mediae et infimae latinitatis*. 1733–1736. Edited by G. Henschel and L. Fauvre. Graz: Akademische Druck-U Verlagsanstalt, 1954.

Eck, D. *India: A Sacred Geography*. New York: Three Rivers Press, 2012.

Pope Francis. *Laudato Si': On Care for Our Common Home*. London: Catholic Truth Society, 2015.

Frembgen, J. "Divine Madness and Cultural Otherness: Diwānas and Faqīrs in Northern Pakistan." *South Asia Research* 26, no. 3 (2006): 235–248.

Harris, M. *Sacred Folly: A New History of the Feast of Fools*. Ithaca, NY: Cornell University Press, 2011.

Huizinga, J. *Homo Ludens: A Study of the Play Element in Culture*. London: Routledge, 1949.

Hynes, W. *Mythical Trickster Figures: Contours, Context and Criticisms*. Tuscaloosa: University of Alabama Press, 2009.

Ivanov, S. *Holy Fools in Byzantium and Beyond*. Oxford: Oxford University Press, 2006.

Johnson, C. "'Base but Nevertheless Holy': Lessons in Liminality from Symeon the Holy Fool." *Studies in Religion* 43, no. 4 (2014): 592–612.

Jung, C. "On the Psychology of the Trickster Figure." In *Collected Works*, vol. 9i, *The Archetypes and the Collective Unconscious*, 255–274. London: Routledge, 1968.

Jung, C. *Psychological Types*. In *Collected Works*, vol. 6. London: Routledge, 1977.

Krueger, D. *Symeon the Holy Fool: Leontius's Life and the Late Antique City*. Berkeley: University of California Press, 1996.

Mawer, S. *The Gospel of Judas*. London: Abacus, 2011.

Pagels, E., and K. King. *Reading Judas: The Gospel of Judas and the Shaping of Christianity*. London: Viking, 2007.

Poulakou-Rebelakou, E., A. Liarmakopoulos, C. Tsiamis, and D. Ploumpidis. "Holy Fools: A Religious Phenomenon of Extreme Behaviour." *Journal of Religion and Health* 53, no. 1 (2014): 95–104.

Radin, P. *The Trickster: A Study in American Indian Mythology*. New York: Philosophical Library, 1956.

Radin, P. *The World of Primitive Man*. New York: Henry Schuman, 1953.

Rahner, H. *Man at Play, or Did You Ever Practise Eutrapelia?* London: Burns and Oates, 1965.

Sviri, S. *The Taste of Hidden Things: Images on the Sufi Path*. Inverness, CA: Golden Sufi Center, 1997.

Thomas, A. "Holy Fools: A Theological Enquiry." Doctoral dissertation, University of Nottingham, UK, 2009.

Tyler, P. M. "Christian Sannyāsa: Dual Belonging or a Bridge Too Far?" In *Hindu-Christian Dual Belonging*, edited by D. J. Soars and N. Pohran. London: Routledge, 2022.

Tyler, P. M. *The Pursuit of the Soul: Psychoanalysis, Soul-making and the Christian Tradition*. Edinburgh: T & T Clark, 2016.

White, D. *The Lost Knowledge of Christ: Contemporary Spiritualities, Christian Cosmology, and the Arts*. Collegeville, MN: Liturgical Press, 2015.

Williams, R. *Looking East in Winter: Contemporary Thought and the Eastern Christian Tradition*. London: Bloomsbury, 2021.

## Notes

1. S. Diamond, "Jung contra Freud: What It Means to Be Funny," in *C. G. Jung and the Humanities: Toward a Hermeneutics of Culture*, ed. K. Barnaby and P. D'Acierno (London: Routledge, 1990), 67.
2. See, inter alia, P. Radin, *The Trickster: A Study in American Indian Mythology* (New York: Philosophical Library, 1956), and C. Jung, "On the Psychology of the Trickster Figure," in *Collected Works*, vol. 9i, *The Archetypes and the Collective Unconscious*, 255–274 (London: Routledge 1968), hereafter Jung, *CW*.
3. For a detailed exposition of the transcendent function within the psyche see P. M. Tyler, *The Pursuit of the Soul: Psychoanalysis, Soul-making and the Christian Tradition*. (Edinburgh: T & T Clark, 2016).
4. Tyler, *Pursuit of the Soul*.
5. Jung, CW, 256.
6. Jung, CW, 260.
7. Jung, CW, 263.
8. Jung, CW, 264.
9. Radin, *Trickster*, 3.
10. Jung, CW, 270.
11. W. Hynes, *Mythical Trickster Figures: Contours, Context and Criticisms* (Tuscaloosa: University of Alabama Press), 2009.
12. See, for example, T. Beidelman, "The Moral Imagination of the Kaguru: Some Thoughts on Tricksters, Translation and Comparative Analysis," in *Mythical Trickster Figures: Contours, Context and Criticisms*, ed. W. Hynes (Tuscaloosa: University of Alabama Press, 2009), 174–192.
13. Hynes, *Mythical Trickster Figures*, 7.
14. Hynes, *Mythical Trickster Figures*, 33.
15. Hynes, *Mythical Trickster Figures*, 24.

16. D. Aycock, "The Mark of Cain," in *Structuralist Interpretations of Biblical Myth*, by E. Leach and D. Aycock (Cambridge: Cambridge University Press, 1983), 124.
17. D. Eck, *India: A Sacred Geography* (New York: Three Rivers Press, 2012), 332–333.
18. S. Sviri, *The Taste of Hidden Things: Images on the Sufi Path* (Inverness, CA: Golden Sufi Center, 1997), 77.
19. Sviri, *The Taste of Hidden Things*, 81.
20. Sviri, *The Taste of Hidden Things*, 85.
21. Sviri, *The Taste of Hidden Things*, 88.
22. Hynes, *Mythical Trickster Figures*, 13.
23. Hynes, *Mythical Trickster Figures*, 4.
24. Hynes, *Mythical Trickster Figures*, 205–206.
25. J. Huizinga, *Homo Ludens: A Study of the Play Element in Culture* (London: Routledge, 1949).
26. Huizinga, *Homo Ludens*, 3.
27. Huizinga, *Homo Ludens*, 6.
28. H. Rahner, *Man at Play, or Did You Ever Practise Eutrapelia?* (London: Burns and Oates, 1965).
29. Rahner, *Man at* Play, 2.
30. Rahner, *Man at Play.*
31. Aquinas, for example, commenting on Ecclesiasticus 32:11–12 ("Run home to your house quickly and do not linger, play and amuse yourself there to your heart's content") states: "That is why the wise man in the above text calls man home to himself—and there play," he says. "Consider here how aptly the contemplation of wisdom is compared to play. There are two reasons for this: first, play gives pleasure, and in the contemplation of wisdom there is the most profound pleasure . . . Secondly, the activity of play is not directed towards some other end, but is sought for its own sake, and this holds true in regard to the pleasures arising from the contemplation of wisdom" (Aquinas, *Expositio super Boethium*, quoted in Rahner, *Man at Play*, 2). In this respect Rahner comments: "We cannot truly grasp the secret of *Homo ludens* unless we first, in all reverence, consider the matter of *Deus ludens*, God the creator who, one might say, as part of a gigantic game, called the world of atoms and spirits into being, for not even the most inspired gesture of man at play can be other than a clumsy, childish imitation of the *Logos* who, since the beginning of time, has made play before the face of the Father" (Rahner, *Man at Play*, 3). The theme, I would argue, is at the heart of the present volume.
32. The malaise and unease with the natural world is nicely encapsulated by Pope Francis in the introduction to his Encyclical *Laudato Si'*: "This sister [the earth] now cries out to us because of the harm we have inflicted on her by our irresponsible use and abuse of the goods with which God has endowed her. We have come to see ourselves as her lords and masters, entitled to plunder her at will. The violence present in our hearts, wounded by sin, is also reflected in the symptoms of sickness evident in the soil, in the water, in the air and in all forms of life. This is why the earth herself, burdened and laid waste, is among the most abandoned and maltreated of our poor; she 'groans in travail' (*Rom* 8:22). We have forgotten that we ourselves are dust of the earth (cf. *Gen* 2:7); our very bodies are made up of her elements, we breathe her air and we receive life and refreshment from her waters" (*Laudato Si'*, 2).

33. See, inter alia, S. Mawer, *The Gospel of Judas* (London: Abacus, 2011), and E. Pagels and K. King, *Reading Judas: The Gospel of Judas and the Shaping of Christianity* (London: Viking, 2007).
34. As well as the volumes cited here, see in particular Rowan Williams's exposition of the theme in his *Looking East in Winter: Contemporary Thought and the Eastern Christian Tradition* (London: Bloomsbury, 2021).
35. For a good modern version of this see D. Krueger, *Symeon the Holy Fool: Leontius's Life and the Late Antique City* (Berkeley: University of California Press, 1996).
36. C. Johnson, "'Base but Nevertheless Holy': Lessons in Liminality from Symeon the Holy Fool," *Studies in Religion* 43, no. 4 (2014): 592–612.
37. E. Poulakou-Rebelakou, A. Liarmakopoulos, C. Tsiamis, and D. Ploumpidis, "Holy Fools: A Religious Phenomenon of Extreme Behaviour," *Journal of Religion and Health* 53, no. 1 (2014): 98.
38. J. Frembgen, "Divine Madness and Cultural Otherness: Diwānas and Faqīrs in Northern Pakistan," *South Asia Research* 26, no. 3 (2006): 235–248. See also Ankur Barua's essay in the present volume on the role of the *baul* in Rabindranath Tagore's work (" 'You have made me endless, such is thy pleasure': The *Līlā* of Love in the Metaphysical Poetry of Rabindranath Tagore").
39. Other recent studies worth consulting include A. Thomas, "Holy Fools: A Theological Enquiry" (doctoral dissertation submitted to the University of Nottingham, UK, 2009), and S. Ivanov, *Holy Fools in Byzantium and Beyond* (Oxford: Oxford University Press, 2006).
40. Peter Tyler, "Christian *Sannyāsa*: Dual Belonging or a Bridge Too Far?" in *Hindu-Christian Dual Belonging*, ed. D. J. Soars and N. Pohran (London: Routledge, 2022).
41. Jung, *CW*, 260.
42. Jung, *CW*, 257, n. 3.
43. C. Du Cange, *Glossarium ad scriptores mediae et infimae latinitatis*, ed. G. Henschel and L. Fauvre (1733–1736; Graz: Akademische Druck-U Verlagsanstalt, 1954), 1666, quoted in Jung, *CW*, 257.
44. Jung, *CW*, 258.
45. M. Harris, *Sacred Folly: A New History of the Feast of Fools* (Ithaca, NY: Cornell University Press, 2011).
46. Harris, *Sacred Folly*, 54.
47. Harris, *Sacred Folly*, 56.
48. Harris, *Sacred Folly*.
49. Harris, *Sacred Folly*, 60.
50. D. White, *The Lost Knowledge of Christ: Contemporary Spiritualities, Christian Cosmology, and the Arts* (Collegeville, MN: Liturgical Press, 2015), 126–127.
51. Jung, *CW*, 256.
52. And in this respect, we remain sufficiently Jungian to concur with Diamond's quote with which we headed the chapter, that there is a universal aspect to tricksterism which means that, whether we like it or not, it will continue to manifest itself in human affairs, not least in religious spheres.

# 12 The Serious Subject of Play

## PLAY IN DANCE AND MUSIC

*Dominic White, OP*

Music, at least in its classical/traditional forms, is hardly regarded as just amusement. One could not call Bach's organ music or a Mahler symphony flippant or shallow, a mere pastime. Yet in English, French, and German, we *play* this music. Indeed, the creation of art may suffer from *not* having a playful dimension. In *Justine*, the first novel of *The Alexandria Quartet*, Lawrence Durrell comments on a fictitious novel called *Moeurs* by his character Jacob Arnauti:

> What is missing in his work—but this is a criticism of all works which do not reach the front rank—is a sense of *play*. He bears down so hard upon his subject-matter; so hard that it infects his style with some of the unbalanced ferocity of Claudia herself.[1]

We might also play with an idea. Serious thinking is going on, yet, it seems, *precisely in the playfulness*, some unexpected truth or solution may emerge, because it is free from the usual constrictions and projections. But play is not devoid of rules. Play is a serious business. One only need think of the game of hopscotch, in which you can land in a square, or straddle both, but you lose your turn if you step on a line.[2] In this chapter I argue that hopscotch can symbolize the apophatic that lies at the heart of Christian play, a Cusan *coincidence of opposites* which hops continually from one to the other, saying "not this" even as it is also "this or that"—but never exclusively, and never trying to fudge the issue by landing on the line in the middle, but rather, joining together, harmonizing.

In an attempt to restore play to what I believe is its proper place in theology, I continue on the path of Douglas Hedley's ground-breaking work on play, *līlā*, in the Indian tradition, in the Judeo-Christian tradition and in German Idealist philosophy. I then respond with considerations of the medieval cathedral dances, and the remarkable fusion of Hindu *līlā* rhythms with Catholic theology and mysticism in the music of Olivier Messiaen.

## Līlā, Its Critics—and a Synthesis?

*Līlā* is usually translated as play or sport, but with connotations of appearance, grace, body, and/or beauty. From the perspective of Hinduism, especially in its monotheistic form, Hedley sees *līlā* (or *krida*)[3] as a key concept, which, through the authority of the *Mahābhārata*, one of the two great Sanskrit epics, naturally unfolded into Vedāntic metaphysics. In polytheistic Hinduism, sacrifice (including on the part of the gods themselves) is central, but play is important too: So Agni, the fire god, is also a *playful* fire. Indra is the war and storm god, but also a dancer. In monotheistic Hinduism, *līlā* emerges in the third to fourth centuries. In His *ānanda* (bliss) God is playfully creative. He creates the world not out of necessity, nor duty, nor arbitrarily, as if by some random whim or chance, nor again out of *kāma*, desire—because God is already blissful, thus content. Rather, absolute creation arises from "blissful self-affirming creativity."[4]

This is strikingly close to Aquinas's teaching on creation: that God, already complete and fulfilled in Himself, creates freely, from His own will.[5] The Hindu conception above is also close to the idea of *bonum diffusivum sui*, "good spreading itself."[6] For Hans Urs von Balthasar, creation is an overflowing of the mutual love of the Divine Persons of the Trinity.[7] In Advaita (nondual) Vedanta, though, the created world is only *māyā*, illusion: The notion of God as creator is also an illusion, so the notion of God creating the world is "mere sport" in a negative sense.

*Līlā* is also linked to *ashcharya* or wonder (the beginning of philosophy, according to Aristotle)[8] and a sense of bliss in life. In this volume Douglas Hedley notes how for Sri Aurobindo and Rabindranath Tagore *līlā* is the infinite delight of the divine. Following Julius Lipner, Hedley adds, "From a theological perspective, *līlā* is primarily the divine play in the sense that the Godhead is not forced in any way to create or act in the world: The plenitude of divine bliss is the very incentive for creation."[9] Rāmānuja's more positive understanding of creation as theophany can embrace a more "real" play, and affirm the importance of play as a way for creatures to participate in the divine life: God realizes himself by creating. Such a perspective appears to part company with the Christian doctrine of creation, since it seems to imply that God is not fully realized *until* he has created: that is, he lacks something. However, if this is understood more metaphorically (playfully, even) it may not be so far from Christianity.[10] We will return to this question in connection with Jakob Boehme.

Let us note first, though, that from the different streams of Hindu theology a tension is emerging between, on the one hand, divine play as grace-giving and on the other, as God merely playing without any thought for the benefit of creatures. This seems to mirror, and is perhaps connected to, a dialogue about "good" and "bad" play. The Buddha would condemn a list of games as a basis for negligence—including hopscotch (*parihārapatha*).[11] Hedley compares this with the Christian tradition, showing how for Pascal, the balls and hunts of the French aristocratic elite were mere distraction and exposed a spiritual malaise, whereas Kierkegaard associated aestheti*cism* with boredom. We can see in this the compulsion, addiction to distraction, to fill every hole in my life which might otherwise reveal an intolerable abyss. In short, a flight from reality. The Christian theologian Tertullian's critique of the games of the circus, linking them to pagan rites and idolatry, not only shows the idolatry that is at the heart of distraction and addiction, but also, ironically, the sacred origins of games.[12]

Yet Christian Scripture and tradition have something positive to say about play, chiefly in the biblical figure of Wisdom. Douglas Hedley has approached this through the writings of Friedrich Schelling and Jakob Boehme.

## Schelling, Boehme, and the Hebrew Scriptures: Wisdom's Play

Douglas Hedley shows how Schelling recovered in his philosophy the figure of biblical Wisdom, not directly from the Bible, but, as one in the Lutheran Pietist tradition, from the Lutheran mystic Jakob Boehme. Boehme, "the Shoemaker of Görlitz," had a vision around 1600 in which Sophia emerges from the Holy Spirit. According to Stratford Caldecott's concise summary of Boehme's account, Sophia,

> clothed by the desire of God in an eternal, imperishable body becomes "Uncreated Heaven," the Kingdom of Beauty or Body of God, Eternal Nature, in which his Glory is forever manifested. Heaven or Sophia is the model for all subsequent creation.[13]

If anything, Boehme's attempts to explain his visions just make things worse from the point of view of Christian doctrinal orthodoxy—he was no scholar, though something of an autodidact, having read Paracelsus. Balthasar gave up on him.[14] But in his 2020 essay *Wisdom and Playful Zest* [die spielende Lust]*: Schelling and the Legacy of Boehme*, Hedley points out that Schelling's fascination with Boehme is specifically with regard to the idea of a self-differentiation *within* God, so that

> God is presented as a complex unity both as ground (or *mē on*, "not being") and his actualised being. This model of the eternal becoming of God as self-constitution is developed in various drafts known as The Ages of the World.[15]

But Stratford Caldecott re-reads Boehme's writings as *art*: Boehme's is "the active imagination turned towards God."[16] This is what artists do. This is what children do: They play, and their play disrupts our ontologies. So, for example, by playing in a bombsite, a site of death, they make it a place of life again—Wisdom the little child (Prov 8:30, according to one reading).

Theologically there is, nevertheless, a problem here: In what appears to anticipate Alfred North Whitehead's process philosophy, Boehme seems to be saying, like Rāmānuja, that God is realized along with the world, and so it is hard to see any fundamental ontological distinction between God and his creation, between infinite and finite. There is a possible reconciliation through the Greek Christian theological tradition, though, which understands potentiality differently from the Scholastic (Western) insistence on God as *actus purus*, as opposed to *potentia* indicating something unrealized in God's essence. Rather, the Greek Christian tradition sees divine potency in terms of what God can do—*and can choose not to do*.[17] God's potency is His creative power, exercised, as Rāmānuja recognizes, in God's freedom. God is not obliged to create—rather, creation comes from God's playfulness. So reading Boehme as artist, in including being and not-being in God, he recognizes God as *manifested* in creation, in God's creative work, as free and playful. Citing Wolfgang Smith, Caldecott says that "Boehme is viewing 'from below,' or through the lens of nature, realities that in the Kabbalah are treated 'from above,' through commentary on revealed Scripture."[18]

If we take this further and apply it to Trinitarian theology, it offers a playfully dynamic vision of the Trinitarian God, in which all three persons *are* fully God but *are not* each other—the love between the persons overflowing into Creation, as we saw from Hans Urs von Balthasar. Creation images God's internal dynamic playfulness, as does the artist when his/her creativity is turned toward God and graced by a participation in God's creative work, *which is also play, its prima facie opposite.*

Indeed, Boehme's vision takes us not away from the Bible on a tangent, but rather deeper in. The locus classicus for play in the Hebrew Scriptures, or rather the Vulgate translation, is Wisdom speaking of herself as playing, *ludens* (Hebrew *mᵉśaḥeqet*, "play/laugh/rejoice"), before God's throne (Prov 8:30).

Is it a coincidence that Wisdom plays? Wisdom has been a rather neglected figure, often treated as just an "extended metaphor," a personification of God's gift of Wisdom.[19] At the opposite end of the spectrum, the Gnostic tradition, with its tendency to hypostatization, treats her as a spirit: So in the *Pistis Sophia*, she is the little sister of the Logos, who falls into the material world and has to be rescued from it by her brother, who comes in the form of Jesus. Possibly in reaction to this, the majority Christian tradition has read Christ as Wisdom incarnate:[20] After all, "Christ is the power of God and the Wisdom of God" (1 Cor 1:24). He is the Word by whom God created the world. Yet Jesus also says, "Whoever has seen me has seen the Father" (John 14:9). But Jesus is the Son, not the Father; and Jesus breathed out the Spirit on the apostles on Easter night (John 20:22). Continuing to read 1 Corinthians 1, though, we find that Paul "unpacks" God's wisdom as not a wisdom of this age, which none of the rulers of this age understood, "for if they had, they would not have crucified the Lord of glory" (1 Cor 2:8). So Christ—the Messiah, the incarnate Word—is God's *wise act*: and then Paul moves on to speak of the Spirit of God, who makes us spiritual people (*pneumatikoi*) (2 Cor 2:10–13).

Irenaeus, though, reads Wisdom as the Holy Spirit, based on a close reading of Proverbs 8, which, typically of the patristic tradition, connects verses across Scripture by resonance and resemblance. Thus, in Proverbs, Wisdom says that the Lord created her "at/as the beginning of his work" (Prov 8:22) and that she was, in the unpointed Hebrew text, *'MWN* (Prov. 8:30). Depending on which vowels are used, she is *'amon* "like a master worker" or "artisan" or *'amun*, a "beloved little child" depending on where the dot is place on the Hebrew consonant *waw* (W). An agreement or concord *('amanah)* joins people together: hence the LXX *harmozousa*, "joiner" or "harmoniser." Irenaeus, putting together Genesis 1, Proverbs 8, and possibly Wisdom 9:1–2 ("who have made all things by your word, and by your wisdom have formed humankind"), reads the Old Testament as saying that, at the Creation, Wisdom, the Holy Spirit, joined together what the Father had made through the Logos.[21] It is not hard to see how this second reading has come to be understood by Christians as referring to the incarnation of the Logos-master worker by whom God made the world: "In the beginning was the Word . . . all things came into being through him" (John 1:1, 3)—He who was God's beloved child.

The difficulty with Irenaeus's reading is that Wisdom herself says, "The Lord created me at/as the beginning of his work" (Prov 8:22).[22] In the Wisdom of Solomon and Sirach (Ecclesiasticus), which read as expansions of Proverbs, Wisdom is "a breath of the power of God, and a pure emanation of the glory of the Almighty" (Wis 7:25), who, she says, "came forth from the mouth of the Most High" who was "my Creator" (Sir 24:3, 8). A possible distinction is to say that the Holy Spirit is Uncreated Wisdom, and the Wisdom of the Wisdom literature is Created Wisdom, a possible World Soul/*shekinah* figure who connects and fills everything ("alone I compassed the vault of heaven," Sir. 24:5), an idea entertained by Augustine.[23] Created Wisdom appeared not only to Boehme but also to Hildegard of Bingen, as she records in both words and paintings,[24] and to Vladimir Solovyov (recorded in poetry),[25] and was understood by Anne Catherine Emmerich, a Catholic nun, visionary, and contemporary of Friedrich Schelling, as the soul of the Virgin Mary.[26] Wisdom is particularly associated with the Virgin Mary in older Christian traditions, including the readings of the pre–Vatican II (Roman Rite Mass), *and* realized in the virtue of wisdom which is a gift of the Holy Spirit.[27]

To return to the Proverbs passage, the similarity in the *sound* of the Hebrew words based on the root 'MWN is not a coincidence, according to Margaret Barker. She argues that the discourse of the First Temple of Jerusalem had an "intricate word play"—so, for example, the root *šb*' gives *šebua'ah*, "oath," but also *šeba'*, "seven," the sacred number, and of course *šaba'*, the seventh day or Sabbath. Put them together and you have an oath by which God binds the creation together in Sabbath rest, so seven is key to understanding the creation.[28]

In all of this, Wisdom may play, connecting together: in the unpredictable playfulness of the Holy Spirit, who blows where S/He will (John 3:8); in the Virgin Mary, who, according to the apocryphal *Protoevangelium of James*, danced when she was *a little child* on the third step of the Jerusalem Temple, "and all Israel loved her";[29] and in the freedom and indeed seeming folly of the saints, the "Holy Fools" of the Orthodox tradition (cf. 1 Cor 1:23. on "folly to the Gentiles").

According to Sirach 33:15, "the works of the Most High . . . come in pairs, one *the opposite* of the other." We have already seen this in the *coincidentia oppositorum* of God's work *and* play, the hopscotch between this *and* that, between this and *not this*. But this structure is ingrained in the usual couplet structure of the proverbs in the Wisdom literature, for example:

> A wise child makes a glad father,
> But a foolish child is a mother's grief. (Prov 10:1)

Margaret Barker draws attention to the particular "heaven-earth" pairing in Proverbs 8:30–31:

> *A* I was daily his *delight,*
> *B* Playing/laughing before him all the time,
> *B* Playing/laughing in his inhabited earth.
> *A* And my *delight* was with the sons of Adam.[30]

Wisdom *'MWN* the master worker *and/or* child delights to be at the side of *('mn)* God (in heaven) *and* with humankind (literally, "the sons of Adam," note *'adamah* means "earth"). This pair is all one role for Wisdom.[31]

Or, perhaps, on earth as it is in heaven, as in the Lord's Prayer (Mt 6:10)? An *irreducible* pair: neither *just* heaven (by the annihilation of earth) nor *just* earth (by taking heaven "down to earth"). Instead, a quite literally *play-ful* alternation. And if we read this in the context of the Christian canon, when the new heaven and new earth come about, and the Holy City, adorned like a bride and the new dwelling of humankind, descends from heaven (Rev 21:1–8), there will a *union* to be symbolized by the marriage of the Lamb and His Bride (Rev 19:7–9)—just like the *embracing* ABBA structure of Proverbs 8:30–31.

All this shows the possible intellectual significance of play. But is this actually what happens in play? Is biblical Wisdom, is the life of God, *like* play, but in such a way that play becomes a metaphor, or at best an analogy, so that human play gets left behind as it is more unlike divine "play" than like it? At best, does human play simply gesture toward the *serious* business of a theological reality? Or can human play somehow *participate* in divine play, in the playful God? Here I examine two examples, the medieval cathedral dances and the use by composer Olivier Messiaen of Hindu *līlā* rhythms as Catholic theological symbols.

## The Cathedral Dances—the Body's Wisdom?

Play is, of course, not an adult practice, therefore not a serious one. Children have playtime at school and home, and concerns are expressed if children don't play or find it difficult—so, for them, *not playing* is a serious matter. Adults, though, don't play for the sake of it. We may play sport or music, which often have the status of recreation and have their elements of fun, but are not *purely* play—so play, as such, is *not serious* for adults—though we also saw that play is a serious matter for children—you *mustn't* step on the line in hopscotch.

What status, then, can we assign to the medieval dances in at least several French cathedrals? I have discussed these in detail elsewhere,[32] but here I put them in dialogue with Douglas Hedley's work on play and Michael Eisenberg's study of the Easter dances,[33] with my own reconstructions of the dance, and also with Hugo (brother of Karl) Rahner's remarkable study of play,[34] which touches on the cathedral dances but takes them much further.

First, a brief summary of the French cathedral dances. They took place at Easter and sometimes around the Feast of the Holy Innocents (December 28—so a children's feast?). Some survived into the fifteenth century and evolved, in the case of Bayeux, into a game of football still taking place in the cathedral chapter house in the early twentieth century. The most detailed description surviving is that of the dance in the cathedral of Auxerre:

> The dean or his representative, who is dressed like all those present in the [amice], receives the ball from one who is newly baptized or from a newly admitted cleric. All sing the antiphon *Victimae paschali laudes* appropriate to the feast of Easter. Then the dean seizes the ball with his left hand and [performs a *tripudium*] *(tripudium agebat)* solemnly in time to the music. The others join hands and dance around centre [of the labyrinth] *(choream circa daedalum ducentibus)*. While they are dancing, the dean throws the ball to the individual dancers in turn, and they throw it back. The game proceeds to the accompaniment of the organ and the dance. When song and dance are ended, the company goes to lunch.[35]

Note that the dean receives the ball from someone newly baptized or a newly admitted cleric (the youngest, i.e., a *little child*, as in Prov 8:30).

Exactly what the *tripudium* step consisted of is a matter of debate,[36] but the word suggests "three foot," or "triple step," that is, a dance in triple time. For us, the most obvious example might be a waltz, but specific to French folk tradition is the farandole: The dancers lift first the right leg and then the left as they move around, *1* 2 3, 2 2 3 . . .

To reconstruct the dance has obvious challenges: First, we don't have the original location to hand. Even if we did—the labyrinth of Chartres cathedral is perfectly preserved and still used in the spiritual life of the cathedral—we don't have the original cultural and theological context. *Translation* is required, which can employ a knowledge of theological and philosophical tradition to develop the dance. This is to follow Yves Congar's idea of tradition as both what is handed down and the process of handing down[37]—all the more important when the tradition has been interrupted and thus needs to be retrieved.

The first, simplest version is to dance without the ball. I found that because the farandole is an easy step, it gives the assembled group confidence to engage with the dance without worrying about what they're doing with their feet. You kick upward and you naturally look up to the sky; down, and you look to the earth. "On earth as it is in heaven"—just like the great Last Judgement window of Chartres that maps perfectly on to the labyrinth. An *immediate and spontaneous association* via the senses, without having to "think oneself into it."

The second stage of the dance was to add the ball—which needs to be thrown against the direction of travel. Predictably, it got dropped sometimes, with ensuing laughter. Perhaps this is a reminder that, *from the perspective of the Resurrection,* even Original Sin is not so serious: *O felix culpa,* "O happy fault that earned so great, so glorious a Redeemer," sings the deacon in the great preface of the Easter Vigil, the Exsultet[38]—just the night before the dance would have taken place.

The third stage of the dance I developed at a weekend workshop given with the Benedictine nuns of Dinklage, Germany. It wasn't practical to use a ball, so instead we copied the "hand over wrist" gesture of Christ of the Anastasis (Resurrection) icon, in which He grabs Adam and Eve in an almost flying movement and raises them up from Hades. We found that joining hands in this way, we stabilized each other's movement, and had a sense of being raised up to heaven *without losing contact with the earth*. In other words, earth was raised up to heaven with us.[39] Could this suggest an experiential origin for Plotinus's use of the image of a dance moving around the leader in the center (very like the cathedral dance), to describe how the soul is lifted up beyond the difference of different bodies to be united with Intellect?[40]

I venture to suggest that this experience of the third stage of the cathedral dance might overcome two aporias in the Divine Dance of Plotinus as discussed by Stephen Clark in this volume. First, the question of whether we look up (and escape to) to the heavenly dance to resign ourselves to our enmeshment in the earthly dance. Being embodied, earthly humans, we can't step outside nature's dance—but maybe dance enables us *to take nature up* to heaven even as we join in in the dance? The second aporia is whether we resist or go along with a flawed and fallen world. Instead, the dance transforms earth by taking it up to heaven and uniting heaven and earth: neither looking exclusively to heaven, nor exclusively to earth (nor again to an image, which Clark acknowledges can be our focus more on the *image* of our achievements or failures than the reality). But rather, as Clark says, there is a looking to an *elsewhere* on which, according to Plotinus, the dancer's attention is focused.[41] For in the dance there is a third beyond the dyad of heaven and earth, a third which is transformative through us of heaven and earth, and we ourselves are transformed in that cosmic dance.

To return to the Anastasis gesture, my appropriation of it may seem arbitrary, but the image of Christ the dancer is an ancient one in the patristic tradition (with clearly a (Neo-) Platonist antecedent). Hippolytus and Gregory of Nyssa are the great exponents, Gregory notably arguing that Christ is the leader of the dance (*choregos*), restoring humankind to the angelic dance from which we fell. And for Hippolytus, this is a round dance[42] (just like the cathedral dance), as it is also depicted in Fra Angelico's *The Last Judgement.* Rahner demonstrates the Platonist origins of this tradition in the dance which was the rotating movement of the stars, the *musica mundana*,[43] but clearly sees more in it than merely a Platonization of Christian tradition, because then he makes a mystical turn: For Rahner—recalling the "dancing figures of the Bible," he argues that "pious men dimly sense the great dance that moves before the eyes of God."[44] In other words, to understand the origins of the cosmic dance does not just require source criticism, but openness to the possibility of a common, perhaps universal mystical intuition. After all, the Jewish apocryphon 1 Enoch, which has no demonstrable source relationship with the Platonic tradition, speaks of the angels (*which are stars*, cf. Rev 1:20) revolving around the house of God (1 Enoch 71:8–9).

Eisenberg, we have seen, reads the cathedral dances as "performatic," involving the material, gestural, communal, and so on, that which is thoroughly removed from the discursive logocentric realm,[45] and the dances do indeed demonstrate liminality; this is all rather serious, one might say, self-conscious. But Rahner has found a greater depth in capturing both the playfulness and seriousness of the dance:

> Sacral play has always taken the form of a dance; for in the rhythm of body and music are conjoined all the possibilities of embodying and expressing in visible form the strivings and aspirations of the mind—and also, of chastely veiling and protecting them.[46]

So it is play, and children (teach us again to) play, for unless you become as little children, you shall not inherit the Kingdom of Heaven (Mt 18:3). *Sacral* play—not some strategy to make more fun for children a liturgy perceived as old, boring, and staid, but rather, a sacral play which takes adults back to the nonverbality of childhood play *and* beyond the verbal and logocentric to mysteries that cannot be spoken. And therefore, this *is* a serious matter, something perhaps intuited by children in the "wrongness" of stepping on the lines in hopscotch. Rahner reminds us that offense against the mysteries is called "dancing them away" (*exorcheisthai*).[47]

This might also explain the better known patristic condemnations of dance:[48] It is not dance *itself* that is being condemned, but *dancing wrongly.* Enoch saw the chaos caused by the rebellious chiefs of the stars who changed their courses and appeared at the wrong times (1 Enoch 80:6). Occult dances that seek a frenzied escape from the exterior world[49] or the dance of Christ and his apostles that replaces the drastic embodiment of the Last Supper and Crucifixion in the Gnostic *Acts of John*[50] contrast in their unreality with the bodily "raising up" of Adam and Eve by the dancing Christ in the Anastasis icon. Rahner recognizes in the gesture and movement of the Christian liturgy a slow dance.[51] And is it a coincidence that in the Roman Rite the "solemn" (i.e., full) version of the liturgy is led by the thurifer, bearing incense, a symbol of Wisdom (Sir 24:15), the harmonizer (Prov 8:30)—which makes us think of music and choirs, the *choros*, that is, the dance?

## The Play of the Impossible? Olivier Messiaen's *Līlā* Music

The oeuvre of the French composer Olivier Messiaen (1908–1992) strongly reflects his Catholic faith and theological curiosity, especially the extended meditation-cycles *The Ascension*, *The Nativity of the Lord*, and the hard-to-translate *Les Corps Glorieux: Sept visions brèves de la vie des*

*Ressuscités* ("The Bodies in Glory: Seven Brief Visions of the Life of the Risen Ones"). While rooted deeply in the great French organ tradition and Gregorian chant, Messiaen employed revolutionary techniques of harmony, rhythm, and structure. His rhythms are of special interest to us here, since, starting with *The Nativity* (1935) he worked with Hindu rhythms, many of which have titles based on *līlā*, for example, *Gajalîla* ("play/game of the elephant"). He drew these from the treatise *Samgîta-ratnâkara* of Sharngadeva (1175–1247), via Albert Lavignac's *Encyclopédie de la Musique*.[52] To begin with, Messiaen was unaware of their symbolic meanings, choosing the rhythms intuitively, and only starting to work explicitly with their symbolism in *Colours of the Heavenly City* (1963). He was attracted, though, by the fundamental principle of Hindu rhythm. Unlike in Western music which takes a bar or measure and divides it into smaller notes with a beat, Hindu music does the opposite: It has a primary note value, which is the shortest possible (Indian *mâtra*) and forms the basic unit of a rhythmic pattern. In particular, Messiaen imagines a first note, a single beat, with eternity before and after; then, a second beat, longer than the first, as any beat is prolonged by the silence which follows it.[53] Time and eternity: already in the metaphysical and theological, and Jean Marie Wu sees an additional symbolism of the musical note as a present linking past and future.[54]

This is well illustrated in the opening of *Dieu Parmi Nous* ("God among Us"), the final meditation of *The Nativity*. Here Messiaen uses two rhythms, *râgavardhana* ("colour/desire/love increasing/growing") for the opening chords, and *laksmiça* ("mark, sign, token") for the descending pedal motif. With the combined rhythmic drive and then the long-held chord with the movement underneath it, there is a sense of time and eternity united, past and present, heaven and earth: and above all, God and human united in the sign and actual visibility of God in His incarnation as the man Jesus Christ.[55] Messiaen, like the medievals, is also sensitive to number symbolism. For example, 3 and 5 both represent divinity, thus 3 represents the Trinity. 5 is the number of Hindu Shiva, destroyer of death, and thus a symbol of (connection with?) Christ, destroyer of death.[56]

And Messiaen goes a step further: Rather than just reproducing the Hindu rhythms, he *plays* with them, "either by the lengthening of a note, the addition of a short note-value, or by the addition of a short rest"—what he calls the principle of "added values."[57] The playfulness of his style is undeniable in *Dieu Parmi Nous*: after the thunderous opening, there are a few quiet bars (450–453, "Slow, with charm"—we'll come back to that), then a florid motif (454, "Lively and joyful"), reminiscent of Messiaen's beloved birdsong, and where he is clearly having fun. Messiaen weaves the three themes of the opening, the quiet bars and the florid motif together until the piece concludes in an ecstatic toccata (505 to end).

Here we find more play: Not only in the toccata section of *Dieu Parmi Nous* but throughout many of his works, Messiaen's harmonies are very jazzy, although scholars are coy about this (in none of the scholarly works I consulted could I find "jazz" in the index), and most prefer to focus on Messiaen's synaesthetic sense of harmonic color expressed in his Modes of Limited Transposition.[58] Now, while the harmonies in *Dieu Parmi Nous* can indeed be so attributed, especially to Messiaen's Mode 2, which alternates tones and semitones, the result is "blue" thirds and sevenths, added-sixth chords, all essential to the jazz which was filling the cafés of Europe when Messiaen was writing *The Nativity*. This is but one challenge to the apparent seriousness of Messiaen's work, and indeed he has sometimes been accused of not taking suffering seriously: His work seems all glory—where is the theology of the Cross?[59]

In an essay titled "Messiaen's Saintly Naïveté," Sander van Maas picks up on Paul Griffiths's coining of this term, in response to "a tune of banal perkiness" in Messiaen's *Quartet for the End of Time*: "It takes a sublime, even saintly *naïveté* to accept materials from Massenet and Glenn Miller, then use them to praise Christ as if they had never been employed for any baser purpose. . . . The challenge of the religious artist is to make all things sacred."[60] It is also easy to forget that Messiaen suffered the loss of his first wife to early dementia, amnesia, and a long ensuing institutionalization, and that he wrote the *Quartet*, with its "perky" tune, in a Nazi prisoner of war camp where his health also suffered severely.[61] Even amid suffering, the Resurrection was always more powerful. Indeed, Christ is the one who makes *all* things new (Rev 21:5), for God has put all things (*panta*) under Christ's feet (Eph 1:22).

A more serious challenge is cultural appropriation. Messiaen takes sacred rhythms from another religion, for a long time not even bothering to investigate what they might mean—and then, when he starts to employ them consciously, are the symbolisms really translatable from Hinduism into Catholicism? It was in fact a Hindu friend who translated the names of the rhythms for Messiaen, and then found that Messiaen had unconsciously come close to the symbolic meanings of some of them—such as *Gajalīlā* signifying "illumination of the mind" or divine enlightenment.[62] There is no sense of indifference, disrespect, or Catholic triumphalism in Messiaen's attitude to Hindu rhythms, but rather a humble apophaticism. Messiaen was often fascinated by *limitation* and *impossibility* in music: As he played with Hindu rhythms and Greek meters—another interest—he found that some could be reversed but others not, because they were palindromes (such as long-short-long). His modes, for all their color, are limited in their transposability—his Mode 2 only three times, compared with the eleven times of the major or minor modes of classical Western music. He called this "the *charm* of impossibilities."[63] But what is more surprising is that he actually didn't care: He thought that the listener is essentially uninterested in "the technical machinations of the music"—there's no time in concert to inspect the nontranspositions and nonretrogradations—the listener just won't be interested.[64] Rather, Messiaen said to Claude Samuel,

> It's not essential for listeners to be able to detect precisely all the rhythmic procedures of the music they hear just as they don't need to figure out all the chords of classical music. . . . The moment that they receive a shock, realize that it's beautiful, that the music touches them, the goal is achieved.[65]

Indeed,

> to be charmed will be his [*sic*, i.e., the listener's] only desire. And that is precisely what will happen; in spite of himself, he will submit to the strange charm of impossibilities: a certain effect of tonal ubiquity in the nontranspositions, a certain unity of movement (where beginning and end are confused because identical) in the nonretrogradation, all things which will lead him progressively to that sort of theological rainbow which the musical language, of which we seek edification and theory, attempts to be.[66]

Messiaen's game is to hide the technique and let the music gesture toward the reality. Indeed, one can see this in a certain *theologia crucis*:—maybe precisely in the playful quality of Messiaen's music there is the kenosis of one who does not take himself too seriously, who does not care if he is considered an irreverent child playing with café music and kitsch—and moreover, one whose faithful and joyful hope in the Resurrection makes him forgetful of his own suffering. There is an echo of the Christ who emptied Himself, taking the form of a slave (Phil 2:7). We can also see this in Messiaen's intuitive approach to Hindu rhythms, which does not seek to "master" them, nor impose a syncretism which would be little more than an intellectual straitjacket. Rather, he plays with the rhythms with a sense of wonder—perhaps also with a Sophianic capacity to connect (Wisdom the harmonizer), since the "basic unit" rhythmic structure strongly resembles the Gregorian chant that was Messiaen's bread and butter as a church musician. Thereby he goes to the essence of the Hindu rhythms, that is, to divine play.

What though of the "charm of impossibilities"? "Charm is deceitful" (Prov 31:30), but just as in Proverbs there is the contrast of Dame Folly and Wisdom, can there be a holy charm? "The hidden meaning of Messiaen was the 'charm of impossibilities' available in the complexity of the rhythms," says Andrew Shenton:[67] It is the *not* this, *not* that, always jumping from one side to the other, apophatic hopscotch, gesturing toward but never capturing the ineffable playing One who charms us to heaven in the Cusan coincidence of opposites.[68]

## Playing to Rethink Knowledge? Toward a Conclusion or a Beginning

In this chapter, we have looked at play from different perspectives, and we have seen examples of playing well and playing badly. From Indian traditions we see that God plays, and human play can be a participation in divine play. Play can also be a distraction or escape, and for some Hindu theologians God's play is indifferent to the benefit to creatures, and not grace-giving. But for other Hindu theologies, play can be participation in the sheer freedom of God in His creativity. In harmony especially with the Greek Christian theology of creation, God creates not because He has to, nor with a predetermined system, a kind of productionism, but rather out of the potentiality to do this *or* that *or* something else entirely, a potentiality that emanates from God's freedom.

We found in the Judeo-Christian tradition and the German Idealists—the two bridged by Schelling's great influence, the mystic Jakob Boehme—that Wisdom plays before God as God creates. And Wisdom plays in the *wordplay* of Hebrew vowels: with different pointing, she is both a little child playing before God *and* a master craftsperson who *joins together* heaven and earth, God and humankind. Human play is not merely some pale imitation or vague reminiscence of divine play, but a participation. This is also why play needs its rules—rules that do not stifle, but rather free us up for participation in the cosmic dance of the stars. These rules also *protect* that play from the disorderly movement of the fallen angels that Enoch saw causing chaos.

In the play of the Cathedral Dances we saw again a precise though simple set of rules in the form of a choreography, and one which had a strong theological backing in the patristic tradition of the Angelic Dance, itself a baptism of the Platonic *musica mundana* (a baptism not too difficult to achieve if one reads the Platonic stars/gods as the angels-who-are-stars of Judeo-Christian apocalyptic). It is significant though that the sources for the choreography do not *explain* the dance: You cannot just read about it and then abstract from what you read. You have to do the dance, with your body. The three versions attempted in my reconstructions and development of the tradition—playfully—suggested a (re-)union of heaven and earth; dropping the ball as a "happy fault" understanding of the Fall in the light of the Resurrection; and finally, the raising of humankind to heaven *with the earth* through the addition to the dance of the Anastasis gesture.

The Cathedral Dances also show us, *precisely in their humor,* the seriousness and ascesis of divine play. In order to experience, for example, the "happy fault" of dropping the ball, we have to put aside all strategies of argument and interpretation which may present themselves as rational and logical but often mask a desire to restrict the material of theology or even exclude certain material ("cookie-cutter" approaches). All pre-planned productionist schemes, all intellectual foreclosures must die on the Cross—along with our self-consciousness in participating in the dance—in order to rise not as fools but with the immediacy of little children, unexpectedly accepted together, and becoming creative master craftspeople through the grace of the divinizing transformation that is the grace of the Resurrection.

Olivier Messiaen's playful music-making demonstrates similar themes. He works *with* the limitations of modal and rhythmic structures, which by their limitedness can symbolize the objectivity of the structure of the cosmos—God made it *this* way, not *that.* Yet, by virtue of our being made in the image and likeness of God, we human beings are creative. Because of Original Sin, human interventions in the world and in each other's lives can be destructive rather than creative; but by divine grace and especially the grace of divinization (*theosis*), the *likeness* of the Creator God is restored in us. Thus, we can play, as Messiaen plays using addition and subtraction, *with and as part of* the evolution of the universe, the evolution which is integral to God's creative work.

As both master composer and in his childlike immediacy, Messiaen is very like the biblical figure of Wisdom: His primary response to Hindu rhythms was intuitive rather than cerebral, yet he sometimes came close to their actual meanings. He cannot have been unaware of the jazzy sound of many of his harmonies, or the possible kitschiness of added-sixth final chords and "perky" melodies. There is something of the naughty child. Also, as we saw, the utterly kenotic child, who does not care whether people think his music kitsch or not, or whether they understand his musical structures—and who, in the glorious light of the Resurrection, forgets his own suffering. A putting aside of glory in the light of Resurrection hope.

Furthermore, in Messiaen's appropriation of the unlikely, there is the *recapitulative* work of Christ who unites things in heaven and things on earth (Eph 1:12). This takes us back to Wisdom as *speculative* (cf. Wis 7:26), as recognized by Schelling and Hedley—literally a mirror (*speculum*) but also playing with the possible images the mirror can give—as we see in an earthly art reflecting God in the writings of Boehme.

It also takes us back to Wisdom the harmonizer. In the game of hopscotch, in the dance of the cathedrals, in the harmonic and rhythmic games of Messiaen's music, there is neither chaotically unbounded plurality, nor reductionism, nor fudge, nor an apophaticism so extreme that the "not" is absolutized and we end up with atheism and nihilism. So you must not stand on the lines *between* the two squares, which are *distinct* and *different*. You dance with *this* step in *triple* time, not in a different step in double time or just doing your own thing in the initial freedom but high risk of loneliness, which is the solo disco dance. The irreducibility of difference paves the way for the unity of harmony, in which the unity is beautiful precisely because of the wise and sometimes surprising coming together of different elements. The late Fr. Raphael Armour pointed out to me that in the Anastasis icon Christ is not just raising Adam and Eve from Hades, but bringing them back together,[69] *reuniting*, without merging their difference, the couple whose relationship was damaged by the Fall (Gen 3:16). It may not be a coincidence that much of Messiaen's music is dance-like—one need only think of *Force et Agilité des Corps Glorieux*[70]—and notice that the bodies are plural, even though they move in the unity of monody, recalling the action of singing chant together.

Going further, this playful harmony is an introduction to Godself, the Holy Trinity, One *and* Three, yet the Father is *not* the Son, the Son *not* the Spirit, and so on. And the divine hide-and-seek of Christ: "who has seen me has seen the Father" (John 19:30), and the Holy Spirit is breathed out by Christ on the Cross and on Easter evening (John 19:30, 20:22), yet Christ is neither the Father nor the Spirit. *Deus absconditus* . . .

In conclusion, I want to consider two serious objections to the theology of play that I have developed in this essay. First, that it is so far removed from the ways we normally practice philosophy and theology as to be unconnectable, and thus risks appearing eccentric and irrelevant. The second objection is that it fails as Christian theology in that it does not distinguish between Christian and Hindu divine play and therefore fails to guard the *uniqueness* of Christ.

So no, we don't do theology by dancing or playing/listening to music. Rather, painstakingly and over many centuries we have carefully analyzed the meaning of words in context, have insisted on intellectual rigor and especially on logical entailment, or at least an acknowledgment of what is speculative (in the everyday sense) or intuitive. This is one of the developments that has saved us from religious fundamentalism and all the death and destruction that this has brought. I write this in a country where Catholics and Protestants executed each other in the most vile ways: Now we do theology together and pray together.

But we have also found in the experience of secularization a gulf between, on the one hand, everyday spiritual belief and practice—even the beliefs and practices of "the pew"—and on the other, academic theology, which can often be regarded as abstract, irrelevant, and boring. Have we, in our arguments, become too cerebral and too logocentric? Thomas Aquinas, schooled in the verbality—and courtesy—of the scholastic disputation, nevertheless held that all knowledge comes to us through the senses: indeed, that the intellect must be *converted* (*convertat se*) to the images which come to it from the senses.[71]

This is where play saves us: We can talk about play, we can make intellectual *connections* (Wisdom *harmozousa*), but ultimately, *play needs to be experienced.* In other words, if you want to understand play, you need to play. Of course, Aquinas's restriction of knowledge to images from the senses is in the context of "natural theology," that is, what we can know about God without Christian faith: Thus, he is not excluding supernatural, "infused" knowledge, such as the mystics might have, but nor is he reducing, still less excluding, the possibility of suprarational or supernatural experience coming through the senses. In the play of games, of dance, in the "hopping between", the *not* this, *not* that, we are actually in apophatic theology, awaiting the third which graces us, ineffably, with the ineffable harmony.

Play takes us beyond words. As Hugo Rahner says,

> The Greeks used the dance to give . . . concealed and cryptic expression to the *arreta*, the unspeakable things of the mysteries; for they knew that there are certain insights and intimations which go beyond the powers of speech and may only be expressed in some kind of comely action.[72]

And the visionary of 2 Corinthians 12:2–4 was taken up to the Third Heaven and heard things which cannot be spoken (*arrēta rhēmata*). What he or she heard could be spoken *about* by Paul, *gestured toward*, but not exhausted by the saying. This is why Christianity has to be bodily—in the liturgy, in humble participation in the Body of the Church, in hearing and speaking the Word, *and that Word made flesh* as perhaps symbolized by the cleric leading the Easter dance, standing right in the middle of it. And Christianity is bodily too in the practical love of neighbor, especially of the weakest and most marginalized, as well as in the joyful metanoia of dropping the Easter ball.

Now for the second objection: whether this theology of play adequately distinguishes between Hindu and Christian divine play, with consequences for the uniqueness of Christ. Is not Rahner risking a sort of mystical perennialism, whereby difference of doctrine is ultimately unimportant because of the apparent convergence of mystics, whether Hindu, theurgical Platonist, or Christian? And this in such a way that is not only practically ineffable, but morally so—that is, not only can it not be spoken but you can't speak about it? Mystical freedom becomes tyranny?

One of the reasons that interreligious dialogue, and what is often called "theology of religions," arose in the Catholic Church in the twentieth century was through the experience of European missionaries who were deeply challenged by the spiritual depth of the "heathen" they went to preach to.[73] And if the Spirit of God blows where S/He will, what Christian can say that a Hindu cannot have a genuine experience of God, the playing, creative God? Again, can any Christian say for certain that some Christians who claim to have mystical experiences are not bogus or suffering from psychosis? And what about the false visions of the devil who appears as an angel of light (2 Cor 11:14, just a chapter before the mystic of 2 Cor 12)?

Hinduism and Christianity alike acknowledge that there can be good play and bad play, good dance and bad dance. There is a *moral* dimension here, and, for the Christian, that does need an ascesis, a metanoia of kenosis, even in the most spiritually and artistically gifted. Without this, there is pride, the sin of Satan, leader of the fallen angels.

And this leads us back to the Easter dance. We recall that in Judeo-Christian apocalyptic, the angels are stars, and therefore the cosmic dance, long known in many cultures, is a dance with the angels, if we follow the interpretation of God speaking to the gods in Psalm 82:1 as God speaking to the angels. But is our dance, here and now, with the angels of God or with the fallen angels? Is it a fear-driven attempt to escape the physical world in a frenzied dance, the perfect fear that casts out love? In a rigidity and formalism that rejects freedom? A self-centered, prideful bottom-up ascent? Or *being raised up together* like Adam and Eve in the Anastasis? Paul warns the Ephesians that their battle is not against earthly powers, but the Powers and Principalities, angels who by nature are all the more powerful than human beings, and thus, as fallen angels (Eph 1:21; Col 1:16, 2:10) all the more dangerous—and hence the battle against them (Eph 6:10–17). Only God can overcome for us the fallen angels, and therein lies the soteriological necessity of the Incarnation.[74] It might explain too why a number of medieval churches, including Chartres cathedral, one of the places of the Easter dance, has Zodiac windows:[75] Christ has overcome the influence of the fallen/angels stars, and fills all the creation.

We cannot conclude from this that the mystical experiences of non-Christians are false: The Spirit blows where S/He will, and "By their fruits you shall know them" (Mt 7:16). Rather, in Christ who is God made human, all that is good is taken up, harmonized, and made new by the God who is eternally playing, and teaching us to play with music and dance, words, ideas, and with each other.

## Bibliography

*The Apocryphal New Testament: A Collection of Apocryphal Christian Literature in an English Translation*. Edited and translated by J. K. Elliott. Oxford: Clarendon, 1993.

Aquinas, Thomas. *The Disputed Questions On Truth (De Veritate)*. Translated by Robert W. Mulligan. Chicago: Henry Regnery, 1952.

Aquinas, Thomas. *On the Truth of the Catholic Faith (Summa Contra Gentiles)*. Translated by James F. Anderson. Garden City, NY: Doubleday, 1955–57.

Aquinas, Thomas. *Summa Theologiae*. Edited and Translated by the English Dominican Friars. London: Eyre & Spottiswoode, 1963.

Aristotle. *Metaphysics*, books I–IX. Translated by Hugh Tredennick. Loeb Classical Library. Cambridge, MA: Harvard University Press, 1933.

Athanasius. *Against the Gentiles (Contra Gentes).* Translated by E. P. Meijering. Leiden: Brill, 1984.

Augustine. *Confessions.* Translated by R. S. Pine-Coffin. London: Penguin, 1961.

Augustine. *Sermons.* Translated by Edmund Hill. New York: New City Press, 1990–.

Balthasar, Hans Urs von. *Theodrama,* vol. 2. 1976. Translated by Graham Harrison. San Francisco: Ignatius Press, 1990.

Balthasar, Hans Urs von. *Theodrama,* vol. 4. 1980. Translated by Graham Harrison. San Francisco: Ignatius Press, 1994.

Barker, Margaret. *Creation: A Biblical Vision for the Environment.* London: T&T Clark, 2010.

Barker, Margaret. *The Great Lady: Restoring Her Story.* Sheffield: Phoenix, 2023.

Bartholomew Craig G., and Ryan P. O'Dowd. *Old Testament Wisdom Literature: A Theological Introduction.* Downers Grove, IL: InterVarsity Press, 2011.

*Long Discourses of Brahmajāla Sutta.* In *The Long Discourses of the Buddha: A Translation of the Dīgha Nikāya.* Translated by Maurice C. O'Walshe. Boston, MA: Wisdom Publications, 1995.

Caldecott, Stratford. *The Radiance of Being: Dimensions of Cosmic Christianity.* Tacoma, WA: Angelico Press, 2013.

Congar, Yves. *Tradition and Traditions: An Historical and a Theological Essay.* 1960/1963. Translated by Michael Naseby and Thomas Rainborough. London: Burns & Oates, 1966.

Cselényi, István. *The Maternal Face of God: Explorations in Catholic Sophiology.* Kettering, OH: Angelico Press/Sophia Perennis, 2017.

Dingle, Christopher. *The Life of Messiaen.* Cambridge: Cambridge University Press, 2007.

Dunn, James. *The Theology of Paul the Apostle.* Grand Rapids, MI: Eerdmans, 1998.

Durrell, Lawrence. *The Alexandria Quartet.* 1957. New Edition. London: Book Club Associates, 1972.

Eisenberg, Michael. "Performing the Passion: Music, Ritual, and the Eastertide Labyrinth." *Trans: Revista Cultural de Música,* 13 (2009). Online only at www.sibetrans.com/trans/a59/performing-the-passion-music-ritual-and-the-eastertide-labyrinth#_edn22 (accessed 29 October 2021).

Emmerich, Anne Catherine. *The Life of the Blessed Virgin Mary.* Translated by M. Palairet. London: Burns & Oates, 1954.

Griffiths, Paul. *Olivier Messiaen and the Music of Time.* London: Faber & Faber, 1985.

Hedley, Douglas. *Wisdom and Playful Zest* (die spielende Lust)*: Schelling and the legacy of Boehme.* Friends of Sophia Conference, 2020. Available online at https://www.friendsofsophia.com/events/conference2020/#hedley (accessed January 28, 2025).

Hildegard of Bingen. *Book of Divine Works.* In *Hildegard of Bingen: An Anthology.* Edited by Fiona Bowie and Oliver Davies, Translated by Robert Carver. London: SPCK, 1990.

Hildegard of Bingen. *Scivias.* Translated by Mother Columba Hart. New York: Paulist, ca. 1990.

John Scotus Eriugena. *Periphyseon = On the Division of Nature.* Translated by Myra L. Uhlfelder. Eugene, Oregon : Wipf & Stock, 2011.

Irenaeus. *Against the Heresies.* Translated by Dominic J. Unger and John J. Dillon. New York: Paulist, ca. 1992–.

Lebeuf, Jean. Items in *Mercure de France,* May 1726. Translated by E. Mehl. "Baseball in the Stone Age." *Western Folklore* 7, no. 2 (1948).

Mainoldi, Ernesto Sergio. "Creation in Wisdom: Eriugena's Sophiology beyond Ontology and Meontology." *Proceedings of the International Conference on Eriugenian Studies in Honor of E. Jeauneau.* Turnhout: Brépols, 2014.

Maas, Sander van. "Messiaen's Saintly Naïveté." In *Messiaen the Theologian*, edited by Andrew Shenton, 41–59. Aldershot: Ashgate, 2010.

Messiaen, Olivier. *The Technique of My Musical Language.* Translated by John Satterfield. Paris: Leduc, 1958.

Morrison, Tessa. "The Labyrinthine Path of Pilgrimage." *Peregrinations* 1, no. 3 (2005), https://digital.kenyon.edu/perejournal/vol1/iss3/6/ (accessed 21 October 2021).

Plotinus. *Enneads.* Translated by A. H. Armstrong. Loeb Classical Library. Cambridge, MA: Harvard University Press, 1967.

Pseudo-Dionysius. *On the Divine Names and Mystical Theology.* Translated by John D. Jones. Milwaukee: Marquette University Press, 2011.

Rahner, Hugo. *Man at Play, or Did You Ever Practise Eutrapelia?* 1963–1964. Translated by Brian Battershaw and Edward Quinn. London: Burns & Oates, 1965.

*The Roman Missal.* 2008. English translation according to the Third Typical Edition. London: Catholic Truth Society, 2011.

Samuel, Claude. *Olivier Messiaen: Music and Color: Conversations with Claude Samuel and Olivier Messiaen.* 1986. Translated by E. Thomas Glasow. Portland, OR: Amadeus, 1994.

Schloesser, Stephen. "The Charm of Impossibilities: Mystic Surrealism as Contemplative Voluptuousness." In *Messiaen the Theologian*, edited by Andrew Shenton, 163–182. Aldershot: Ashgate, 2010.

Shenton, Andrew. *Olivier Messiaen's System of Signs: Notes towards Understanding His Music.* Aldershot: Ashgate, 2008.

Sherlaw Johnson, Robert. *Messiaen.* London: J. M. Dent & Sons, 1975.

Smith, Wolfgang. *Christian Gnosis: From Saint Paul to Meister Eckhart.* Tacoma, WA: Angelico Press/Sophia Perennis, 2011.

Solovyov, Vladimir. "Three Rendezvous." In *The Religious Poetry of Vladimir Solovyov*, translated by Boris Jakim and Laury Magnus. San Rafael, CA: Semantron Press, 2008. Also in *The Postil* Magazine, August 1, 2017, https://www.thepostil.com/three-rendezvous-a-poem-by-vladimir-solovyov/ (accessed 1 March 2021)

Tyler, Peter. *Confession: The Healing of the Soul.* London: Bloomsbury Continuum, 2017.

*Chandogya Upanishads.* In *The Twelve Principal Upaniṣads: Text in Devanāgari; and Translation with Notes in English from the Commentaries of Śaṅkarācārya and the Gloss of Ānandagir.* Edited and translated by Edward Röer and others. 2nd edition. New Delhi: D. K. Printworld, 2000.

White, Dominic. "Dance in Christianity: A *Ressourcement.*" *Sobornost* 35, no. 1–2 (2013): 81–122.

White, Dominic. *The Lost Knowledge of Christ: Contemporary Spiritualities, Christian Cosmology, and the Arts.* Collegeville, MN: Liturgical Press, 2015.

White, Dominic. "An Overview of Sophiology." https://www.friendsofsophia.com (accessed 29 October 2021).

Wu, Jean Marie. "Mystical Symbols of Faith: Olivier Messiaen's Charm of Impossibilities." 1998. In *Messiaen's Language of Mystical Love*, edited by Siglind Bruhn, 85–120. New York: Routledge, 2012.

## Notes

1. Lawrence Durrell, *The Alexandria Quartet*, new ed. (1957; London: Book Club Associates, 1972), 67. Claudia is Jacob's wife.
2. See "How To Play Hopscotch: Learn the Basic Rules and Five Variations," *Parents Magazine*, https://www.parents.com/fun/activities/hopscotch/.
3. *Chandogya Upanishad*, 7.25.2.
4. Douglas Hedley, "Play in East and West," in this volume.
5. Thomas Aquinas, *Summa Theologiae* 1.44–46, especially 46.1.
6. An idea developed by Thomas Aquinas, from Pseudo-Dionysius (*On the Divine Names* 700B–704A): see especially *Summa Contra Gentiles* 3.24 (also 1.37), *De Veritate* 21, a. 1, obj. 4, and ad 4.
7. See Hans Urs von Balthasar, *Theodrama*, vol. 4, trans. Graham Harrison (1980; San Francisco: Ignatius Press, 1994), 328–332 (also 319–328).
8. Aristotle, *Metaphysics* 982b.
9. Hedley, "Play in East and West," in this volume.
10. Cf. John Scotus Eriugena, *Periphyseon* III 678C-D on God realizing Himself in creation; see Ernesto Sergio Mainoldi, "Creation in Wisdom: Eriugena's Sophiology Beyond Ontology and Meontology," *Proceedings of the International Conference on Eriugenian Studies in Honor of E. Jeauneau* (Turnhout: Brépols, 2014), 183–222 (esp. 209–211). My thanks to Daniel Soars for drawing my attention to Scotus.
11. *Long Discourses of Brahmajāla Sutta*, 1.1.
12. Tertullian, *On the Games*, 6–13.
13. Stratford Caldecott, *The Radiance of Being: Dimensions of Cosmic Christianity* (Tacoma, WA: Angelico Press, 2013), 252.
14. See Hans Urs von Balthasar, *Theodrama*, vol. 2, trans. Graham Harrison (1976; San Francisco: Ignatius Press, 1990), 420.
15. Douglas Hedley, *Wisdom and Playful Zest* [die spielende Lust]: *Schelling and the legacy of Boehme*, Friends of Sophia Conference, 2020, available online at https://www.friendsofsophia.com/events/conference2020/#hedley (accessed January 27, 2025).
16. Caldecott, *The Radiance of Being*, 252.
17. See István Cselényi, *The Maternal Face of God: Explorations in Catholic Sophiology* (Kettering, OH: Angelico Press/Sophia Perennis, 2017), 17.
18. Caldecott, *The Radiance of Being*, 252, citing Wolfgang Smith, *Christian Gnosis: From Saint Paul to Meister Eckhart* (Tacoma, WA: Angelico Press/Sophia Perennis, 2011), 142–144.
19. James Dunn, *The Theology of Paul the Apostle* (Grand Rapids, MI: Eerdmans, 1998), 271; Craig G. Bartholomew and Ryan P. O'Dowd, *Old Testament Wisdom Literature: A Theological Introduction* (Downers Grove, IL: InterVarsity Press, 2011), 237–239.
20. E.g., Athanasius, *Against the Gentiles*, 40.2, on Christ as the Word and wisdom of the Father. In the Roman Breviary this is paired with Sirach 42:15–43:12, on creation as the Lord's work (Week 1, Thursday). The previous day pairs Wisdom's hymn to herself (Sir 24:1–23) with Irenaeus on the Word of God (*Against the Heresies*, 4.6.3, 5.6.7).
21. Irenaeus, *Against the Heresies*, 4.20.1.
22. Manuscripts differ: *en archei* ("at the beginning"); *archēn* ("as the beginning").
23. Augustine, *Confessions*, 12.9, 11, 15.

24. Hildegard, *Book of Divine Works* 1.2; see also *Scivias* I.6.
25. Vladimir Solovyov, "Three Rendezvous," in *The Religious Poetry of Vladimir Solovyov*, translated by Boris Jakim and Laury Magnus (San Rafael, CA: Semantron Press, 2008).
26. Anne Catherine Emmerich, *The Life of the Blessed Virgin Mary*. trans. M. Palairet (London: Burns & Oates, 1954), 43, 63.
27. See Dominic White, "An Overview of Sophiology," https://www.friendsofsophia.com (accessed 29 October 2021).
28. See Margaret Barker, *Creation: A Biblical Vision for the Environment* (London: T&T Clark, 2010), 179–187.
29. *Protoevangelium of James*, 7.1, in *The Apocryphal New Testament: A Collection of Apocryphal Christian Literature in an English Translation*, ed. and trans. J. K. Elliott (Oxford: Clarendon, 1993), 60.
30. Margaret Barker, *The Great Lady: Restoring Her Story* (Sheffield: Phoenix, 2023), 344. I am indebted to Margaret Barker for sharing this work with me before its publication, as well as her advice on the Hebrew.
31. Barker, *The Great Lady*, 344.
32. Dominic White, "Dance in Christianity: A *Ressourcement*," *Sobornost* 35, no. 1–2 (2013): 81–122—on the Easter dances, see 81, 107–109; Dominic White, *The Lost Knowledge of Christ: Contemporary Spiritualities, Christian Cosmology, and the Arts* (Collegeville, MN: Liturgical Press, 2015), 1, 115–116, 119.
33. Michael Eisenberg, "Performing the Passion: Music, Ritual, and the Eastertide Labyrinth." *Trans: Revista Cultural de Música*, 13 (2009).
34. Hugo Rahner, *Man at Play, or Did You Ever Practise Eutrapelia?* trans. Brian Battershaw and Edward Quinn (1963–1964; London: Burns & Oates, 1965).
35. Jean Lebeuf, *Mercure de France*, May 1726, 243–4, items 921–2, trans. E. Mehel, cited in Eisenberg. I have slightly amended the translation, which is moved into the present tense for the sake of vividness.
36. Eisenberg citing Tessa Morrison, "The Labyrinthine Path of Pilgrimage," *Peregrinations* 1, no. 3 (2005),The tripudium has been reconstructed as a processional dance at St. Gregory of Nyssa Episcopal Church in San Francisco: https://www.youtube.com/watch?v=ByI_6kzoIk8 (accessed 25 October 2021).
37. Yves Congar, *Tradition and Traditions: An Historical and a Theological Essay*, trans. Michael Naseby and Thomas Rainborough. (1960/1963; London: Burns & Oates, 1966), 237–270.
38. *The Roman Missal*, English translation according to the Third Typical Edition (2008; London: Catholic Truth Society, 2011), 395.
39. White, *The Lost Knowledge of Christ*, 115–116, 119.
40. Plotinus, *Enneads* 6.9.8; cf. also 3.2.16.
41. Plotinus, *Enneads* 4.4 [28].33.
42. Hippolytus, *Paschal Homilies*, 6; *On the Songs of Songs*, 11; Gregory of Nyssa, *Treatise on the Titles of the Psalms* 86.58–59.
43. Philo, *On Flight*, 45–46, *On the Cherubim*, 23; Rahner, *Man at Play*, 72–75.
44. Rahner, *Man at Play*, 77.
45. Eisenberg, :Performing the Passion."
46. Rahner, *Man at Play*, 66.

47. Rahner, *Man at Play*, citing Clement of Alexandria, *Stromata* I.ii.21.2.
48. E.g., John Chrysostom, *Homilies on Matthew* 48[49].3; Gregory of Nazianzen, *Orations* V.35; Augustine, *Sermons* 326.1.
49. White, *The Lost Knowledge of Christ*, 109.
50. *Acts of John*, 94–96. See White, *The Lost Knowledge of Christ*, 120–123.
51. Rahner, *Man at Play*, 79.
52. Robert Sherlaw Johnson, *Messiaen* (London: J. M. Dent & Sons, 1975), 10.
53. Sherlaw Johnson, *Messiaen*, 32.
54. Jean Marie Wu, "Mystical Symbols of Faith: Olivier Messiaen's Charm of Impossibilities," in *Messiaen's Language of Mystical Love*, ed. Siglind Bruhn (New York: Routledge, 2012), 95–98.
55. See Bernhard Schneider's recording at https://www.youtube.com/watch?v=-oQqEbWubcQ, bars 447–449 (accessed 26 October 2021); also Sherlaw Johnson, *Messiaen*, 50.
56. See Sherlaw Johnson, *Messiaen*, 41.
57. Sherlaw Johnson, *Messiaen*, 32–33.
58. E.g., Sherlaw Johnson, *Messiaen*, 41; for the Modes see 16–17.
59. Stephen Schloesser, "The Charm of Impossibilities: Mystic Surrealism as Contemplative Voluptuousness," in *Messiaen the Theologian*, ed. Andrew Shenton (Aldershot: Ashgate, 2010), 163–182.
60. Sander van Maas, "Messiaen's Saintly Naïveté," in *Messiaen the Theologian*, ed. Andrew Shenton (Aldershot: Ashgate, 2010), 41–59, citing Paul Griffiths, *Olivier Messiaen and the Music of Time* (London: Faber & Faber, 1985), 102.
61. Sherlaw Johnson, *Messiaen*, 61; Christopher Dingle, *The Life of Messiaen* (Cambridge: Cambridge University Press, 2007), 76, 98–101, 141, 153.
62. See Andrew Shenton, *Olivier Messiaen's System of Signs: Notes towards Understanding His Music* (Aldershot: Ashgate, 2008), 55, citing Claude Samuel, *Olivier Messiaen: Music and Color: Conversations with Claude Samuel and Olivier Messiaen*, trans. Thomas Glasow (1986; Portland, OR: Amadeus, 1994, 77.
63. Shenton, *Olivier Messiaen's System of Signs*, 55, citing Samuel, *Olivier Messiaen*, 77.
64. Shenton, *Olivier Messiaen's System of Signs*, 55.
65. Shenton, *Olivier Messiaen's System of Signs*, 58, citing Samuel, *Olivier Messiaen: Music and Color*, 83.
66. Shenton, *Olivier Messiaen's System of Signs*, 58, citing Olivier Messiaen, *The Technique of my Musical Language*, trans. John Satterfield. (Paris: Leduc, 1958), 21.
67. Shenton, *Olivier Messiaen's System of Signs*, 55.
68. See Nicholas of Cusa, *The Vision of God*, *passim*.
69. Personal conversation, 28 October 2021.
70. https://www.youtube.com/watch?v=kVy8nrkxeIY (accessed 28 October 2021).
71. Thomas Aquinas, *Summa Theologiae* 1.84.7.
72. Rahner, *Man at Play*, 66.
73. For example, Swami Abhishiktananda (Fr. Henri Le Saux)—see Peter Tyler, *Confession: The Healing of the Soul* (London: Bloomsbury Continuum, 2017), 104–134.
74. White, *The Lost Knowledge of Christ*, 135–142.
75. White, *The Lost Knowledge of Christ*, 130.

# Afterword

## DIVINE *LĪLĀ* AND HUMAN PLAY

*Michelle Voss*

In 2002, captivated by the enchanting and unfathomable divine actions known as *līlā* in Hindu traditions, I wrote a master's thesis, "Divine Delight and Imaginative Imitation: A Comparative Theology of Play," at Emory University.[1] The abandon of divine creativity, which frames even destructive cosmic forces as manifestations of divine sport, was an intriguing detour from the seriousness of my Calvinist upbringing. *Līlā* invited me to rethink several central Christian tenets and, later, to delve more deeply into devotional and aesthetic themes in Hindu and Christian traditions.[2]

*Deus Ludens* is the first collection on the topic of *līlā* in Hindu and Christian traditions. Following several waves of major studies in each tradition, this fresh treatment brings the range of approaches together in a generative manner. This Afterword will locate the collection in relation to earlier offerings and consider how its contributions reflect changes in the scholarly context.

### Playing in the Waves

The nineteenth century saw a rediscovery of the aesthetic that gave new life to scholarly interest in play. No longer content with modern working conditions and the Enlightenment's severance of mind from body and reason from emotions, Romantic philosophers such as J. C. F. von Schiller centered aesthetics in human meaning-making. Play theories and game theories sprang up in divergent disciplines, including sociology, philosophy, mathematics, literature, religion, and art, so that "an emergent mythology of post-Puritan, post-Christian, postmodern [humanity]" seemed to be emerging to unite the "theoretical disciplines."[3] For example, Johan Huizinga attempted to trace the origin of all cultural phenomena to the play of "primitive man."[4] Gerardus van der Leeuw's analysis of visual and performance art also linked play and culture by mapping the breakup of the original unity of these activities with religious practice. Such nostalgia for a more playful humanity likely reveals more about modern needs than about ancient civilizations; yet whether or not their anthropological analysis was correct, these theorists were trying to retrieve something their society had apparently lost: the spirit of play in a world of work.

The mid-twentieth century witnessed a spate of Christian theological works on the possibilities of play. The reasons for this sudden interest are varied. In part, it was a continuation of the application of play theory to diverse fields of study that had begun with Huizinga.[5] In the United States, theological engagement with play studies between 1950 and 1970 developed in the intersection of the "leisure revolution" and the crisis of the "death of God." The middle class suddenly found themselves with shorter work weeks and a growing leisure industry to help them occupy their newfound free time.[6] At the same time, widespread questioning of authority, both religious and political, led to a search for new modes of doing theology.

For example, Hugo Rahner's 1949 study, *Man at Play*, begins with a consideration of *Deus ludens* in Plato and biblical Wisdom themes, and then turns to the human imitation of divine play. He retrieves the forgotten Aristotelian virtue of *eutrapelia*, a "well-turning" that marks the median between the poles of humorlessness and buffoonery, seriousness and levity, love of the world and detachment from it.[7]

In contrast to Rahner's sacramental approach, which locates play within the theistic framework of the church, two decades later Sam Keen shifted focus to the human individual. His reevaluation of what it means to live an authentic human life is sparked by protest against the all-powerful, benevolent God who allowed so much suffering. Turning to the sacred in the natural world, he sought to insert wonder back into the modern outlook. His model of the authentic life bears clear resemblances to theories of play: spontaneity, celebration, embodied meaning, immediacy, and absorption in a story or game.[8]

Jürgen Moltmann's *Theology of Play* focuses on the ethical, agonistic aspects of play. Characteristically driven by eschatology in his work, a vision of liberated existence ushered in by the resurrection of Christ shapes his treatment of play. He speaks back to prevailing aesthetic play theories that minimize or neglect the realities of suffering in the world and notes that too often play comes into the service of oppressors. Moltmann develops his theology of play with attention to the purposefulness of God's activity. Humans are free to respond in doxology to God's free actions on our behalf. Obedience to God arises out of adoration and praise rather than coercion or fear. History is God's playground, and all created beings are co-participants in the game. When God and creation rest on the Sabbath, they experience a foretaste of the new creation, in which God will reconcile all things and become manifest in them.[9]

Such works, both in Europe and the United States, exhibited the desire to connect theology with experience and to balance an overwhelming traditional emphasis on the ethical with a sense of the aesthetic. Studies of humor flourished around the same time, with Conrad Hyers, Harvey Cox, and others initiating an ongoing field of study that highlights the role of humor in scripture, Christian liturgy, and festivals as a way of dealing with the incongruities of life.[10]

In contrast with the anthropocentric focus of twentieth-century Christian theologies of play, Hindu traditions have been speaking of God's play for millennia. Following David Kingsley's major study of Kṛṣṇa *līlā* in 1979, several important works on the topic emerged in the mid-1990s by David L. Haberman, Don Handleman, David Shulman, William Sax, and others.[11] Many of the essays in this volume build on these important analyses of Indian traditions.

## A Fresh Influx of *Līlā*

By taking the Indian concept of *līlā* as the category of comparison rather than some loose translation of the term such as "play" as I did in my master's thesis, *God at Play* differs from comparative studies that impose Western, particularly Christian, categories on other traditions. By gathering voices, texts, and phenomena that might not otherwise have been put into conversation with one another, the volume highlights what it calls "*līlā*-shaped themes" or "echoes" of this important Indian philosophical and theological category in an increasingly connected intellectual world. As such, this volume not only deepens and complexifies the scholarship on *līlā* but is also an important contribution to comparative studies of religion and comparative theology.

What is learned by taking *līlā* as the category of comparison now? How do the conversations in this volume augment, confirm, or modify the earlier scholarship?

Of the possible sub-themes of *līlā*, God's creative activity receives the most attention here. While prominent in Indian theorizing about the divine freedom to create, Jews and Christians also have recourse to the semi-divine figure of Wisdom, whose play is the work of creation in the biblical book of Proverbs. Contemporary interpreters from both traditions find this a generative theological playground.[12] Here, Jessica Frazier draws out the metaphysical implications of *līlā* as expressing "key insights into the natural creativity, artistic sophistication, and dramatic value of existence itself." By examining the metaphysical significance of *līlā* in relation to other themes in the Caitanya Vaiṣṇava school, which is known primarily for its dramatic and emotional aesthetics, she paints a picture of a dynamic, full, creative divinity that stands apart from other Vaiṣṇava theistic interpretations. She also insightfully connects this vision with contemporary philosophical interests in emergence that are becoming integral sources for reflection across traditions.[13]

In the prevalent interpretation of *līlā*, God does not create out of necessity but acts in a free and unconstrained manner to generate the worlds. Similarly, as Bernard McGinn explains, prominent medieval Christian scholastics "thought of God's creative activity as totally spontaneous and completely self-determining" and occasionally described the relationship between the creator and the creation in terms of play. Themes such as the world's "dependence on God; the nature of God's decision to create; . . . the duration that God determines for the world"; and a "dialectic" of divine transcendence and immanence are *līlā*-shaped.[14]

Cases of *līlā* treated here nuance and even challenge the interpretation of *līlā*'s purposelessness and absolute freedom. Ankur Barua's reading of Tagore highlights a paradox of divine *līlā*: "The Lord who has no need whatsoever somehow needs our loving response." Sucharita Adluri and Francis X. Clooney both demonstrate that the emphasis for Śrīvaiṣṇavas of South India, including Rāmānuja and Vedānta Deśika, does not rest on the unpredictable, unconstrained, and purposelessness of divine sport. Rather, Viṣṇu's causality ultimately accords with his compassion and grace and, therefore, "may be just as well or better characterized by . . . nothing less than purposeful, utterly gracious action."

Theodicy weaves through the volume as another important sub-theme. Suffering is a byproduct of divine *līlā*. This theme is not limited to the Vaiṣṇava imagination but appears as well in Śaiva understandings of the establishment of the city of Madurai via the divinely mandated destruction of a beautiful forest ecology. Srilata Raman explicates sacred geography and divine presence in the city in relation to "the unfathomable eruptions of Śiva's deeds." Taking a *māyā*-centric rather than *līlā*-centric approach, Rachel Fell McDermott's essay wonders whether *Deus ludens* (or, in the case of the Great Goddess, *Dea Deludens*) is a pastorally helpful teaching in relation to the apparently cruel way the Goddess's play binds creatures in the dance of worldly attachment. The "Līlā Solution" to theodicy is ultimately not very satisfying if it simply lets divinity off the hook. McDermott finds that in a pastoral context, *līlā* functions best if a devotee already accepts it as a theological framework. Alternately, devotees such as those who have dealt with suffering by understanding it as the all-encompassing Goddess can become examples for others who are suffering.

The comparative dimension of this collection yields some important takeaways, including a complication of the category of analysis. *Līlā* defies easy translation, and its multivalence in Hindu traditions proffers many points of contact for comparative study. For example, Clooney's reading of *līlā* as grace pulls us back from an easy translation of the term as "play" or "sport." Ankur Barua proposes "structured spontaneity," which captures well the theological nuances that thinkers from both traditions have tried to convey. Drawing on this multivalence, Douglas Hedley relates *līlā*'s creative, theodical, mystical, and aesthetic aspects to these themes in Plotinus, a thinker who has been foundational for much of Western and Christian thought. Other comparisons and points of contact will likely occur to readers of these essays.

Daniel Soars's recognition of the volume's incompleteness might be read as recruiting for new players to take up this game and play additional rounds. As we see here, Hindu traditions field the more experienced players. The Vedic, Śaiva, Vaiṣṇava, and Śākta teams represented *must* take up the theme of *līlā* in some way because of its ubiquity in Hindu contexts, particularly in the Vaiṣṇava theological tradition and the medieval and modern traditions of Bengal. The "Western" interlocutors here skew Neoplatonist and Catholic. There are few parallel Lutheran, Orthodox, process, or liberation treatments of creativity and play to parallel this august heritage. One reason for the paucity of this theme is that the dominant telling of the Christian story is dead serious: The divine intervention to remedy human transgression results in the torture and death of the incarnate deity. To treat a matter such as the crucifixion as divine sport seems to trivialize the severity of the situation, the magnitude of Christ's sacrifice, and by extension the gravity of the suffering of creatures. This volume's attention to the grace and purpose of divine *līlā* could permit Christian thinkers from across the theological spectrum to take another look at the relation between the "structured spontaneity" of divine action and the problem of evil.

## Has the Playing Field Changed?

Christian scholars interested in *līlā*-shaped themes have frequently framed play in contrast to human work. We have seen that the nineteenth-century Romantic turn to the aesthetic was a response to the Enlightenment and modern working conditions, just as mid-twentieth-century treatments of play responded to the "leisure revolution" and the crisis of the "death of God." There was the perception in the latter wave that North Americans and Europeans had achieved a level of material comfort that afforded time and resources for relaxation, fun, and sport. Greater secularization and a loosening of religious structures had also freed them for the pleasures previously regulated by moralistic asceticism.

These earlier waves of theorizing on work and play presumed a relatively comfortable socioeconomic position, either emerging or newly achieved within the middle class. Of course, the attitudes and dispositions of *līlā*-shaped activity have never been bound to a single cross-section of society. Nevertheless, as some anticipated then, the understanding that leisure is something one *should* do has expanded into billion-dollar industries. Even more than then, play has become work. The obligation and financial burden of vacation travel rest more heavily amid rising costs of living. Social media influencers have exacerbated the moral superiority of the fit and the indispensability of expensive diets and accessories. Workplaces capitalize on the now-conventional wisdom that the individual's responsibility for "self-care" is the best way to maintain ever-higher standards of productivity. Spaces for freedom, creativity, spontaneity, adventuresome risk, and joyful absorption—for *līlā*—seem more elusive than ever.

Previous theologians of play also wrote in an emerging post-Christian world, in the milieu that first produced Nietzsche's dancing God and then full-blown theologies of the death of God. For them, Christianity remained the primary referent. However, neither Christianity nor religion disappeared as anticipated. Today more theological perspectives are gaining a hearing: This collection's interest in the Indian category of *līlā* is expanding and creatively combining the philosophical and theological repertoires.

The academy is also becoming more aware that theory is produced in places it never recognized before. Peter Tyler introduces several faces of the trickster, a cross-cultural motif with much to teach about these themes. We might add more, such as the subversive role of the Br'er Rabbit tales in African American traditions, or Nanabush and Coyote, who highlight the humor in absurd situations in Anishinaabe thought.[15] These figures do more than poke fun at the serious and powerful members of society. Sometimes they stand as revolutionary markers of worldviews in which productivity, accumulation, and work were never the primary problematic in the first place.

The present volume focuses primarily on how God plays (*Deus ludens*). As noted above, Christian teaching that humanity is created in the image of God often leads to reflection on how divine activity informs human ethics and purpose. Here, we see these impulses combined in a spiritual thinker like Tagore: "Divine *līlā* is the cosmological template for quotidian enactments of human *līlā*," Barua writes of his philosophy; "just as God does not remain enclosed in a cosmic aloofness but surrenders Godself to human devotees, human beings too should step out of the egoistic encirclements of their everyday lives and find themselves, along the path of love, in and through the other." Despite the limitations of the earlier waves, this aspect of earlier Christian forays into theologies of play invites further expansion.

Without fully recapitulating the Christian tendency toward anthropocentrism on this topic, I invite future scholars of *līlā* to consider such questions about human spiritual development once again. How might the wisdom of these traditions inform human working and playing in novel contexts such as pandemics and climate crisis? What difference does it make if human beings are participants in a reality created by the God who plays in certain ways? Might contemplation of divine ease and playfulness serve as an antidote for certain manifestations of human seriousness, including the seriousness of our current ideological era and late capitalist cultures of work and productivity? Could the Goddess's awesome power and Śiva's inscrutability teach us that we still do not quite know the game the universe is playing? How can the Vaiṣṇava emphasis on the divine freedom to love and graciously respond temper critics' ethical and theodical worries—about play's frivolity and carelessness as well as its function as an escape valve within unjust systems of power? How might human attitudes toward both work and leisure shift if divine *līlā* were reframed as creative and loving responsiveness to others, as Tagore advocated?

## Bibliography

Cox, Harvey. *The Feast of Fools: A Theological Essay on Festivity and Fantasy.* New York: Harper & Row, 1969.

Dahl, Gordon J. "Protestant Responses to a Leisure Revolution, 1945–1970." Ph.D. diss., University of Minnesota, 1974.

Dumont, Alf. *The Other Side of the River: From Church Pew to Sweat Lodge.* Toronto: United Church Publishing House, 2020.

Haberman, David L. *Acting as a Way of Salvation: A Study of Raganuga Bhakti Sadhana.* New York: Oxford University Press, 1998.

Handleman, Don, and David Shulman. *God Inside Out: Siva's Game of Dice.* New York: Oxford University Press, 1997.

Huizinga, Johan. *Homo Ludens: A Study of the Play-Element in Culture.* New York: Roy Publishers, 1950.

Hyers, M. Conrad. *The Comic Vision and the Christian Faith: A Celebration of Life and Laughter.* New York: Pilgrim Press, 1981.

Hyers, M. Conrad, ed. *Holy Laughter: Essays on Religion in the Comic Perspective.* New York: Seabury Press, 1969.

Johnson, Elizabeth A. *She Who Is: The Mystery of God in Feminist Theological Discourse.* 1992. New York: Crossroad, 2017.

Keen, Sam. *Apology for Wonder.* New York: Harper & Row, 1969.

Keen, Sam. *To a Dancing God.* Harper & Row, 1970.

Kinsley, David. *The Divine Player: A Study of Kṛṣṇa Līlā.* Delhi: Motilal Banarsidass, 1979.

Miller, David L. *Gods and Games: Toward a Theology of Play.* New York: Harper & Row, 1970.

Moltmann, Jürgen. *Theology of Play.* Translated by Reinhard Ulrich. New York: Harper & Row, 1971.

Neale, Robert E. *In Praise of Play: Toward a Psychology of Religion.* New York: Harper & Row, 1969.

Rahner, Hugo. *Man at Play.* Translated by Brian Battershaw and Edward Quinn. New York: Herder and Herder, 1967.

Sax, William, ed. *The Gods at Play.* New York: Oxford University Press, 1995.

Sydnor, Jon Paul. *The Great Open Dance: A Progressive Christian Theology.* Eugene, OR: Pickwick, 2024.

Voss Roberts, Michelle. "Divine Delight and Imaginative Imitation: A Comparative Theology of Play." MTS thesis, Emory University, 2002.

Voss Roberts, Michelle. *Tastes of the Divine: Hindu and Christian Theologies of Emotion.* New York: Fordham University Press, 2014.

Winnicott, Donald Woods. *Playing and Reality.* London: Tavistock Publications, 1982.

## Notes

1. Michelle Voss Roberts, "Divine Delight and Imaginative Imitation: A Comparative Theology of Play," MTS thesis, Emory University, 2002. The literature review in this Afterword draws on this unpublished thesis.

2. Particularly in Michelle Voss Roberts, *Tastes of the Divine: Hindu and Christian Theologies of Emotion* (New York: Fordham University Press, 2014).
3. David L. Miller, *Gods and Games: Toward a Theology of Play* (New York: Harper & Row, 1970), 4.
4. Johan Huizinga, *Homo Ludens: A Study of the Play-Element in Culture* (New York: Roy Publishers, 1950).
5. E.g., Robert E. Neale, *In Praise of Play: Toward a Psychology of Religion* (New York: Harper & Row, 1969); and Donald Woods Winnicott, *Playing and Reality* (London: Tavistock Publications, 1982), which develops this interest in his studies of early childhood development.
6. Gordon J. Dahl, "Protestant Responses to a Leisure Revolution, 1945–1970" (Ph.D. diss., University of Minnesota, 1974).
7. Hugo Rahner, *Man at Play*, trans. Brian Battershaw and Edward Quinn (New York: Herder and Herder, 1967), 91–105. This was first published at *Der Spielende Mensch* in the *Eranos-Jahrbuch* in 1949.
8. Sam Keen, *Apology for Wonder* (New York: Harper & Row, 1969); Sam Keen, *To a Dancing God* (Harper & Row, 1970).
9. Jürgen Moltmann, *Theology of Play*, trans. Reinhard Ulrich (New York: Harper & Row, 1971).
10. M. Conrad Hyers, ed., *Holy Laughter: Essays on Religion in the Comic Perspective* (New York: Seabury Press, 1969); M. Conrad Hyers, *The Comic Vision and the Christian Faith: A Celebration of Life and Laughter* (New York: Pilgrim Press, 1981); Harvey Cox, *The Feast of Fools: A Theological Essay on Festivity and Fantasy* (New York: Harper & Row, 1969).
11. David Kinsley, *The Divine Player: A Study of Kṛṣṇa Līlā* (Delhi: Motilal Banarsidass, 1979); David L. Haberman, *Acting as a Way of Salvation: A Study of Raganuga Bhakti Sadhana* (New York: Oxford University Press, 1998); Don Handleman and David Shulman, *God Inside Out: Siva's Game of Dice* (New York: Oxford University Press, 1997); William Sax, ed., *The Gods at Play* (New York: Oxford University Press, 1995).
12. Elizabeth Johnson offers one influential Catholic development of these themes. See Elizabeth A. Johnson, *She Who Is: The Mystery of God in Feminist Theological Discourse* (1992; New York: Crossroad, 2017).
13. For example, Jon Paul Sydnor's constructive Christian theology of creation in *The Great Open Dance: A Progressive Christian Theology* (Eugene, OR: Pickwick, 2024) explicitly draws on the thinking of the Viśiṣṭādvaita Vedānta teacher Rāmānuja, who appears across the present volume.
14. Bernard McGinn, "Creating without a 'Why': Divine Play as Metaphor for Creation in John Scottus Eriugena, Thomas Aquinas, and Meister Eckhart," in this volume.
15. See Alf Dumont, *The Other Side of* the *River: From Church Pew to Sweat Lodge* (Toronto: United Church Publishing House, 2020) for the trickster as a character in one Ojibwe Christian life.

# CONTRIBUTORS

SUCHARITA ADLURI is a scholar of South Asian religions and Professor in the Department of Philosophy and Religious Studies at Cleveland State University. She has written a monograph titled *Textual Authority in Classical Indian Thought: Ramanuja and the Vishnu Purana* (Routledge, 2014). Her recent publications focus on religious reading and commentary in Vedānta traditions.

ANKUR BARUA is Senior Lecturer in Hindu Studies at the Faculty of Divinity, University of Cambridge. He researches various aspects of Vedāntic Hindu worldviews in premodern and contemporary South Asia. Recent publications include *The Hindu Self and Its Muslim Neighbors: Contested Borderlines on Bengali Landscapes* (Lexington Books, 2022); and *Exploring Hindu Philosophy* (Equinox, 2023).

STEPHEN R. L. CLARK is Emeritus Professor of Philosophy at the University of Liverpool, and Honorary Research Fellow in Theology and Religious Studies at the University of Bristol. His principal recent works include *Plotinus: Myth, Metaphor and Philosophical Practice* (University of Chicago, 2016); *Cities and Thrones and Powers: Towards a Plotinian Politics* (Angelico Press, 2022); and *How the Worlds Became: Philosophy and the Oldest Stories* (Angelico Press, 2023).

FRANCIS X. CLOONEY, SJ, is Parkman Professor of Divinity and Professor of Comparative Theology at the Harvard Divinity School. His primary areas of Indological scholarship are theological commentarial writings in the Sanskrit and Tamil traditions of Hindu India. Recent publications include *Reading the Hindu and Christian Classics: Why and*

*How It Matters* (University of Virginia Press, 2019) and his memoir, *Hindu and Catholic, Priest and Scholar: A Love Story* (T&T Clark/Bloomsbury, 2024).

RACHEL FELL MCDERMOTT is Professor in the Department of Asian and Middle Eastern Cultures, Barnard College, Columbia University. She is the author and editor of several books on Hindu Goddess traditions, and she is also keenly interested in Comparative Theology. Her most recent book, co-authored with Daniel Polish, is *A Hindu-Jewish Conversation: Root Traditions in Dialogue* (Lexington, 2024). Her current project engages Hindu-Muslim relations in Bengal and Bangladesh.

JESSICA FRAZIER is Lecturer in the Study of Religion at the University of Oxford and a member of the Oxford Centre for Hindu Studies. Her research explores key philosophical themes across cultures, from Indian classical theories of Being to twentieth-century phenomenology. Her publications include *Hindu Worldviews: Theories of Self, Ritual and Divinity* (Bloomsbury, 2016), and *Categorisation in Indian Philosophy: Thinking Inside the Box* (Ashgate, 2014).

BERNARD MCGINN is the Naomi Shenstone Donnelley Professor Emeritus at the Divinity School of the University of Chicago where he taught for thirty-four years before retiring in 2003. He has written extensively on patristic and medieval theology, especially the history of spirituality and mysticism.

DOUGLAS HEDLEY is Professor of the Philosophy of Religion at the University of Cambridge, and Director of the Cambridge Centre for the Study of Platonism. As well as a monograph on Samuel Taylor Coleridge: *Coleridge, Philosophy, and Religion: Aids to Reflection and the Mirror of the Spirit* (Cambridge University Press, 2000), Hedley has written a three-volume work on the religious imagination: *Living Forms of the Imagination* (T&T Clark, 2008); *Sacrifice Imagined: Violence, Atonement, and the Sacred* (Continuum, 2011); and *The Iconic Imagination* (Bloomsbury, 2016). He has held visiting professorships in France, Germany, the USA, Canada, and India.

SRILATA RAMAN is Professor of Hinduism at the University of Toronto. Her areas of interest are Tamil and Sanskrit Vaiṣṇava and Śaiva intellectual formations from the late medieval to the early colonial period, including the emergence of nineteenth-century socioreligious reform and colonial sainthood. Her publications include the monographs *Self-Surrender to God in Śrīvaiṣṇavism* (Routledge, 2007) and *The Transformation of Tamil Religion* (Routledge, 2023).

DANIEL SOARS teaches in the Divinity Department at Eton College and is book reviews editor for the *Journal of Hindu-Christian Studies*. Recent publications include a co-edited volume titled *Hindu-Christian Dual Belonging* (Routledge, 2022) and a monograph titled *The World and God Are Not-Two: A Hindu-Christian Conversation* (Fordham, 2023).

DANIEL J. TOLAN is a Fellow at The Polonsky Academy for Advanced Study in the Humanities and Social Sciences at The Van Leer Jerusalem Institute. He received his MPhil and PhD from the University of Cambridge's Faculty of Divinity as a member of Clare College, and his publications can be found in the *Harvard Theological Review*, *Vigiliae Christianae*, *The International Journal of the Platonic Tradition*, and *Studia Patristica*.

PETER TYLER is Professor of Pastoral Theology and Spirituality and Director of the Centre for Initiatives in Spirituality and Reconciliation (InSpiRe) at St Mary's University, Twickenham, London. A registered psychotherapist in private practice, he has contributed extensively to the current dialogue between psychology and theology. Latest publications include *The Living Philosophy of Edith Stein* (Bloomsbury, 2023) and *John of the Cross: Carmel, Desire and Transformation* (Routledge, 2024).

MICHELLE VOSS is Professor of Theology at Emmanuel College in the Toronto School of Theology. She is a scholar of comparative theology, with a particular focus on Christian and Hindu contexts, and has also written widely about aesthetics, gender, and embodiment. Recent works include *Body Parts: A Theological Anthropology* (Fortress, 2017) and *The Handbook of Hindu-Christian Relations*, which she edited with Chad Bauman (Routledge, 2020).

DOMINIC WHITE OP, a Dominican friar, is a Fellow of Blackfriars Hall, Oxford, a Research Fellow of the Margaret Beaufort Institute of Theology, Cambridge, and Prior of Blackfriars Priory, Oxford. His publications include *The Lost Knowledge of Christ: Christian Cosmology, Contemporary Spiritualities and the Arts* (Liturgical Press, 2015), and *How Do I Look? Theology in the Age of the Selfie* (SCM, 2020). He is a composer, and co-founder of the Friends of Sophia group.

# INDEX


absence (versus presence), 130n1, 153, 156–159, 169, 173
Adluri, Sucharita, 7, 89, 179
Advaita, 7, 33, 141, 162, 164, 178, 180, 265
aesthetic: dimensions of *līlā*, 8, 21, 25, 32; theory, 34, 37, 181, 189, 289
Anastasis (Resurrection), 272–274, 279–280, 283
angel, 258, 273, 279, 283
animals, 208, 248, 255
*The Anxious Generation*, 13
Apollo, 221, 225, 234, 242n73, 242n75
apophatic, 67, 264, 277, 280, 281
Aquinas, Thomas: and Aristotle, 251; on creation, 49–52, 68–69; on God, 57–58, 265; and Gregory Palamas, 99–104; on knowledge, 281; and Meister Eckhart, 52–53
archetype, 244, 252
art, 32, 35, 189, 230
Augustine: on creation, 43, 269; and Neoplatonism, 22, 24, 235
Aurobindo, 24–25, 35–38, 265
*avatāra*, 8, 97, 99, 112

Bādarāyaṇa, 4, 34, 109
Barker, Margaret, 269–270
Barua, Ankur, 8, 179, 250–253
Bauls, 163, 254
Being: absolute, 6, 178, 180, 187; in *Chāndogya*, 92–93, 156; and existence, 120; finite being, 31, 49–50, 55, 99; God's, 45, 129; in Origen, 64–66; in Plotinus, 67–68; principle of, 32–33, 52; in Rāmānuja, 110–112; source of, 37
beauty, 226, 231, 265
Bengal Renaissance, 23
*Bhagavad Gītā*, 36, 38, 97–98, 183
*Bhāgavata Purāṇa*, 8, 33, 182–183
*bhakti* (devotion), 94, 153, 166
Bhaṭṭācārya, Kamalākānta, 138
Bhedābheda, 178–185, 188
Boehme, Jakob, 24, 266–269, 278, 280
Boersma, Hans, 89, 100–104
Brahman: and devotion, 153and *līlā*, 4, 35, 37, 159; and Viṣṇu, 109–110; and world, 92, 111, 136, 183
*Brahmasūtra*, 5–7, 10, 15n13, 95, 109–110, 113, 120
Bréhier, Émile, 26, 38

Cabasilas, Nicholas, 226
Caitanya Vaiṣṇava, 36, 71; on the divine nature, 185–187; and play, 178–184
Caldecott, Stratford, 266–267
Cambridge Platonists, 22–24, 37, 235
*Caṇḍī*, 136–138
Carter, Sydney, 146
causation, 8, 28, 181, 185, 189
Chander, Vineet, 141, 146
*Chāndogya Upaniṣad*, 91–93, 156, 178, 183
children: and anxiety, 13; and games, 228–229, 267, 271, 274; and Jesus, 145; in Plato, 26; and Plotinus, 235; in Tagore, 161
chorus, 222, 225
Clark, Stephen R. L., 33, 273

Clooney, Francis X., 113, 129, 140, 179
*coincidentia oppositorum*, 249, 270
compassion: creation as an act of, 96–97; and *līlā*, 108n28, 112, 115, 120, 123–124; as quality of Brahman, 113–114, 118, 121–122; and Śiva, 207; in Vedanta Deśika, 126–129; and Viṣṇu, 116–117, 119. See also *dayā*
conductor (*koruphaios*), 225
contemplation, 11; in Aquinas, 52, 262n31; in Origen, 72; in Plotinus, 25–30; in Rāmānuja, 93
contingency, 6, 11, 13, 44, 61n22, 179, 180, 188
creation ex nihilo, 6, 45–50, 89, 102
Cudworth, Ralph, 23–24
Cusa, Nicolas of, 278

dance, 9, 25; and the feast of fools, 255–258; and the Goddess, 136–139; and Jesus, 145–146; and Kṛṣṇa, 159; and medieval cathedral dances, 271–274, 279–283; and music, 230–232; in Plotinus, 32–34, 221–222, 225–226; and Śiva, 198, 212
*dayā* (mercy): and creation, 119; definition, 115; goddess, 116; and incarnation, 120; and liberation, 122; and *līlā*, 127–129; in the *Rāmāyaṇa*, 125–126; and Viṣṇu, 117–119
*Dayāśataka (Hundred Verses to Compassion)*, 109, 115
delude, 136, 137, 148n4
demiurge, 22, 33, 44, 248
dependence (of world on God), 44, 49–51, 75, 111, 192n2, 292
desire (*kāma*): in Rāmānuja, 109–113, 131n7, 159; in Tagore, 166; in Vedānta Deśika 117, 129
destiny, 226
*Devī-Māhātmya*, 136–137, 144, 148n7
dialectic, 44–47, 51, 53–55, 162
Diamond, Stanley, 244
Dionysus, 30, 242n75
distinction (between world and God), 44, 46, 49–53, 75, 128, 267
drama: in Caitanya Vaiṣnavism, 179, 181–182, 187–189; and *līlā* 34–37; in Plotinus, 30–31, 227
Durgā, 135, 143, 144
Durrell, Lawrence, 264

Eckhart, Meister, 6, 24, 43, 47, 52–57
Edgar, Brian, 12, 145
Eliot, T. S., 233, 242n71
emanation, 11; in Aquinas, 49–50; and creation, 22, 25, 41n3, 63, 83n49; in Eckhart, 54; in Eriugena, 46; in Origen, 65; in Plotinus, 67–70, 83n50
emergence, 186–188
*enantiodromia*, 247
Enoch (Book of), 273–274
Eriugena, John Scottus, 46–49, 55
eternity, 45, 52, 54, 275
*eutrapelia*, 10, 12, 251, 290
evil: in Origen, 73–74; in Plotinus, 228–229; problem of, 30, 37, 141, 145–146
exemplarism, 65–66, 73, 81n24, 81n29
exitus/reditus, 46

feast of fools (*festum stultorum*), 245, 255–256, 259
Ficino, Marsilio, 26
Frazier, Jessica, 8, 57, 71, 75, 85n80, 111, 143
freedom (of divine action), 3, 5, 45, 48, 267, 278; and grace, 104; and *līlā* 90, 173; in Origen, 63–65, 69, 77
fun, 12, 248, 251, 271, 276

geography (sacred), 197, 211
Gerson, Lloyd, 68–69, 77, 223
*Gitanjali*, 155, 161, 168
Golden Rule, 232–233
Gosvāmī, Rūpa, 143, 181, 185
grace, 7; in Christian theology, 279; and *dayā*, 109, 115, 126, 128; *līlā* as, 89–90, 99–105, 139, 178
Green Man, 249
Griffiths, Bede, 24–25

Haidt, Jonathan, 13
harmony (musical), 32, 164, 230, 275, 280
Hedley, Douglas, 178, 231, 264–267, 271
Hengstermann, Christian, 65, 71
holy fools, 160, 250, 253
Holz, Harald, 64
*Homo Ludens*, 10, 26, 251
hopscotch, 264, 266, 271, 274, 280
Huizinga, Johan, 10, 26, 39, 251, 290

humour, 181, 251
Hynes, William, 247–248, 250

icchā (wish/desire/will), 117, 165, 167
illusion, 33, 35–36, 136, 144, 146, 265
incarnation, 10, 75, 269; as divine play, 112–114; and *līlā* 119–122. See also *avatāra*
intelligibility, 73
Irenaeus, 69, 268–269

jazz, 276, 280
Jung, Carl: and the Feast of Fools, 255–256; on the trickster, 244–249, 258–259
justice, 36, 121, 123–126, 211

Kālī, 135, 137–140, 143–144
Kar, Minati, 144
karma, 7, 96–97, 110–112, 124, 129, 158
Khiḍr, 249
Kinsley, David, 135, 144
Krishna/*Kṛṣṇa*: and the Goddess, 139–140; and the *gopīs*, 22, 34, 38, 143

laughter, 11, 168, 248, 250–251
liberation: and divine mercy, 122–124; and the Goddess, 140, 144, 146; from *saṃsāra*, 112, 115, 117; and Śiva, 203
*libertas ingenita*, 65, 71, 77
*līlāvibhūti*, 89, 95, 99, 107n16, 111, 214
*liṅga*, 148n5, 200, 207
Lipner, Julius, 3–6, 89–90, 105, 109, 198, 265
liturgy, 10, 16n36, 255, 257, 274, 291
*Logos*, 29–30, 53, 64, 73–77, 268–269
love: in Christianity, 236, 282; divine, 22, 161, 169; in Eckhart, 56; of God, 159; making love, 136; in Rūpa Gosvāmī, 181; and separation, 158; in Tagore, 161–168

Madurai: description of, 205; and the Pāṇṭiya kings, 204; Śiva's creation of, 197–200, 211–212, 214–215
*Mahābhārata*, 209–210, 265
*māyā*, 33–36, 39, 140, 146
McDermott, Rachel Fell, 7, 179, 293
McGinn, Bernard, 71, 75, 189
meditation, 95–96
mercy. See *dayā*
Messiaen, Olivier, 265, 270, 274–280
*A Midsummer Night's Dream*, 246
*mokṣa*. *See* liberation
Moltmann, Jürgen, 10–12, 145, 290–291
More, Henry, 37
music, 31, 36; and dance, 230, 257, 274; Olivier Messiaen, 274–278, 280; and play, 264
mysticism, 265

Nammāḻvār, 107n15
Narasiṃha, 121, 249
Naṭarāja, 34, 146
nature, 25, 27–29, 73, 100–102, 273
Neale, Robert E., 145
necessity: in Plotinus and Aquinas, 68–69, 77; and *līlā*, 95, 173, 265, 292
Neoplatonism, 22, 27; and Eriugena, 46; and Plotinus, 221–237
Newman, John Henry, 236n92
Nicholas of Methone, 67, 73
nothing(ness)/nihil, 47–48, 52, 55
*Nous* (~Spirit), 28, 66, 70, 229, 232, 236, 237, 241n49

ontology, 100, 111, 178, 189
Origen, 6, 24; on creation as revelation, 74–77; and divine exemplarism, 64–67; and divine volition, 69–74; and play, 63–64

*paideia*, 26, 64
paint(ing), 124, 127, 134n55
Palamas, Gregory: and Aquinas, 89, 95; on creation and vision of God, 99–104
panentheism, 99, 102
pantheism, 30, 46, 102
Pāṇṭiya (dynasty), 199, 201, 204–205, 209–211, 213–214
pantomime, 227, 231–232, 241n61
Parañcōtimuṉivar, 197–199, 203, 206
participation, 33, 37, 49–51, 53, 81n24, 278
Paul, St., 69, 253, 260, 268, 282–283
Peacocke, Arthur, 189
Plato, 26, 39, 273. *See also* Cambridge Platonists; demiurge; Neoplatonism; participation

play: in Aquinas, 52; and children, 267; in Christian theology, 145, 282; and divine creativity, 112, 114, 186, 188–189; and drama, 30–32; and the Goddess, 136–140, 146; in Bede Griffiths, 24, 274; in Johan Huizinga, 26; importance of, 10, 250–251; and Krishna, 38, 157, 161; in Oliver Messiaen, 275–278; in Origen, 63–64; in Plato, 26, 39, 234; in Plotinus, 26–27; in Hugo Rahner, 251; in Rāmānuja, 35–36; scholarship on, 289–295; versus seriousness, 28; and theodicy, 36–37, 140–143; as translation of *līlā*, 1–2, 6–7, 21, 25, 57, 90, 97, 105, 155, 265; and the trickster, 248, 259; as a virtue, 11–12, 228; and well-being, 13, 281; of Wisdom, 268–270
Plotinus, 21–22, 25–26; on dance, 273; on divine will, 67–69; on drama, 30–31, 37; on how to live, 235–236; on nature, 29; on play, 27–28; on stars, 222–225
poetry: and the Āḷvārs, 214; and devotion, 197; and Kālī 137; and Umā, 139, 153; and Vedānta Deśika 115–116; and Vladimir Solovyov, 269
Porphyry, 221–223, 235
*prakṛti*, 136
primitive, 246–247
principle (principium), 52–54, 61n32
process philosophy, 267
Proclus, 63, 66–67
Proverbs (Book of), 10, 39, 268–270
psychoanalysis, 245
psychopomp, 244, 247, 249
*pūjā* (devotional worship), 154
Purāṇas, 33, 136, 183, 197
purgatory, 239n18
*pūrṇa* (fullness), 85n80, 180, 186

Rādhā, 143–144, 193n7
Radin, Paul, 244–247
Rahner, Hugo, 10–11, 251, 271, 273–274, 282, 290
Ramakrishna, 24, 143–144
Raman, Srilata, 249, 292
Rāmānuja, 90; commentary on *Brahmasūtra*, 6, 109, 159–160, 179; on compassion/mercy, 113; on the divine nature, 111, 267; on *māyā*, 35; on *tat tvam asi*, 92–93; on vision of God, 94–97, 102
*rasa*, 35, 140, 186. *See also* aesthetic
*rāsa līlā* (circle dance), 8–9, 157–158, 160, 213
rationality, 75
refuge (*prapatti*), 114–115, 117–118, 121, 124–129, 142
Roy, Rammohan, 23
rules, 232, 264, 278–279

sacrament, 100–104
Śākta: and absence of *līlā*, 135–136, 139; Bengali devotional poetry, 137–139; *Devī-Māhātmya*, 136–137; and illusion, 146; and the problem of suffering, 143–145; Śītalā, 139
*śakti* (power), 85n80, 135–136, 180, 183, 185
salvation: and incarnation, 113, 122; and the Goddess, 139; and mercy, 124, 127; in Platonism, 237; as play, 24, 35
*Saṃkalpasūryodaya*, 127
Śaṃkara: commentary on *Vedāntasūtras*, 4; on *līlā*, 35; and monism, 38–39, 184
*saṃsāra* (transmigration), 7, 110, 115, 126
*śarīraśarīribhāva* (body-self ontology), 111
*satkāryavāda*, 184. *See also* causation
Sax, William, S., 3, 21, 140
Schelling, Friedrich, 266–267, 269, 278, 280
Scipio's Dream, 222
self-manifestation (the world as divine), 89–90, 92, 103
Sen, Ramprasād, 137, 139
separation, 158, 161, 165–167, 169, 171, 174, 188
seriousness, 11–12, 28, 251, 274, 276
Shakespeare, William, 36, 246
sidereal, 223–225, 230
Silesius, Angelus, 57
Śītalā, 135, 139, 143
Śiva: and *līlā*, 197–198; Lord of Dance, 34, 146; and Madurai, 199–215, 249; and Śakti, 136. See also *liṅga*; Madurai; Naṭarāja
Soars, Daniel, 57, 293
Sophia (Wisdom), 10, 266
soul: and the divine, 36, 55–56; individual, 31–32, 112, 128, 136, 146; in Origen, 69, 76; and Plotinus, 221, 223; in Proclus, 66;

and psychoanalysis, 245; in Rāmānuja, 93; of the world, 28, 231, 269
Spinoza, Benedict, 183, 185, 193n14
spontaneity: and divine creativity, 52, 56–57, 178; and Kṛṣṇa 161; and *līlā* 2–3, 11–12, 21, 29, 153–154
stars: and angels, 278–279, 283; in Plotinus, 221–225, 228, 273
Stoicism, 21, 28, 30–32
subordinationism, 64
*Śvetāśvatara*, 156, 183, 187
Śyāmā Saṅgīt, 137
Symeon the Fool, 253–254

Tagore, Debendranath, 23
Tagore, Rabindranath, 34, 38, 153–155, 265, 292; and Bauls, 163; devotional songs, 168–173; on divine presence and absence, 158–161; and love, 164–168; on transcendence and immanence, 156–157; and Vaiṣṇavism, 161–162
*talapurāṇam*, 197
Tamil, 9, 90, 115, 132n30, 197–198, 214
Tantras, 136
*tat tvam asi*, 92
theatre, 30, 37
*Tirumoḷi*, 214
*Tiruviḷaiyāṭaṟpurāṇam*, 197, 199
Tolan, Daniel, 6
Transfiguration, 100–103
trickster, 160, 244–245; as agent of change, 250; animal aspects of, 252; concept of, 245, 248; and deception, 253; and feast of fools, 255; and holy fools, 253; in Jung, 246–247; in Shakespeare, 246; theological aspects of, 251, 256, 258–259
Tyler, Peter, 9, 160, 295

Umā, 139
unconscious (the), 246

Vaiṣṇavism, 111, 115, 129, 162
Vedānta. *See* advaita; Bhedābheda; Caitanya Vaiṣṇava; Rāmānuja; Śaṃkara; *Viśiṣṭādvaita*
Vedānta Deśika, 89, 97, 109, 214; on creation, 119–120; on incarnation, 121–122; on liberation, 122–124; on *līlā* and mercy, 114–119, 127–129
*Vedāntasūtras*. See *Brahmasūtra*
*Vedārthasaṃgraha*, 91–95, 98, 117
Vidyābhuṣaṇa, Baladeva, 187
*viḷaiyāṭal/viḷaiyāṭṭu*, 197–198
violence (divine), 210–211, 235, 216n6
Virgin Mary, 269
vision (of God): in Aquinas, 100; in Palamas, 101–103; in Rāmānuja, 90–96, 99. *See also* Boehme, Jakob; Boersma, Hans
*Viśiṣṭādvaita*, 7, 90, 96, 109–110, 124, 179
Viṣṇu: and creation, 109–111, 120, 159, 214; and *dayā* (mercy), 115–119, 129; and incarnation, 125, 249; and liberation, 122–123
volition, 63–73, 117
voluntarism, 24, 25
Von Balthasar, Hans Urs, 265, 268
Vṛṣagiri/Vṛṣācala (pilgrimage site), 115–127

Watts, Alan, 228
Westcott, B. F., 24
White O. P., Dominic, 229, 257–258
Whitehead, Alfred North, 267
will (divine), 24, 67, 73, 75, 110, 117, 131n7, 167
Wisdom, 10, 39; Aquinas on contemplation of, 262n31; divine figure, 51–54, 66, 266–271, 278–280, 292

*Yādavābhyudaya*, 127

Comparative Theology / *Thinking Across Traditions*

SERIES EDITORS
*Loye Ashton and John Thatamanil*

Hyo-Dong Lee, *Spirit, Qi, and the Multitude: A Comparative Theology for the Democracy of Creation*
Michelle Voss Roberts, *Tastes of the Divine: Hindu and Christian Theologies of Emotion*
Michelle Voss Roberts (ed.), *Comparing Faithfully: Insights for Systematic Theological Reflection*
Francis X. Clooney, S.J., and Klaus von Stosch (eds.), *How to Do Comparative Theology*
F. Dominic Longo, *Spiritual Grammar: Genre and the Saintly Subject in Islam and Christianity*
S. Mark Heim, *Crucified Wisdom: Theological Reflection on Christ and the Bodhisattva*
Martha L. Moore-Keish and Christian T. Collins Winn (eds.), *Karl Barth and Comparative Theology*
John J. Thatamanil, *Circling the Elephant: A Comparative Theology of Religious Diversity*
Catherine Cornille (ed.), *Atonement and Comparative Theology: The Cross in Dialogue with Other Religions*
Daniel Soars, *The World and God Are Not-Two: A Hindu–Christian Conversation*
Daniel Soars (ed.), *God at Play: Līlā in Hindu and Christian Traditions*

www.ingramcontent.com/pod-product-compliance
Lightning Source LLC
Chambersburg PA
CBHW020354080526
44584CB00014B/1018